The Middle East and North Africa

The Middle East and North Africa

A Political Geography

ALASDAIR DRYSDALE
University of New Hampshire

GERALD H. BLAKE
University of Durham

New York Oxford
OXFORD UNIVERSITY PRESS
1985

OXFORD UNIVERSITY PRESS

Oxford   New York   Toronto
Delhi   Bombay   Calcutta   Madras   Karachi
Kuala Lumpur   Singapore   Hong Kong   Tokyo
Nairobi   Dar es Salaam   Cape Town
Melbourne   Auckland

and associated companies in
Beirut   Berlin   Ibadan   Mexico City   Nicosia

Published by Oxford University Press, Inc.,
200 Madison Avenue, New York, New York 10016

Library of Congress Cataloging in Publication Data
Drysdale, Alasdair.
The Middle East and North Africa.
Includes bibliographies.
1. Near East—Politics and government.   2. Africa,
North—Politics and government.   3. Near East—
Administrative and political divisions.   4. Africa,
North—Administrative and political divisions.   5. Geog-
raphy, Political.   I. Blake, Gerald Henry.   II. Title.
DS62.8.D79   1985   956   84-1095
ISBN 0-19-503537-2
ISBN 0-19-503538-0 (pbk.)

Printing (last digit): 9 8 7 6 5 4 3 2 1

Printed in the United States of America

Preface

This book is intended to serve two objectives simultaneously: first, to enrich understanding of political phenomena within the Middle East and North Africa by offering a spatial perspective; and second, to help to fill a noticeable gap in the political geographic literature on the region.

Political geography texts are essentially of three types. First, there are general introductions to the subdiscipline; these are written principally for students and are typically organized around its dominant concepts, theories, or subject areas. Most of their examples are drawn from North America and Europe. Second, there are more advanced, specialized, topically based works written for professional political geographers and advanced students. These might deal with such subjects as national integration problems, elections, the oceans, boundaries, and locational conflict. Third, there are regional political geographies, like this text, written mainly for students. Relatively few books fall into this category, and those that do vary greatly in their approach. Some take a country-by-country approach, whereas others (like this book) arrange their material topically.

Although there are no books that deal exclusively with the political geography of the Middle East and North Africa, there are, of course, several that cover the general geography of the region. Unfortunately, Fisher's classic text, *The Middle East: A Physical, Social and Regional Geography*, virtually ignores political geography. Beaumont, Blake, and Wagstaff have only one chapter on the political map in *The Middle East: A Geographical Study*. Possibly no other major world region has attracted so little attention from political geographers. This lacuna seems all the more surprising in view of the region's global importance and the numerous instances in which political conflicts within it have geographic origins or dimensions.

One is compelled to employ geographic terms and concepts to describe and explain many current political relationships or problems within the Middle East and North Africa. Any account of the Arab-Israeli conflict or the Iran-Iraq War would be incomplete without an accompanying map or sensitivity to the spatial perceptions of the parties involved. Similarly, it is well nigh impossible to explain the global political significance of the Turkish, Hormuz, Bab al-Mandab, and Tiran straits, or the Suez Canal without reference to their geographic context. Countries are profoundly conscious of their place in the world. The maps that usually accompany television or newspaper reports about political events in the Middle East and North Africa are not simply for decoration or background. Their inclusion suggests that geographic context is itself relevant. Maps can have an explanatory function. A geographic perspective not only adds an extra dimension to understanding political problems, but also it can sometimes go to the very heart of these problems.

How to render Middle Eastern place names in English always presents a problem. There are formal rules for transliterating Arabic, Persian, and other languages, and the U.S. Board on Geographic Names publishes approved spellings. However, following these rigidly often means using unfamiliar forms instead of commonly accepted ones (e.g., Tarabulus instead of Tripoli, Al-Qahirah instead of Cairo, and Al-Iskandariyah instead of Alexandria). We have, therefore, decided to use familiar English spellings of countries, most major cities, and many other geographic features. In other instances, we have tried to approximate the correct transliteration but without long vowels, diacritical marks, and certain consonants that have no English equivalents. For personal names, we have tried to stay close to the original (Husayn rather than Hussein, Nasir rather than Nasser, and Khumayni rather than Khomeini for instance). Similarly, we prefer Shi'i to Shiite and Sunni to Sunnite. Finally, it must be recognized that toponyms can be loaded with political significance: the first step to appropriating territory is appropriating its name. There are certain cases in which no matter what name one uses, one will offend someone. To Israel, the West Bank is Judea and Samaria and part of the "administered territories" rather than the "occupied territories." Conversely, to Arabs, Israel is Palestine. The Gulf between Iran and the Arabian peninsula is the Persian Gulf to Iranians, but the Arabian Gulf to Arabs. (We prefer to call it simply the Gulf.)

We define the area covered in this book in Chapter 2. However, it is necessary here to explain our use of certain regional terms. "North Africa" encompasses all the Arab countries bordering the Mediterranean from Morocco in the west to Egypt in the east. Three of these countries (Morocco, Algeria, and Tunisia) are referred to as the Maghreb. Strictly speaking, all other countries in this book outside North Africa are in Southwest Asia. However, the term "Southwest Asia," although correct, is less familiar than the less precise "Middle East." Unfortunately, definitions of Southwest Asia and the Middle East are not completely congruent. In particular, most scholars would place Egypt, which is in North Africa, within the Middle East, and many would also include Libya and Sudan. Therefore, the Middle East and North Africa overlap to a certain extent in popular usage. We have tried to use regional terms as they are generally understood.

Children at the beach delay getting out of the water until the last possible moment. "Just five more minutes," they call. Writing about the political geography of the Middle East and North Africa is not very different. "Just five more months," one is tempted to ask an editor. By then the situation may be clearer in Lebanon. Or the West Bank. Or in the Iran-Iraq War. The rush of events is so rapid and unrelenting that to stop constantly updating a manuscript requires more than a little self-discipline. Eventually, one recognizes the futility of delay and simply hopes the region's political map will stop evolving at the same time one decided to stop writing. Besides, our intention is less to be "current" than it is to provide students with some of the background necessary to understand and interpret the significance of future events themselves. Our basic goal is to encourage students to look at the world from a geographic perspective as a matter of habit.

Our editor, Joyce Berry, had to keep her eye on not one water splasher, but on two conspiring ones who were, moreover, on opposite shores of the Atlantic. We divided our efforts largely on the basis of special interests developed through several years of teaching and research. Alasdair Drysdale focused on national and regional integration, the Arab-Israeli conflict, and petroleum; Gerald Blake focused on the Middle East and North Africa's global context, the evolution of the state system, boundaries, and offshore political geography. We offered detailed comments on one another's drafts, so that considerable cross-fertilization of ideas occurred.

We would like to express our thanks to several people. Joyce Berry, our editor, offered encouragement and sound advice when they were most needed. Joan Knizeski-Bossert did an excellent job of coordinating production. Andrew Yockers' copy-editing was particularly careful and thorough. We would also like to thank Kathy Kuhtz. Many colleagues took a close interest in what we were writing. Particular thanks are owed to William H. Wallace, Dick Lawless, and our anonymous readers. Jonathan Mitchell undertook the time-consuming calculations on which Table 4.2 is based. Arthur Corner, George Brown, David Cowton, and David Hume of the Cartography Unit at Durham University's Department of Geography drew the maps with great skill. Our typists, Suzanne Gagnon and Margaret Bell, typed and retyped the manuscript with infinite patience. Suzanne Gagnon's enthusiasm, efficiency, carefulness, and unfailing humor made everything easier and will not be soon forgotten. Above all, our wives, Catherine Baker and Brenda Blake, did not give up on us, and we are indebted to them for their patience and support through many months of writing.

Durham, New Hampshire   A.D.
Durham, England   G.B.
April 1985

Contents

Part III. Integration   147

Part IV. Critical Issues   261

List of Figures

List of Tables

The Setting

1

Introduction

The Nature and Scope of Political Geography

Political geography has been defined and redefined over the years as
its focus has shifted. Today, most of its practitioners would agree that
it fundamentally involves the spatial analysis of political phenomena and
that it is concerned with the spatial attributes of political process.[1] Many
political geographers eschew a precise definition altogether, character-
izing their work in the broadest terms as political studies that use the
techniques and ideas associated with their spatial perspectives.[2] At root,
political geographers (like all geographers) believe that location matters
and that they should show the spatial causes and effects of political
processes.[3]

Most definitions are intentionally broad because political geography
is itself diverse, encompassing a wide variety of research topics and
methods. The field of observation ranges from the local (microscale) to
the international and even global (macroscale). One scholar might investigate spatial variations in voting patterns in an urban area or evaluate the optimum location for a public facility within a county. Another
might examine national integration problems in a Third World country
or assess superpower global geostrategic views. Both could describe
themselves as political geographers with equal justification.

In a sense, political geography's roots are ancient. The Greek philos-
opher Aristotle, the Arab historian Ibn Khaldun, and the French phi-
losopher Montesquieu all explicitly considered geographic factors in their
writings about politics and the state. The "father" of political geography, however, is generally considered to be the German Friedrich

3

Ratzel (1844–1904), who left a deep imprint. In its early phase, political geography focused on the supposed interrelationships between politics and the physical environment, particularly terrain and climate. This led to a simplistic, pseudoscientific, and deterministic approach. Ratzel, for example, likened political entities to biological organisms and suggested that "laws" governed the spatial growth of states. His ideas about states' territorial "destinies" profoundly influenced Rudolph Kjellen and Karl Haushofer, two European political geographers whose "science" of geopolitics, in turn, found official Nazi support because it purported to justify Germany's territorial aggrandizement. Environmental determinism similarly tainted the global geostrategic theories of Sir Halford Mackinder and others (these theories still have some influence over superpower thinking). Currently, there is a resurgence of interest among political geographers in the environment but from an altogether different perspective. Rather than speculating about how the environment shapes politics, political geographers now ask how politics shapes the environment. They might look at political responses to transboundary atmospheric or water pollution, congressional voting patterns on environmental issues, the international management of a river basin, or conflict over the control of a vital natural resource. The ecological tradition remains strong.

Until the early 1960s, political geography was dominated by studies of the morphology (or the formal and structural attributes) of political regions, particularly the state. Most research focused on the tangible features of the political map, such as state size and shape, boundaries, capital cities, core areas, and administrative systems. Boundary and territorial disputes received considerable attention. However, many political geographers grew increasingly dissatisfied with aspects of this static, overly descriptive, and state-based approach, which all too often relied on classification rather than analysis. Excited by methodological developments elsewhere in geography, they sought to invigorate the subdiscipline by greater use of quantitative methods, changing the scale of observation away from the global and state to the local level and emphasizing dynamic processes. They also introduced new behavioral approaches. Political geography has been greatly enriched and broadened by these fresh ideas and techniques. Instead of merely tracing a particular boundary's evolution and describing its static morphological characteristics, for instance, political geographers would now be more likely to examine its permeability, its effect on spatial interaction patterns, and how it is perceived. Instead of describing a state's formal political geographic features, they would be more likely to examine the integrative and disintegrative forces acting on it. Whole new areas of research have opened up: electoral geography (voting patterns and the spatial organization of electoral systems), locational conflict (where to site public facilities most efficiently or equitably), decision making (where decision makers come from and the geographic consequences of their decisions), public policy (geographic variations in government expenditures), territoriality (perceptions and defense of space), conflict resolution (the avoidance or management of disputes over territory or resources), new frontiers (the division of the oceans and air space), spatial integration (the unification of states and groups of states), and numerous other topics. Nevertheless, it is easy to exaggerate differences between the "old" and "new" political geography and to neglect continuities and commonalities. All political geographers, regardless of their specialty, continue to focus on the political organization of space. Collectively, they might not be so preoccupied with the state as a unit of territorial organization, but few would deny the continuing need to investigate problems at this scale.

In this book, we deal primarily with state and international problems both because these are of such extraordinary importance in the Middle East and North Africa and because local-level political geographic studies and data are absent or scarce. We favor a process-oriented political geography rather than a formal-structural approach. At the same time, the relevance of "traditional" political geographic subjects, such as boundary and territorial disputes, in the Middle East and North Africa is obvious. Anyone concerned with issues of international conflict and cooperation is obliged to take an active interest in the political map and its many imperfections. The state remains a basic, universal unit of political geographic organization. Because states still retain a monopoly over the "legitimate" means of violence, the way they interact determines whether we live in peace or war.

The need to continue studying problems of the world political map was explicitly recognized at a conference of 44 political geographers from 18 countries in Oxford, England, in July 1983. The meeting had two goals: to discuss research agendas for the 1980s and to submit a proposal for the establishment of a political geography specialty group within the International Geographic Union (IGU). The group unanimously passed a statement saying:

> In view of the urgent need to increase co-operation between nations and peoples in the face of underlying stresses and conflicts, and to promote peace and well-being when confronted by national and internal inequalities and uneven prospects, there is justification for a search, on the widest possible front, for a fuller *understanding of the political problems of territory, the oceans and human resources.* (Italics in original)[4]

A priority research agenda for an IGU political geography specialty group was also set out. Because it represents a collective and current view of what political geographers who deal with issues relating to the world political map should study, it is worth repeating in full. Topics to be the focus of study include[5]:

1. The evolution of the present system of states and the location and nature of their frontiers and boundaries;

2. Contemporary changes:
   (i) The development of supranational organizations and institutions;
   (ii) The Law of the Sea and the geographic extension of effective state control;
   (iii) Regionalism, nationalism, and related movements;
3. The role of territory and spatial strategies in the creation of nations' collective identities;
4. Geographical contributions to the study of peace;
5. Geographical variations in the nature of the state and political processes;
6. Local government and local administrations;
7. National and international environmental policy; and
8. The relationships of states to economic, social and cultural processes.

We have not tried to write a book organized around this list. Not all of these topics are pertinent to a political geography of the Middle East and North Africa, and others that are important to understanding the basic problems of the region are inevitably not included on such general agenda. Nevertheless, our coverage, if not our organization, coincides to a large degree with this list, placing the book in the mainstream of current political geography.

No political geographer would suggest that geography provides the wherewithal to an understanding of all political processes and problems. That would be both naive and deterministic. Nevertheless, a surprisingly large number of conflicts in the Middle East and North Africa result from the way in which space is politically organized. It is not hard to demonstrate the geographic origins of many political conflicts. Peter Haggett, the British geographer, has illustrated the many potential geographic sources of international stress in a fictitious landlocked country, Hypothetica (Figure 1.1).[6] Although he did not have the Middle East and North Africa in mind, he might as well have had because important examples of virtually every type of trouble spot can easily be found in the region. In a sense Haggett's model serves as a partial checklist of many of the topics covered in this volume.

Organization of the Book

This book is divided into four parts. In the first, entitled "Setting," we place the Middle East and North Africa in their global context (Chapter 2). The next six chapters fall within Parts II and III and are entitled, respectively, "Partition" and "Integration." These topics are the central, interrelated themes of the book and provide a framework for examining the political organization of space and political spatial pro-

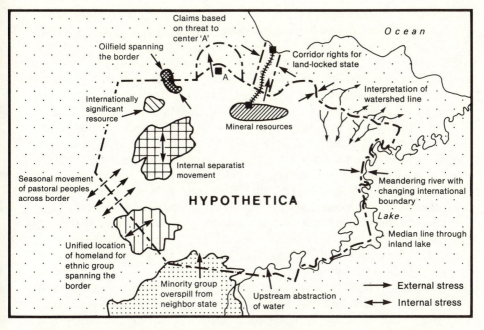

Figure 1.1 Geographic sources of international stress. (After Peter Haggett, *Geography: A Modern Synthesis*, revised third edition, 1983, p. 477, Figure 19.10. Copyright © 1983 by Peter Haggett. Reprinted by permission of Harper & Row, Publishers, Inc.)

cesses. The most obvious feature of the political organization of space in the Middle East and North Africa is the region's division into states—sovereign territorial entities with their own governments, national identities, and land and offshore boundaries. The political map is the outcome of the partitioning and repartitioning of space and of centrifugal forces that promote territorial division. At the same time, centripetal forces are working to integrate those spaces defined by partition lines. National and supranational integration aggregate areas, just as partition disaggregates them.

The three chapters in Part II examine the way in which the political map of the Middle East and North Africa has evolved through the process of partition. Chapter 3 describes antecedents of the modern state and the intrusion of the European colonial powers, who were largely responsible for dividing the region into its present-day states. The growth of nationalism and the birth of independent states after the demise of colonialism are also described here. The next two chapters examine the partition lines themselves: namely, land and offshore boundaries. Particular attention is given to describing territorial disputes. Besides being an obvious way in which geography and politics intersect, these are a significant source of international stress.

The three chapters of Part III examine the other side of the coin: the coalition of areas rather than their separation. Chapter 6 looks at national integration problems, processes, and prospects generally, identifying the principal centripetal and centrifugal forces that unite and divide countries. Special emphasis is given to the problems of nation building in states that are culturally diverse or affected significantly by political regionalism. Chapter 7 analyzes in depth the integration problems of five disparate countries: Lebanon, Israel, Saudi Arabia, Sudan, and Libya. These case studies illustrate the importance of considering centripetal and centrifugal forces together: forces that interact in complex ways. Chapter 8 then examines integration at the regional scale, looking specifically at prospects for Arab unity. If the political partitioning of the Middle East and North Africa is ever reversed, it will be because the Arabs succeed in dissolving the boundaries that separate them. After outlining the bases of pan-Arabism, the chapter attempts to account for the lack of success in redrawing the political map and describes the network of regional institutions that are gradually tying the Arab countries together functionally.

Certain critical regional issues manifestly have global importance. In particular, many Americans and Europeans have begun to take an interest in the region because the Arab-Israeli dispute, possibly more than any other local conflict, runs the risk of provoking a global superpower confrontation and because the Middle East and North Africa have a large share of the world's proven oil reserves. We have grouped the two chapters on these subjects in Part IV, entitled "Critical Issues." If there is an implied secondary theme of the book, it is the relevance of geographic factors to the intensification and amelioration of conflict and, to a lesser extent, the prospects for cooperation. This theme, which runs through Parts II and III, is explicit in the last section. From a political geographic standpoint, the Arab-Israeli dispute involves conflict over the *control of territory*, whereas the history of petroleum development in the region can be explained partly in terms of a conflict between foreign oil companies and Middle Eastern governments over the *control of a natural resource*. Obviously, numerous other instances of territorial and resource conflicts are discussed elsewhere in the book. Similarly, other critical issues, such as Lebanon's civil war and the Iran-Iraq conflict, receive attention in prior sections. In a sense, therefore, Part IV is defined rather arbitrarily. We felt that although the Arab-Israeli conflict and petroleum could have been treated earlier in the book and fitted into our partition-integration framework, they deserved to be singled out for more detailed attention. Our conclusion, which speculates about future changes in the region's political geography, also fits well into the critical issues rubric.

Notes

1. See definitions by Roger E. Kasperson and Julian V. Minghi (eds.), *The Structure of Political Geography* (Chicago: Aldine Publishing Co., 1969): xi; and S. B. Cohen and L. D. Rosenthal, "A Geographical Model for Political Systems Analysis," *Geographical Review* 61(1971): 6. Martin Ira Glassner and Harm de Blij, in their *Systematic Political Geography*, 3rd ed. (New York: John Wiley & Sons, 1980), provide a large selection of definitions, see p. 3.

2. See, for example, comments in Alan D. Burnett and Peter J. Taylor (eds.), *Political Studies from Spatial Perspectives* (New York: John Wiley & Sons, 1981): 4.

3. Richard Muir, *Modern Political Geography* (London: Macmillan, 1975): 2.

4. Association of American Geographers, *Political Geography Specialty Group Newsletter*, October 15, 1983: 2–3.

5. Ibid.

6. Peter Haggett, *Geography: A Modern Synthesis*, 3rd ed. (New York: Harper & Row, 1983): 477.

Selected Bibliography

Beaumont, Peter, Blake, Gerald H., and Wagstaff, J. Malcolm. *The Middle East: A Geographical Study.* London: John Wiley & Sons, 1976.

Bergman, Edward F. *Modern Political Geography.* Dubuque, Iowa: William C. Brown Co., 1975.

Burnett, Alan D., and Taylor, Peter J. (eds.). *Political Studies from Spatial Perspectives.* New York: John Wiley & Sons, 1981.

Cox, Kevin R. *Location and Public Problems.* Chicago: Maaroufa Press, 1979.

East, W. Gordon, and Prescott, J. R. V. *Our Fragmented World: An Introduction to Political Geography.* London: Macmillan, 1975.

Fisher, William B. *The Middle East: A Physical, Social and Regional Geography*, 7th ed. London: Methuen and Co., Ltd., 1978.

Glassner, Martin Ira, and de Blij, Harm. *Systematic Political Geography*, 3rd ed. New York: John Wiley & Sons, 1980.

Kasperson, Roger E., and Minghi, Julian V. (eds.). *The Structure of Political Geography.* Chicago: Aldine Publishing Co., 1969.

Muir, Richard. *Modern Political Geography.* London: Macmillan, 1975.

Muir, Richard, and Paddison, Ronan. *Politics, Geography, and Behaviour.* New York: Methuen, Inc., 1981.

Norris, Robert E., and Haring, L. Lloyd. *Political Geography.* Columbus, Ohio: Charles E. Merrill Publishing Co., 1980.

Pounds, Norman J. G. *Political Geography*, 2nd ed. New York: McGraw-Hill, 1972.

2

The Middle East and North Africa:
The Global Context

There could scarcely be a more appropriate part of the world in which to test the usefulness of politico-geographic perspectives than the Middle East and North Africa. No region of comparable size has received so much anxious attention in recent years. Why should this region seem to have been the scene of so much violence and political change? What has made it the focus of great power interest? Have geographic characteristics influenced events? Many have sought the answer to these questions but all too often in the context of distorted and inaccurate views of the region. Interestingly, there seems to be a recognition that the geographic setting is important, as shown by the frequent adoption of pseudogeographic terms, such as chokepoints, crossroads, critical interfaces, and arc of crisis, by the media.[1] Though such terms are probably bandied about too readily, they underline the fact that, even at the global scale, geographic realities have some bearing on the politics of the region. This chapter is an attempt to highlight some of these realities, such as distance, physical and cultural diversity, and relative location.

The Region Defined

Although the term "Middle East" has been traced back with certainty only to 1900, it may have been in use in Britain's India Office since the mid-nineteenth century.[2] It first came into prominence when used by the American naval historian A. T. Mahan in 1902 to describe a region around the Gulf that, as seen from Europe, was neither "Near East" nor "Far East." Mahan was discussing the geographical implications of Russian influence in Iran and of German plans to build a railway to Baghdad. Although the commonly accepted definition of the Middle East now encompasses a far greater area than that of Mahan, the geostrategic overtones of the term linger on. The Middle East became familiar in the United States and Europe in World War II when both the British and the Allied headquarters in Cairo—known as H.Q. Middle East—covered large parts of northern and eastern Africa as well as Iran, Turkey, and all the Arab states east of the Suez Canal. If any more exposure was needed to fix the region indelibly in the popular mind, it resulted from the region's being the source of more than a quarter of the world's oil production as well as the possessor of more than 60 percent of the world's known oil reserves.

A half dozen North African states are also discussed in this book for a number of reasons.[3] They are historically and culturally inseparable from the Middle East. They share a common language with the Arab-speaking states, a common religion in Islam, and political aspirations within the Arab community that also broadly coincide. Both North Africa and the Middle East are key oil-producing regions; states in both regions belong to the Organization of Petroleum Exporting Countries (OPEC) and the Organization of Arab Petroleum Exporting Countries (OAPEC).[4] The Mediterranean Sea is also an important common factor.

The Middle East and North Africa, as we have defined them, are neither physically nor culturally bounded regions, although their physical environment and cultural patterns endow them with a distinctive regional identity. There is no standard definition of the Middle East. It is commonly taken to refer to Turkey, Iran, Israel, and the Arab states east of Suez together with Egypt and Libya.[5] Sudan and Cyprus are sometimes included, less often Morocco, Algeria, and Tunisia. However the region may be defined, it is not a closed political system. Culturally, the Middle East in certain areas extends far beyond the outer limits of some of the states of the region, whereas in other areas—as in southern Sudan—different cultural regions impinge on it. The geopolitical influence of the Middle East and North Africa extends into Afghanistan, Pakistan, and the Indian Ocean as well as into the Sahara and the Horn of Africa. No grouping of states can claim to belong to so many geopolitical realms. The coastal states of North Africa are African, Mediterranean, Islamic, and Arab—all influenced politically and economically by nearness to Europe. Most of the states of the Middle East are in Asia, but they have strong ties with the Euro-Mediterranean world or the Afro-Indian Ocean world or both. All but Cyprus, Israel, and Lebanon are Islamic; only Cyprus, Iran, Israel, and Turkey are not Arab.

The Significance of Location

The coming together of the Eurasian and African continental land masses along an axis through the Mediterranean and Red seas has created one of the world's great human and physical junctions. Europe and Africa are separated by a few miles of water at the Strait of Gibraltar in the west. Europe and Asia are separated by the narrow Turkish Straits in the east. But for the Suez Canal, Africa and Asia would be joined at the Isthmus of Suez; they are separated by only a few miles at the southern end of the Red Sea at Bab al-Mandab. The Strait of Gibraltar, the Turkish Straits, and the Isthmus of Suez have been strategic crossing points for invading armies for centuries. In time of peace, they are vitally important for the movement of people and goods between the continents and within the region. The Turkish Straits are already bridged, and there are tunnels under the Suez Canal. Discussions are also in progress concerning a possible fixed link across the Strait of Gibraltar in the form of a bridge or tunnel. In the modern world, commercial links between Europe, Africa, and Asia are heavily dependent on sea and air communications; the closeness of Europe and North Africa encourage a high level of interaction.

Intercontinental trade between Europe and Africa and Asia has varied in style and scale over the centuries, but it has nearly always been important. In the past, it meant the painstaking transportation of silks and spices from the east overland through Asia. Similarly, slaves, ivory, and gold were brought across the Sahara by camel caravans for the markets of Europe. In modern times, trade has meant the exchange of oil and natural gas for modern technology and manufactured goods. Quite apart from such commercial interaction, the Middle East has acted as a passage between Europe and the East. To a lesser extent North Africa has been a transit link between Europe and black Africa. The transit function of the Middle East is best understood by glancing at the population distribution of the "world island" (Eurasia and Africa). Two marked concentrations of population stand out, one in western Europe, the other from the Indian subcontinent to the Far East. The Middle East stands astride the routes between the two by land, sea, and air—at the heart of the "world island."

The opening of the Suez Canal in 1869 linked the Atlantic and Indian oceans via the Mediterranean and Red seas (see Chapter 5). As a result, global perception of distance changed radically, and the Middle East acquired great geopolitical significance for the maritime powers. The saving in time and distance, which primarily means lower fuel costs, is up to 40 or 50 percent for certain voyages (Table 2.1). The advantages for commercial shipping are clearly attractive, particularly for smaller ships, but the canal's strategic value to naval ships is also important. Transfer of naval units from the Mediterranean Sea to the Indian Ocean

Table 2.1
Distances Between Selected Ports

	Via the Cape of Good Hope (nautical miles)	Via the Suez Canal (nautical miles)	Distance Saving (percentage)
London to			
Bombay	10,800	6,300	42
Kuwait	11,300	6,500	42
Melbourne	12,200	11,000	10
Calcutta	11,700	7,900	32
Singapore	11,800	8,300	30
Marseilles to			
Bombay	10,400	4,600	56
Melbourne	11,900	9,400	21
New York to			
Bombay	11,800	8,200	31
Singapore	12,500	10,200	18
Ras Tanura, Saudi Arabia	11,900	8,300	30

Source: Adapted from W. B. Fisher, "Suez Canal," *Encyclopedia Britannica*, 15th ed., p. 768.

via the Suez Canal takes 17 to 18 fewer days than the voyage via the Cape of Good Hope, South Africa.

Communications are greatly assisted by the fact that the region is flanked by the Atlantic and Indian oceans and interpenetrated by five bodies of water: the Mediterranean, Red, Caspian, and Black seas and the Gulf. Far from creating barriers, the region's seas have generally been intensively used for commerce. Concomitantly, they have also been the scene of numerous naval and military struggles to control the main trade routes.[6] It is also worth remembering that the region's vast interior deserts were by no means impenetrable—even before the coming of modern roads and transport. The recognized camel caravan routes were traveled regularly, with towns on the desert margins functioning rather like ports.

Physical Background

The Middle East and North Africa lie roughly between latitudes 20° north and 40° north in a transitional climatic zone between equatorial and midlatitude climates. Because of general atmospheric circulation patterns, a characteristic of these latitudes is the prevalence of aridity, with minimum amounts of rainfall registered at about 30° north. Scarcely any precipitation occurs during the summer months. The implications of widespread aridity are many. The population of the region is relatively sparse and discontinuous in its distribution. Nomadism was widespread until recent decades, leaving a legacy of tribal values and attitudes in society. Where settled agriculture was practiced using irrigation, delicate infrastructures developed that became highly vulnerable in time of war. Scarce water resources often led to local quarrels, despite the existence of elaborate legal codes concerning their ownership and allocation. Such quarrels over water, as with land, could easily erupt into regional conflict. Today, there are serious international disputes over the allocation of water resources in several river basins as well as numerous local troubles over water.

The Middle East and North Africa are geologically extremely complex, chiefly because they occupy part of the earth's crust where three tectonic plates meet. As a result of the convergence of these plates, great ranges of high fold mountains have been thrown up, notably in the Maghreb and in the northern tier states of Turkey and Iran. Although these ranges present a magnificent sight, particularly when snow-clad, they are formidable barriers to travel. Peaks in the High Atlas of Morocco rise to over 13,000 feet (4000 meters). The Taurus range in southern Turkey rises to over 12,000 feet (3700 meters) in places. Mount Ararat in Turkey's eastern highlands reaches nearly 17,000 feet (5200 meters), and the region's highest peak, Mount Damavand in the Elburz Mountains along the southern shore of the Caspian Sea, reaches 18,400 feet (5600 meters). The broad, long Zagros range of western Iran is also impressive in scale, reaching over 13,000 feet (4000 meters). It is not always appreciated that there are also important mountainous regions outside the northern Middle East; the Yemen Highlands, for example, have peaks of over 12,000 feet (3700 meters), and Mount Hermon in Syria is over 9800 feet (2800 meters). The region's mountain systems have often provided refuge for persecuted minorities or have been the stronghold of dissidents and brigands. In modern times, they have been the core areas from which anticolonial and antigovernment movements have sprung. Mountains have played an important role in the political geography of the Maghreb, Turkey, Cyprus, Lebanon and Iraq. The close proximity of highland and lowland and sea and desert have given much of the region terrains that can provide mobility for the attacker and security for the defender at the same time.

Population and Peoples

Large tracts of arid and semiarid land ensure that the Middle East and North Africa are not extensively populated (Table 2.2). The total 1984 population of 278 million was about 5.6 percent of the world popula-

Table 2.2
States of the Region: Area, Population, and GNP 1984

	Area (sq mi/sq km)	Area Rank	Population (millions)	Population Rank	Percent Urban	GNP (per capita) 1982 (US$)
North Africa	3,271,306 (8,472,682)	—	123.8	—	42	
Algeria	919,600 (2,381,764)	2	21.4	5	52	2,350
Egypt	386,663 (1,001,457)	6	47.0	2	44	690
Libya	679,364 (1,759,553)	4	3.7	15	52	8,510
Morocco	254,817 (659,976)	8	23.6	4	41	870
Sudan	967,500 (2,505,825)	1	21.1	6	21	440
Tunisia	63,362 (164,107)	14	7.0	10	52	1,390
Southwest Asia	2,432,905 (6,301,224)	—	154.2	—	53	
Bahrain	231 (598)	22	0.4	21	81	9,280
Cyprus	3,572 (9,251)	20	0.7	20	53	3,840
Iran	634,000 (1,642,060)	5	43.8	3	55	—
Iraq	167,957 (435,009)	10	15.0	7	68	—
Israel	7,992[a] (20,699)	18	4.2	12	87	5,810
Jordan	37,000[a] (95,830)	15	3.5	14	60	1,690
Kuwait	9,375 (24,281)	17	1.6	17	90	19,870
Lebanon	3,400 (8,806)	21	2.6	13	78	—
Oman	105,000 (271,950)	11	1.0	19	8	6,090
P.D.R. Yemen[b]	111,075 (287,684)	9	2.1	16	38	470
Qatar	4,000 (10,360)	19	0.3	22	87	21,880
Saudi Arabia	864,800 (2,239,832)	3	10.8	8	70	16,000
Syria	71,498[a] (185,180)	13	10.1	9	48	1,680
Turkey	301,383 (780,582)	7	50.2	1	45	1,370
United Arab Emirates	36,193 (93,740)	16	1.5	18	81	23,770

Table 2.2 *(continued)*
States of the Region: Area, Population, and GNP 1984

	Area (sq mi/sq km)	Area Rank	Population (millions)	Population Rank	Percent Urban	GNP (per capit 1982 (US
Yemen A.R.[c]	75,290 (195,001)	12	5.9	11	38	500
(Gaza)	139 (360)	—	0.5	—	90	—
Total	5,704,211 (14,773,906)		278.0			

[a] Pre-1967 areas.
[b] People's Democratic Republic of Yemen
[c] Yemen Arab Republic.
Source: Adapted from *1984 World Population Data Sheet.* Washington, D.C.: Population Reference Bureau, 1984.

tion in a region occupying just over 10 percent of the earth's surface. Although the region covers a far greater area than the United States, (see Figure 2.1) it has only 40 million more people. The average population size in the region's 22 states is under 12 million. The largest populations are in Turkey, Egypt, and Iran, which globally rank 18th, 19th, and 24th, respectively. These three states possess 52 percent of the region's population. Individually they each have sufficient manpower to be eligible for consideration among Cohen's emergent second-order powers, although other factors are likely to prevent them from achieving this status in the near future.[7] The region also includes some of the smallest states in the world both by area and population (Qatar, Bahrain, Cyprus, Oman, the United Arab Emirates [U.A.E.], and Kuwait). On the other hand, the population of the region as a whole is growing rapidly because death rates have fallen, whereas birth rates remain high. The average growth rate is 2.8 percent per annum. This means a doubling of population in about 25 years. Roughly 40 to 45 percent of the population is under 15 years old, and yet to have their children. The expected increase in population far exceeds that projected in the United States, Western Europe, and the Soviet Union (see Table 2.3). Some 64 percent of the region's population lived in Arab states in 1984, which could rise to over 66 percent by the end of the century.

Rapid population increase coupled with urban growth provides an essential backdrop to the political geography of the region. Oil-producing states with large populations wish to press ahead with major and costly development projects that call for maximization of oil prices for short-term goals. The less populous producers prefer to keep prices down in the interests of long-term global economic stability. Large population increases have also led to a high degree of dependence on imported food in many states. At the same time, urbanization has significantly redistributed the population geographically and sharply decreased the

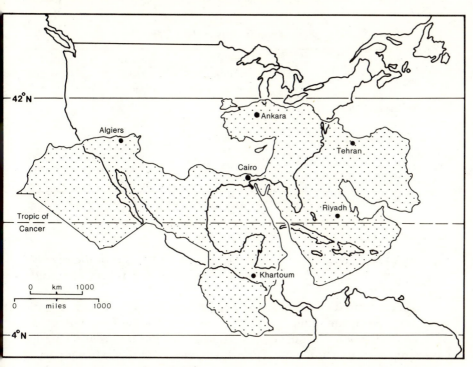

Figure 2.1   The Middle East and North Africa compared with North America by area and latitude. (After Robert A. Harper and Theodore H. Schmudde, *Between Two Worlds: An Introduction to Geography*, third edition. Copyright © 1984 by Kendall/Hunt Publishing Co., Dubuque, Iowa. Reprinted with permission of the authors.

percentage of people engaged in agriculture. Political awareness tends to be greatest among urban populations, who comprise 42 percent of North Africa's population and 53 percent of the Middle East's population.

Although 18 states of the Middle East and North Africa are officially Arab, cultural distribution patterns within the region are complex. Not all Arab states are exclusively inhabited by Arabs, and Arab minorities live outside the recognized Arab states. The peoples of the region have become so mixed racially that it is no longer useful to identify racial groups. The Arabs are probably as mixed racially as the inhabitants of Western Europe. Language is a more useful guide to the variety of peoples and can provide some indication of political aspirations. The dominant regional languages are Arabic, Turkish, and Persian (Figure 2.2). Arabic is a Semitic language that spread out from the Arabian peninsula with successive waves of conquerors and replaced existing languages in all but a few areas south of the Taurus and Zagros mountains. Berber is still widely spoken in parts of Morocco and Algeria; Kurdish in sections of Iraq and Syria; and a variety of African tribal lan-

Table 2.3
Population Increases 1984–2000

	Population in 1984 (millions)	Population in 2000 (millions)	Increment
Middle East and North Africa	278	423	+145
Arab states	179	280	+101
Non-Arab states	99	143	+ 44
United States	236	268	+ 32
Soviet Union	274	316	+ 42
Western Europe	155	156	+ 1

Source: *1984 World Population Data Sheet.* Washington, D.C.: Population Reference Bureau, 1984.

guages in southern Sudan. Altogether, about 57 percent of the region's inhabitants speak Arabic, although as Chapter 8 explains, the colloquial form varies spatially.

Invaders from the central Asian steppes introduced varieties of Altaic and Indo-European languages to the northern Middle East, largely replacing indigenous languages. In Asia Minor, ancient Asiatic tongues were replaced by Hittite and Turkish languages. Turkish, being part of the Altaic family, bears no resemblance to Arabic, although the two share some words as a result of an intertwined history and common Islamic faith. Since the 1920s, Turkish has been written in the Roman script. It is the dominant language of only one country in the region, Turkey. However, Turkish languages are widely spoken in neighboring Central Asia. Over the Iranian Plateau intrusive languages, like Persian, Kurdish, Afghan, and Pushtu, replaced indigenous languages. Persian, which belongs to the Indo-European family, bears little similarity to Arabic. However, it is written by using essentially the same script, and many Iranians learn basic Arabic in school because of its significance within Islam. The movements of peoples who spread these languages throughout the region were completed centuries ago. The introduction of Hebrew as the language of Israel is a small exception. This ancient Semitic language, which has a unique script (although it is part of the same family as Arabic), has been successfully revived in modern times as an element in the nation-forming process of the Jewish state.

The Region in the Global System

The World of Islam

Although estimates vary considerably, there are probably about 750 million Muslims in the world today or about 1 in 6 of the world's pop-

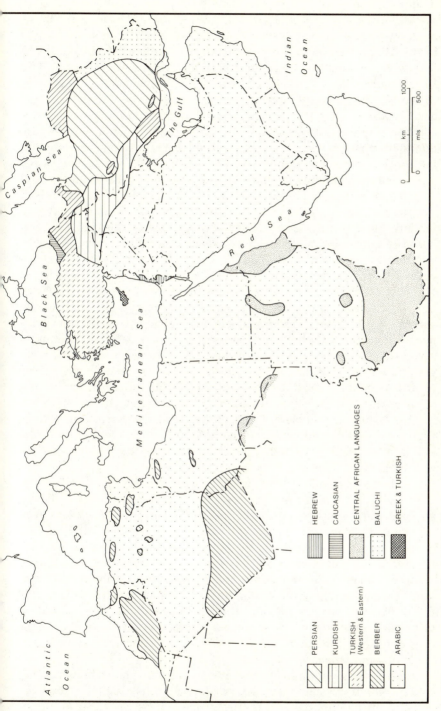

Figure 2.2 Languages of the Middle East and North Africa. (After Peter Beaumont, Gerald Blake, and J. Malcolm Wagstaff, *The Middle East: A Geographical Study*. New York: Wiley, 1976, p. 5. Copyright © 1976 by John Wiley & Sons, Inc. Reprinted by permission of the publisher.)

19

ulation.[8] There are 50 states that have large Muslim populations; 40 of these describe themselves officially as Islamic states. About half of these, accommodating about one quarter of the world's Muslims, are located in the Middle East and North Africa. By far the largest Muslim populations are outside the region in Indonesia, Bangladesh, Pakistan, and India (Figure 2.3). On the other hand, about 93 percent of the peoples of the Middle East and North Africa are Muslim. Less than 3 percent are Christians, about 3 percent adhere to tribal religions—chiefly in southern Sudan—and less than 2 percent are Jews. Because of its predominant position within the region, the Islamic religion is an integrating force of particular significance (see Chapter 8). The culture of the region is fundamentally Muslim. The Middle East is the birthplace and core region of Islam; its focal point is the pilgrim city of Mecca, which the faithful are supposed to visit once during their lifetime. Before modern transport, the lands closest to Mecca yielded the greatest number of pilgrims, and unity was most keenly felt at the center.

Although Islam unites the Middle East and North Africa, it also divides it between the Sunni and Shi'i branches. About 90 percent of Muslims are Sunnis. The schism in Islam dates almost from its beginning in the seventh century, originating in a dispute over who would succeed the Prophet Muhammad as Caliph (Successor) of Islam. Sunnis believed the Caliph should be selected on the basis of community consensus; Shi'is believed that the succession should be hereditary, beginning with Ali, Muhammad's son-in-law and the first Imam. Sunnis regard Ali as their fourth Caliph. The Sunni-Shi'i difference should not be overstated. All Muslims, regardless of sect, believe in the "Five Pillars" of Islam. Nevertheless, the schism has created fierce local rivalries from time to time and explains some of the political complexity of the Middle East, especially where geographical proximity of the two groups is most marked (Figure 2.3).

Iran is overwhelmingly Shi'i and has a large majority of all Shi'is in the region. Shi'is also form the majority in Iraq and Yemen A.R. and are important minorities in Syria, Lebanon, Turkey, and eastern Arabia. To complicate matters, the Shi'i are also split into a large number of sects, mostly on the basis of the line of succession after Ali. The most important are the Imamis or "Twelvers," who await the return of a "hidden" Imam to restore justice and righteousness in the world.[9] Another branch are the Zaydis, though their influence today is confined to the two Yemens. Finally, the Alawis, Druzes, and Isma'ilis, whose beliefs are somewhat obscure, consider themselves (but are not always considered by others) to be Shi'i. They are concentrated in Syria, Lebanon, and Israel.

The divisions within Islam are most significant in relationships between communities at village and town level. Internationally, they can occasionally be important, as in the current war between Iraq and Iran. Today, there is an increasing tendency for Islamic states to cooperate

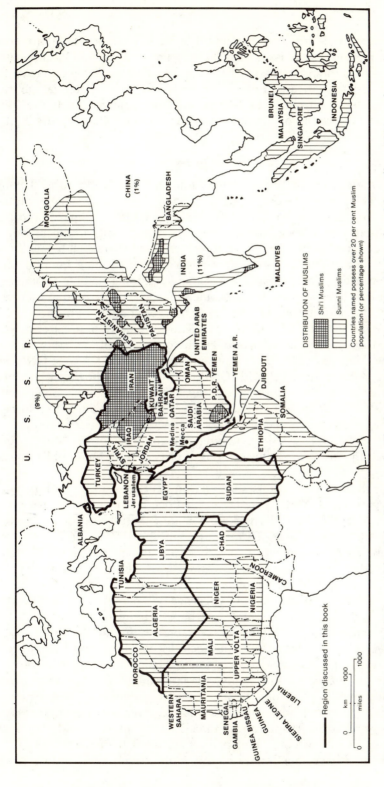

Figure 2.3 The world of Islam. (After John Paxton, ed., *The Statesman's Yearbook 1981–82*. London: Macmillan, 1981, endcover.)

in cultural and economic spheres. Islamic summit meetings are convened regularly, there is an Islamic Development Bank, and Islamic states have shown themselves willing to support Islamic political movements, as in Afghanistan and Eritrea. There is enormous potential for the worldwide mobilization of Islamic political feeling, which the geographical contiguity of so many Muslims could facilitate (Figure 2.3).

The Third World

As a whole, the countries of the Middle East and North Africa belong to the Third World.[10] They are still generally at an early stage of industrialization and heavily dependent on the export of primary products and the import of food, consumer goods, equipment, and technology. Literacy rates, particularly among women, tend to be well below those of the industrialized countries. Almost all exhibit acute internal geographic and social inequalties. Yet there are some notable anomalies, as Table 2.2 shows. The high-income oil exporters are among the richest countries in the world, measured by gross national product (GNP) per capita, with U.A.E., Qatar, and Kuwait ranking first, second, and third, respectively, in the world. At the other end of the scale, Sudan, the two Yemens, and Egypt have among the world's lowest GNP per capita. A preoccupation with GNP per capita can, however, be misleading. Many states in the region register high per capita GNP's only because of their small populations. This is strikingly illustrated in Figure 2.4, which shows the world political map in relation to absolute size of national GNP. By this reckoning, the countries of the Middle East and North Africa do not appear out of place among the world's poorer states.

Four countries—Egypt, Israel, Syria, and Turkey—do not conform with the typical Third World economy, in that one fifth or more of their gross domestic product are derived from manufacturing industry. By contrast, the manufacturing sector in Sudan and the two Yemens is extremely poorly developed. In fact, these 3 states are among the 31 states classified by the U.N. as the world's least developed countries (or LLDC's). Despite these anomalies and contrasts, the region is included in the South (see Figure 2.4) in what has become known as the North-South dialogue. More important perhaps is the central location of the region within the South, and its favorable location on the fringe of the privileged North. There has been much discussion in recent years about the urgent need to transform economic relationships between the rich North and the poor South to give the latter a better deal. Future world stability may depend on the ability and willingness of the advanced countries to evolve a new world economic order. The geographic location of the North African and Middle Eastern states should give them a better chance of going into partnership with their neighbors of the North than have most states of the South. Some have already made special agreements with the European Economic Community (EEC), and such arrangements could multiply. In time, the region could develop into a zone of rising prosperity between the poorer states of Africa and Asia, a role already symbolized by the fact that it is both a giver and receiver of aid.

The oil price increases of the 1970s gravely affected many Third World countries who had to pay more for goods from the industrial countries as well as for energy imports. The oil exporters of the Middle East and North Africa along with other exporters have been blamed by certain developing states for damaging their development prospects. Although financial aid from the oil producers may have compensated somewhat for these price increases,[11] much goodwill between the oil producers and the poorer consumers has been lost, and there is little sense of Third World solidarity between them.

Geopolitical Views of the World

Political geographers have made several attempts to devise global geopolitical models of the relationships between states. What do they reveal, if anything, of the place of the Middle East and North Africa in the state system of the world? In some ways, it is tempting to dismiss these models as inaccurate, subjective, or antiquated, but they continue to be featured as an explanatory framework in books on political-geographic issues in the region. Are they valid?

Almost all discussions of global geopolitical perspectives begin with Halford J. Mackinder, largely because of his influence on subsequent ideas. Early this century, while the American historian A. T. Mahan was developing his ideas about seapower in international strategy, the British geographer Mackinder was restating the importance of land-power. Indeed, his views were partly a response to Mahan's views. Mackinder's basic thesis was that the inner area of Eurasia is the pivot region of world politics. With its abundant resources, it is also beyond the reach of the maritime powers. Mackinder noted that this pivotal area was surrounded by a marginal crescent, which embraced the Middle East (Figure 2.5a). If the pivot state should ever gain control of the marginal lands, thus gaining access to the sea, "the empire of the world would then be in sight."[12]

Although Mackinder modified his views in later years his basic model remained unchanged, with the land-based power competing for influence in a marginal crescent to which the maritime powers have access. The Mediterranean and Middle East would be key regions in the struggle. Mackinder's concepts have been overtaken by advances in arms technology, but Western strategists are apparently still behaving as though his model is valid.[13] The U.S. policy of post-World War II containment, according to which alliances and bases have been established throughout the Eurasian marginal crescent, is designed to prevent the

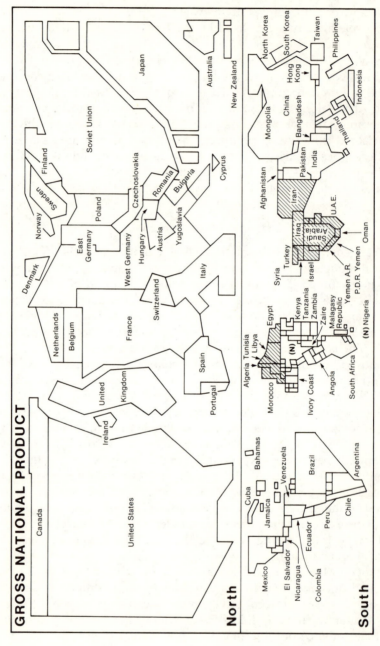

Figure 2.4a

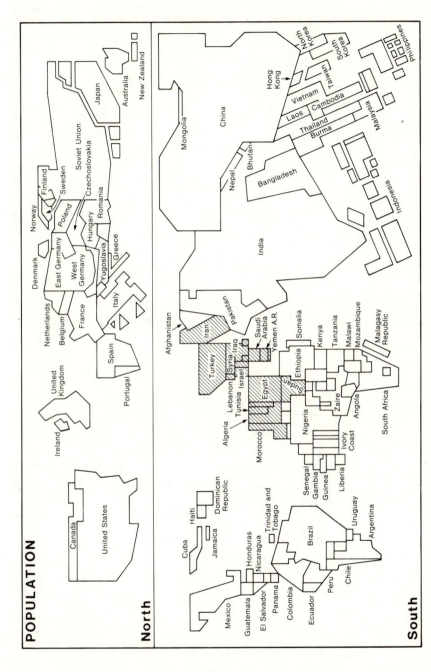

Figure 2.4b   World gross national product (GNP) and world population. (After *Newsweek*, October 26, 1981.)

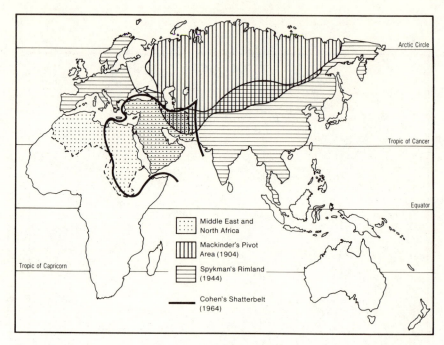

Figure 2.5a Geopolitical views of the world: Mackinder, Spykman, and Cohen.

Figure 2.5b View from the U.S.S.R.

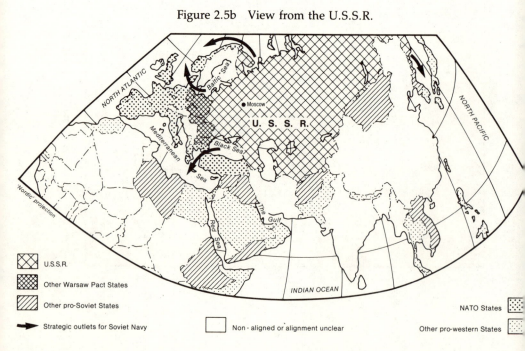

outward expansion of this heartland power, the U.S.S.R. (Figure 2.5b). Several political geographers have suggested refinements of Mackinder's ideas, all of which emphasize the significance of the marginal crescent in global geopolitics. During World War II, N. J. Spykman advocated that the United States adopt policies that would promote American influence in the marginal crescent, which he called "the rimland"[14] (Figure 2.5a). Another American geographer, D. W. Meinig, suggested that some rimland states were inward-looking toward the heartland, and others outward-looking toward the oceans. Thus, the choice of allies in the rimland could be a complicated matter, and the orientation of individual states might change through time.[15]

Ideas of heartland and rimland and the struggle between landpower and seapower to secure control of the marginal states have little validity in the modern world for a number of reasons. First, the landpower (the U.S.S.R.) has built an ocean-going fleet, and the struggle with the maritime powers is now being conducted far beyond the margins of Eurasia. Second, the advent of intercontinental ballistic missiles has meant that the heartland power is no longer immune to attack from land or sea. Third, Mackinder's alarming and deterministic assumption that the heartland power is endemically expansionist—to the point of world domination—cannot be justified. Nevertheless, the Middle East, but not North Africa, clearly falls within a critical belt of states that are *perceived* by the superpowers to be particularly sensitive. Here, the United States anticipates and fears territorial expansion by the heartland power, whereas the U.S.S.R. deeply resents and fears U.S. influence in borderland states regarded as vital to Soviet security. How far Mackinder and his disciples stoked these fears is impossible to say. The truth remains, however, that the Middle East rimland is still seen as a key strategic region in the global power struggle, quite apart from concerns over access to oilfields.[16]

S. B. Cohen suggested a rather less controversial scheme of world geostrategic regions in which the Middle East along with Egypt, Sudan, and part of Libya, are characterized as "the Middle East shatterbelt." (Figure 2.5a) A shatterbelt is defined as "a large strategically located region . . . occupied by a number of conflicting states . . . caught between the conflicting interests of the Great Powers."[17] Part of western Libya and the Maghreb are grouped with Western Europe in a region known as "maritime Europe and the Maghreb". To date, Cohen's inclusion of the Maghreb with Europe has not been justified, except in the sense that it is farther from the U.S.S.R. than is the Middle East, and the rivalry is, therefore, less intense and the stakes are lower. Thus, although the Maghreb can be seen as part of the worldwide pattern of superpower competition, the Middle East is a crucial contact zone between Eurasia and the maritime world. As with other world views mentioned earlier, Cohen's has two weaknesses in relation to its application to the Middle East and North Africa. First, the global perspective

tends to obscure the infinitely complex and pertinent geopolitical relationships within the region itself. In reality a mosaic of related and
overlapping geopolitical spheres exists. Second, global geostrategic
models are so preoccupied with superpower rivalry that the geopolitical perspectives of the people of the region are distorted or ignored altogether. A better grasp of these perspectives might cause external
powers, particularly the United States, to rethink their policies in the
region. The following sections consider this theme.

Geopolitical Views Within the Region

The states of the Middle East and North Africa have no single geopolitical perspective, but a variety of views conditioned by history, political ideology, and geographic location. Yet most states share certain attitudes that virtually amount to a composite outlook on the world. They
have always resented interference from outside powers in the region's
economic and political life. The intrusion of Cold War politics, which
bring no obvious benefits (except to certain elites) and a great many
risks, is generally deplored. As part of the Islamic world these states
do have a sense of solidarity with communities in Africa and Asia.
Equally important, there is a golden age to look back upon, a time when
Arab and Persian civilizations exported art, medicine, and science to a
backward Europe. This sense of having once been at the center of the
world is reinforced by the fact that Judaism, Christianity, and Islam—
whose adherents number more than half the world's population—emanated from the Middle East. Although academics and strategists from
developed capitalist and Communist societies have found it useful to
fit the Middle East and North Africa into their global geopolitical
schemes, such attempts are rare within the region. The real geopolitical
preoccupations of the people are regional, not global. Long-standing
political cleavages and traditional rivalries dominate relationships between states. Some of these divisions are illustrated in Figure 2.6. For
example, Arab states adjacent to Israel have been incensed by the growth
of a Jewish state at the heart of the Arab world, but they are also concerned with practical questions of territorial security and the political
influence of Palestinians living on their soil. Behind these frontline states,
a second ring of states, equally anti-Zionist, is rather less fearful of Israeli territorial expansion but alert to the possibilities of commando raids
or air strikes. Another example is in the Gulf region where the Arab
states do not fear the U.S.S.R. or the United States half so much as
they fear Iranian military and ideological expansionism. The Iran-Iraq
War has served to concentrate minds on regional dangers, and the Gulf

Figure 2.6   Geopolitical regions and subregions of the Middle East and North
Africa.

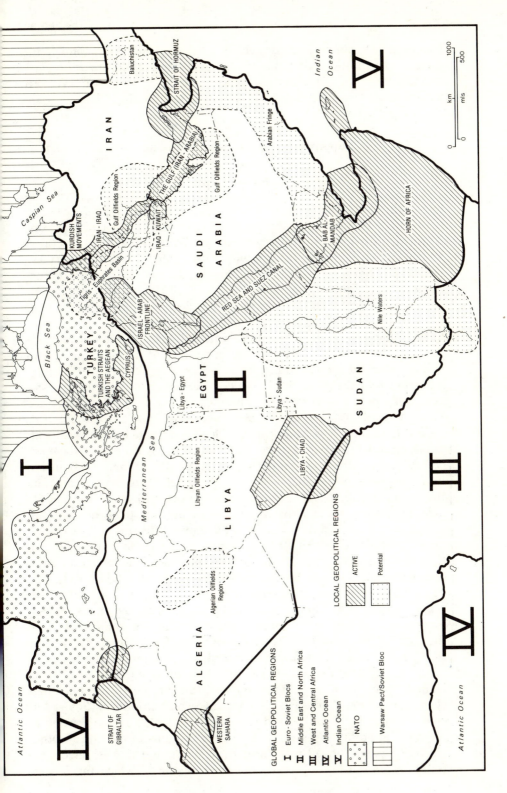

GLOBAL GEOPOLITICAL REGIONS

I   Euro - Soviet Blocs
II Middle East and North Africa
III West and Central Africa
IV Atlantic Ocean
V   Indian Ocean

NATO

Warsaw Pact/Soviet Bloc

LOCAL GEOPOLITICAL REGIONS

ACTIVE

Potential

Atlantic Ocean
Caspian Sea
Black Sea
Mediterranean Sea
Indian Ocean

IRAN
TURKEY
CYPRUS
SAUDI ARABIA
EGYPT
LIBYA
ALGERIA
SUDAN

Baluchistan
STRAIT OF HORMUZ
Arabian Fringe
HORN OF AFRICA
KURDISH MOVEMENTS
IRAN - IRAQ
Gulf Oilfields Region
THE GULF (IRAN - ARABIA)
Gulf Oilfields Region
IRAQ - KUWAIT
BAB AL - MANDAB
RED SEA AND SUEZ CANAL
Tigris Euphrates Basin
ISRAEL - ARAB FRONTLINE
TURKISH STRAITS AND THE AEGEAN
Nile Waters
Libya - Egypt
Libya - Sudan
LIBYA - CHAD
Libyan Oilfields Region
Algerian Oilfields Region
WESTERN SAHARA
STRAIT OF GIBRALTAR

km 0 500 1000
mis 0 500

I   II   III   IV   V

Cooperation Council was formed as a regional response. Similar instances confirm the importance of local geopolitics in North Africa, such as Morocco's struggle with the Polisario guerilla movement in Western Sahara and Libya's military involvement in neighboring Chad.

Superpower Involvement in the Region

The U.S.S.R.

Just as the United States takes a keen interest in what happens close to home in Central America and the Caribbean, the Soviet Union is concerned with the affairs of the Middle East. With over 1400 miles (2200 kilometers) of common border with Turkey and Iran, the everyday business of border security with states to the south is a major preoccupation. In addition, there are 750 miles (1200 kilometers) of Caspian Sea coastline in Iranian hands and 550 miles (880 kilometers) of land boundary in Soviet-occupied Afghanistan to be watched. The importance of these borderlands to Soviet national security is not always appreciated by outsiders. Prior to the overthrow of the Shah of Iran in 1979, the United States had intelligence-collecting facilities strung along Iran's border with the U.S.S.R. Several U.S. electronic monitoring stations still operate in Turkey, which as a member of the North Atlantic Treaty Organization (NATO) is perceived to be hostile to the U.S.S.R. Indeed until the 1960s American missiles were located on Turkish soil. On several occasions in the past, Russian (or Soviet) troops have occupied parts of the Ottoman Empire, Turkey, Persia, and Afghanistan in the interests of national security.[18] Although there is no immediate threat to the U.S.S.R. from conventional ground forces in the Middle East, fears about the massive arms sales by the U.S. to client states are genuine. Such weapons could be requisitioned for use by the United States in wartime. Soviet strategic thinking also has to take account of the fact that short-range missiles or medium-range bombers and fighter bombers could strike at Soviet cities from inside the Middle East. The nearest Soviet territory is less than 200 miles (320 kilometers) from Tehran, 300 miles (480 kilometers) from northern Syria, 500 miles (800 kilometers) from the Mediterranean, and 600 miles (960 kilometers) from the Gulf—as the crow flies. The creation of the Rapid Deployment Force (RDF) has generated even more fear of U.S. intentions in the region.

As long as what the Soviets call the "imperialist powers," led by the United States, retain significant influence in the region through their client states, the Middle East will remain a high priority in Soviet foreign policy. Of all Third World regions, the Middle East is regarded as the most important by the U.S.S.R. both in terms of aid and in other efforts to extend Soviet influence. Arms sales, and to a lesser degree technical assistance, have been the chief means by which the Soviets forged friendships. The building of the Euphrates Dam in Syria and the Aswan High Dam in Egypt are monuments to Soviet engineering skills and political ambitions. But the U.S.S.R. has had a number of disappointments since it first became involved in the Arab world in 1955 after the United States refused to supply weapons to Egypt and finance the High Dam at Aswan. Egypt turned to the U.S.S.R. for help; many years of cooperation ensued until President Sadat asked the Soviet advisers to leave in 1972 and ended the Treaty of Friendship in 1976. Syria and Iraq each have a Treaty of Friendship with the U.S.S.R., signed in 1980 and 1972, respectively. But both states have presented the Soviet Union with problems, not least by being at loggerheads with one another. The Iran-Iraq War has also posed a dilemma because the U.S.S.R. would prefer to be on good terms with both countries. Even so, about 70 percent of Iraq's arms are still of Soviet origin. Syria, at the heart of the Arab world, is a potentially useful ally, but it has always followed an independent course and frequently goes against Soviet wishes (e.g., in Lebanon).

The U.S.S.R. also has good relationships with Algeria, Libya, and the People's Democratic Republic of Yemen (P.D.R. Yemen). The first two, Algeria and Libya, are hostile to communism. The P.D.R. Yemen is the only avowedly Marxist country in the region. In some ways, it is the most useful of all Middle Eastern states for Soviet purposes, giving it a foothold in the pro-Western Arabian peninsula and affording the Soviet navy excellent facilities in Aden and on Socotra Island.

The prime Soviet strategic interest in the Middle East has little to do with oil, at least at present. Rather, it is to prevent the region from becoming a base from which to launch attacks against the Soviet heartland. A secondary role of the region for the U.S.S.R. is for the transiting and deployment of ships of the Soviet Black Sea fleet. The Black Sea fleet provides units for the Mediterranean Sea and the Indian Ocean. Otherwise, the nearest Soviet naval bases are in the Baltic or in the Far East. Although the number of Soviet ships in these seas is never great, they play a key role in the Soviet Union's global political and military thinking. Both are of crucial importance in relation to tanker and other shipping routes; in both regions, the Soviet Union must show the flag to offset the more obvious presence of the Western navies. The political role of the Soviet navy is perhaps particularly important in the Indian Ocean, where the superpowers compete to expand their influence.

The Soviet Union has learned a lot about the dangers and pitfalls of Middle Eastern politics and is very reluctant to become physically involved beyond the level of advisers. But it could do so. Soviet forces theoretically possess the capability to seize the Turkish Straits or occupy the major oilfields or do both. The necessary infrastructure exists for such a massive invasion of the region, and Soviet airlifting capacity is prodigious. Short of World War III, such events are extremely unlikely so long as U.S. military behavior in the region does not become too provocative. Meanwhile, the U.S.S.R. recognizes that the region possesses some of the most glittering geostrategic prizes in the world.

Soviet influence in the region as a whole is relatively small, and is likely to remain so, in part because of the role of Islam. Most Muslims emphatically reject Communist ideology because of its atheism, and Communist parties in the region are generally small, ineffective, and invariably illegal. Fears in the West, especially in the United States, that communism is likely to spread through the region if unchecked are therefore misplaced. Another factor is that Soviet products and technical assistance are usually considered inferior to those from the West. Consequently, the value of Soviet trade, even with friendly states, is far below trade with Western Europe, the United States, and Japan. To the extent that the U.S.S.R. has allies in the region, this is largely because of the limited alternatives available, notably for the supply of weapons, and because of the consistent Soviet support for the Arabs in the Arab-Israeli dispute.

Finally, it is worth remembering that there are some 23 million Sunni Muslims in the Soviet Union, largely located in Central Asia, across the border from Iran and Afghanistan. They are regarded as a potential source of resistance to the goals of communism and are discouraged from practicing their religion. Almost all mosques have been closed, and pilgrimage to Mecca is forbidden. Although isolated from their fellow believers in the Middle East, the Soviet government fears that an Islamic religious revival of some sort might lead to political unrest in Soviet Central Asia.[19]

The United States

The starting point for consideration of the United States and the Middle East and North Africa must be distance. From the eastern seaboard of the United States across the Atlantic to North Africa and the Mediterranean is over 3000 miles (4800 kilometers). Yet the western Mediterranean is only halfway from the United States to the Gulf. Steaming at about 15 knots, a ship can reach Tangier, Morocco, from New York in eight or nine days. It may take another six days to traverse the Mediterranean to the Suez Canal, and at least four days to pass through the canal and the Red Sea to Aden. From Aden to the Strait of Hormuz at the entrance to the Gulf may take four more days. Thus, without allowing for port calls or any other delays, the voyage from New York to the Gulf takes about three weeks. Civil aircraft flying time from New York to destinations in North Africa is between 8 and 10 hours. From Cairo to Riyadh, for example, would add another 2 or 3 hours, or at least 4 hours to destinations in the Gulf from Cairo. All these times assume the availability of direct flights. Military transport aircraft would be slower and would require stopover facilities en route, for example, in the Azores or Morocco.

In spite of distance, there is a high level of intercommunication between the United States and certain states of North Africa and the Middle East. The United States is one of the chief exporters of manufactured goods to the region, rivaling France, Japan, the United Kingdom, and West Germany. Israel, Saudi Arabia, and Turkey are the chief trading partners. Trade with Iran also used to be important. U.S. supplies to the region include large quantities of military equipment. Approximately 20 percent of all America's imported oil is obtained from the Middle East. A fair number of Americans also visit the region as tourists, business executives, technical experts, and in various military roles. The Middle East, rather more than North Africa, has been given intensive media coverage in the United States on particular occasions, for example, during the October 1973 War, during the Iranian hostage crisis (1979–1981), and during the deployment of U.S. Marines in Lebanon (1982–1984).

The United States has a number of interrelated motives for its heavy involvement with the region. Containment of the Soviet Union and combating the spread of Soviet influence are top priorities, regardless of the reality of the threat. U.S. policy is predicated on rarely questioned assumptions about Soviet expansion and the vulnerability of the Middle East. American involvement only gained momentum with the gradual decline since the 1950s of British influence. In 1955, the United States masterminded the Baghdad Pact, a defense alliance among Britain, Turkey, Iraq, Iran, and Pakistan that effectively completed the encirclement of the Soviet Union with U.S. allies from the Philippines to Europe. The pact lasted only until 1958, when Iraq withdrew, and the remaining members formed a new alliance, the Central Treaty Organization (CENTO). When British forces withdrew from the Gulf region in 1971, the United States became extremely active in cultivating Iran and Saudi Arabia as local allies in the region. Both states, but especially Iran, received massive supplies of weapons and military assistance. This concentration of armaments in the Soviet Union's backyard was regarded as highly provocative. At about the same time, the United States negotiated with Britain to build military facilities on the Indian Ocean island of Diego Garcia. The U.S. "twin pillar" policy received a sharp setback with the fall of the Shah in 1979, and there is currently great determination not to allow Saudi Arabia to go the same way.

Support for Israel is a second major plank in U.S. Middle East policy. There are 6 million Jews in the United States who play a vital role in shaping national policies toward Israel and the Middle East generally. U.S. aid to Israel, particularly the supply of arms, has been colossal (see Chapter 9), but it does not mean that the United States has unlimited power to influence Israeli policy. Regionally, Israel represents a considerable liability for the United States. The special relationship between the two states has greatly damaged American relationships with the Arab world. The need to rush supplies to Israel in the event of another war with the Arabs would pose the U.S. Government with some difficult decisions. It is not surprising that successive American administrations have sought a negotiated peace between Israel and her enemies.

Since 1979, several events have focused American attention sharply, almost obsessively, on the Gulf region: the fall of the Shah in 1979, the Soviet invasion of Afghanistan, and the outbreak of the Iran-Iraq War in 1980.[20] There were fears of further Soviet gains in the region, of the spread of the Islamic revolution from Iran to neighboring states, and of general political instability. The result of these events could be to deprive the United States or its allies in Western Europe or Japan of much needed supplies of oil. In January 1980, President Jimmy Carter declared that his administration was willing to use any means necessary to defend the vital interests of the United States in the Gulf region.[21] This policy has been continued under President Ronald Reagan, and the mobile RDF has been greatly expanded and upgraded several times. To move the 400,000 men of the RDF and their equipment implies access points en route, possibly in Morocco, Turkey, Egypt, Israel, and Oman, and continuing use of Diego Garcia, where supplies and equipment are prepositioned.[22] In addition to the RDF, the United States maintains a powerful naval force in the Mediterranean in the shape of the Sixth Fleet, which operates from bases chiefly in Spain and Italy. Its function is to support NATO's southern flank in the Mediterranean and to protect U.S. interests in general. The U.S. Navy has facilities at a number of strategic locations in the region. Those in Egypt are of particular interest, having been made available to the United States only after 1976, when Egypt expelled the Soviet Union. This swift turnabout in superpower fortunes admirably illustrates the unpredictability of Middle East politics and the changing strategic value of places.

It may seem excessive to have concentrated so much on the United States and the U.S.S.R., but their influence overshadows the politics of the Middle East, and is likely to continue to do so in the future. Ironically, it was the superpowers of an earlier era, Britain and France, who were largely instrumental in creating the system of states that have given today's nuclear superpowers a choice of client states in the shatterbelt. In many cases, superpower patronage has exacerbated local and regional rivalries and sometimes even cynically exploited them. Moreover, as Chapters 6 and 8 will show, Great Power interference over the years has done little to solve problems of national or regional integration and has sometimes created new problems. It is, therefore, basic to an understanding of the region's political geography to know how the contemporary pattern of states emerged.

Notes

1. "Crescent of crisis" is a distasteful term to the people of the region because of the symbolism of the Crescent in Islam and the implied association of the faith of Islam with crises (e.g., see the cover of *Time*, 15 January 1979).

2. See C. R. Koppes, "Captain Mahan, General Gordon, and the origins of the term 'Middle East,' " *Middle Eastern Studies* 12(1976): 95–98.

3. Altogether, twenty-two states have been chosen for study in this book; these states are collectively called "the region."

4. Members of OPEC in the region are: Algeria, Iran, Iraq, Kuwait, Libya, Qatar, Saudi Arabia, and the United Arab Emirates (U.A.E.). Members of OAPEC are: Algeria, Bahrain, Egypt (suspended since 1979), Iraq, Kuwait, Libya, Qatar, Saudi Arabia, Syria, Tunisia, and the U.A.E.

5. Peter Beaumont, Gerald H. Blake, and J. Malcolm Wagstaff in *The Middle East: A Geographical Study* (London: John Wiley & Sons, 1976) include these states. William B. Fisher in *The Middle East: a Physical, Social and Regional Geography*, 7th ed. (London: Methuen and Co., Ltd. 1978) includes Sudan and Cyprus.

6. A classic work on seapower in the Mediterranean is Ferdinand Braudel's *The Mediterranean and the Mediterranean World in the Age of Philip II*, 2 vols. (London: Fontana-Collins, 1972).

7. Saul B. Cohen, "A New Map of Global Geopolitical Equilibrium: A Developmental Approach," *Political Geography Quarterly* 1(1982): 223–241.

8. R. V. Weeks (ed.), *Muslim Peoples: A World Ethnographic Survey* (Westport, Conn., and London: Greenwood Press, 1978). Cited by John I. Clarke, "Islamic Populations." Paper presented at the Annual Conference of the Institute of British Geographers, Durham, Eng., January 1984: 1–14.

9. Throughout the centuries the hidden Imam or Mahdi is thought to have appeared in Muslim countries from time to time.

10. For an excellent survey of definitions of the Third World see J. P. Dickenson, C. G. Clarke et al., *A Geography of the Third World* (London: Methuen and Co., Ltd. 1983).

11. See Ibrahim F. I. Shihata, *The Other Face of O.P.E.C.: Financial Assistance to the Third World* (London: Longman, 1982).

12. Halford J. Mackinder, "The Geographical Pivot of History," *Geographical Journal* 23(1904): 431–444; and Halford J. Mackinder, *Democratic Ideals and Reality* (New York: Henry Holt, 1919; republished 1942).

13. See Robert E. Walters, *The Nuclear Trap* (Harmondsworth, Eng.: Penguin Books, 1974).

14. Nicholas J. Spykman, *The Geography of the Peace* (New York: Harcourt Brace, 1944).

15. Donald W. Meinig, "Heartland and Rimland in Eurasian History," *Western Political Quarterly* 9 (1956): 553–569.

16. William Kirk has observed that the subtropical zone extending through the Mediterranean basin and corresponding fairly precisely with the rimland has been the zone of civilizations and innovation. Remarkably, it appears to have its counterpart in Central America. See William Kirk, *Geographical Pivots of History* (Leicester, Eng.: Leicester University Press, 1965). The idea is also discussed in Norman J. G. Pounds, *Political Geography*, 2nd ed. (New York: McGraw-Hill, 1972): 433–434.

17. Saul B. Cohen, *Geography and Politics in a World Divided*, 2nd ed. (New York: Oxford University Press, 1973): 253. For a critique of Cohen's idea of geostrategic regions see J. R. V. Prescott, *The Geography of State Policies* (London: Hutchinson, 1968).

18. See Chapter 3. Russian attempts to reach the Turkish Straits in 1877–78, incursions into Persia in 1920–21, occupation of parts of Iran in World War II are examples.

19. With large numbers of Muslims (23 million), Armenian Christians (4 million) and Jews (2 million), the Soviet Union should have a good understanding of some of the peoples of the Middle East.

20. Publishing books and papers on Gulf security became a minor industry. See David Newman, Ewan Anderson, and Gerald Blake, *The Security of Gulf Oil: An Introductory Bib-*

liography. Occasional Paper 13. (Durham, Eng.: University of Durham Centre for Middle Eastern and Islamic Studies, 1982): 1–55.

21. In January 1957, a similar commitment was made by President Eisenhower ("The Eisenhower Doctrine"), though it referred to the "Mid East," not exclusively to the Gulf, and it pledged economic and military assistance to fight communism in the region.

22. The logistics of a RDF operation would be formidable. Diego Garcia is 2500 miles (4000 kilometers) from the Gulf. Two months' supplies for 12,000 men are held there. An airborne battalion could reach the Gulf from the United States in 48 hours. Within 45 days, five to seven divisions could be in place, though there are plans to reduce this to 30 days by 1987. See "Buildup on the Arc of Crisis," *South* (March 1983): 9–17.

Selected Bibliography

Al-Ebraheem, Hassan A. *Kuwait and the Gulf: Small States and the International System.* Washington D.C.: Center for Contemporary Arab Studies; London: Croom Helm, 1984.

Amirsadeghi, Hossein (ed.). *The Security of the Persian Gulf.* London: Croom Helm, 1981.

Ayoob, Mohammed (ed.). *The Middle East in World Affairs.* London: Croom Helm, 1981.

Cohen, Saul B. *Geography and Politics in a World Divided,* 2nd ed. New York: Oxford University Press, 1973.

Dickenson, J. P., Clarke, C. G., et al. *A Geography of the Third World.* London: Methuen and Co., Ltd., 1983.

Duncan, Raymond W. (ed.). *Soviet Policy in the Third World.* New York: Pergamon Press Inc., 1980.

Elliot, S. R., and Lee, I. "Middle East Geopolitics." *Geographical Magazine* 52(1980): 636–646.

Glassner, Martin I., and de Blij, Harm J., *Systematic Political Geography,* 3rd ed. New York: John Wiley & Sons, 1980.

Halliday, Fred. *Arabia Without Sultans.* Harmondsworth, Eng.: Penguin Books, 1974.

Henrikson, A. K. "The Geographical Mental Maps of American Foreign Policy Makers." *International Political Science Review* 1(1980): 495–530.

House, John W. "War, Peace, and Conflict Resolution: Towards an Indian Ocean Model." *Transactions of the Institute of British Geographers* 9(1984): 3–21.

Independent Commission on International Development Issues. *North-South: A Programme for Survival.* London: Pan Books, 1980.

Kaufman, Edy. *The Superpowers and their Spheres of Influence.* London: Croom Helm, 1976.

Kidron, M., and Segal, R. *State of the World Atlas.* Harmondsworth, Eng.; Penguin Books, 1981.

Kliot, Nurit, and Waterman, Stanley (eds.). *Pluralism and Political Geography: People, Territory and State.* New York: St. Martin's Press, 1983.

Legum, Colin (ed.). *Strategic Issues in the Middle East.* London: Croom Helm, 1982.

Lewis, J. W. *The Strategic Balance in the Mediterranean.* Washington, D.C.: American Enterprise Institute for Public Policy Research. Foreign Affairs Study No. 29 (March 1976): 1–169.

Luciani, Giacomo (ed.). *The Mediterranean Region.* London: Croom Helm, 1983.

Muir, Richard. *Modern Political Geography.* London: Macmillan, 1975.

Rabinovich, Itamar, and Shaked, Haim. *The Middle East and the United States: Images, Perceptions, and Policies.* New Brunswick, N.J.: Transaction Books, 1980.

Rowley, Gwyn. *Israel into Palestine.* London: Mansell, 1984.

Sella, Amnon. *Soviet Political and Military Conduct in the Middle East.* London: Macmillan, 1981.

Spanier, John. *American Foreign Policy Since World War II*, 8th ed. New York: Holt, Rinehart & Winston, 1980.

Spiegal, Steven L. (ed.). *The Middle East and the Western Alliance*. London: Allen & Unwin Inc., 1982.

Treverton, Gregory. *Crisis Management and the Superpowers*. Adelphi Paper No. 5. London: International Institute for Strategic Studies, 1981.

PART II

Partition

3

The Evolution of the State System: The Partitioning of Territory

The contemporary political geographic landscape of the Middle East and North Africa is only the latest version of a constantly changing pattern of spatial-political arrangements that has gone on for over 5000 years. The region's historical geography is complex. If some cinematic miracle made it possible to film the changing political map for screening in the space of an hour or so, it would create an exciting visual impression. States and empires would appear—now here, now there, spread out, change shape—and then die away. Some states would be consumed from outside, whereas others would shatter into fragments from within. For most of the time, the map would be a kaleidoscope of changing shapes and colors. All the skills of the film producer would be needed to depict some of the territorial arrangements, like no-man's-lands, tributary states, and shared sovereignty. But beyond the reach of states and empires, where tribes and tribal federations held sway, it would be impossible to show the ever-changing mosaic of tiny territorial units.

It would be unprofitable to attempt a historical summary here.[1] Instead, selected historic evidence will be used to answer three questions. First, are there recurrent patterns in the political organization of space, such as core regions, or persistent interstate frontiers? Second, what other types of spatial organization have flourished besides the state? Third, to what extent has the modern political map been inherited from the past?

The Political Organization of Space Before World War I

Four main kinds of autonomous political territory were to be found in the Middle East and North Africa before World War I: *tribal territories, independent states, imperial territories,* and *colonial territories* (Figure 3.1). All have featured prominently in the region's past political geography. As will be seen later, there are problems associated with defining these terms and summarizing the relationship between them. At times, they existed side by side; at other times, they were superimposed uneasily on each other; and, occasionally, they had a formal hierarchical relationship. All these territorial units also possessed their own *internal* spatial arrangements. Within tribal territories, there were usually clan divisions. States and empires were subdivided into provinces or their equivalent and below provincial level into smaller administrative units. The finest examples were in the Persian, Roman, and Ottoman empires. Such territorial arrangements for local government were often far more effective instruments of administration and control than some of the tribal territories and microstates considered in this chapter.

Tribal Territories

Both nomadic and sedentary communities in the region possess elements of tribal organization and tribal values even today.[2] In the past, tribalism pervaded society, even in the towns. Before World War I perhaps 10 percent of the region's population was tribal nomads. In some parts of Arabia, Iran, and Sudan, the proportion was much greater. The overall percentage for the region may have been higher in earlier centuries, but it was probably never above 20 percent. Tribalism spread into sedentary communities by a number of processes. Nomadic groups settled in villages adjacent to their grazing lands throughout history, and many cultivators are conscious of their distant nomadic origins. More dramatically, nomadic tribes periodically burst out of the desert and penetrated deep into settled zones, with devastating consequences. Such invasions have been most common in the northern Middle East, bringing about the sudden nomadization of extensive areas. Iraq was thus overrun in the early Middle Ages, causing destruction of cities and degradation of irrigated farmland from which the region never recovered.[3]

Although both sedentary and nomadic tribal peoples have played an important part in the political geography of the region, nomadic tribes are most relevant. These often succeeded in maintaining genuine territorial independence, particularly in the Arabian peninsula where tribal groupings have affected state boundary delimitation and state structure. Throughout most of the rest of the Middle East and North Africa, nomadic tribes have come under the central authority of state or empire, but they continued to exercise a semiautonomous existence. Governments invariably regarded nomadic tribes with some fear and suspicion, being difficult to tax and sometimes constituting a physical threat to settlements along the desert fringes. In confronting central governments, nomadic tribes enjoyed not only the obvious advantage of mo-

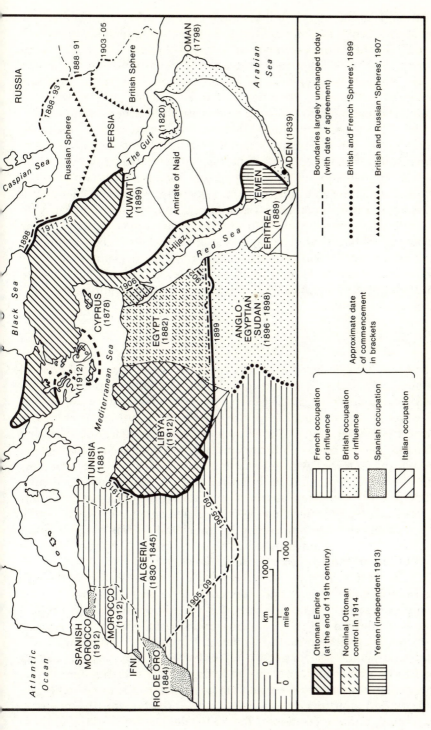

Figure 3.1 The Middle East and North Africa before World War I. (After Peter Beaumont, Gerald Blake, and J. Malcolm Wagstaff, *The Middle East: A Geographical Study.* New York: Wiley, 1976, p. 296. Copyright © 1976 by John Wiley & Sons, Inc. Reprinted by permission of the publisher.)

bility and inaccessibility, but also good organization. Members of the same tribe inhabit a common territory, share a common sentiment derived primarily from a common ancestor, and possess cultural and linguistic similarities. They recognize an obligation to unite in war and to settle internal disputes by arbitration.[4] Neighboring tribes frequently recognized distant kinship ties and intertribal alliances were easily formed, resulting in the creation of powerful tribal federations.

Tribal territories differ from state territories in a number of ways. The boundaries of tribal territory are not precisely defined. In most cases, there was a recognized zone of no-man's-land between the wells and pastures of neighboring tribes. In sparsely populated regions, tribal territories could expand and contract, depending on the availability of pasture and population size. Tribal government was patriarchal, with considerable power bestowed on the tribal head man or shaykh. The center of political power was in and around the tent of the shaykh, migrating seasonally with the rest of the tribe. At the same time, there were usually certain locations in the tribal territory that were regarded as having special significance to the tribe, for example, for burial of the dead or the exchange of goods.

Independent States

The term "state" is used to describe a great variety of types of political organization and scale of territory. In the Middle East and North Africa, almost any political unit that is neither tribal territory nor an empire would probably qualify for the title of state. The state is an autonomous territorial unit, but unlike the tribe, it may encompass several different communities. To maintain itself, the state needs to be able to raise taxes, enforce laws, and recruit an army. Most state governments are, therefore, centralized and depend on paid officials and good communications for effective administration and control. Not that this was always achieved. In fact, many small states sprang up when central government was weak and smooth administration was hardly a priority. States of this kind featured quite often in the history of Morocco and Lebanon, though generally for quite short periods.[5]

The earliest civilizations probably arose in the Middle East in the fifth and fourth millennia B.C. These appear to have been the product of the complex organization needed to exploit the arid but potentially productive alluvial plains of the Tigris-Euphrates basin. Raw materials, such as copper and timber, had to be brought from neighboring highlands, and an irrigation system needed to be devised. Thus, surplus produce had to be exchanged centrally, trade organized, and irrigation implemented. In response to these and other societal needs, three highly significant developments occurred: the emergence of towns, the invention of writing, and the creation of the first states. At the beginning, these states were little more than city-states or urban centers with their tributary food-producing villages; in time, larger states developed. States expanded through conquest, alliances, and annexation; a powerful incentive to expand was provided by the shortage of productive land in Mesopotamia.[6] Before the coming of the great empires, Mesopotamia witnessed a succession of states. This political discontinuity can probably be explained by the vulnerability of the region as a marchland for peoples and armies.[7] Egypt by contrast enjoyed long periods of political stability and empire because it rarely had to face invaders. As states became larger, they embraced peoples of different languages, culture, and religion, and in most of them, there were communities working for, and against, the welfare of the state. As in the modern state, there was conflict between *centrifugal* and *centripetal* forces.

Although these early states had a superficial similarity to the modern state, embracing territory and people and being governed from a core area, there were differences. The degree of central government control often declined with distance from the center of power. In peripheral and inaccessible regions, such as mountains and desert margins, nominal citizens of the state could escape their obligations to the state, particularly when the central government was weak. The Arab historian Ibn Khaldun recognized this when he identified the "lands of the treasury" under formal state control and the "lands of dissidence" beyond, in which state control was only partial.[8]

Imperial Territories

The difference between state and empire is largely a question of scale. Empires arise when there is a concentration of military expertise, manpower, and resources in the hands of a particularly energetic and ambitious people. Empires grow through the subjugation of existing political units, invariably by conquest or the threat of conquest. Once established, they require a far more elaborate government apparatus than the state because of the greater distances involved and the higher cost of administration and maintenance of military supremacy.

Why have there been so many successive empires in the Middle East and North Africa? As with the succession of states previously discussed, part of the explanation lies in the geography of the region. First, the movement of armies by land and navies by sea is not greatly hampered by physical barriers or by adverse seasonal weather conditions. Second, there is no one region with an effective monopoly of political power by virtue of having a large population and exceptional concentration of resources. The earliest empires of Egypt, Babylon, and Assyria were based on the cultivation of the Nile Valley and Mesopotamia. Although these fertile regions enjoyed long periods of political ascendancy, other great empires, such as Persia, sprang up from heartlands in contrasting types of environment and in various locations. If the smaller empires are taken into account, it could be said that almost every part of the region can look back to an age of political power, and all parts of the region have also experienced alien domination. A third explanation for the succession of empires is proximity to Europe and Asia. Several empires have spread into the region from outside, primarily because of seapower in the Mediterranean. The Phoenicians (tenth to sixth centuries B.C.) and later the Greeks and the Romans depended heavily on naval supremacy in the Mediterranean. Many leading cities in classical times were on the coast.

The impetus for the great Arab-Islamic conquests came from the arid interior of western Arabia after the Prophet Muhammad (570-632) had preached the faith of Islam. Less than a century after his death, Islamic armies had conquered most of the Middle East and North Africa and much of Iberia (Figure 3.2). Most of the early Islamic conquests were under the Umayyads (661–750), whose capital was Damascus. During the Umayyad dynasty the empire was centrally governed and the administration dominated by Arabs. Islam and both Arabic language and culture took root and flourished, thus forming the basis for contemporary pan-Arabism. In 750 the Umayyads were overthrown by a revolt in the east that established the Abbasid dynasty (750–1258) as leaders of the Islamic community. Power shifted to Baghdad and the Arabs lost their predominant position. Islamic civilization and culture achieved their greatest glories under the Abbasids before the empire began to disintegrate into self-governing dynasties.

In the twelfth century, the Muslim empire was challenged by the Christian Crusaders from Europe, who sustained a precarious state in the Levant for nearly 200 years. In the thirteenth century, the Middle East was once again caught up in powerful movements from far beyond the region as the Mongols overran Persia and Mesopotamia, thus adding large areas to the vast Mongol Empire, whose heartland was in central Asia. The Abbasid dynasty fell with the destruction of Baghdad by the Mongols in 1258. Among the nomadic peoples retreating before the Mongols were Muslims from Turkestan, who eventually settled in Asia Minor. From about 1300, under their leader Othman, these Muslims began a territorial expansion that continued virtually unchecked until the Ottoman Empire was at its zenith in the late seventeenth century. Ottoman rule extended over most of the Middle East, into Southeast Europe, North Africa, and over much of the Mediterranean Sea (Figure 3.3).[9] In the East, however, the Ottomans failed to defeat the Persians, with whom they waged a series of costly and inconclusive wars.

Small-scale maps of the Ottoman Empire mask the complexities of Ottoman administration. The empire proved far too vast for central

---

Figure 3.2   The expansion of Islam, showing the main lines of advance of the invading armies.

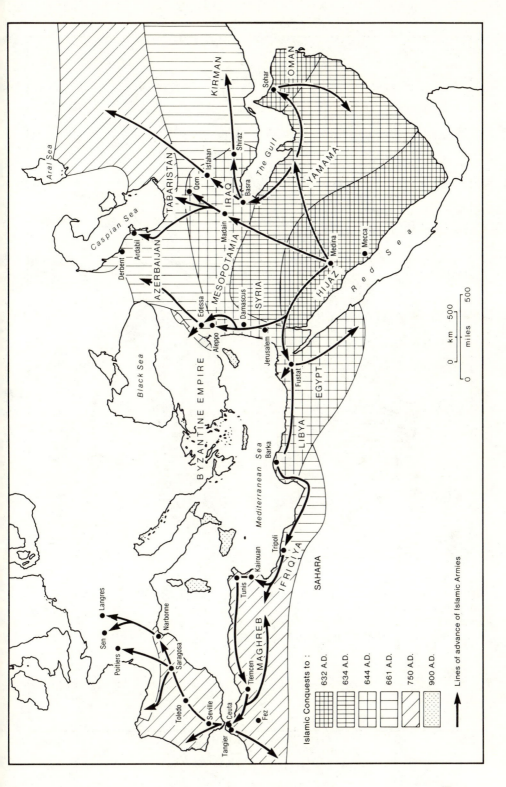

Islamic Conquests to :

	632 A.D.
	634 A.D.
	644 A.D.
	661 A.D.
	750 A.D.
	900 A.D.

Lines of advance of Islamic Armies

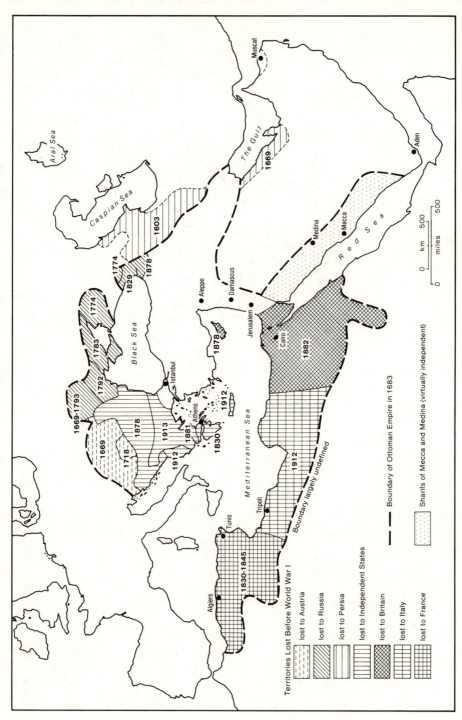

Figure 3.3 The expansion and contraction of the Ottoman Empire.

control by the Sultan, and a great deal of decentralization occurred. Conquered lands were divided into *sanjaks* administered by military officers. A group of *sanjaks* formed an *eyalet* under a governor-general *(beylerbey)*. Many outlying provinces in the Arabian peninsula, eastern Turkey, and elsewhere retained their ruling hierarchies; as long as they paid their taxes, they remained semi-independent. From time to time, provincial governors achieved effective independence. The most celebrated example was Muhammad Ali, an Albanian officer, dispatched by the Ottoman Sultan to Egypt at the time of Napoleon's invasion in 1798. In 1805, after the expulsion of the French, the Sultan recognized Muhammad Ali as Viceroy of Egypt. In subsequent decades, Muhammad Ali implemented far-reaching economic and social reforms, and he created a formidable army. Most of his efforts were designed to turn Egypt into a major military power, and for some years, he and his son Ibrahim Pasha succeeded. They conducted successful campaigns in Arabia, the Sudan, and the Levant, giving Egypt temporary control of the two key routes to India via the Red Sea and the Euphrates Valley. In 1839, however, when Ottoman Turkey was threatened, Britain, Austria, Russia, and Prussia acted jointly to save the Sultan, and Muhammad Ali was forced to accept a limitation on his army and withdraw to Egypt.[10]

From the late seventeenth century, the Ottoman Empire was in decline. A series of reforms in the nineteenth and early twentieth centuries failed to halt the disintegration of the outer margins of the empire. Attempts were made to modernize the army and reestablish control in the provinces, not least by the construction of strategic railways. In 1864, the old *eyalets* were replaced by 27 larger *vilayets* under a *vali* with extensive administrative powers, and local government at all levels was reorganized along French lines. These reforms, however, had come too late; like so many of its predecessors, the empire had outgrown its strength. It might have been saved by vigorous leadership, a powerful army and navy, and efficient administration, but the sultans had become reactionary and ineffective, and their armies were unreliable. Unrest among the Sultan's Christian subjects in the Balkans resulted in independence for Greeks, Serbs, Romanians, and Bulgars. Economic stagnation also hastened Ottoman decline. The opening of the Cape route to India by the Portuguese in 1498 had long deprived the eastern Mediterranean of lucrative transit trade between India and Europe. Another economic weakness was the marked increase of European influence; by the end of the eighteenth century, most trade with Europe was in the hands of Jews and Christians and there was heavy indebtedness to foreign banks. Under the system of Capitulations, large numbers of non-Muslims were encouraged to trade in the empire. Ottoman imports of cheap manufactured goods far exceeded the value of exports of raw materials, while traditional manufacturing suffered disastrously.

The international boundaries that form the framework of the state system of the Middle East and North Africa today are largely the product of the period between 1830 and 1923, when the Ottoman Empire was disintegrating. Several such boundaries are based on former Ottoman administrative divisions, and some provincial capitals became the leading cities of new states. Ottoman laws still govern land and property, personal status, and minority rights in several Middle East states. The issue of who would succeed the Ottomans (the Eastern Question) dominated the foreign policy of the Great Powers for over a century. By World War I, the Ottoman Empire had become so weak that a territorial carve-up by the Europeans was inevitable.

Colonial Territories

European imperial rivalry was worldwide during the nineteenth century, but it was especially strong in the Middle East and North Africa. Not only were these regions readily accessible, but also the economic and strategic prizes they promised were considerable. The Maghreb and Libya were occupied by France, Spain, and Italy, primarily for colonization and trade, though strategic rivalry was also involved. Large numbers of Europeans settled in these territories; at their peak in 1956, they were 1.9 million, or 7 percent of the total population. The European powers had looked forward to an indefinite stay in North Africa: for example, Algeria was administered as part of Metropolitan France and Libya was regarded as Italy's "fourth shore". Rivalry in the Middle East, on the other hand, was dominated by geostrategic considerations. Britain and France were keen to control their routes to India; Russia coveted the Turkish Straits and sought access to the Gulf. Commercial and strategic interests went hand in hand. For example, cotton from Egypt and the Sudan was of crucial importance to the British textile industry. There was no attempt to plant colonies in these countries, though many Europeans lived in the major cities, such as Cairo and Istanbul. The discovery of oil in southern Persia in 1908 added a new dimension to the competing interests of the outside powers in the Middle East, but it was some 50 years before oil was discovered in North Africa.

Colonialism in North Africa

It was inevitable that in an age of European colonial expansion, attention would turn to North Africa, whose economic potential was well known. France and Italy were only a few days' sail away. The first Europeans to establish a foothold were the Portuguese in 1415. Thereafter, Spain and Portugal established and lost a string of strongholds along the Atlantic and Mediterranean coasts of Morocco.[11] The French conquest of Algeria began in 1830, ostensibly to curb the activities of the Barbary pirates in the Mediterranean but in practice to secure trading rights and territorial aggrandizement. Initial Algerian resistance lasted for almost 40 years. French efforts to subdue the people and destroy native culture were ruthless. Nowhere in the region was European political and cultural domination eventually so complete as in Algeria.

France established a protectorate over Tunisia in 1881 to counter growing Italian influence. Three years later, at the Congress of Berlin, Britain waived any interest in Tunisia in return for France's agreement not to interfere in Cyprus, which Britain had acquired in 1878. Frustrated in Tunisia, the Italians began to look to Libya to fulfill their imperial dreams. In 1904, France acknowledged Italy's exclusive interest in Libya in return for Italian recognition of French rights in Morocco. The Italian conquest of Libya began in 1911. Ottoman resistance soon collapsed, but fierce Libyan resistance continued in Cyrenaica under the charismatic leadership of Umar Mukhtar. Once pacified in the 1920s, Libya was energetically colonized, and by 1939, there were 100,000 Italian settlers. Soon after their invasion of Libya, the Italians seized the strategically located Dodecanese islands 15 miles (24 kilometers) off the Turkish coast. These islands offered no economic prospects but controlled the approaches to the Aegean Sea and the Turkish Straits. Their loss was striking evidence of the military weakness of the Ottomans on land and sea.

Morocco had never been part of the Ottoman Empire and was ruled by independent sultans. Although it had considerable economic potential in the cultivable lowland areas, the main attraction for the European powers was geopolitical. France was concerned with the security of Algeria, and Spain, Italy, Germany, and Britain all had an interest in the Strait of Gibraltar. In 1904, Britain agreed to allow France a free hand in Morocco in return for French noninterference in Egypt. France and Spain also agreed to divide Morocco into French and Spanish spheres of influence.[12] In 1912, the Sultan of Morocco was forced to agree to a French protectorate. Spain was granted a protectorate in northern Morocco and the Tarfaya region in southern Morocco was recognized as a Spanish sphere of influence. An International Zone was established around Tangier in 1923 to ensure freedom of navigation through the Strait of Gibraltar (Figures 3.4a and 3.4b). The International Zone was abolished in 1956 and Tangier became part of an independent Morocco.

Colonialism in The Middle East

For two centuries, European interests in the Middle East were largely associated with trade and shipping routes to the East. From the middle of the eighteenth century, the struggle for supremacy in India between France and Britain brought the Middle East into the geopolitical arena. Even before the opening of the Suez Canal in 1869, the transshipment of goods and troops overland via Suez and the Red Sea saved three months on the voyage from Calcutta to London, which took five months via the Cape under sail. Thus, for nearly 150 years, Anglo-French rivalry was one of the chief reasons for European intervention in the Middle East. The other recurrent theme throughout the same period was the fear of Russian expansion to seize the Turkish Straits or parts of Iran.

British Interests

Britain emerged as the dominant power in India from the mid-eighteenth century, but Napoleon invaded Egypt in 1798 with the idea of securing the Red Sea for France and cutting a canal through the isthmus of Suez to hasten the expulsion of the British from India. Napoleon's scheme ended in failure, but it persuaded Britain to play a more active role in the region. In 1802, Britain temporarily occupied Perim Island at the entrance to the Red Sea and persuaded the Sultan of Oman to exclude French subjects from his harbors on either side of the Strait of Hormuz. Britain's territorial acquisitions during the nineteenth century were also extensive (Figure 3.1). In addition, Britain also signed

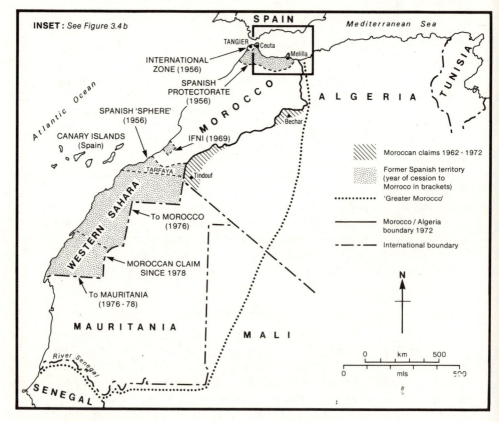

Figure 3.4a Northwest Africa: Spanish colonial territories and Moroccan claims and acquisitions.

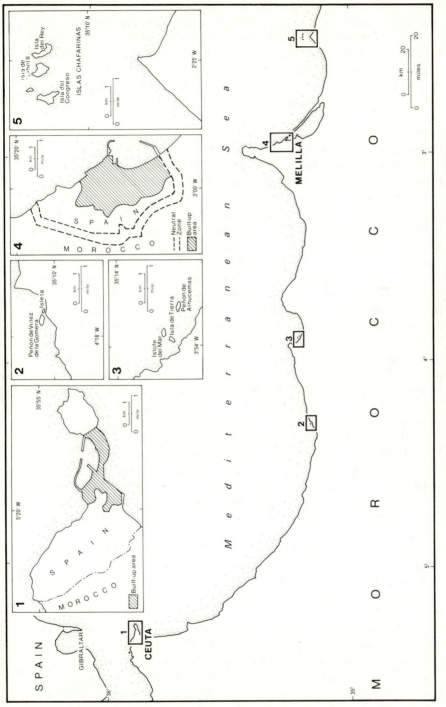

Figure 3.4b   Spanish possessions on Morocco's Mediterranean coast in 1984.

treaties with the small shaykhdoms on the Indian Ocean and Gulf coasts of Arabia excluding rival powers and agreeing to the suppression of slavery and piracy.[13] Britain occupied Egypt in 1882 to protect British financial interests and the Suez Canal at a time of internal unrest. Meanwhile, Sudan broke away from Egypt during the Mahdist rebellion and a joint military expedition established an Anglo-Egyptian condominium over the territory in 1899.

French Interests
France was probably more successful than Britain when it came to cultural and economic penetration of the Middle East. The military successes of Muhammad Ali and Ibrahim Pasha owed much to French officers. In 1840, when the other Great Powers persuaded France to stop supporting Egypt, they frustrated French hopes of establishing a powerful ally. The French may have been particularly disappointed that Ibrahim Pasha was forced to withdraw from Syria because of their traditional concern for the protection of the Maronite Christians. France also had a keen interest in securing supplies of raw silk from the mulberry plantations of Lebanon. Thus, in 1860, when thousands of Maronites were massacred in Lebanon, largely by the Druze, and Damascus a French force landed in Beirut to keep the peace. The Great Powers pressed the Sultan to agree to the establishment of a specially privileged *mutasarrifiyyah* of Lebanon with a Christian governor. French cultural and educational activity flourished in this area for many years. During the 1860s, French influence in various parts of the Ottoman Empire grew in the form of educational and cultural assistance, railway concessions, and trade.

France's greatest triumph was the completion of the Suez Canal in 1869. Britain had opposed the construction of canals and railways on the route to India as being too costly and difficult to protect and because it also controlled the Cape route. The French persisted, and for a time, the Suez Canal was owned and managed largely by them. In 1875, however, the Khedive of Egypt sold his canal shares to Britain to pay off some of his debts, and protection of the canal became a foreign policy priority for Britain for many decades. By 1913, 60 percent of canal shipping was registered in Britain, followed by the Netherlands (6 percent), and France (5 percent).

Russian Interests
By the 1870s, Britain, France, and Russia had become increasingly nervous about each other's intentions in the Middle East. Fear of Russian expansion at the expense of the Ottoman Empire was nothing new. For example, when Ibrahim Pasha was threatening the Ottoman heartland, the Russians advanced to within 150 miles (240 kilometers) of Istanbul before being persuaded to withdraw by Britain and France. The Treaty of Hunkiar Iskelesi (1833) gave Russia the right to control the Turkish

Straits in wartime. The Crimea War (1853–56) was fought by Britain, France, Austria, Turkey, and Sardinia fundamentally to check Russian ambitions. Russia's claim to protect all Orthodox Christians of whatever nationality throughout the Ottoman Empire would almost certainly have provided an excuse for territorial expansion sooner or later. The ultimate goal of such expansion was always assumed to be control of the Turkish Straits. Austria also had vague hopes of controlling the straits, but Russia's economic interests were far stronger. As Russia absorbed parts of the Ottoman Empire around the Black Sea and began to develop the Ukraine, unhindered access to the Mediterranean became essential. By 1914, 60 percent of all Russia's seaborne trade passed the straits, including nearly all grain exports. The European powers were determined not to permit Russian control of the Turkish Straits, which could lead to Russian influence in the Mediterranean.

The Russo-Turkish War of 1877–78 brought Russian troops within 7 miles (11 kilometers) of Istanbul. When the terms of the Russo-Turkish Treaty of San Stefano became known, they were unacceptable to Britain and Austria because Russia would have been left only 70 miles (115 kilometers) from the Dardanelles and with a stretch of Aegean coastline. At the Congress of Berlin, Russia was obliged to accept less favorable arrangements, gaining Bessarabia on the Black Sea coast, but acquiring no territory nearer than 450 miles (725 kilometers) from the straits. Britain's efforts to thwart Russia were rewarded by the occupation of Cyprus, which would be returned to the Sultan if and when Russia withdrew from other recent territorial acquisitions in Asia around Kars. In any event, Cyprus was retained and became a strategically important acquisition in later years.

German Interests

German ambitions surfaced in the Middle East following victory in the Franco-Prussian War. German influence in the Ottoman Empire grew rapidly in the form of arms sales and military aid and German economic and diplomatic activity was widespread. This was typified by the granting of a concession to a German company to extend the railway line from Ankara to the Gulf in 1893. The Germans suggested that Kuwait might be a suitable terminus for the new railway, but eventually Britain, Germany, and Turkey agreed that Basra would be the terminus. Fears of German expansion brought Britain, France, and Russia closer together. In 1904, an Anglo-French entente cleared up many potential sources of conflict between them. In 1907, an Anglo-Russian agreement acknowledged the Gulf as a British sphere of influence; exclusive spheres were also agreed to in Persia (Figure 3.5). The stage was thus being set for a war that would change the face of Europe and the Middle East. Meanwhile, the Sultan kept before him a map of the frontiers of the Ottoman Empire at the time of Sulayman the Magnificent, as a reminder of past glories.

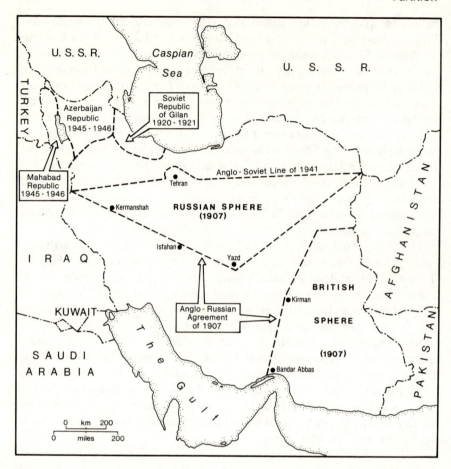

Figure 3.5   Territorial arrangements in Iran, 1907–46. (After Jere L. Bacharach, *A Near East Studies Handbook*. Seattle: University of Washington Press, 1974, p. 81.)

On the eve of World War I, the old political map of the Middle East and North Africa seemed destined for change. Only the central Arabian peninsula remained independent of external influence. Elsewhere, the degree of Ottoman, European, and Russian control varied from outright annexation of colonial territory (as in North Africa) to treaty arrangements (as in the Gulf) and vague spheres of influence (as in Persia). Ottoman sovereignty was still extensive but weakening. World War I was to bring about little more than a change of landlord for many peoples of the region. Among them were increasing numbers who had altogether different ideas about political and territorial arrangements in the region.

The Rise of Nationalism

Although nationalism is probably the most powerful political force in the modern world, it was originally a European idea widely transplanted during the nineteenth and twentieth centuries. Nationalism became the cornerstone of Europe's emerging political system from the mid-seventeenth century as peoples with common characteristics began to be associated with particular territories. Nationalist ideas spread to the Middle East in the second half of the nineteenth century for several reasons. First, the opening of modern schools, particularly in Egypt, Lebanon, and Syria, helped disseminate new ideas. Many of these schools, notably in Lebanon, were Christian mission schools. Second, the introduction of printing presses extended knowledge of political affairs and encouraged a cultural-literary revival. Third, as the old empires began to break up, the idea of self-determination for national groups took root. The Greeks were the first Europeans to break free from the Ottoman Empire after a successful rebellion (1821–30), and other national groups in the Balkans achieved independence before World War I. Although nationalist ideas were held by a small circle of Middle East intellectuals before 1900, it was only after the turn of the century that nationalism became an important political force. Its impact was heightened by the fact that Turkish, Arab, Iranian, and Jewish nationalism emerged at about the same time.

Turkish Nationalism

The gradual decline of the Ottoman Empire provides the background to the emergence of Turkish nationalism. The Ottoman Empire was an Islamic one, whose head, the Sultan, had also been recognized as Caliph (successor to the Prophet) since 1517. All Ottoman citizens were divided into *millets* on the basis of religion (Muslim, Greek Orthodox, Armenian, Catholic, and Jewish), and each *millet* enjoyed a substantial degree of autonomy. Although non-Muslims generally enjoyed peace and security, they could not mix freely in Muslim society or hold high office. An individual's religion rather than race or language determined his or her *millet* status, and the concept of national status based on language and territory had not been conceived.

During the 1860s, a Young Ottoman movement was founded with the aim of bringing about constitutional and social reforms and equal rights for all peoples. The Young Ottomans deeply resented European territorial encroachments and increasing European economic and political domination of the empire. They made little progress in achieving their aims, however, and their movement became increasingly Turkish in character. In 1896, the Young Turks in Istanbul formed a Committee for Union and Progress. In 1908, backed by an army mutiny, they demanded the implementation of reforms previously promised but never fulfilled. The Young Turk movement had been partly provoked by the 1907 Russo-British treaty of friendship, which ended the years of rivalry on which Ottoman survival had depended. Between 1908 and 1912, Ottoman possessions in Europe virtually disappeared. Italy invaded Libya and the Dodecanese Islands, and Greece took Crete. In 1844, Ottoman citizens in Europe had numbered 15 million, compared with 16 million in Asia; by 1912, most of the Europeans were independent. Against this background, the Young Turks at first attempted cooperation with the Arabs of the empire in implementing reforms, but this gradually gave way to a policy of Turkification, which antagonized the Arabs and stimulated Arab nationalism. Turkish language and race began to be emphasized, and the Sultan's Arab advisers and other officials were dismissed.

It was almost inevitable that the Turks would side with Germany during World War I. Germany had supported the idea of a strong Turkey, and an alliance with Germany held out some hope of saving the Ottoman Empire. As imperial rivals of Russia, Britain, and France, the Germans were keen to foster links with the Ottomans. In 1913, they began to reorganize the Ottoman army and the two states planned the coordination of their railway systems. In October 1914, the Ottoman government entered the war on the side of Germany and Austria, thus providing the Allied Powers with an opportunity to acquire Ottoman lands as the spoils of war.

Kemal Ataturk's leadership in saving Turkey from dismemberment after World War I is discussed in Chapter 6. His rejection of the Treaty of Sèvres and his military victories against Greece between 1919 and 1922 gave Turkey territorial coherence and led to an exchange of population with Greece, which left Turkey's population 95 percent Muslim. After Ataturk's victories, Turkish nationalist fervor reached new heights, causing suffering among Turkey's Kurds and Armenians but providing a basis on which to build Turkish national life.

Arab Nationalism

Arab nationalism differs from other Middle East nationalisms because of the immense span of territory inhabited by the Arabs. It consequently embraces a variety of concepts, ranging from the dream of a pan-Arab superstate to local nationalisms, such as Egyptian nationalism.[14] In the sense that some Arabs still hope for a united Arab state, Arab nationalism remains unfulfilled. Whereas there is one Turkish state, one Iranian state, and one Jewish state, there are over 20 Arab states.[15]

It is difficult to pinpoint the birth of genuine Arab nationalism, but the years immediately after the Young Turk movement of 1908 were crucial as the idea of Arab independence grew in response to Turkish nationalism. Even then, only a small number of Arabs regarded Arab national sovereignty outside the Ottoman Empire as a serious possibility. For centuries, most Muslim Arabs had lived happily as Ottoman citizens without discrimination. It should also be remembered that in central and south Arabia and along the Gulf coast, many Arabs remained outside the Ottoman Empire. Although the empire was Turkish based, it was above all an Islamic empire in which Turks and Arabs belonged equally to one Islamic community. Arabs could serve in the Ottoman army, and many reached high office in government employment.

The status of Arabs changed rapidly with the policy of Turkification, which became steadily more extreme from 1909 on. Arab political parties and societies sprang up in Beirut, Damascus, Baghdad, and Cairo to protect Arab rights. Some Arabs advocated autonomy within the Ottoman Empire, others sought binational partnership with the Turks in a reformed Ottoman Empire. Only a few called for Arab separation. Such ideas were now more easily spread with the proliferation of Arab newspapers; between 1904 and 1914, the number of newspapers in Lebanon, Syria, Palestine, and Iraq rose from 35 to 356. Arab nationalism was still largely confined to an educated minority, but it was fanned by the anti-Arab behavior of the Turks. The Arab military revolt in the Hijaz began in the same year, with British encouragement. After World War I, the Arabs were politically separate from the Turks for the first time in centuries. Over most of the Arab world, Ottoman-Muslim rule had been replaced by rule from Christian Europe, and Arab nationalism was still far from its goal of independence.

Iranian Nationalism

The relative geographic isolation of Iran, surrounded by high mountain ranges and sea, has helped create and preserve a distinctive Iranian national character and culture. Iranians share the Islamic faith and can look back proudly on centuries of common history. Although there is wide linguistic diversity with Turkish, Arabic, and Kurdish spoken by large minority groups, Persian is the largest linguistic group, and most educated Iranians from all ethnic groups speak Persian.

Nationalism was not a significant force in Iran before 1890. When it emerged, it was a mixture of antiforeign feeling, desire for social reform, and for an end to tyrannical government—as in Turkey. During the nineteenth century, Iran's rulers had granted generous concessions to foreigners for the exploitation of Iran's resources. Britain and Russia in particular were keen rivals for political and economic influence in Iran. Russia was interested in gaining access to the ports on the Gulf, whereas Britain saw a Russian presence in Iran as a threat to the trade routes to India. From 1890, there was growing popular opposition to Iran's dependence on foreigners, partly as a result of a concession granted to a British company to manage the Persian tobacco industry. In 1906, the

Shah raised a huge loan from Russia, which sparked a revolution led by clergy and merchants, and he was forced to accept a constitution providing for parliamentary rule. The constitutional experiment ended in 1912 as a result of internal opposition and Anglo-Russian hostility. Attempts to reduce foreign interference failed; in 1907, Britain and Russia had divided Iran into spheres of influence; from 1912–19, they virtually ruled Iran as colonial powers.

In 1921, the weak Qajar regime was ousted in a coup that ultimately led to the enthronement of Reza Khan as Shah of Persia in 1925. He did much to unite and stabilize Iran, and by improving education and communications, he created the basis for national consciousness. Nationalism was still confined to a minority, but events during and after World War II generated a wave of nationalist feeling that embraced the masses for the first time. Britain and Russia had again occupied Iran in 1941, which was bitterly resented. After the war, popular national feeling was turned against the Anglo-Iranian Oil Company; in 1951, it was nationalized. Although this ended in failure, the depth of Iranian nationalism and hostility to foreign interference had been clearly demonstrated. The same intense feelings surfaced again after the 1979 revolution, directed chiefly against U.S. influence.

Other Nationalisms

Jewish nationalism and the quest for a Jewish national home are discussed in Chapter 9. The possibility of establishing a Jewish homeland in Argentina, Angola, Uganda, Cyprus, or Sinai were all rejected in favor of Palestine. But it should be noted that the national idea attracted relatively few Jews to Palestine. By 1918, when the Jewish population of the United States was over 3 million, there were only 70,000 Jews in Palestine compared to 700,000 Arabs. Many more Jews remained in Eastern Europe and Russia or settled in Western Europe. Their long-distance material and moral support for Zionism helped bring about the birth of Israel in 1948.

Two other peoples in the Middle East have aspired to statehood, the Kurds and the Armenians. Neither has enjoyed external support in the way the Jews have, and they remain stateless. Both groups are discussed in Chapter 6, but some brief comments relevant to the political map are appropriate here. Kurdish nationalists have sometimes made excessively large claims to a homeland, but on a strict basis of language and culture, a Kurdish state would be quite small and landlocked (Figure 3.6). Similarly, the Armenians made grand claims for a state at the time of World War I, but the area proposed for them under the treaty of Sèvres was small and insecure (Figure 3.7). The status of the Armenians in the Soviet Republic of Armenia has generally been far superior to that of the Kurds in neighboring Middle East states.

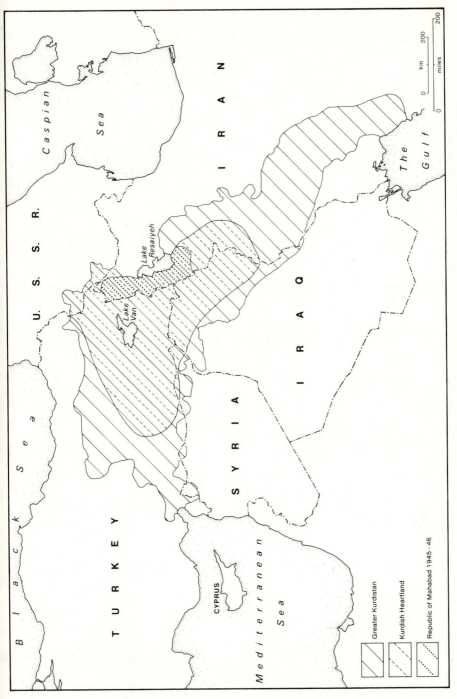

Figure 3.6 Greater Kurdistan, the Kurdish heartland, and the Republic of Mahabad, 1946.

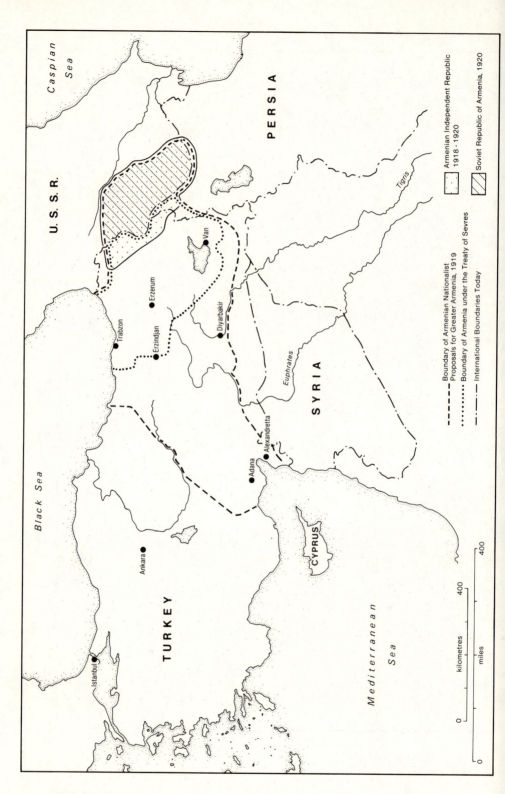

Caspian Sea

U.S.S.R.

PERSIA

Tigris

Van

Erzerum

Trabzon

Erzindjan

Diyarbakir

Euphrates

SYRIA

Alexandretta

Adana

Black Sea

Ankara

TURKEY

CYPRUS

Istanbul

Mediterranean Sea

Armenian Independent Republic 1918 - 1920

Soviet Republic of Armenia, 1920

Boundary of Armenian Nationalist Proposals for Greater Armenia, 1919

Boundary of Armenia under the Treaty of Sevres

International Boundaries Today

kilometres

miles

0   400

0   400

World War I and the Balkanization of the Middle East

During World War I, Britain made a series of promises that the postwar peace conferences could not reconcile. First, there were the series of letters exchanged by Sir Henry McMahon and the Sharif Husayn of Mecca between July 1915 and January 1916 that promised Arab independence in return for revolt against the Turks. Second, the Balfour Declaration of November 1917 pledged British support for the idea of a Jewish national home in Palestine. Third, Britain, France, and Russia drew up the secret Sykes-Picot agreement to divide the central Middle East between them. Following the 1917 Bolshevik Revolution, the Russians exposed the deal. The Arabs were angered and dismayed by this double-dealing. The Sykes-Picot agreement had been negotiated between the end of the Husayn-McMahon correspondence but before the start of the Arab Revolt. Each power would govern two areas, one of which would be administered directly and the other under Arab government with British or French protection. France's share was to include the Cilicia region of Turkey. On Russia's insistence, much of Palestine was to be under some international regime (Figure 3.8). Between them, Britain and France would dominate the central Middle East from the Mediterranean to the Gulf. Although the Sykes-Picot agreement was modified considerably in practice, it established a framework for the future map of the Arab Middle East.

At the end of hostilities in 1918, the conquered Ottoman territories were put under an Occupied Enemies Territories Administration (OETA) pending a peace agreement. Because there were delays in concluding a peace treaty, Britain and France convened the Supreme Council of the League of Nations, which announced its decisions at San Remo in 1920. Britain and France assumed the right to govern conquered territories on behalf of the League of Nations. Britain took the mandates for newly created Palestine, Transjordan, and Iraq, giving it control of a land bridge between the Mediterranean and the Gulf. The terms of the mandate for Palestine, quoting the Balfour Declaration, were drafted by Britain and endorsed by the Conference of San Remo. France was given the mandate for Lebanon and Syria but had to take Damascus by force and remove Emir Faysal from the throne to which he had been elected by the General Syrian Congress in 1920. With this, British wartime promises to support Arab independence in areas liberated from Turkish control were irrevocably broken. In 1921, Faysal's brother Emir Abdallah advanced from the Hijaz as far as Amman to raise a rebellion against the French. The British offered to recognize him as ruler of

---

Figure 3.7   Various proposals for an Armenian state after World War I. (After David M. Lang and Christopher J. Walker, *The Armenians.* London: Minority Rights Group, 1978, p. 12.)

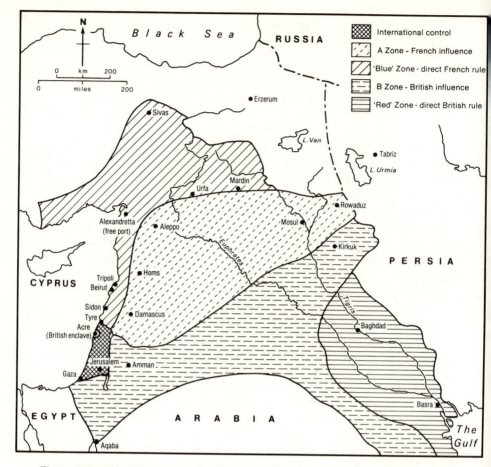

Figure 3.8   The Sykes-Picot agreement, 1916, dividing the central Middle East into colonial spheres of influence and control. (After Jere L. Bacharach, *A Near East Studies Handbook*. Seattle: University of Washington Press, 1974, p. 70.)

Transjordan in return for abandoning his plan, which he did, thus founding Jordan's Hashimite dynasty.

The 1920 Treaty of Sèvres between Ottoman officials and the victorious allies would have confirmed French occupation of Cilicia. Elsewhere, parts of what is today Turkey were placed under Greek and Italian occupation and much of eastern Turkey was assigned to the Armenian Republic. A small Kurdish state was also proposed, subject to a plebiscite that was never held. The Turkish Straits zone was to be demilitarized and internationalized (Figure 3.9). The 1923 Treaty of

Figure 3.9   Proposals for carving up Turkey in the Treaty of Sèvres.

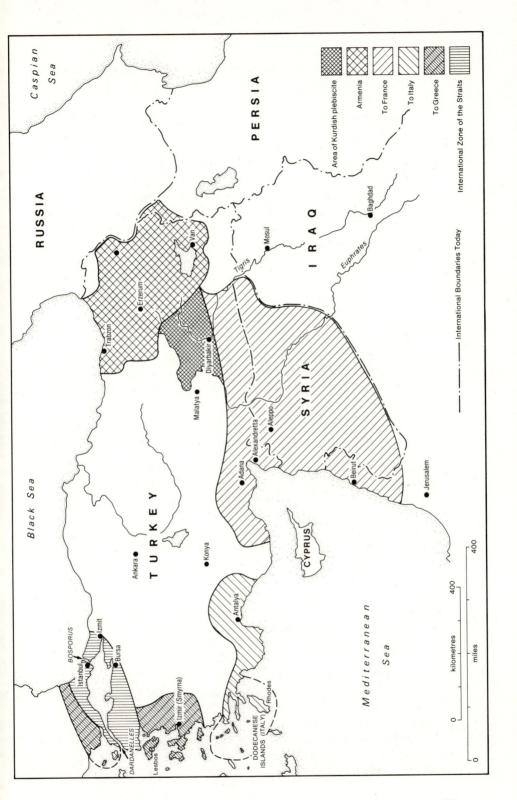

65

Lausanne, however, revised these territorial arrangements, fixing Turkey's borders much as they are today. The territorial gains made by Turkey in the Lausanne Treaty were crucial to the future economic potential and security of the state. All that remained to be cleared up was the *vilayet* of Mosul, which was originally in the French zone. In 1925, the Supreme Council of the League of Nations formally awarded Mosul to Iraq, and in the 1926 Treaty of Mosul, Turkey and Britain accepted the new boundary. France gave up Mosul to Britain in return for a free hand in Syria and a stake in the Iraq Petroleum Company.[16]

The European powers had, thus, imposed their own arbitrary boundaries on the central Middle East without reference to the people of the region. These bore no relationship to physical or cultural features. The Jews and the Turks had reason to be satisfied. The Arabs felt betrayed and frustrated, whereas the Kurds and Armenians remained stateless.

The Birth of Independent States

Immediately after World War I, only Turkey, Persia, North Yemen, and central Arabia were independent of European control. Elsewhere, Europe dominated the region politically. Between 1932 and 1971, all the region's states became independent.

The Central Middle East

In the context of 5000 years of political history, British and French rule in the central Middle East was short lived; excluding Cyprus, it lasted on average only 23 years. The French mandate in Syria was an unhappy affair; Arab nationalists bitterly opposed the French administration. From 1925 until 1927, there was open rebellion, beginning in the Jabal Druze region in the south and spreading to the major cities. Thousands of lives were lost, and the French twice bombarded Damascus to regain control. The surrender of the Hatay region to Turkey in 1939 was also deeply resented by the Syrians. France's most important effect on the political map was the creation of Lebanon. The autonomous *mutasarrifiyyah* of Lebanon created in 1864 was enlarged by the French, roughly doubling its size and population. The new Lebanon had a small Christian majority with sufficient Muslims to guarantee the need for French protection, thus setting the stage for future conflict.[17] The Lebanese declared independence after the fall of France in 1941, but the French did not formally agree until 1946. Syria also became independent of France in 1946.

The British were as unwelcome in Iraq as the French in Syria. They had hoped that Iraq would become a lucrative prize, with the promise of oil and control of the approaches to India via the Gulf. But the new state proved almost ungovernable, particularly after 1926 when the *vilayet* of Mosul was allocated to Iraq. Mosul province had oil, discovered in 1927, and a rebellious Kurdish population. Britain wanted one but not the other and was involved in suppression of Kurdish rebellions by force on three occasions. In 1930, the British mandate ended, though Royal Air Force bases remained in Iraq by agreement until 1956. Meanwhile, foreign oil interests, including American companies, began to dominate the economic life of Iraq.

Britain's mandate in Palestine and Transjordan began in 1922. The transformation of Palestine from a predominantly Arab territory to a Jewish state is discussed later. The territorial changes associated with the birth and expansion of Israel in 1948 and 1967 are among the biggest changes to the political map, and they are certainly the most important in their wider repercussions. Transjordan was something of an artificial state, even before the advent of Israel cut it off from the Mediterranean Sea, and was conceived by Britain as the western end of a strategic land and air corridor to Iraq and the Gulf.

The Northern Tier States

The signing of the humiliating Treaty of Sèvres by the Sultan's representatives in 1920 created a huge wave of support for the nationalists in Turkey. Their convincing military victories over the Greeks also persuaded the Italians and French to leave Turkish soil, though Italy retained the Dodecanese Islands. Russia returned the frontier provinces of Kars and Ardahan. In 1923, the office of Sultan was abolished and Turkey became a republic. A further step towards Turkish independence occurred in 1936 when a new Straits Convention was signed at Montreux that gave Turkey the right to remilitarize the straits and the International Straits Commission was abolished.

At the end of World War I, Persia was a weak but self-governing state under Russian and British influence. The 1907 Anglo-Russian agreement on spheres of influence lapsed after the Russian Revolution in 1917, but Russian interest in the north of Persia continued. In 1920, Russian troops established the short-lived small Soviet Republic of Gilan inside Persia (Figure 3.5). During the interwar period, Persia[18] relied heavily on German assistance in modernizing the country to such an extent that Britain and the Soviet Union again occupied Iran during World War II, assisted by U.S. troops. The Russians used their influence to establish the two autonomous republics of Azerbaijan, with a Turkish-speaking population, and Mahabad, with a Kurdish population. Soviet troops withdrew from Iran in 1946 under pressure from the United Nations and the United States, and the autonomous republics collapsed. They probably had little chance of survival; the Republic of Mahabad in any case only contained one third of the Kurds in Iran and was far from being a Kurdish national home. During the post-World War II period,

U.S. influence in Iran increased massively until the overthrow of the Shah in 1979, when it ended abruptly.

Britain's occupation of Cyprus was intended to be a short-term geo-political expedience. Until 1914 when the island was made a British Crown Colony, it was still theoretically only on lease from the Ottoman Sultan. In 1915, Britain offered Cyprus to Greece in return for support in the war, but the offer was declined. During the years immediately preceding Cypriot independence in 1960, Britain fought a determined Greek Cypriot terrorist campaign (EOKA) to bring about union with Greece. The Turkish minority in Cyprus was equally strongly opposed to being incorporated into Greece, as we will see later; in 1974, Turkey invaded Cyprus to protect its interests. The Turkish Federated State of Cyprus is not recognized internationally, but it has administered the north for almost a decade. The political map of Cyprus is complicated by Britain's two sovereign bases, which were retained as part of the independence arrangements in 1960.

The Arabian Peninsula

Political change in the Arabian peninsula since World War I has been dominated by the emergence of Saudi Arabia and the declining role of Britain in the peripheral states of the peninsula. The broad outline of the political map was established in this period, although long stretches of desert boundary between Saudi Arabia and neighboring states have yet to be delimited.[19] Before World War I, Abdul Aziz Ibn Saud had already succeeded in uniting the tribes of the Najd in central Arabia. Next, he extended his rule south into the Asir region and then north into the territory of the Jabal Shammar. Finally in 1924–25, he defeated Sharif Husayn of the Hijaz (Figure 3.10). In 1927, the Treaty of Jiddah recognized Ibn Saud as "King of the Hijaz, the Najd, and its Dependencies." The name "Kingdom of Saudi Arabia" was adopted in 1932.

Britain had managed to negotiate a complex series of treaties with most of the important rulers of the small coastal states of Arabia from the beginning of the nineteenth century. The latest of these was with the ruler of Qatar in 1916. These treaties gave Britain effective control of the foreign relations of the emirates and responsibility for their security as well as certain commercial privileges. Britain's treaties with Kuwait ended in 1961 and with Bahrain, Qatar, and the Trucial States in 1971. The United Arab Emirates (U.A.E.) was created in 1971 from seven of the former Trucial States, with strong encouragement from Britain. Although an uneasy federation of unequal partners, the U.A.E. has survived and gained political credibility.

Aden Colony and Aden Protectorate became the independent People's Republic of South Yemen (P.R.S.Y.) in 1967, but not before the British had engaged in urban guerilla warfare with nationalist groups in the streets of Aden. The P.R.S.Y. was renamed the People's Demo-

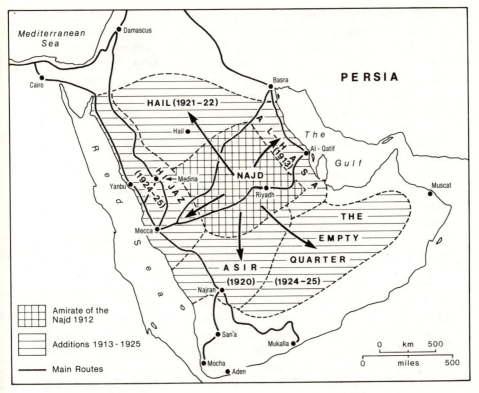

Figure 3.10   The emergence of Saudi Arabia under Ibn Saud, 1912–25.

cratic Republic of Yemen (P.D.R. Yemen) in 1970. North Yemen had become partially independent in 1918. As a mountainous country, relatively densely populated by fiercely independent tribes, North Yemen (now Yemen Arab Republic) is not amenable to central government. Between 1962 and 1969, North Yemen was racked by a republican/royalist civil war, following the deposition of Yemen's traditional leader, the imam.

North Africa

Egypt was still nominally an Ottoman possession on the eve of World War I, although occupied and administered by Britain. With the outbreak of war in 1914, Egypt was proclaimed a British protectorate, but it won independence in 1922. Britain, however, maintained the right to station troops in the Suez Canal Zone until 1956.

Britain did not restore the Sudan to Egyptian administration following the defeat of the Mahdist rebellion in 1898; for some years, it was governed as an Anglo-Egyptian condominium. Sudan only obtained its independence in 1956.

The Italians were the last to gain colonial territory, and the first to lose it. The conquest of Libya was not really complete until 1932. In 1939, Libya was formally incorporated into metropolitan Italy; by 1943, the Italians were driven out of Libya as part of the Allied campaign in North Africa. The British took over the administration of Cyrenaica and Tripolitania and the French became responsible for Fezzan. After World War II, the United Nations decided to grant independence to Libya with a federal constitution. Libya became independent in 1951, heavily dependent on foreign funds until the advent of oil revenues about a decade later.

Morocco and Tunisia became independent in 1956 after 44 years and 75 years of French rule, respectively. France retained the strategic naval base of Bizerta in Tunisia until 1963. The Spanish Zone and the International Zone around Tangier also reverted to Morocco in 1956, although Ceuta and Melilla remained in Spanish hands. Algeria's path to independence was much less straightforward because the French saw Algeria as part of France, with over 1 million European settlers. About 40 percent of the cultivated area was owned by Europeans, compared with 20 percent in Tunisia and only 8 percent in Morocco. Algeria was of some strategic importance as well; in 1960, the Algerian Sahara had been used as the testing ground for France's first nuclear weapons. Above all, perhaps, oil was discovered in Algeria in 1956; when exports began in 1961, France was the chief market. France, therefore, put up a strong fight to retain Algeria in the face of one of the most determined struggles for national independence by any colonized people. After 8 years of bitter fighting, Algeria achieved independence in 1962.

The political map of North Africa still had, in 1985, one major area of uncertainty in Western Sahara, formerly Spanish Sahara (Figure 3.4a). Following Spain's withdrawal from Spanish Sahara in 1976, the territory was partitioned between Morocco in the north and Mauritania in the south. In 1978, Mauritania withdrew from the southern part of Western Sahara, leaving Morocco to claim the whole territory. However, as we will see in Chapter 4, many of the territory's 80,000 inhabitants support a guerilla war against Moroccan forces.

Conclusion

In drawing conclusions from this brief discussion of historical geography, it helps to distinguish between the experiences of North Africa, Turkey and Iran, the Arabian peninsula, and the central Middle East (the Fertile Crescent). Generalizations about these subregions are difficult enough, but generalizations are virtually meaningless when applied to the region as a whole.

Without European intervention, what spatial-political patterns might have emerged? Direct European influence on the political map began first in North Africa. Here, autonomous states based on present-day Moroccan, Tunisian, and Egyptian territories would probably have survived. Each of the regions formerly enjoyed long periods of political independence, owing in part to geographic factors such as Morocco's remoteness from centers of power in the east and its high mountain barriers, Tunisia's favorable location in the central Mediterranean, and Egypt's densely populated ecumene surrounded by desert. Algeria and Libya would probably have been divided into several smaller states, possibly along the lines of Libya's former provinces, with two coastal states and one inland.[20] Left to themselves, the people of the Nile basin would similarly have reached alternative solutions to their organization of space. Certainly, the arbitrary division along latitude 22° north makes little sense.

In some ways, the northern-tier states of Turkey and Iran show a greater degree of continuity than other territories, in spite of their national integration problems. Broadly speaking, modern Turkey is bounded by long-standing frontier regions with Russia and Iran, following effective mountain barriers. In the west, the boundaries of Turkey mark out the Greek-speaking world of Christian Europe, although this was achieved by large population transfers in the 1920s. Turkey's southern border coincides roughly with a zone of transition from Turkish-speaking uplands to the Arabic-speaking lowlands of the Fertile Crescent. Modern Iran is the rump of a large Persian state whose domain once extended far into Russia and to the southern shore of the Gulf. But the heartland of the Persian state, secure within a girdle of mountain ranges, has not changed greatly for centuries, and an uneasy frontier with the Arab world has long persisted along the western foothills of the Zagros and along the Gulf coast.

The experience of Arabia has been different. Traditionally, there were tribal territories and federations of tribes, with a number of peripheral maritime city-states. Tribal populations were concentrated in certain physically favored environments—the rain-fed Yemeni highlands, the interior oases of central Arabia, and the highlands of Oman. Discontinuity of population, the prevalence of nomadism, and the absence of trunk routes, which are so important elsewhere in the region, may help explain the persistence of small political units. Britain's treaties with the peripheral shaykdoms doubtless helped their survival; they certainly kept Persia out of the Gulf in the nineteenth century. But the most important influence on the political map of Arabia was the indigenous national movement under Ibn Saud, spreading from core to periphery, which created the Kingdom of Saudi Arabia. Here, the personality of one man coupled with a powerful idea in Wahhabism were crucial.

It was in the central Middle East that European influences created the greatest impact on the map, bringing Syria, Iraq, Jordan, and Lebanon into being, and later Israel. It is conceivable that in time an Arab Fertile Crescent state might have emerged, stretching from the Mediterranean to the Gulf and lying between Turkey and an Arab desert kingdom to the south. But in the aftermath of World War I, the central Middle East was Balkanized. As will be discussed later, Iraq, Syria, and Jordan were all geographically disadvantaged states in some way, and they did not conform to geographic realities. More than any other region, the center has been the scene of conflict and instability during the last 60 years. On the other hand, a united Arab state in the region might have experienced regional rivalry between a Damascus-based Mediterranean wing and a Baghdad-based Gulf wing. There is no natural focus of power in between.

Apart from the central Middle East, therefore, there may be more historic continuity than is sometimes appreciated in the modern political map. The Europeans however took matters further than these broad outlines by defining precise and permanent boundary lines, raising more local problems between neighboring states. This is not to say that unbounded territories, as typified by tribal organizations, could have survived long in the modern world but that boundaries could have been drawn up with more sensitivity to human and cultural factors, as will be shown later.

Notes

1. For an introductory overview of historical geography, see the historical atlases in the bibliography.

2. Tribalism is still a major factor in the internal politics of Sudan, the two Yemens, and Morocco. Thus, when rural commune boundaries were established in Morocco in 1960, one third of them reflected tribal divisions. See William Zartman, *Government and Politics in Northern Africa* (London: Methuen and Co. Ltd. 1964): 29.

3. See William C. Brice, *South-West Asia.* (London: University of London Press, 1966): 74–81.

4. See E. E. Evans-Pritchard, *The Nuer: A Description of the Modes of Livelihood and Political Institutions of a Nilotic People* (Oxford: Oxford University Press, 1940).

5. See, for example, D. Seddon, "Tribe and State: Approaches to Maghreb History," *Maghreb Review* 2(1977): 23–40; P. J. Vatikiotis (ed.), *Revolution in the Middle East and Other Case Studies* (London: Allen & Unwin Inc., 1972); and P. K. Hitti, *Lebanon in History: From Earliest Times to the Present*, 2nd ed. (London: Macmillan, 1962).

6. Robert Carneiro, "A Theory of the Origin of the State," *Science* (August 21, 1970): 733–738.

7. Harm J. de Blij, *Geography: Regions and Concepts*, 3rd ed., (New York: John Wiley & Sons, 1981): 335–339.

8. Edward F. Bergman, *Modern Political Geography* (Dubuque, Iowa: William C. Brown Co., 1975).

9. Ottoman naval supremacy was demonstrated by the seizure of Rhodes from the Knights of St. John in 1522, but Ottoman efforts to take Malta (notably in 1565) failed.

10. Another remarkable example was the Karamanli family of Tripoli who exercised independent rule over parts of Libya from 1710 to 1835. Their dependence on piracy brought conflict with the maritime powers, including the United States. In 1801 the U.S.

ship *Philadelphia* went aground while blockading Tripoli harbor, and 200 American seamen were taken prisoner. In 1804, the U.S. consul in Tunis, William Eaton, accompanied by a detatchment of marines and mercenaries marched on Tripoli in a brave but unsuccessful attempt to free them. The episode was important in stimulating the United States to build a bigger navy. See Seaton Dearden, *A Nest of Corsairs* (London: John Murray, 1976).

11. Britain occupied Tangier from 1662 to 1684. Spain acquired Ifni (579 square miles; 1500 square kilometers) in 1860 and Spanish Sahara (106,000 square miles; 275,000 square kilometers) in 1885. Ceuta and Melilla remain Spanish today.

12. Germany disliked these arrangements and, in 1911, dispatched a warship to the Atlantic port of Agadir in an unsuccessful protest.

13. The most important treaties were those with: Oman (1802), the Trucial States (1869), Bahrain (1878), Qatar (1878), and Kuwait (1899).

14. "Egypt for the Egyptians" was first heard in Cairo in 1877. See George E. Kirk, *A Short History of the Middle East* (London: Methuen University Paperbacks, 1964).

15. 18 Arab States are considered in this book; in addition, Djibouti, Mauritania, Palestine, and Somalia are members of the Arab League.

16. France had already been promised a share in the Iraq Petroleum Company at the San Remo Conference in 1920. The Treaty of Mosul divided the shares between Britain (52.5%), the United States (21.25%), and France (21.25%). George Antonius, *The Arab Awakening* (London: Hamish Hamilton, 1961).

17. Some Syrians still regard Lebanon as part of Syria. The Syrian Foreign Minister Abd al-Halim Khaddam was once quoted as saying, "Lebanon used to be part of Syria and we shall take it back at the first serious attempts at partition" (*The Times* [London], 22 January 1976). This is discussed in more detail in Chapters 6 and 7.

18. Persia was renamed Iran in 1935.

19. The Arabian peninsula may also witness future changes to the political map. For example, unification of the Yemens or changes in membership of the U.A.E.

20. Until 1963, Libya was a federal state with each of its three provinces (Tripolitania, Cyrenaica, Fezzan) having considerable autonomy. In 1963, federalism was abolished, and the state was divided into 10 *muhafazats*.

Selected Bibliography

Antonius, George. *The Arab Awakening*. London: Hamish Hamilton, 1961 (reprint of 1938 edition).

Bacharach, Jere L. *A Near East Studies Handbook*. Seattle: University of Washington Press, 1974.

Boateng, E. A. *A Political Geography of Africa*. Cambridge: Cambridge University Press, 1978.

Cottam, Richard W. *Nationalism in Iran*, 2nd ed. Pittsburgh: University of Pittsburgh Press, 1979.

Cottrell, Alvin J. (ed.). *The Persian Gulf States*. Baltimore: Johns Hopkins University Press, 1980.

Dawn, Ernest C. *From Ottomanism to Arabism*. Urbana: University of Illinois Press, 1973.

Dempsey, M. W. *The Daily Telegraph Atlas of the Arab World*. London: Nomad Publishers, 1983.

Fisher, W. B. *The Middle East: A Physical, Social and Regional Geography*, 7th ed. London: Methuen and Co., Ltd., 1978.

Glubb, Sir John B. *The Great Arab Conquests*. London: Hodder & Stoughton, 1963.

Goldschmidt, Arthur. *A Concise History of the Middle East*. Boulder, Colo.: Westview Press, 1979.

Haddad, William and Ochsenwald, William (eds.). *Nationalism in a Non-National State: The Dissolution of the Ottoman Empire*. Columbus: Ohio State University Press, 1977.

Helmreich, Paul C. *From Paris to Sèvres: The Partition of the Ottoman Empire at the Peace Conference of 1919–1920*. Columbus: Ohio State University Press, 1974.

Hitti, Philip K. *History of the Arabs*, 10th ed. New York: Macmillan, 1970.

Hottinger, Arnold. *The Arabs*. London: Thames & Hudson Inc., 1963.

Hourani, Albert. *Emergence of the Modern Middle East*. Macmillan: London, 1981.

Karpat, Kemal. *An Inquiry into the Social Foundations of Nationalism in the Ottoman State: From Social Estates to Classes, from Millets to Nations*. Research Monograph No. 39. Princeton, N.J.: Center for International Studies, Princeton University, 1973.

Kedourie, Elie. *In the Anglo-Arab Labyrinth*. Cambridge: Cambridge University Press, 1976.

Kirk, George E. *A Short History of the Middle East*. London: Methuen University Paperbacks, 1964.

Kushner, David. *The Rise of Turkish Nationalism: 1876–1908*. London: Frank Cass, 1977.

Lebon, J. H. G. "South-West Asia and Egypt," in W. G. East, O. H. K. Spate, and C. A. Fisher (eds.), *The Changing Map of Asia*, pp. 53–126. London: Methuen and Co., Ltd., 1971.

Lewis, Bernard. *The Emergence of Modern Turkey*. London: Oxford University Press/Royal Institute of International Affairs, 1961.

———. *The Arabs in History*, 3rd ed. London: Hutchinson, 1964.

Mansfield, Peter. *The Arabs*, rev. ed. New York: Penguin Books, 1978.

Peretz, Don. *The Middle East Today*, 4th ed. New York: Praeger Publishers, 1983.

Sachar, Howard M. *The Emergence of the Middle East, 1914–1922*. New York: Alfred A. Knopf, Inc., 1969.

Sykes, Christopher. *Crossroads to Israel*. London: William Collins Publishers, Inc. 1965.

U.S. Department of State. *The Spanish State*. Geographic Report No. 8, June 1962. Washington, D.C.: U.S. Department of State, 1962.

Zeine, Zeine N. *The Emergence of Arab Nationalism*. Beirut: Khayyat's, 1966.

Historical Atlases

Barraclough, Geoffrey (ed.). *The Times Atlas of World History*. London: Times Books, 1978.

Brice, William, C. (ed.). *An Historical Atlas of Islam*. Leiden, The Netherlands: E. J. Brill, 1981.

Groellenberg, L. H. *Atlas of the Bible*. London: Thomas Nelson, 1956.

Kinder, Hermann, and Werner, Hilgemann. *The Penguin Atlas of World History*. Harmondsworth, Eng.: Penguin Books, Vol. I, 1974, Vol. II, 1978.

Roolvink, R., et al. *Historical Atlas of the Muslim Peoples*. Amsterdam: Djambatan, *ca.* 1960.

Van der Heyden, and Scullard, H. H. (eds.). *Atlas of the Classical World*. London: Thomas Nelson, 1959.

Van Der Meer, F. and Mohram, Christine. *Atlas of the Early Christian World*. London: Thomas Nelson, 1959.

4

Interstate Land Boundaries

State sovereignty in the modern world encompasses land, sea, and air. The boundaries of the state extend in a vertical plane upward to define national airspace and downward to define sovereignty below ground. Coastal states may also claim sovereignty over the airspace, the water-body, and the seabed and subsoil of their territorial waters. All states attach great importance to the land, but interest in airspace and terri-torial waters varies considerably with geographic location and air and naval power. In the Middle East and North Africa, the possibility of finding oil, gas, or mineral resources has accelerated the quest for pre-cisely defined national boundaries, both onshore and offshore. Off-shore boundaries are discussed in Chapter 5.

As the point of contact between neighboring states, international boundaries play a prominent part in shaping their political and eco-nomic relationships. Boundaries are frequently the cause of interstate tension, and they powerfully affect the degree of interaction between peoples inhabiting adjacent regions. Towns and villages in the vicinity of boundaries may decline or prosper depending on whether their nat-ural hinterlands have been distorted by a boundary or whether they have acquired new functions associated with border crossings. Unlike some geopolitical phenomena, boundaries often possess the added fas-cination of being visible in the landscape as boundary stones, pillars or fences, or in the form of natural features adopted by the boundary makers for convenience. In certain long-established border regions, contrasting man-made landscapes have evolved on either side of the line. Political geographers have, therefore, devoted a great deal of time and energy to boundary studies, concentrating primarily on their origins, evolution, physical form, and function. The famous dictum that "good fences make good neighbors" has been aptly applied to international boundaries.[1] How good then are the fences in the Middle East and North Africa?

Political Frontiers

It is often suggested that the concept of the boundary line is alien to the Middle East and North Africa. To a large extent this is true. Certainly, at the local level in regions where nomadism was prevalent, precise tribal boundaries were rarely recognized, though rights to particular wells and pastures were known and generally respected. In sedentary communities, however, boundary lines were used to define land ownership, and where irrigation was practiced, plots were laid out with geometric precision—as in the Nile valley. The idea of exercising total sovereignty over territory to precisely defined boundaries was rarely extended to state level.[2] In most cases, it was impossible for governments to maintain full control of all the lands they claimed; along the margins of the desert and in the mountains, there were invariably tribes who lived beyond the reach of central authority. State control tended to diminish with distance from the main seat of power. With few exceptions, therefore, the states and empires of the past were bounded by political *frontiers* rather than by boundary lines. In a political frontier region, the geographic limits of jurisdiction are poorly defined, often advancing and retreating with fluctuations in the military power of the regime.[3]

As elsewhere, two main types of political frontier can be identified in the Middle East and North Africa: *frontiers of separation* and *frontiers of contact*.[4] In the sparsely populated regions, frontiers of separation were most common. Tribes or tribal federations were separated from one another by extensive areas of arid no-man's-land. In more populous regions, frontiers of contact were usual, for example, in Sinai, where for centuries the great powers of the day fought for control. Sinai is a key link between Egypt and the Fertile Crescent. Conflict in Sinai most frequently left a frontier region between the rival powers, sometimes near Egypt, sometimes near Palestine, but there was rarely a boundary line.[5]

Boundary Status

The states of the Middle East and North Africa are outlined by over 21,000 miles (34,000 kilometers) of land boundaries. On small-scale atlas maps and in the press and television, these boundaries are generally depicted with a precision and boldness that is misleading. Probably only about one third of the total length of these boundaries has been agreed to between states and marked out on the ground, whereas several stretches are actively disputed. In the context of centuries of political turmoil, the contemporary boundaries of the region are extremely youthful, many of them having been delimited in the early years of the twentieth century. In general, boundary alignments were made earlier in North Africa than in the Middle East during the French, British, and Italian colonial adventures before World War I. In the Middle East, extensive boundary alignment was necessary to implement the peace agreements following World War I. The average age of boundaries in the region is less than 70 years, 40 boundaries having been delimited in this century. Despite their alien origin and youthfulness, the present system of boundaries is probably here to stay. It is, therefore, appropriate to examine how well established the boundaries are and how well they function.

Interstate boundaries tend to evolve through various stages to reach full maturity, though not every boundary necessarily passes every stage. A fully mature boundary is one recognized by both parties, is demarcated, and is effectively administered and maintained. In this sense, many Middle East and North Africa boundaries will probably never reach full maturity. S. B. Jones suggested that boundaries may pass three stages in their development: *allocation, delimitation,* and *demarcation.*[6] In effect, these are stages of increasing concern with the detail of the boundary. Allocation represents the initial understanding between states as to their territorial claims. Lines may be crudely drawn on maps, but no accurate field survey has been attempted. When delimitation occurs, the boundary line is defined with precision and formally agreed to by the parties. If it is not a geometric line, field surveys will be conducted to site the boundary with reference to physical features. Next, boundary demarcation may be carried out, marking the boundary on the ground. In certain sensitive areas or where population densities are high, this may mean the construction of fences to mark the boundary and also prevent movement across it. Such boundaries have to be regularly patrolled and maintained to be effective.[7] Thus, some political geographers have proposed the addition of a fourth stage called *administration*.

Only three boundaries in the region remain to be allocated; Saudi Arabia-Oman, Saudi Arabia-People's Democratic Republic of Yemen (P.D.R. Yemen), and Saudi Arabia-Yemen Arab Republic (Yemen A.R.). The two former are probably the most obscure boundaries in the region. Both are about 450 miles (725 kilometers) long, passing chiefly through uninhabited deserts, where even oil exploration is severely handicapped by physical conditions. There is probably some official understanding as to where the border will run in each area, but the alternative boundary lines shown tentatively on maps and in atlases may be hundreds of miles apart. One perplexing result is that vastly different estimates are given for the areas of the states involved. It may be years before these boundaries are delimited, though Saudi Arabia has shown great determination in recent years to sort out other boundary problems, reaching formal agreements with Jordan and Qatar (1965), Kuwait (1969), the United Arab Emirates (U.A.E.) (1974), and Iraq (1981). In 1982, Saudi Arabia and Oman agreed to shelve all territorial questions as part of a security pact, but their boundary remains undefined. When Saudi Arabia's boundaries with the two Yemens are eventually delimited, they will have to take into account tribal allegiances in regions where there are long-standing tribal rivalries.

Table 4.1 (derived from Figure 4.1) summarizes boundary status in 1984. Several problems arise in preparing such a table, notably obtaining accurate information and classifying boundaries of mixed status. More than one third of the boundaries in the region are already demarcated, and all but three are delimited. Many of the remaining boundaries may never be demarcated because of cost or impracticability. No attempt has been made to collect data on "administered boundaries." Here again, access to information and problems of definition are insuperable. Many boundaries are undoubtedly assiduously administered for short stretches, those near important crossing points or in militarily sensitive areas. Israel's boundaries with her Arab neighbors are administered to a degree reminiscent of stretches of the Iron Curtain in Europe, being fenced, patrolled, and inspected daily.

Recent decades have witnessed a growing realization in the Middle East and North Africa that uncertainties over boundaries—particularly boundary disputes—are a hazard in international relations that can be eliminated. Thus, a number of boundary agreements have been reached in addition to the Saudi Arabian examples mentioned above. Among the most important was the 1981 Iraq-Saudi Arabia agreement, which

Table 4.1
Boundary Status in 1984

	Number of Boundaries
Not allocated	3
Allocated and delimited	13
Allocated, delimited, and demarcated	23[a]
Allocated, delimited, and partially demarcated	5
Disputed or partially disputed	5
Armistice lines	4
Total	53

[a] Including Ceuta and Melilla.
Source: Derived from Figure 4.1.

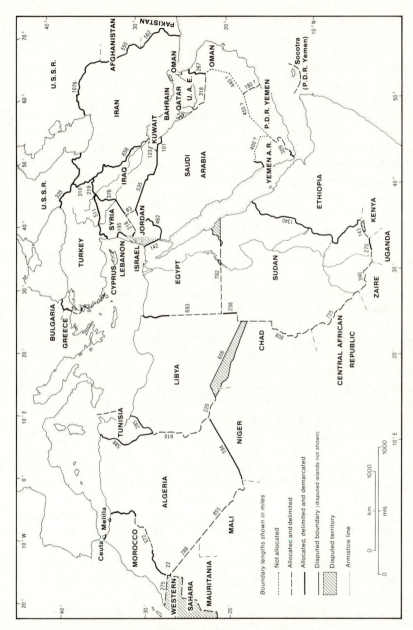

Figure 4.1 The Middle East and North Africa: Boundary status in 1984.

ended nearly 60 years of uncertainty over their 530-mile (850-kilometer) border. The agreement provides for the equal division of the former Saudi Arabia-Iraq neutral zones. In 1972, Morocco and Algeria agreed on their 970-mile (1560-kilometer) boundary after years of bitter dispute, which had involved heavy fighting in 1962–63. Also in 1972, Sudan and Ethiopia agreed in principle on their complex 1300-mile (2100-kilometer) boundary.

Surprisingly, few boundary agreements have incorporated territorial exchanges to benefit both parties. One creative boundary adjustment was achieved by Jordan and Saudi Arabia in the 1965 Treaty of Amman, which lengthened Jordan's narrow Gulf of Aqaba coastline by 15 miles (24 kilometers).[8] In return, Jordan ceded inland desert areas to Saudi Arabia (Figure 4.2). Similarly, Saudi Arabia's agreement with the U.A.E. gave Saudi Arabia access to the Gulf east of Qatar (Figure 4.6).

Boundary Classifications

In the opinion of two of the most respected writers on international boundaries, boundary classifications are of little value because each boundary is unique and is often too complex to be amenable to simple categorization.[9] A further objection is that geographers have ignored the more important functional aspects of boundaries in their preoccupation with classifications. These criticisms appear to be particularly relevant when it comes to studying Middle East and North African boundaries in detail. For this reason only two classification systems are considered here, that proposed by Boggs and that proposed by Hartshorne.[10] At least they provide a useful framework for discussion and an introduction to terms that have become widely accepted.

Boggs adopted a fourfold classification on the basis of boundary form: *physiographic, anthropogeographic, geometric,* and *complex* (or *indeterminate*). A physiographic boundary follows physical features: a river, mountain range, lake, or marsh, for example. Although these features may have the advantage of being visible in the landscape, physiographic boundaries are rarely ideal. In mountainous terrain, difficulties can arise from the use of the crestline from peak to peak, which may not coincide with the watershed. River boundaries are notoriously problematic, not only because of position (whether along the midpoint, the deepest navigable channel, or along the left or right bank), but also because of what happens when the course of the river changes. To give a small example, in 1982–83, the river Jordan changed course by several dozen yards in the northern Jordan Valley as a result of exceptionally heavy winter floods. Several acres of land were lost from the west bank and in places sections of Israel's security road ended up on the Jordanian side of the river.

Anthropogeographic boundaries coincide with man-made features,

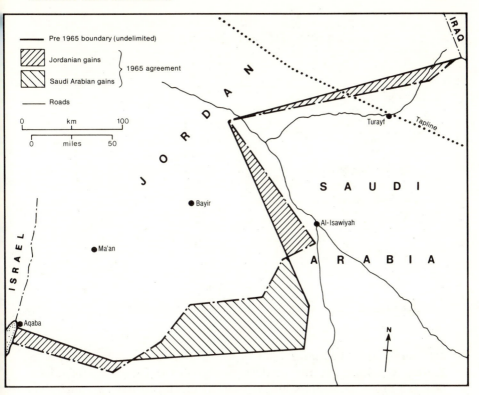

Figure 4.2 Exchange of territory under the Jordan-Saudi Arabia Treaty of Amman in 1965, giving Jordan improved access to the Gulf of Aqaba. (After Martin J. Glassner and Harm J. de Blij, *Systematic Political Geography*, third edition, p. 72. Copyright © 1980 by John Wiley & Sons, Inc. Reprinted by permission.)

such as roads, railways, and canals, or they follow tribal, religious, or ethnic divisions between peoples. Geometric boundaries are either based on lines of latitude or longitude, as with Egypt's western and southern boundaries, or lines joining certain specified geometric points, as with the Syrian-Iraqi boundary. Complex or indeterminate boundaries are a combination of any of the above types. Close examination of Middle East and North African boundaries reveals no fewer than 36 complex boundaries.[11] In the preparation of Table 4.2, it was, therefore, found preferable to disregard individual boundaries and add together boundary lengths in each category to give a more accurate picture of boundary types for the region as a whole. In cases where the same stretch of boundary apparently coincides with physical, human, or geometric criteria at the same time, it is "indeterminate."

About 35 percent of the boundary lines in the region are physiographic, chiefly following rivers, wadis, and watersheds. Physical features have been extensively utilized in the mountainous borderlands

Table 4.2
Morphometric Classification of Boundaries

	Miles (Kilometers)		Percentage of Total	
Physiographic				
Wadis and rivers	3,600	⎫	17	⎫
	(5,800)	⎪		⎪
Watersheds	3,100	⎬ 7,420	15	⎬ 35
	(5,000)	⎪ (11,940)		⎪
Edge of plain or plateau	720	⎪	3	⎭
	(1,160)	⎭		
Anthropogeographic	850		4	
	(1,370)			
Geometric	12,300		58	
	(19,800)			
Complex/indeterminate	730		3	
	(1,170)			
Total	21,300		100	
	(34,300)			

between Turkey and Iran. Some of these boundaries, notably between Turkey and Iran, are the modern versions of centuries-old frontiers. Because physical features are so prominent and in conventional warfare may provide an obstacle to invading forces, they are often thought of as good boundaries. The idea of "natural" physical boundaries for states was once popular, but it is now a dated and discredited concept. The Israelis, however, have continued to argue the case for "defensible borders," primarily as justification for their boundary along the Jordan rift valley. But there is no such thing as a natural boundary; all boundaries are arbitrary. Whether or not a boundary makes a good fence depends on its stage of development, not its physiography. A mature geometric boundary properly recognized and administered may be far more open and stable than a disputed physical boundary.

The most characteristic feature of international boundaries, both in the Middle East and North Africa, is the prevalence of geometric boundaries. To a large extent, these are confined to desert regions. In most cases, they were drawn by rival colonial powers without detailed knowledge of local human activity or topography.[12] For certain uninhabited regions, this was probably the simplest solution; it is likely that Saudi Arabia's desert boundaries with Yemen A.R., P.D.R. Yemen, and Oman will be straight lines; this was assumed when calculating boundary types in Table 4.2. Altogether, there are two dozen exclusively geometric boundaries and about a dozen others that are geometric for at least one third of their length. In total, 58 percent of the boundary lines in the region are geometric. Only a small proportion of boundary lines are anthropogeographic. The most obvious case is the Turkey-Syria boundary, which parallels the Baghdad railway for about 240 miles (390 kilometers) in accordance with a 1926 Franco-Turkish agreement. Similarly, part of the Libya-Algeria boundary follows an ancient caravan route for about 80 miles (130 kilometers).[13] Other anthropogeographic boundaries in the Middle East include the 1959 U.A.E.-Oman boundary, which reflects tribal affiliations. Several short stretches of boundary between Lebanon and Syria and Turkey and Syria were also devised by using existing village boundaries.

Hartshorne[14] chose a fivefold boundary classification based on the relationship between the boundary and the cultural landscape. A *pioneer* boundary is drawn in a completely uninhabited region. An *antecedent boundary* is drawn before intensive human settlement and prior to the development of most of the cultural landscape. *Subsequent boundaries* are established after cultural patterns have been formed and take these into account, whereas *superimposed boundaries* disregard cultural features. *Relict* boundaries are less important, being abandoned boundaries still discernible in the landscape. Hartshorne's classification is most useful in regions with relatively high population densities and a well-developed cultural landscape, such as Europe or North America. Although it can be partially applied to the Middle East and North Africa, there are serious limitations that make its application rather unprofitable. The vast majority of the boundaries in the region are superimposed boundaries created by the colonial powers. The only exceptions are the relatively short anthropogeographic boundaries discussed above, which correspond to Hartshorne's subsequent boundaries. The Israeli-Jordan armistice line from 1949–67 was a particularly badly superimposed boundary: it cut off many Arab villages from their lands, wells, and pastures (Figure 4.3).[15]

Superficially, geometric boundaries traversing arid areas appear to be antecedent or pioneer boundaries, but these terms are misleading. They were intended to describe situations in which pioneer settlement was advancing into virgin territory, as in nineteenth-century North America. The arid zones of the Middle East and North Africa already had cultural elements appropriate to low-density population and an arid zone economy—oases, wells, caravan tracks, pastures, and nomadic migration routes. Every boundary impinged on such features at some point, though their impact may not be so evident as in closely settled regions. Several superimposed boundaries have subsequently influenced transport networks, including oil pipelines, but this provides insufficient basis on which to regard them as antecedent boundaries.

Both these boundary classifications emphasize the degree to which the contemporary system is discordant with the underlying physical and human landscapes. Nevertheless, it is unlikely to change too much. Having achieved national independence, most governments seem to prefer to preserve territorial integrity behind artificial boundaries than

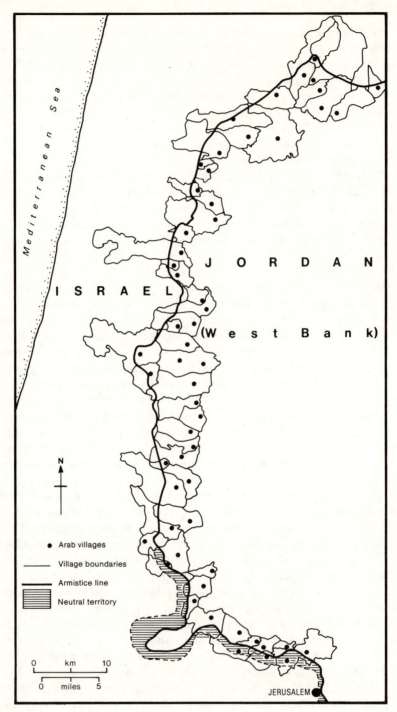

Figure 4.3 The effects of the Israel-Jordan armistice line of 1949–67 on Arab
village lands. (After Moshe Brawer, *The "Green Line": The Boundary of the West
Bank.* Tel Aviv: Tel Aviv University Research Project on Peace, 1980, p. 9.)

84

to embark on risky unions or major territorial conflicts. This view was officially stated by the Organization of African Unity in 1963 and by the Conference of Non-Aligned Countries in Cairo in 1964. Mutual respect for boundaries as they existed at the time of independence has not always been maintained, however, and disputes have occurred.

Boundary Disputes

Unfortunately, boundary delimitation and demarcation—and the formal agreements accompanying them—do not guarantee any state immunity from boundary disputes. Poor boundaries can easily be used as the pretext for quarrels between states; when the boundaries themselves seem physically and legally secure, allocation of resources or some aspect of the functioning of the boundary may cause disagreement. Thus, S. B. Jones wrote that "a boundary like the human skin, may have diseases of its own or may reflect the illnesses of the body."[16] Prescott[17] recognized four types of boundary dispute, all of which can be found in the Middle East and North Africa today. First, *positional disputes* concern the precise location of the boundary; these may arise from different interpretations of legal documents or from shifts in the location of physical features used to mark the boundary. Positional disputes often result from shifts in river channels, sandbanks, and islands. Second, *territorial disputes* occur when neighboring states claim the same border territory, usually on the basis of history or geographic necessity, such as access to the sea or national security. The most obvious example in the Middle East is the dispute between Israel and the Arabs over Palestine (see Chapter 9). In positional and territorial disputes, a change in boundary location is usually being sought. Third, *functional disputes* arise out of differences concerning the effect of the border on the movement of people and goods and out of local difficulties over land use and management. Fourth, *transboundary resource disputes* may arise from the exploitation of water, minerals, oil, or pasture by one state at the expense of another. The most common examples in the Middle East occur when offshore oil and gas fields straddle an international boundary. An onshore example is the oil field under the Iraq-Kuwait boundary, which Kuwait has accused Iraq of illegally exploiting—but there are more offshore than onshore problems of this kind. Functional disputes and transboundary resource disputes are rarely solved by a change in the location of the boundary.

Positional Disputes

Positional boundary disputes are uncommon in this region. The quarrel between Iraq and Iran over their boundary along the river Shatt al-Arab is a classic example. The problem concerns the last 50 miles (80 kilometers) or so before the river reaches the Gulf. For much of this stretch, the river is several hundred yards wide (Figure 4.4). The Iran-Iraq boundary has been the subject of many treaties, the earliest in 1639. Britain and Russia tried to bring about a final demarcation of the boundary between the Ottoman Empire and the Persians in the 1847 Treaty of Erzerum. In this treaty, the Ottoman island of Khizr was ceded to Persia, but by implication the Shatt al-Arab river boundary ran along the eastern bank. This was confirmed by a 1913 protocol between Turkey and Persia, which clearly gave the Ottomans full sovereignty over the Shatt al-Arab apart from some small islands and the anchorage opposite the port of Khoramshahr. In 1937, it was also agreed that a 4-mile (6.5-kilometer) stretch of river opposite Iran's growing oil port of Abadan was to have a midstream boundary. In spite of the agreement, many minor incidents occurred, often as a result of Iran's refusal to recognize Iraqi sovereignty over the lower course of the river.

In 1975, the two states agreed to a midstream boundary throughout the Shatt al-Arab in return for an Iranian promise to stop supporting Kurdish rebels in northern Iraq. Following the 1979 Iranian revolution, relations between the two states deteriorated. The boundary became a symbol of their hostility. Border incidents occurred with increasing frequency, more than 560 being reported by Iraq in 1979 and 1980. Iranian troops occupied four small pockets of Iraqi territory. In response, Iraq abrogated the 1975 midstream agreement in 1980. The two states then plunged into full-scale war. Iraq's rights to the Shatt al-Arab were used as justification for its invasion of Iran. The war's underlying causes had little to do with a positional boundary dispute. They lay, partly at least, in centuries of Arab-Persian rivalry, reinforced latterly by the bitter personal animosity between Iraq's President Saddam Husayn and Iran's Ayatallah Khumayni. The outcome of the war and future boundary arrangements along the Shatt al-Arab have yet to be resolved.

There are many other minor uncertainties and disagreements in the region concerning the position of boundary lines, but they mostly involve technical, not major political questions. For example, since Egypt's reoccupation of Sinai, completed in 1982, questions have been raised about the 142-mile long (228-kilometer) Egypt-Israel boundary. Israel casts doubt on the accuracy of Turkish, British, and Egyptian maps attached to the 1906 agreement that established the original Palestine-Egypt boundary—15 small border areas are, thus, disputed. Among these is a 700-yard (640-meter) stretch of coastline at Taba, near Eilat, where the Israelis have built a luxury hotel on land now claimed by Egypt.

Territorial Disputes

Although examples of territorial disputes abound in the region, they differ in character and scale. Morocco's claim to Western Sahara involves 103,000 square miles (267,000 square kilometers) and is one of

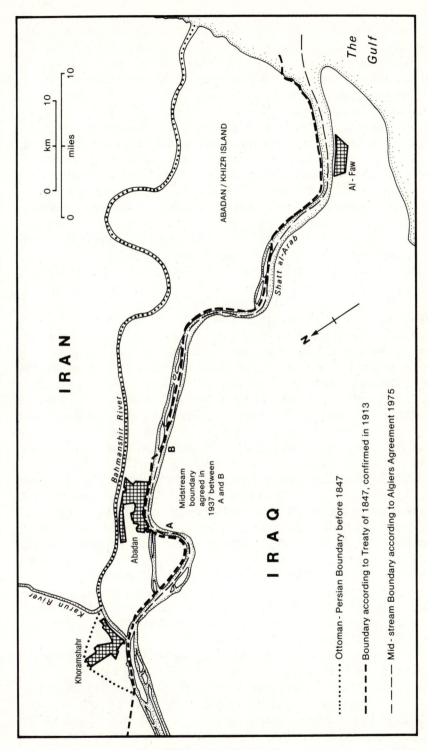

Figure 4.4   The Iran-Iraq boundary along the Shatt al-Arab.

the largest active territorial claims in the world. Following Spain's withdrawal from Spanish Sahara in 1976, the territory was partitioned between Morocco in the north and Mauritania in the south. The 80,000
inhabitants were not consulted, and many of them embarked on a war
of liberation spearheaded by the Polisario Front, who renamed the territory the Sahrawi Arab Democratic Republic (S.A.D.R.). In 1978,
Mauritania withdrew from the southern half of Western Sahara, leaving Morocco to claim the whole territory. From a Moroccan viewpoint,
this did not seem unreasonable because large parts of Algeria, Mauritania, and Western Sahara were once part of a "Greater Morocco" (Figure 3.4a). Until 1969, Morocco actually claimed Mauritania on these
grounds. Although history provided the basis for Moroccan claims to
Spanish Sahara, there were also strong economic motives. The phosphate mines at Bu-Craa in the north are among the richest in the world
and a potential source of huge export earnings.

The position in Western Sahara in 1985 is complex. The Moroccans
occupy all the coastal settlements and one or two inland towns, such
as Bu-Craa and Smara. In the capital at El Ayoun, there are signs that
Western Sahara is becoming integrated administratively and economically with Morocco, though the town is surrounded by an elaborate de-
fensive perimeter. Large tracts of desert, on the other hand, are controlled by the Polisario Front. The Algerians have given strong support
to the Polisario Front in the past, but in 1983, they appeared to be seeking a negotiated settlement of the problem.[18] Morocco has agreed in
principle to a referendum, but none has been held. Although the
S.A.D.R. has earned diplomatic recognition from more than 50 states,
Morocco remains in control of all the key centers and productive areas.

In 1975, Libya occupied a large tract of territory in northern Chad
known as the Aouzou strip (Figure 4.5). Libya's de facto boundary with
Chad is now 650 miles (1050 kilometers) long. The region contains valuable iron ore and uranium deposits, but the basis of Libya's claim is
legal. The pre-1975 Libya-Chad boundary had been agreed to by France
and Italy in 1919. An agreement between France and Italy in 1935 would
have given Libya the Aouzou strip. However, the treaty had not been
ratified when World War II broke out in 1939, and it was never implemented.[19] Libya's occupation of this remote, sparsely populated desert
territory is likely to become permanent. Indeed, the dispute went almost unnoticed until Libyan forces advanced deeper into Chad in 1983
and became embroiled in Chad's civil war.

The dispute between Saudi Arabia, Oman, and Abu Dhabi over the
Buraimi oasis is one of the best documented territorial disputes in the
Middle East. Buraimi comprises nine villages with a settled population
of mixed tribal origin. It was also an important focus for nomadic tribes
belonging to two major groups, the Bani Yas and the Manasir. As an
important route center, Buraimi also had ties with tribes throughout
eastern Arabia. Traditionally, territorial boundaries were of little signif-

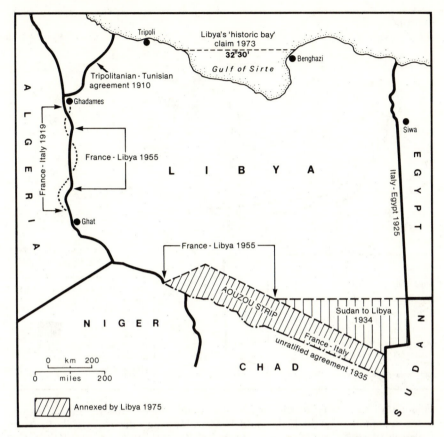

Figure 4.5 Libya's boundaries and the Aouzou strip in northern Chad, which was occupied by Libyan troops in 1975.

icance in this region. Tribal allegiance defined political relationships, not territory. Thus, the coming of modern states coupled with the search for oil necessitated the alignment of boundary lines that could not be reconciled with complex tribal allegiances.[20] Using tribal allegiances, Abu Dhabi, Oman, and Saudi Arabia were able to claim all or part of the Buraimi region. Until 1971, when the U.A.E. was formed, Britain acted on behalf of Abu Dhabi. Negotiations over the boundary between Abu Dhabi and Saudi Arabia lasted 40 years, and involved oases, tribes, and oil fields. The dispute received international publicity in 1955 when a British-led force acting on behalf of the rulers of Abu Dhabi and Oman ejected a contingent of armed Saudis from one of the Buraimi oases, which they had occupied in 1952. In the absence of any agreement with Saudi Arabia, Britain laid down a boundary on behalf of Abu Dhabi in 1955. In 1974, the U.A.E. and Saudi Arabia reached agreement on their boundary, using the 1955 alignment as a guideline. No detailed maps

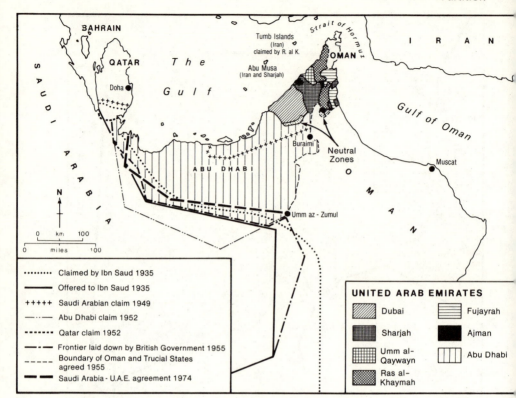

Figure 4.6   Various proposals for interstate boundaries in eastern Arabia. (After Peter Beaumont, Gerald Blake, and J. Malcolm Wagstaff, *The Middle East: A Geographical Study,* p. 305. Copyright © 1976 by John Wiley & Sons, Inc. Reprinted by permission.)

have been published, but the boundary apparently comprises straight lines throughout its length of over 320 miles (515 kilometers). The Saudis achieved valuable access to the Gulf coast east of Qatar as part of the deal, and a major oil field has been left on either side of the boundary. The line lies more than 100 miles (160 kilometers) south of Buraimi (Figure 4.6). The Oman-Abu Dhabi boundary leaves six Buraimi villages in Abu Dhabi and three in Oman, disrupting the rational development of what is clearly a single geographic entity.

A territorial dispute in the Gulf region that created much international anxiety was Iraq's claim to Kuwait. Since Kuwait won full independence from Britain in 1961, Iraq has periodically claimed sovereignty over the shaykhdom on the grounds that it was part of Basra province in Ottoman times. In 1961, British and Arab League forces deterred an Iraqi invasion. The Iraqi claim has never been formally dropped. Iraq has also pursued claims to Warbah and Bubiyan islands (see Chapter 5). According to agreements reached in 1932, these islands belong to Kuwait. Numerous border incidents have occurred since Iraq first pressed claims in 1971. In 1972, for example, an Iraqi army brigade attempted to build a road through Kuwaiti desert territory to the Gulf; Arab pressure forced the Iraqis to withdraw.[21]

Finally, two territorial problems associated with the Sudan-Egypt border are worth mentioning (see Figure 4.1). First, there is the Wadi Halfa salient, a finger of territory about 15 miles (24 kilometers) long. Sudan claims that this was transferred permanently from Egypt in 1899, but Egypt believes the transfer was an administrative convenience, not a transfer of sovereignty. Much of the area is now under the waters of Lake Nasir. Second, there is the question of two administrative boundaries in the east established in 1902 to facilitate the management of tribal grazing areas. These enabled Egypt to administer land south of the international boundary, and Sudan to administer a larger area to the north. Although the legal position seems clear, both states now tend to regard the administered areas as sovereign territory, as shown by maps printed in the respective countries. The large eastern territory adjacent to the sea is of special importance for its possible effect on rival claims to the Red Sea seabed.

Functional Disputes

Three types of functional dispute can be identified: those associated with formalities at legal crossings, illegal crossings, and problems generated by the boundary at the local level, such as access to fields or wells. The degree of control exercised at border crossings varies between states and often mirrors changes in the political relationship between the states. Excessive delays to travelers, tedious formalities, unnecessary harassment, or confiscation of goods are familiar techniques whereby one state can penalize the citizens of another. Unfortunately, many Middle East and North African borders have a bad reputation in this respect, thus greatly impeding interaction between neighboring regions. The frustrations experienced by West Bank Arabs entering and leaving Israel via the Jordan River bridge exemplify the problem.

Illegal border crossings are easily made where boundaries pass through vast areas of desert. Disputes often develop when one state fails to prevent or encourages illegal movements harmful to the interests of its neighbor. Israel has constantly complained that her Arab neighbors permit Palestinian fighters to cross into Israel. Thus, the entire 55 miles (88 kilometers) of the Israel-Lebanon border has been strongly fenced to keep out infiltrators, but this has not prevented Israeli incursions into Lebanon. There are many other instances of the illegal movement of guerilla fighters, weapons, and supplies across international boundaries, for example, between Algeria and Western Sahara, Libya and Sudan, Iran and Iraq, and P.D.R.Y. and Oman. Apart from weapons, many other kinds of goods are smuggled, often depending on the mobility and geographic knowledge of the bedouin.[22] In recent years, conventional smuggling has been supplemented by lucrative drug smuggling. The Middle East lies astride the main international drug route between Europe and North America and the world's major heroin and hashish-producing areas in the East. The crops from which the drugs are derived (opium poppy and hemp) also grow in parts of the Middle East and locally produced drugs are smuggled into Europe.

Thousands of illegal migrants cross boundaries by clandestine routes in the hope of finding work in the oil-rich states. A particularly large number have originated in the Y.A.R., and the Saudis believe greater efforts could be made by the Yemeni authorities to prevent these migrants from leaving. Many states nurse grievances against their neighbors for similar reasons. A common cause is when sanctuary is given to persons or groups hostile to a neighboring government: Iranian exiles in Turkey, Syrians in Jordan, and Iraqi Kurds in Iran are some examples.

The third group of functional boundary disputes occur where boundaries have been superimposed on established rural or urban land use patterns and created local hardship: Cyprus and Israel provide graphic examples. Since the Turkish invasion of 1974, Cyprus has functioned as a partitioned state. The cease-fire line between the Turkish north and the Greek south was crudely superimposed, dividing the capital city of Nicosia and crossing some of the best farmland in Cyprus without any regard for land ownership. The Turkish administration has offered to modify the cease-fire line in five locations to overcome some of the worst anomalies, but no progress has been made in the absence of an overall settlement.[23] It is some comfort to the Cypriots that the cease-fire line is not intended to be permanent.

The inhabitants of the city of Rafah in the Gaza strip enjoy no such comfort. As part of the Egyptian-Israeli Sinai boundary agreement, Rafah has been partitioned and its 60,000 Arab inhabitants shared between Egypt and Israel. A broad no-man's-land has been bulldozed through the town, brutally disrupting economic and social life. Permission to cross the boundary is not always easy to obtain.[24]

Jerusalem was the most infamously divided city in the Middle East between 1949 and 1967 when the old city was in Jordanian hands and most of the new city was in Israeli hands (Figure 4.7). A no-man's-land lay between the two sides; in places, high concrete walls screened one side of the city from the other. The boundary followed the 1949 armistice line.

Transboundary Resource Disputes

The most significant transboundary resource disputes in the region concern river-basin management. Such disputes raise particularly thorny problems in a region where there is an acute water shortage. The dis-

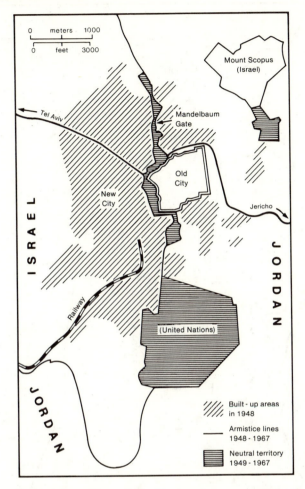

Figure 4.7 Divided Jerusalem, 1949–67, showing no-man's-land and the Israeli exclave on Mount Scopus. (After Martin Gilbert, *The Arab-Israel Conflict: Its History in Maps*, third edition. London: Weidenfeld, 1979, p. 53.)

pute between Turkey, Syria, and Iraq over allocation of the waters of the Euphrates is a striking example (Figure 4.8).

Construction of the massive Euphrates Dam at Tabqa (Al-Thawra) in Syria was completed in 1973 with Soviet assistance. The dam will enable Syria to double the area under irrigation and will supply the bulk of the country's electricity. Its importance to Syria's development is, therefore, considerable, but Iraq claims that Syria and Turkey, which are upstream, are taking an unfair share of the Euphrates water. Syria plans to extract 247 billion cubic feet (7 billion cubic meters) of water, and the projected Ataturk (Karababa) Dam in Turkey will require another 353 billion cubic feet (10 billion cubic meters). Allowing for addi-

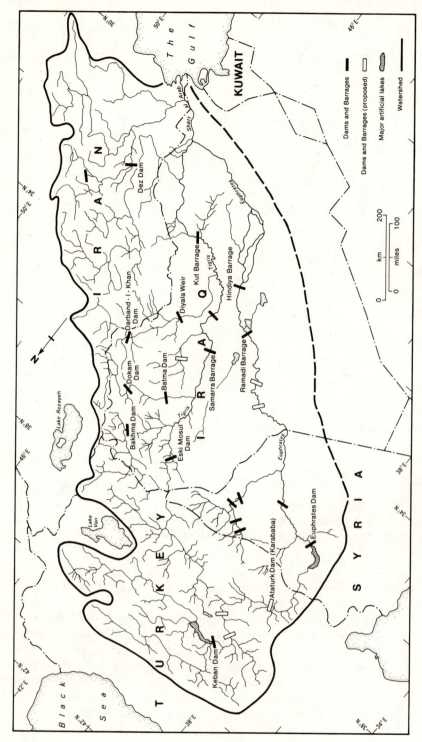

Figure 4.8 The basin of the Tigris and Euphrates rivers.

94

tional evaporation from the dams, the amount of Euphrates water entering Iraq will be reduced from 1059 billion cubic feet (30 billion cubic meters) to 388 billion cubic feet (11 billion cubic meters) when both plans in Turkey and Syria are in full operation. The Iraqis claim that their minimum future water requirement will be 459 billion cubic feet (13 billion cubic meters). They also argue that water quality is deteriorating with increased amounts of saline water draining from Syrian irrigation projects. Technical and managerial solutions could partly solve this dispute, but as long as Syria and Iraq remain politically at loggerheads, it will be a major source of friction between them.

Syria, too, is concerned about what happens upstream in Turkey. Early in 1984, only three of the Tabqa Dam's eight electricity-generating turbines were operating because of Lake Asad's low water level. Although unusually low rainfall was partly to blame, Syria also asserted Turkey was using too much Euphrates water. Syria even asked oil-rich Arab states not to provide Turkey with any loans to construct the Ataturk Dam unless agreement was reached over dividing the river's waters. In 1984, it also called for the establishment of a multinational Euphrates River Authority and for a trilateral meeting to discuss riparian rights.

The Nile basin is a second important example (Figure 4.9). The average annual discharge of the Nile where it enters Egypt is 3000 billion cubic feet (85 billion cubic meters). About 882 billion cubic feet (25 billion cubic meters) are derived from headwaters of the White Nile in Sudan and Uganda; the remaining 2118 billion cubic feet (60 billion cubic meters) are derived from the Blue Nile (1765 billion cubic feet or 50 billion cubic meters) and the Atbara (353 billion cubic feet or 10 billion cubic meters), which rise in Ethiopia. Egypt's rapidly growing population is almost entirely dependent on water originating in neighboring countries, and one of the prime concerns of Egyptian foreign policy has been protecting these sources. Under the 1929 Nile Waters Agreement, Egyptian rights were fully protected; Sudan was not permitted to build any further storage capacity without Egypt's permission. At that time, water was plentiful. Egypt consumed about 1694 billion cubic feet (48 billion cubic meters) and Sudan about 141 billion cubic feet (4 billion cubic meters) per annum; about one third of the Nile waters reached the Mediterranean unused.

The proposal to build a major new dam at Aswan necessitated revision of the 1929 agreement. The Agreement for the Full Utilization of the Nile Waters was accordingly signed in 1959. Under this agreement, which is still in operation, Egypt would receive 1960 billion cubic feet (55.5 billion cubic meters) and Sudan 653 billion cubic feet (18.5 billion cubic meters), a far greater proportional increase than Egypt's and more water than Sudan then required. Some 353 billion cubic feet (10 billion cubic meters) were written off to evaporation and seepage at the reservoir. The Aswan High Dam was completed in 1970; to date, there has been no conflict over the 1959 allocation. Some experts, however, are

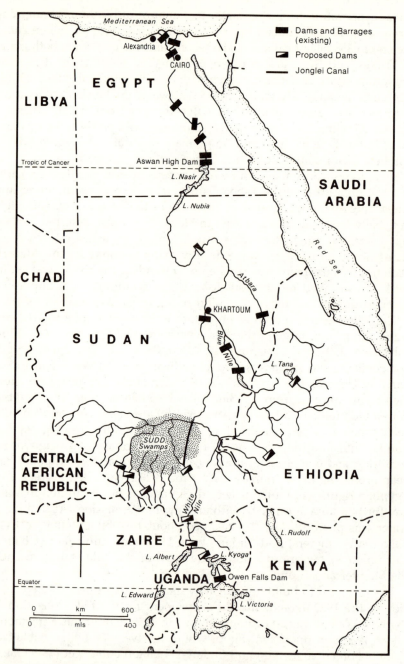

Figure 4.9   The basin of the Nile, showing sites proposed for dam projects. (After Peter Beaumont, Gerald Blake, and J. Malcolm Wagstaff, *The Middle East: A Geographical Study*, p. 93. Copyright © 1976 by John Wiley & Sons, Inc. Reprinted by permission.)

forecasting competition for Nile water before the end of the century among Egypt, Sudan, and Ethiopia as a result of rising demands based on new irrigation schemes, population increase, and higher standards of living (Table 4.3).

The question of future demand for Nile water is extremely complex and controversial, but figures of the kind shown in Table 4.3 are bound to feature more and more in the geopolitics of the Nile basin.[25] Although Ethiopia was bound by agreements between Britain and Italy before World War II not to undertake works on the Nile headwaters without consultation, no such understanding exists today, and Ethiopia is considering fairly ambitious water development plans. At the same time, large-scale irrigation plans in Sudan could be greatly stimulated by investment from the Arab world. In 1974, the Arab Fund for Social and Economic Development drew up plans for a large project to grow food for the Arab world, using Sudan's substantial reserves of soil and water. Such a plan might release certain Arab countries from dependence on imported food, which obviously has a powerful political appeal.

The basin of the Jordan River is divided between Lebanon, Syria, Jordan, and Israel (Figure 4.10). By world standards, the Jordan is a small stream, whose total discharge is equivalent to about 2 percent of the annual flow of the Nile or to about 7 percent of the Euphrates in Syria. To Jordan and Israel, however, the Jordan River is crucial, representing one third the volume of Israel's other water resources, and three times the volume of Jordan's. Before the 1967 boundary changes, three major tributaries of the Jordan rose outside Israel (Table 4.4). Since 1967, the Banias has been in Israeli-occupied territory. When Britain and France delimited the northern Syria-Palestine boundary in 1923, the Dan springs were deliberately left within Palestine, which has since proved a great benefit to Israel.

The Jordan basin is ideally suited to integrated development for irri-

Table 4.3
Water Balances in the Nile, 1985–90 (in billion cubic feet and billion cubic meters)

	Optimistic	Cautious	Pessimistic
Egypt	+557.7 (+15.8)[a]	−240.0 (−6.8)	−497.8 (−14.1)
Sudan	−112.9 (−3.2)	−289.5 (−8.2)	−342.4 (−9.7)
Ethiopia	−35.3 (−1.0)	−70.6 (−2.0)	−141.2 (−4.0)
Deficit/surplus	+409.5 (+11.6)	−600.1 (−17.0)	−981.3 (−27.8)

[a]Figures in parentheses are in billion cubic meters.

Source: Adapted from John Waterbury. *Hydropolitics of the Nile Valley.* Syracuse, N.Y.: Syracuse University Press, 1979, p. 239.

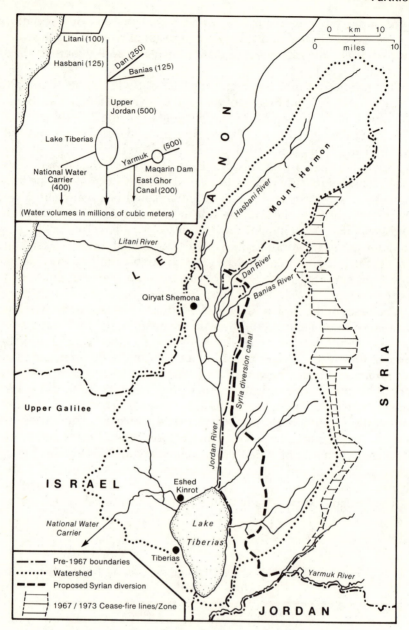

Figure 4.10 Basin of the Jordan and the Litani rivers.

gation and hydroelectric power, using Lake Tiberias as a natural storage reservoir. Several imaginative schemes have been proposed, all of which foundered because of the deep enmity between the Arabs and Israel. The last attempt to persuade the parties to participate was made by the representative of the president of the United States in 1955, Am-

Table 4.4
Major Tributaries of the Jordan River

Tributary	Source of Headwaters	Discharge[a]
Hasbani	Lebanon	4,871 (138)
Banias	Syria	4,271 (121)
Dan	Israel	8,648 (245)
Yarmuk	Jordan, Syria	17,368 (492)

[a]In millions of cubic feet; millions of cubic meters given in parentheses.

Source: C. G. Smith. "The Disputed Waters of the Jordan," *Transactions of the Institute of British Geographers* 40 (1966), pp. 111–128.

bassador Eric Johnston. He failed, but the proposed allocation of water in Johnston's plan (Jordan 52 percent, Israel 36 percent, Syria 9 percent, and Lebanon 3 percent) appears to have been used as a guideline by the states in their own schemes.[26]

In the absence of regional agreement, Jordan began construction of a canal from the Yarmuk to irrigate the east Jordan Valley in 1958. In the same year, Israel began construction of a National Water Carrier as part of a national master plan for water, whose key feature was the diversion of large amounts of water from Lake Tiberias to irrigate the Negev desert in the south. Both Jordan and Israel's schemes have been highly successful, although Israel's water-diversion plans have constantly met fierce Arab opposition. In 1964, an Arab summit meeting resolved to divert the headwaters of the Jordan tributaries outside Israel. Syria's diversion attempts resulted in a series of large-scale border clashes. Israel will be reluctant to see Syria in control of the Banias springs again and may consider that control of the Hasbani headwaters constitutes an argument for remaining in southern Lebanon. Many Lebanese fear that Israel's dream of diverting the Litani's headwaters might be revived. The Litani waters flow into the Mediterranean Sea underutilized and could be diverted into the Hasbani River by means of a tunnel, giving Israel an extra 17.6 billion cubic feet (500 million cubic meters) a year.[27]

Nonstate Territories and Boundaries

When territorial disputes reach deadlock, states may agree to a partial surrender of sovereignty in limited areas. The most common forms are *demilitarized zones* and *neutral territories*. In demilitarized zones, claims to territory may not be disputed, but demilitarization is undertaken by state *A* in the interests of state *B*. In neutral territories, however, land ownership is in contention, and the parties mutually concede equal

rights, equal access, and demilitarization. Where armed conflict has occurred, the belligerent states may agree on the establishment of a demilitarized *buffer zone* between them. An independent force may be asked
to police the buffer zone to ensure observance of the cease-fire agreements. A fourth type of nonstate territory is the *international zone.* An
international zone was established around Tangier from 1923–56 to ensure the safety of shipping passing through the Strait of Gibraltar. The
same idea was adopted for the Turkish Straits between 1923 and 1936
to ensure free passage. Britain's occupation of the Suez Canal Zone until 1956 was not an international operation, but the motives were much
the same, and it meant partial surrender of its sovereignty by Egypt.

The Iraq-Saudi Arabia and Kuwait-Saudi Arabia neutral zones were
prominent features of the map of the Middle East until recently. The
Iraq-Saudi Arabia neutral zone was established in 1922 as a demilitarized area in which tribes from both states would have equal rights to
water and pasture. No oil has been found there, and it was agreed to
divide the zone equally in 1975. The Kuwait-Saudi Arabia neutral zone
was also established in 1922, with rights of access for nomads from both
states. Oil has been exported since 1954 by concessionaires operating
on behalf of both states, who enjoy equal rights to the resources. In
1966, it was decided to partition the neutral zone, and a boundary was
delimited and demarcated in 1969. All oil revenues from the former
neutral zones are divided equally between Saudi Arabia and Kuwait.

There are at least three other small neutral territories surviving in the
region. A narrow neutral zone dating back to 1860 separates Morocco
from the Spanish enclave of Melilla (Figure 3.4b). In 1970, as part of an
overall boundary agreement Dubai and Abu Dhabi delimited a neutral
zone where several wells were in dispute. Ajman and Oman also share
a neutral zone (Figure 4.6).

Before the Arab-Israeli war of 1967, there were a number of neutral
territories along Israel's boundaries incorporated in the 1949 armistice
agreements. Examples can be seen on Figures 4.3, 4.7, and 4.11. Though
small, these territories caused considerable difficulties for U.N. observ-
ers, often over access to cultivable land.[28] Neutral territories may be
useful in certain circumstances, but they are notoriously difficult to administer, and, in some cases, the neutral land lies totally idle. The neutral territory in divided Jerusalem in the 1948–67 period was a derelict,
war-damaged eyesore.

Buffer zones physically separate two potentially hostile states to reduce the possibility of armed conflict. The buffer-zone concept has been
adopted at both macroscales and microscales. British and Russian spheres
of influence in Persia between 1912–17 were separated by an agreed
buffer zone to reduce the risk of competing political interests boiling
over into open war. Today, Afghanistan is sometimes seen as a *buffer
state* between the Soviet Union and the pro-Western world. These grand
geopolitical uses of the buffer concept are beyond the scope of this
chapter. Our concern here is with buffer zones at the microscale. There

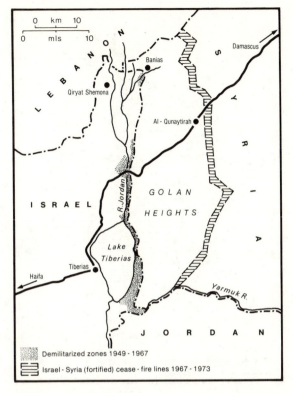

Figure 4.11   Israel-Syria armistice lines, 1949–73.

can be *formal buffer zones*, bounded by recognized boundaries, or *informal buffer zones*, less well defined but fulfilling a similar function. Territories controlled by Israeli-backed Christian militias in southern Lebanon after 1976 provided an informal buffer zone between Israel and Palestinian and Syrian forces to the north.

Buffer zones established between Israel and Egypt in Sinai and between Israel and Syria in the Golan region are superb examples of formal buffer zones. (Figure 4.12). In 1974, a Syria-Israel disengagement agreement created a demilitarized buffer zone policed by the United Nations as well as two zones where the forces of the two sides were restricted. The entire zone, more than 20 miles (32 kilometers) wide, is a kind of buffer zone between Syria and Israel. Similar arrangements were made in Sinai during Israel's phased return of the territory to Egypt.

Boundaries as Barriers

Boundaries act as barriers to the movement of people, goods, and ideas. The degree to which a particular boundary affects such movements can

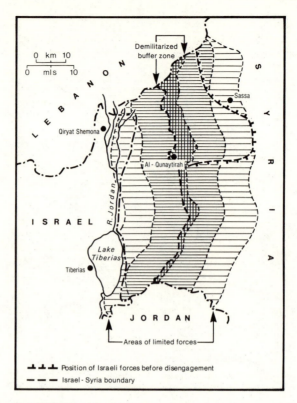

Figure 4.12   The 1974 Israel-Syria disengagement agreement, showing demilitarized buffer zone and area of limited forces. (After Martin Gilbert, *The Arab-Israel Conflict: Its History in Maps*, third edition. London: Weidenfeld, 1979, p. 100.)

be described as its permeability. The permeability of boundaries in the Middle East and North Africa varies enormously from state to state and can change markedly through time. Unfortunately it is impossible to evaluate boundary permeability with any precision. To do so would require data on transborder movements, which are not always readily available, and data on what movements might be expected if no boundary existed. The latter could be roughly calculated by using gravity interaction models. On a regional scale, this would be a major undertaking.[29] Clearly, a low level of transborder activity may reflect economic rather than political limitations, and some permeable or open boundaries may be little used. It would also be wrong to assume that high permeability is always beneficial; an impermeable boundary may be essential to protect the state from arms or drug smuggling or infected livestock.

  If data on cross-border movements could be assembled, they would show that several boundaries are almost completely impervious to the passage of people and goods, notably those between Syria and Israel, Egypt and Libya, Sudan and Libya, and the two halves of Cyprus. They would show a number of boundaries where movement is restricted for political reasons, as between Egypt and Israel, P.D.R. Yemen and Saudi Arabia, and Turkey and the Soviet Union. Some boundaries would display abnormal permeability in the form of military traffic and supplies (Morocco and Western Sahara, Israel and Lebanon, Syria and Lebanon, Iran and Iraq). At the other end of the spectrum, there are a larger number of boundaries across which interaction is maintained at a relatively high level, including Saudi Arabia's boundaries with her Arabian peninsula neighbors, Algeria and Tunisia, and Egypt and Sudan. Several such boundaries have been closed wholly or partially at times of political tension. The Morocco-Algeria boundary was partially closed from 1975 until 1983. Other boundary closures have included those of Greece and Turkey, Syria and Iraq, Syria and Jordan, and Iraq and Jordan.

Middle East and North African boundaries have affected the migration patterns of desert nomads and have also had a largely negative effect on existing urban centers. As a general rule, traditional tribal movements appear to have continued long after the imposition of boundary lines. Indeed, in parts of the Middle East, provision was made in certain boundary agreements for the recognition of nomadic rights.[30] On the other hand, governments have always tended to dislike nomadism, and sedentarization has been actively encouraged. The compulsory sedentarization of tribes along the Iran-U.S.S.R. boundary under Reza Shah (1925–41) ended any movement across the border. In North Africa, cross-border movements were sometimes stopped by the authorities or permission became necessary. After 1948, movements in and out of Israel were forbidden. Some boundary lines, thus, prevented or deterred nomadic movements, accelerating the decline of traditional lifestyles (at least in certain tribal communities), but the decline of nomadism was brought about by many other factors as well.[31] Modest movements of nomads across international boundaries still occur but on a much reduced scale.

The superimposition of a boundary system onto an existing urban network inevitably affected the functions of a number of towns in the region. Those that suffered most were the large-and medium-size centers whose spheres of influence would have been quite extensive. Damascus and Aleppo, for example, lost some of their former hinterlands after the creation of the post-World War I Syrian boundaries with Lebanon, Palestine, Transjordan, Iraq, and Turkey. Several towns in Turkey's partially enclosed Hatay region lost parts of their hinterlands to Syria when the boundary was redrawn in 1939. But the most conspicuous examples resulted from the creation of Israel and the impervious nature of Israel's boundaries with the Arab world. Israel became an effective barrier between the eastern and western wings of the Arab world, and it profoundly affected the geographic development of several towns and villages. Jerusalem, Haifa, and Ashdod in Israel as well as Hebron, Aqaba, and Gaza are obvious examples. Worse still, Syria's administrative center of the Golan region at Al-Qunaytirah has never recovered from proximity to the Israel-Syrian boundary, and it has been a ghost town since 1967.

Conclusion

The longer interstate boundaries survive, the more they become etched into the political and cultural landscape. This process is going on in the Middle East and North Africa. As a whole, the boundary system of the region is youthful and in places remains to be allocated or properly delimited, but it is, nonetheless, far more extensively recognized and demarcated than is often realized. Although boundaries in the Arab world may be anathema to some, today they embrace territories with their own deepening nationalisms and self-interest, and they are profoundly influencing the economic infrastructure of individual states. Considering the length and number of boundaries involved and the strained relations between certain states, the incidence of land-boundary disputes is quite small—in this sense, many are "good fences." Indeed, maritime boundary disputes are currently more numerous. But the examples cited in this chapter are not exhaustive. The 33 internal boundaries of the member states of the U.A.E. are still largely unsettled and have not been discussed. In addition, there are many positional and functional disputes only known at the local level. Nor have problems of transboundary resources been exhausted; the waters of several smaller river basins, such as the Helmand River on the Iran-Afghanistan border, are disputed. Finally, violations of airspace should be noted. This unseen aspect of modern boundary disputes deserves more attention; for example, it has often figured in the Greece-Turkey dispute in the Aegean and in the Israeli raid on Iraq's nuclear power station in 1981, which was a violation of the airspace of at least two Arab states. Similarly, the U.S. Airborne Warning and Control System (AWACS) reconnaissance aircraft sent to Saudi Arabia in 1981 operate without regard for international boundaries.

Notes

1. From Robert Frost's poem "Mending Wall," *North of Boston* (London: David Nutt, 1914): 13.

2. Lack of cartographic know-how was an added problem: an early Ottoman map of Egypt shows thick, uncertain-looking boundary lines, as if drawn by a child. See Gideon Biger, "The First Map of Modern Egypt: Mohammed Ali's Firman and the map of 1941," *Middle Eastern Studies* 14 (1978): 323–324.

3. The term "settlement frontier" is sometimes used to describe the process of advanc-

ing colonization and state control in new lands. See J. R. V. Prescott, *The Geography of Frontiers and Boundaries* (London: Hutchinson, 1965): 34–40.

4. Lord Curzon of Keddleston, "Frontiers," *The Romanes Lecture, University of Oxford, 1907* (London: Oxford University Press, 1908).

5. In the first century A.D., however, there was a demarcated and fortified line in Sinai between Roman-occupied Judea to the north and the Nabateans in the desert to the south.

6. S. B. Jones, *Boundary-Making: A Handbook for Statesmen, Treaty Editors, and Boundary Commissioners* (Washington D.C.: Carnegie Endowment for International Peace, 1945): 5.

7. For example, in the six years following the demarcation of the Turco-Persian boundary in 1913–14, local tribesmen destroyed nearly all the boundary pillars on three occasions. See C. H. D. Ryder, "The Demarcation of the Turco-Persian Boundary in 1913–14," *Geographical Journal* 66(1926): 238.

8. For a historic view of the Gulf of Aqaba see, Naval Intelligence Division, *Palestine and Transjordan, 1943*, Admiralty Geographical Handbook Series (London: Admiralty, 1943). This series is an invaluable source of data on pre-World War II boundaries for many Middle East and North African states.

9. See Notes 3 and 6 above: Prescott, op. cit., pp. 23–24. Prescott cites S. B. Jones, op. cit., as holding this view (p. 24).

10. S. W. Boggs, *International Boundaries: A Study of Boundary Functions and Problems* (New York: Columbia University Press, 1940); Richard Hartshorne, "Suggestions on the Terminology of Political Boundaries," *Annals of the Association of American Geographers* 26(1936): 56–57.

11. Where available, U.S. Department of State boundary studies were consulted; for other boundaries 1:250,000-scale maps were examined.

12. "The curious kink in the frontier that was drafted to divide the new amirate of Transjordan from what was to become Saudi Arabia is known as 'Winston's hiccough' because, according to legend, it was drawn by the secretary of state with pen and ruler after an exceptionally good lunch in Jerusalem." Peter Mansfield, *The Arabs*, rev. ed. (New York: Penguin Books, 1978): 219. Winston's hiccough can be seen on Figure 4.2.

13. See Bureau of Intelligence and Research, *International Boundary Study No. 163: Syria-Turkey*, 1978 and *International Boundary Study No. 1: Algeria-Libya*, 1961 (Washington, D.C.: U.S. Department of State).

14. See Note 10 above: Hartshorne, op. cit.

15. Figure 4.3 is based on a map in M. Brawer, *The "Green Line": The Boundary of the "West Bank" (Judea and Samaria)*, Research Project on Peace (Tel Aviv: Tel Aviv University, 1980).

16. See Note 6 above: S. B. Jones, op. cit., p. 3.

17. See Note 6 above: Prescott, op. cit., pp. 107–133.

18. Libya has also supplied the Polisario Front via a formidable road through the Algerian Sahara. The Libyans may not be so keen on a negotiated settlement as the Algerians. See *Africa Guide, 1981* (Saffron Walden, Eng.: World of Information, 1981): 248–251.

19. In spite of this, some maps and atlases published in the 1940s and 1950s show the unratified 1935 Libya-Chad boundary.

20. The difficulties were demonstrated in the 1950s when the British set about defining the boundaries of the emirates comprising the Trucial States: "The British official [Julian Walker] would drive to isolated villages and encampments and then ask the elders there to which of the seven rulers in addition to the Sultan of Oman they owed allegiance. A consensus on this matter would prompt Walker to simply encircle such a village or encampment, using whatever landmarks were available. He would then submit to the Brit-

ish authorities his recommendations as to which of the states this piece of land should belong." Ali Mohammed Khalifa, *The United Arab Emirates: Unity in Fragmentation* (London: Croom Helm, 1979), p. 100.

21. In 1977, rather surprisingly, a Kuwaiti minister declared that "there are a few hundred Iraqis on our side of the frontier here and there, but we do not consider it a major crisis." *Christian Science Monitor*, 23 February 1977, p. 26.

22. Bedouin genius for smuggling was revealed during Israel's phased withdrawal from Sinai in 1979 and 1980. Israeli officials discovered over 200 stolen cars buried in the sand awaiting the boundary to be moved. Many more cars had clearly been buried in this way in Israeli territory and dug up again in Egyptian territory for sale in Egypt free of customs duty. See *New York Times*, 8 February 1980, pp. A1, A3.

23. There are three other international boundaries in Cyprus: the de jure boundaries between the Republic of Cyprus and the United Kingdom Sovereign Bases of Akrotiri and Dhekelia, which remained British territory when Cyprus became independent in 1960, and the de facto boundary between the Turkish Federated State of Cyprus and the United Kingdom Sovereign Base of Dhekelia. (The British Sovereign Base boundaries were excluded when calculating Tables 4.1 and 4.2.)

24. In the first eight months after its opening, about 300,000 people used the Rafah crossing, including a large number of Arab residents of the occupied territories. *(The Jerusalem Post*, 28 December 1982, p. 2). Crossing difficulties were reported in *New York Times*, 27 February 1983, p. A14.

25. The construction of the Jonglei Canal along the eastern fringe of the Sudd Swamps (Figure 4.9) will save 70.6 billion cubic feet (2 billion cubic meters) for each country; this is accounted for in Table 4.3.

26. About 23 percent of the flow of the Jordan River is derived from inside Israel. The Johnston allocation of 36 percent to Israel was based on estimated water requirements of the four states.

27. Israel was reported to be actively investigating the project in 1983; the river and surrounding land would be expropriated under the guise of security needs in southern Lebanon. See *Middle East Economic Digest*, 13 May 1983, p. 52.

28. See J. S. Haupert, "Political Geography of the Israel-Syria Boundary Dispute 1949–67," *Professional Geographer* 21(1969): 163–171.

29. For an interesting attempt to quantify the barrier effect of the United States-Canada boundary by using telephone calls, see J. Ross McKay, "Interactance Hypothesis and Boundaries in Canada: A Preliminary Study," *Canadian Geographer* 2(1958): 1–8.

30. See "The Boundaries of the Nejd: A Note on the Special Conditions," *Geographical Review* 17(1927): 128–134. Also, Douglas L. Johnson, *The Nature of Nomadism*, Department of Geography Research Paper No. 118 (Chicago: University of Chicago, 1969).

31. "The boundary marks that were set up by the conquerors, who would only recognize the existence of Algerians, Tunisians, or Tripolitanians, formed frontiers that shattered the mental framework of bedouin life, even before the superiority of the occupier began to affect the economic substructure." Andre Marel, *Les confins Saharo-Tripolitains de la Tunisie (1881–1911)*, Vol. 2 (Paris: P.U.F., 1965): 355. Quoted by Martine Muller, "Frontiers: An Imported Concept: An Historical Review of the Creation and Consequences of Libya's Frontiers," in J. A. Allan (ed.), *Libya Since Independence*, pp. 165–180 (London: Croom Helm, 1982).

Selected Bibliography

Abdullah, Muhammad M. *The United Arab Emirates.* London: Croom Helm, 1978.

Beeley, Brian W. "The Greek-Turkish Boundary: Conflict at the Interface." *Transactions of the Institute of British Geographers* 3(1978): 351–366.

Boggs, S. W. *International Boundaries: A Study of Boundary Functions and Problems.* New York: Columbia University Press, 1940.

Brawer, Moshe. "The Geographical Background of the Jordan Water Dispute," in Charles A. Fisher (ed.), *Essays in Political Geography*, pp. 225–242. London: Methuen and Co., Ltd. 1968.

———. *The "Green Line": The Boundary of the "West Bank" (Judea and Samaria).* Research Project on Peace. Tel Aviv: Tel Aviv University, 1980.

Brownlie, Ian. *African Boundaries: A Legal and Diplomatic Encyclopaedia.* London: C. Hurst and Co., for the Royal Institute of International Affairs, 1979.

Bureau of Intelligence and Research. *International Boundary Study Series.* Washington, D.C.: Office of the Geographer, U.S. Department of State. (Many Middle East and North Africa boundaries have featured in the series since 1961.)

Cooley, John K. "The War Over Water." *Foreign Policy* 54(Spring 1984): 3–28.

Drury, Michael P. "The Political Geography of Cyprus," in John I. Clarke and Howard Bowen-Jones (eds.), *Change and Development in the Middle East*, pp. 289–304. London: Methuen and Co., Ltd., 1981.

East, W. Gordon, and Prescott, J. R. V. *Our Fragmented World.* London: Macmillan, 1975.

Gilbert, Martin. *The Arab-Israeli Conflict: Its History in Maps*, 3rd ed. London: Weidenfeld and Nicolson, 1979.

Glassner, Martin I., and de Blij, Harm J. (eds.). *Systematic Political Geography*, 3rd ed. New York: John Wiley & Sons, 1980.

Hodgson, Robert D., and Stoneman, Elvyn A. *The Changing Map of Africa*, 2nd ed. Princeton, N.J.: D. Van Nostrand Co., 1968.

Jones, S. B. *Boundary-Making: A Handbook for Statesmen, Treaty Editors, and Boundary Commissioners.* Washington, D.C.: Carnegie Endowment for International Peace, 1945.

Karmon, Yehuda. *Israel: A Regional Geography.* Chichester, Eng.: John Wiley & Sons, 1971.

Kasperson, Roger E., and Minghi, Julian V (eds.). *The Structure of Political Geography.* Chicago: Aldine Publishing Co., 1969.

Kelly, J. B. *Eastern Arabian Frontiers.* London: Faber and Faber Inc., 1964.

Litwak, R. *Security in the Persian Gulf (2): Sources of Inter-State Conflict.* London: International Institute for Strategic Studies, 1981.

Lynn-Price, David. *Conflict in the Maghreb: The Western Sahara.* Conflict Studies No. 127. London: Institute for the Study of Conflict, 1981.

Melamid, Alexander. "The Economic Geography of Neutral Territories." *Geographical Review* 45(1955): 359–374.

———. "Political Boundaries and Nomadic Grazing." *Geographical Review* 55(1965): 287–290.

Muir, Richard. *Modern Political Geography.* London: Macmillan, 1975.

Prescott, J. R. V. *The Geography of Frontiers and Boundaries.* London: Hutchinson, 1965.

———. *The Geography of State Policies.* London: Hutchinson, 1968.

———. *Boundaries and Frontiers.* London: Croom Helm, 1978.

for its sauerkraut!Reyner, Anthony S. "The Case of an Indeterminate Boundary: Algeria-Morocco," in Charles A. Fisher (ed.), *Essays in Political Geography*, pp. 243–251. London: Methuen and Co., Ltd. 1968.

Ryder, C. H. D. "The Demarcation of the Turco-Persian Boundary in 1913–14." *Geographical Journal* 66(1926): 227–242.

Sevian, Vahe J. "The Evolution of the Boundary Between Iraq and Iran," in Charles A. Fisher (ed.), *Essays in Political Geography*, pp. 211–223. London: Methuen and Co., Ltd., 1968.

Smith, C. G. "The Disputed Waters of the Jordan." *Transactions of the Institute of British Geographers* 40(1966): 111–128.

Waterbury, John. *Hydropolitics of the Nile Valley.* Syracuse, N.Y.: Syracuse University Press, 1979.

Widstrand, Carl G. (ed.). *African Boundary Problems.* Uppsala, Sweden: Scandinavian Institute of African Studies, 1969.

Wilkinson, John C. "The Oman Question: The Background to the Political Geography of South-east Arabia." *Geographical Journal* 108(1971): 361–371.

5

Offshore Political Geography:
The Partitioning of the Oceans

Slowly over the past two decades, the states of the Middle East and North Africa have been extending their domains seaward. Drawn initially by the prospect of offshore resources, particularly oil, they have become increasingly aware of the wider implications of offshore activity, notably the environmental implications and questions of national security. Until the emergence of the United Nations Treaty on the Law of the Sea in 1982, offshore boundary delimitation was not given high priority, especially outside the Gulf.[1] Following the treaty, however, maritime boundary delimitation is likely to proceed in dozens of cases. In many instances, the process will be lengthy and difficult; in some instances, associated land boundary disputes may be revived. Eventually, a completely new political map of the region will crystallize, each state with its offshore domain. Geopolitical analyses of the future will have to take into account state sovereignty in three dimensions—land, sea, and air (Figure 5.1). Certain states will find themselves the legal custodians of enormous areas of seabed and possibly considerable wealth, whereas others will regard themselves as losers in the new dispensation. Either way, offshore political geography is bound to feature prominently in relations between states over the coming decades, creating both opportunities for cooperation and risks of conflict.

Historically, commercial and military superiority were often maintained through seapower, particularly in the Mediterranean world. Today, the strategic importance of the seas that interpenetrate the region is global. Only the landlocked Caspian Sea is of little interest to states outside the region. The Mediterranean and Red seas provide a highway between the Atlantic and the Indian oceans via the Suez Canal.

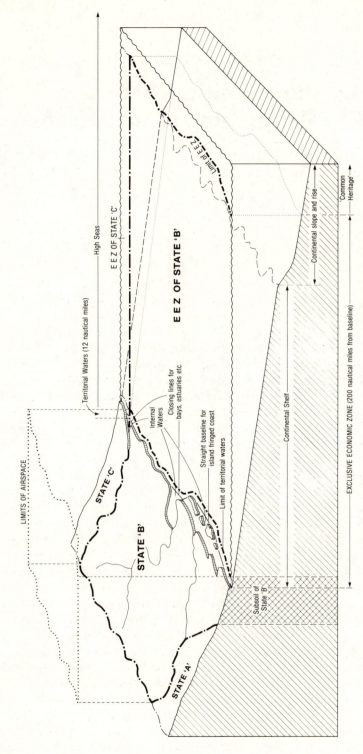

Figure 5.1 The limits of state jurisdiction, onshore and offshore.

The Black Sea and Mediterranean provide the Soviet Union, Romania, and Bulgaria with access to the world's oceans. The Gulf and the Indian Ocean have acquired special importance as oil transportation routes, especially to the industrialized countries of Western Europe, Japan, and the United States. Control of shipping lanes has already been a contributory factor in three wars in the Middle East: between Iraq and Iran in 1980 and between Egypt and Israel in 1956 and 1967.

Access to the Sea

States with the longest coastlines do not necessarily possess the largest areas of seabed. Much depends on the relative location of other states.

Table 5.1
Land Area and Coastal Length

	Land Area		Coastal Length		Land Area per Length of Coast	
	Sq. Miles	Sq. Kilometers	Miles	Kilometers	Sq. Miles per Mile	Sq. Kilometers per Kilometer
Bahrain	231	598	78	125	2.9	4.8
Cyprus	3,572	9,251	334	534	10.7	17.3
Qatar	4,000	10,360	235	376	17.0	27.5
Lebanon	3,400	8,806	121	194	28.0	45.4
Israel[a]	7,992	20,699	143	229	55.9	90.4
Kuwait	9,375	24,281	156	250	60.0	97.1
U.A.E.	36,193	93,740	435	696	83,2	134.7
Oman	105,000	271,950	1,156	1,850	90.8	147.0
Tunisia	63,362	164,107	639	1,022	99.2	160.6
Turkey	301,383	780,582	2,211	3,538	136.3	220.6
P.D.R. Yemen	111,075	287,684	753	1,205	147.5	238.7
Morocco	254,817	659,976	1,030	1,648	247.4	400.5
Egypt	386,663	1,001,457	1,505	2,408	257.0	415.9
Yemen A.R.	75,290	195,001	281	450	268.0	433.3
Iran	634,000	1,642,060	1,139	1,822	556.6	901.2
Saudi Arabia	864,800	2,239,832	1,515	2,424	570.8	924.0
Libya	679,364	1,759,553	1,047	1,675	649.0	1,050.5
Syria[a]	71,498	185,180	94	150	760.6	1,234.5
Algeria	919,600	2,381,764	686	1,098	1,340.5	2,169.2
Sudan	967,500	2,505,825	446	714	2,169.2	3,509.5
Jordan[a]	37,000	95,830	17	27	2,176.4	3,549.2
Iraq	167,957	435,009	12	19	13,996.0	22,895.0

[a] Pre-1967 areas.

Source: Adapted from G. H. Blake. "Offshore Politics and Resources," in John I. Clarke and H. Bowen-Jones (eds.), *Change and Development in the Middle East.* London: Methuen and Co., Ltd., 1981, pp. 113–129.

A long coastline, on the other hand, provides scope for the rational development of ports, and it reduces the risk of interference with shipping by neighboring states. Table 5.1 indicates landmass in proportion to length of coastline as a crude indicator of the degree of maritime access. A more revealing index might be the proportion of national populations living within 50 miles (80 kilometers) or so of the coast. On this ranking, Libya and the People's Democratic Republic of Yemen (P.D.R. Yemen) would appear higher in the table, Turkey and Egypt rather lower.[2] Certain states are particularly well placed geopolitically by having coastlines on more than one major ocean. Morocco (Atlantic and Mediterranean), Turkey (Black Sea and Aegean), Israel and Egypt (Red Sea and Mediterranean), and Saudi Arabia (Red Sea and the Gulf) all enjoy access to two oceans. Oman and the United Arab Emirates (U.A.E.) (the Gulf and the Indian Ocean) are similarly fortunate, but their advantage is greatly diminished by the discontinuity of their national territories and the absence of suitable ports. Although no state in the region is landlocked, Jordan and Iraq have severely restricted access to the sea, resulting in unwelcome economic costs and political dependence.

Jordan became virtually a landlocked state in 1948 when all links to the coast through Israel were completely severed. During the British mandate over Palestine, there were no political or economic barriers to movement between Jordan and the Mediterranean coast; Haifa served as the country's leading port. Since 1948, one of Jordan's most pressing tasks has been the development of two alternative trade routes: one via Damascus in Syria to Beirut in Lebanon, the other via Aqaba on Jordan's short Gulf of Aqaba coastline. Unfortunately, Syria has occasionally closed its airspace and border to Jordanian traffic and the port of Beirut has become almost useless as a result of fighting in Lebanon. Aqaba's importance has increased accordingly. Before 1948 Aqaba was a tiny isolated settlement in an undeveloped part of Jordan, but its role as a port has steadily expanded, except during the period when the Suez Canal was closed from 1967 to 1975. For a short time during and immediately after the 1970 civil war in Jordan, exports could neither cross Syria nor transit the Suez Canal, so phosphate shipments to Europe had to go round southern Africa. In 1965, Saudi Arabia ceded Jordan 15 miles (24 kilometers) of coast on the Gulf of Aqaba, thus enhancing Jordan's only direct access to the sea.

Iraq's only outlet to the sea is via the Gulf, where possession of about 36 miles (58 kilometers) of low-lying coast permits port building only with difficulty. Unlike Jordan, Iraq has no convenient alternatives, even when political relations with neighboring states are normal. In the absence of good coastal ports, river ports, such as Basra, have been traditionally important to Iraq, and control of the river Shatt al-Arab has been a major policy objective, causing conflict with Iran over several decades (see Chapter 4). Iraq has also become anxious about access to

Umm Qasr, which is reached via a channel bordered by Iraq and Kuwait. Since 1970, Iraq has claimed the two Kuwaiti islands of Bubiyan and Warbah, whose possession would enable Iraq to control the Umm Qasr channel and claim a greater share of the Gulf seabed. Kuwait has rejected Iraq's claims and the recent proposal that Iraq rent the islands on a 99-year lease.

The Iran-Iraq War has served to underline Iraq's restricted access to the sea. Seaborne trade via the Shatt al-Arab and ports of Umm Qasr and Al-Faw has almost ceased. The bulk of Iraq's oil exports are via the trunk pipeline through Turkey. As discussed more fully in Chapter 10, the pipeline via Syria has proved unreliable, and the Iraqis are now considering constructing an additional pipeline across the Arabian peninsula. Since the outbreak of the Gulf war, large quantities of imported goods have been reaching Iraq through Aqaba, including vital war materials.

National Interests Offshore

The maritime interests of coastal states have developed considerably from the days when trade and shipping routes were the chief concern. The continental shelf and adjacent waters have become an integral part of the resource base of a number of states. Offshore jurisdiction is also regarded as necessary for state security and environmental management. Thus, the slow process of maritime boundary delimitation is already well under way and at least two dozen disputes concerning boundaries, islands, and fisheries were unresolved in 1985. More disputes will emerge in future as the U.N. treaty begins to be applied.

Oil and Gas

The growing importance of offshore oil and natural gas production has underlined the need for precise international maritime boundary delimitations. Offshore oil production amounted to about one quarter of the region's total in the early 1980s (Table 5.2). The Mediterranean is not yet a large producer of offshore oil, but the exploitation of promising areas has been delayed by protracted boundary disputes, notably between Libya and Tunisia and between Libya and Malta. Offshore exploration is still intensive in the Mediterranean and in the Gulf of Suez-Red Sea region. The Gulf has large reserves and offshore production can be foreseen for many years.

Fishing

The region's marine fisheries have been exploited for centuries. By world standards, the fisheries of the region are not prolific; the catch is less

Table 5.2
Offshore Oil Production, 1983

	Barrels per Day (thousands)	Percent of Total Production
Saudi Arabia	2,100.00	39.4
Abu Dhabi	338.46	42.5
Divided Zone (Saudi Arabia/Kuwait)	216.00	55.4
Egypt	508.65	65.6
Dubai	323.00	96.4
Qatar	129.20	38.5
Iran[a]	350.00	26.5
Tunisia	39.16	33.9
Sharjah	6.94	100.0

[a] 1981 data.

Sources: British Petroleum Statistical Review of World Energy 1984. London: British Petroleum, 1984/5; and "Worldwide Offshore Daily Average Oil Production," *Offshore,* July 20, 1984, 57.

than 2 percent of the world total. By far the largest catches are landed by Morocco, Oman, P.D.R. Yemen, and Turkey. Greater demand for fish and better fishing techniques have markedly increased the quantity of fish landed, and almost every country has plans to exploit marine fisheries more intensively in the future. The desire to protect fish stocks has been one reason for the extension of national territorial water claims and the declaration of exclusive fishing zones. Some serious disputes have already occurred over fishing grounds. The worst incidents have involved Spain and Morocco following Morocco's extension of exclusive fishing from 12 to 70 nautical miles in 1973. There have also been incidents between Italy and Tunisia on several occasions since 1975. More disputes are likely to occur as the 1982 Law of the Sea Treaty introduces a standard 200 nautical mile exclusive economic zone (EEZ) for each coastal state.

Seabed Minerals

Although knowledge of seabed minerals in the region's waters is still sketchy, there are interesting possibilities, particularly in the Mediterranean. Valuable mineral resources are known to exist in the Red Sea where metal-bearing muds were first located in 1963 at depths below 7000 feet (2134 meters). The chief minerals are zinc, copper, silver, lead, iron, and gold, worth over $3 billion (U.S.). In 1974, Sudan and Saudi Arabia agreed to exploit these minerals jointly. Although the largest deposits are on Sudan's side of the Red Sea median line, the two states have agreed to regard seabed below 1000 meters (or 3281 feet) as com-

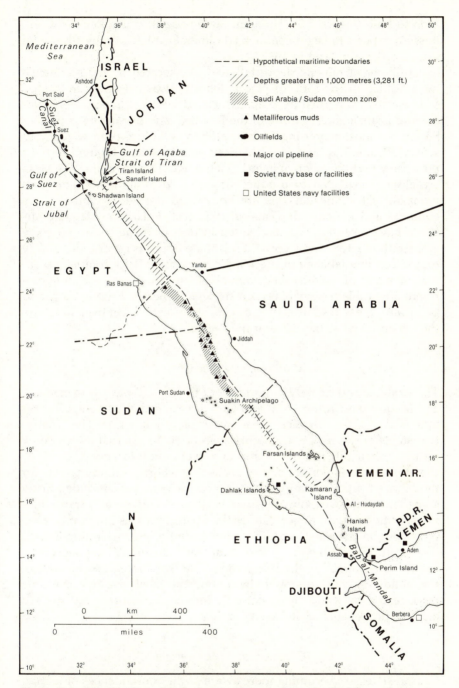

Figure 5.2   The Saudi Arabia/Sudan common zone in the Red Sea, where mineral extraction has begun. (After Gerald Blake, *Maritime Aspects of Arabian Geopolitics*. London: Arab Research Centre, 1982, p. 3.)

mon to both (Figure 5.2). The joint Sudan-Saudi Arabia Red Sea Commission expects to begin commercial mineral exploitation by 1988; pilot extraction commenced in 1982.

A number of mineral deposits have been located on the Mediterranean seabed in the form of placer deposits (washed down from land sources), hydrothermal deposits associated with volcanoes, metalliferous muds analogous to those of the Red Sea, and phosphate deposits.[3] So far, the most promising finds appear to be in European waters, but several Middle East and North African states are also thought to have potentially useful offshore minerals (Figure 5.3). Placers off the Nile Delta are already extracted to produce tin, iron, zirconium, titanium, and monazite. Chromite deposits are known off northern Cyprus as are chromite and mercury deposits off the coast of Turkey. Metalliferous muds have recently been discovered in deeps off the coast of Turkey and south of Crete and Cyprus. Phosphate deposits occur quite widely on the continental shelf of the Maghreb countries. The commercial future of many of these seabed minerals is uncertain, though they represent a possible reserve of certain strategic minerals. Economically and politically, these resources give coastal states extra incentives to secure the maximum possible share of the seabed.

Military Uses of the Oceans

The strategic and military importance of the region's seas is enormous. The Mediterranean, Red Sea, and Gulf are the foci of both superpower and local rivalries in which naval power plays a key role. The twenty-two states of the region are highly susceptible to external influence by virtue of their differing ideologies and geopolitical locations. There is, therefore, competition for access to bases, anchorages, and markets for the sale of weapons. Arms acquired in recent years have included many ships and naval weapons, with Israel, Egypt, Turkey, and Iran building significant naval forces. Under the Shah, Iran was intent on developing one of the most modern navies in the world, including a large hovercraft fleet. At the same time, local merchant and fishing fleets have grown substantially in the last decade. The five strategic waterways of the Middle East are undoubtedly among the most sensitive maritime passages in the world. They not only influence maritime strategy, but also political events in the coastal states.

Environmental Management

Coastal states are becoming more aware of the consequences of marine pollution. In the early 1970s, Mediterranean pollution was reaching alarming levels, threatening tourism and fishing. The semienclosed Mediterranean Sea is peculiarly lacking in natural defense mechanisms against pollution because of limited additions of freshwater, small tides,

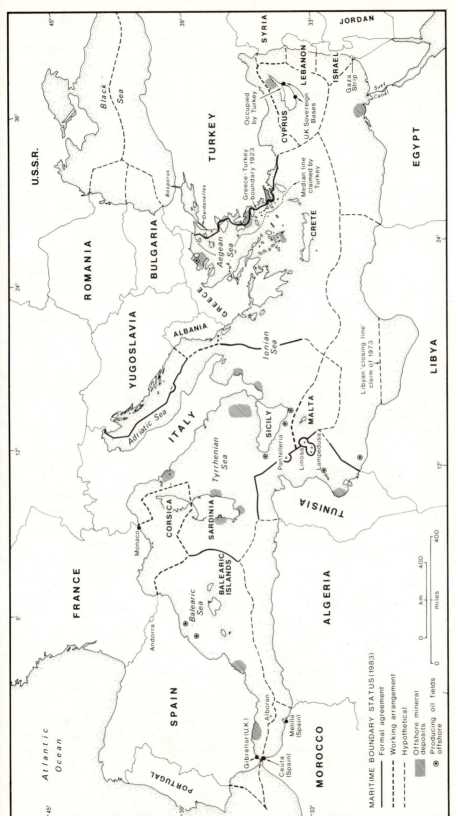

Figure 5.3 The partitioning of the Mediterranean Sea.

and weak currents. A resident population of about 100 million around the Mediterranean basin is supplemented by an annual influx of a similar number of tourists and some of the northern coasts are heavily industrialized. Oil is the most conspicuous source of pollution. About 3 billion barrels of oil are transported across the Mediterranean each year. Some 6 million barrels of oil of all kinds find their way into the sea, much of it in ballast water from tankers.[4] Other sources of pollution include huge quantities of organic waste, much of which reaches the sea untreated, which causes beaches to be closed and creates local health hazards from time to time. More dangerous are the chemical pollutants from agriculture and industry washed down by the rivers of northern Europe.[5] In 1976, the European Economic Community (EEC) and 16 Mediterranean states signed a Convention in Barcelona pledging themselves to tackle the problem. Only Albania did not sign. Since then, several important measures have been taken by means of legislation, monitoring, and research. A Regional Oil Combating Center has been established in Malta to fight oil pollution. The willingness of states to cooperate over the protection of the environment when they are often at loggerheads on other questions is evidence of the seriousness of the pollution problem.

Pollution has also reached critical levels in the Gulf, whose coastal regions are undergoing some of the most rapid urban and industrial development in the world. The Gulf is also a semienclosed sea, with high rates of evaporation and only limited inputs of freshwater. Because of its smaller size and shallow waters, the Gulf has an even more fragile environment than the Mediterranean. In 1978, as a result of initiatives taken by the U.N. Environmental Program, all the Gulf coastal states agreed to cooperate to protect their marine environment under the Kuwait Regional Convention. A Gulf Regional Organization for Protection of the Marine Environment (ROPME) was set up in 1981 to implement an action plan. Much practical progress has been achieved, including the establishment of an emergency center in Bahrain.

All coastal states near tanker routes or with offshore oil installations fear a major accident resulting in massive oil pollution. The possibility was all too graphically illustrated in March and April 1983 when several Iranian offshore oil platforms were damaged by Iraqi attacks, resulting in the unchecked flow of between 2000 and 10,000 barrels of crude oil a day. Efforts to stop the flow were thwarted by the continuation of hostilities between Iraq and Iran. Although early reports of the size of the slick may have been exaggerated, it caused serious damage to marine life, beaches, and such coastal installations as desalination plants and refineries. There were already signs in 1983 that commercial fisheries were suffering badly.[6] The Gulf oil slick may have been one of the worst ecological disasters of recent years.[7] Iraqi and Iranian attacks on tankers in 1984-85 also raised serious environmental concerns.

The Red Sea and Gulf of Aden are still relatively clean. An action plan for these seas was drawn up in 1976 at a conference in Jiddah convened by the Arab League Educational, Cultural, and Scientific Organization (ALECSO). In 1982, seven coastal states of the Red Sea region signed a Convention for the Conservation of the Red Sea and the Gulf of Aden. As with the Gulf and Mediterranean, there is a high degree of commitment to environmental cooperation by the coastal states, though Israel is not allowed to participate.

National Jurisdiction Offshore

Unlike national jurisdiction on the land, offshore jurisdiction is not absolute, except in internal waters. A state may exercise jurisdiction in a number of overlapping offshore zones for specific purposes. The rights of coastal states and other maritime users are governed by conventions that can be variously interpreted. Nor can maritime boundaries be demarcated—even today they rarely are shown on maps and charts. However, national offshore zones and rights will become more clearly defined as the 1982 U.N. treaty influences the de facto behavior of signatory and nonsignatory states.[8] Considerable efforts will be made to fix international maritime boundaries precisely. Six types of state jurisdiction occur in the region's waters: internal waters, territorial seas, contiguous zones, exclusive fishing zones, continental shelves, and EEZs. The new treaty attempts to standardize state practice with regard to these types of jurisdiction.

Internal Waters

Internal waters generally include estuaries and certain bays.[9] The coastal state has absolute jurisdiction over the seabed, waters, and airspace of internal waters. Some bays can be treated as internal waters, even if they are too large to qualify under the U.N. Convention of 1958 on the grounds of being "historic waters." Essentially, historic waters must be seen to have been intensively used by the coastal state for long periods of time without being challenged by another state. Libya's claim that the Gulf of Sirte is a historic bay and, therefore, internal waters is not accepted by the United States. In 1981, the U.S. Navy insisted on its right to maneuver in the Gulf of Sirte, inside the Libyan closing line across the mouth of the Gulf, and two Libyan aircraft were destroyed while attempting to challenge this asserted right.

Territorial Seas

The earliest states to claim territorial seas in the region were Turkey (1914), Palestine (1924), Iran (1934), Cyprus (1935), Jordan (1943), and Egypt (1951). Most states initiated claims after the first U.N. Conference on the Law of the Sea in 1958 recognized the right of coastal states to a territorial sea. In most cases, the original claim of 3 or 6 nautical miles was subsequently increased. In territorial seas, sovereignty is exercised over the waters themselves, the seabed, the subsoil, and the airspace above. Ships of all states, however, enjoy the right of "innocent passage" through the territorial sea. The right of innocent passage has been the subject of fierce debate in international law, and practices differ considerably between states in spite of certain rules laid down in 1958. P.D.R. Yemen and Algeria, for example, require foreign warships to obtain permission before entering their territorial seas.

The need for territorial seas has become increasingly pressing: to control smuggling, immigration, pollution, and dumping; to enforce health regulations; to regulate shipping; and for national security. Offshore resources of all kinds also need to be protected as improved technology makes their exploitation ever-more attractive. There has hitherto been no international consensus as to a standard width for territorial seas (Table 5.3). The new treaty proposes a standard 12-nautical-mile territorial sea. Half a dozen Middle Eastern states would benefit from this, but, in reality, the political and economic gains are limited.

Delimitation of territorial seas is complicated by the adoption of straight baselines by a number of states. These are permitted where coastlines are deeply indented or if there is a fringe of islands. Baselines are normally at the low watermark, though there are rules for using closing-lines across the mouths of bays and other inland waters. The straight baseline can greatly extend the outer limit of territorial waters, but the conventions agreed to in 1958 to discourage such abuse are frequently disregarded or misinterpreted.[10] For example, by liberal interpretation of such terms as "bay" and "island," Saudi Arabia and Oman appear to have enclosed large areas of internal waters, which the 1958 Convention does not strictly allow. The international debate concerning the introduction of a standard 12-mile limit has focused a great deal on possible threats to freedom of navigation as a result of the extension of territorial waters into international straits.[11]

Contiguous Zones

Beyond the territorial waters, a state may exercise the control necessary to prevent infringement of customs, fiscal, immigration, or sanitary regulations. According to the 1958 Convention, such contiguous zones should not extend beyond 12 miles from the baseline from which the territorial sea is measured. In fact, seven Middle East states claim contiguous zones for customs and sanitary purposes beyond 12 miles, several of which are connected with health regulations associated with seaborn pilgrims traveling to Mecca (Table 5.3). Lebanon has made no territorial sea claim; in the absence of this, claims to 6 nautical miles for security and fishing are of interest.

Table 5.3

National Offshore Claims on the Eve of the Adoption of the U.N. Convention on the Law of the Sea, 1982 (in nautical miles[a])

	Territorial Sea	Exclusive Fishing	Exclusive Economic Zone (EEZ)	Contiguous Zone
Algeria	13 (1963)	as T.S.[b]	—	—
Bahrain	3 (?)	as T.S.	—	—
Cyprus	13 (1964)	as T.S.	—	12 (1964) customs, criminal
Egypt	12 (1958)	as T.S.	—	18 (1958) customs, sanitary
Iran	12 (1959)	To edge of shelf	—	—
Iraq	12 (1958)	as T.S.	—	—
Israel	6 (1956)	as T.S.	—	—
Jordan	3 (1943)	as T.S.	—	—
Kuwait	12 (1967)	as T.S.	—	—
Lebanon	Undeclared	6 (1921)	—	—
Libya	12 (1959)	as T.S.	—	—
Morocco	12 (1973)	200 (1980)	—	—
Oman	12 (1977)	200 (1977)	200	—
P.D.R. Yemen	12 (1970)	200 (1978)	200 (1978)	24 (1978) customs, criminal
Qatar	3 (?)	To continental self boundary	—	—
Saudi Arabia	12 (1958)	To continental shelf	—	18 (1958) fiscal, sanitary
Sudan	12 (1960)	as T.S.	—	18 (1970) customs, fiscal, sanitary
Syria[c]	35 (1981)	as T.S.	—	18 (1963) customs, sanitary
Tunisia	12 (1973)	as T.S.	—	—
Turkey	6[d] (1964)	12 (1964)	—	—
U.A.E. (Sharjah)	3 (?) 12 (1970)	as T.S. as T.S.	— —	— —
Yemen A.R.	12 (1967)	as T.S.	—	18 (1967) customs, sanitary,

[a] 1 nautical mile = 1.15 statute miles = 1853 meters.

[b] T.S. = territorial sea.

[c] Syria's claim to a 35-nautical-mile territorial sea was reported in *Middle East Economic Digest*, 11 September 1981, p. 51. The move is likely to antagonize Cyprus.

[d] 12 nautical miles in the Black Sea and the Mediterranean.

Sources: John Paxton (ed.), *The Statesmans' Yearbook 1981–82*. London: Macmillan, 1981, pp. xxv–xxviii; and Bureau of Intelligence and Research. *National Claims to Maritime Jurisdictions*. Limits in the Seas No. 36. Washington, D.C.: U.S. Department of State, May 1981.

Exclusive Fishing Zones

States have exclusive rights to fish in their own territorial waters. Beyond territorial waters, they may claim complete control over the exploitation of fish stocks in an exclusive fishing zone. Only eight such claims have been made in the region (Table 5.3). Coastal states rarely insist on the right to exclusive fishing, but rather on the right to control fishing, thus conserving stocks. Concessions to fish have been granted by P.D.R.Yemen and Oman in specified areas in their 200-mile exclusive fishing zones. P.D.R. Yemen had agreements with Japan and the Soviet Union in the 1960s and with Iraq in 1977. Oman had similar agreements with Japan in 1976 and 1977 and with South Korea in 1978. The introduction of the EEZ gives states the right to exclusive exploitation of fisheries to a limit of 200 nautical miles.

Continental Shelves

Continental shelves vary greatly in width, representing natural inequalities with regard to offshore opportunities. Coastal states have the exclusive right to the mineral resources of the seabed, the subsoil, and to sedentary species of marine life (e.g., oysters and sponges) of their continental shelves beyond the limits of the territorial waters. Continental shelf rights do not automatically extend to nonsedentary living resources or to the airspace, and the laying of cables and pipelines by other states is permitted. The outer limit of continental shelf jurisdiction was ill defined before the 1982 treaty. The U.N. Convention of 1958 specified that it applied to a depth of 200 meters (656 feet), "or beyond that limit to where the depth of the superadjacent water admits of the exploitation of the natural resources of the said area." Exploitation in depths far below 200 meters (656 feet) is clearly quite feasible today, and national claims, thus, began to encroach on seabed that the United Nations regards as "the common heritage of mankind." In the seas of the Middle East and Mediterranean no continental shelves extend beyond 200 nautical miles. If they did, the treaty would allow the coastal state a share of the resources up to 350 nautical miles offshore.

The Gulf is a classic case of a continental shelf effectively partitioned between the coastal states (Figure 5.4). Continental shelf boundaries in the Gulf are generally based on median lines, though different criteria can be applied by mutual consent. In practice, many problems arise, and several boundaries in the Gulf have yet to be agreed to, even after 15 to 20 years of doubt.

Exclusive Economic Zone (EEZ)

The proposal to allow every state the exclusive right to all resources, living and nonliving, to a distance of 200 nautical miles offshore is the

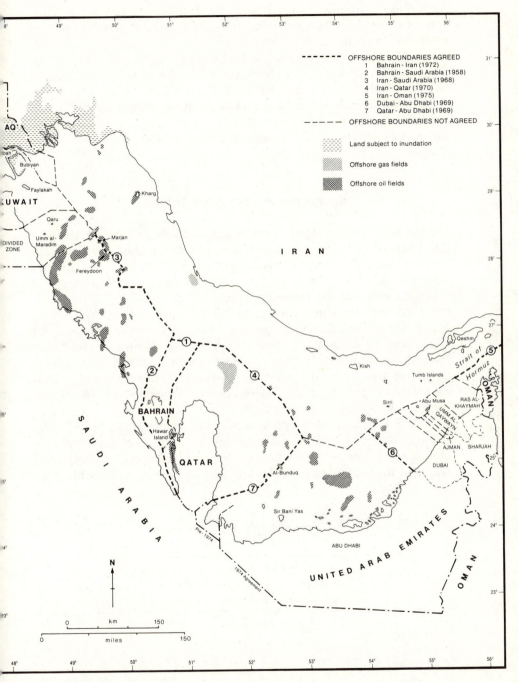

Figure 5.4 Maritime boundaries and offshore oil fields in the Gulf.

most radical provision of the 1982 treaty. The passage of ships and air-craft of other states are unaffected in the EEZ, but the coastal state may establish fixed installations associated with the exploitation of re-sources, which could impede the free passage of ships. In the region, only the P.D.R.Yemen and Oman (in the Indian Ocean) and Morocco (in the Atlantic Ocean) can claim an EEZ up to 200 miles. It remains to be seen whether there will be a gradual extension of state control within the EEZ's as the maritime powers fear; certainly, coastal states will be taking a closer interest in the activities of other states in their offshore zones.

Boundaries and Boundary Disputes

During the 1980s the states of the region will seek to establish the pre-cise limits of their offshore jurisdiction. More than 100 boundaries are involved, only 10 of which have so far been formally agreed to and de-limited (Table 5.4). The absence of a formal agreement does not nec-essarily mean that the boundary is actively disputed. In many cases, there has not been much urgency to delimit maritime boundaries. With the advent of the 1982 treaty, there will be a strong incentive for states to fix their maritime limits, even if they do not sign the treaty. Many more disputes are likely to arise, most of which should be relatively easy to resolve. The most intractable disputes are those associated with rival claims to islands or fundamental political differences between states concerning the status of territory.[12]

Table 5.4 distinguishes between adjacent and opposite boundaries. Adjacent boundaries divide the territorial sea, continental shelf, and EEZ of neighboring states. Under the new treaty, all existing continental shelf claims in the seas around the Middle East and North Africa will, in ef-

Table 5.4
Maritime Boundaries

	Adjacent		Opposite		
	No Formal Agreement	Agreed and Delimited	No Formal Agreement	Agreed and Delimited	Total
The Gulf	13	2	9	5	29
Indian Ocean	7	0	5	0	12
Red Sea	8	0	7	0	15
Mediterranean Sea	19	1	23	1	44
Black Sea	1	1	3	0	5
Atlantic Ocean	1	0	2	0	3
Total	49	4	49	6	108

Source: Derived from Figures 5.2, 5.3, 5.4.

fect, be superceded by the more favourable EEZ to a distance of 200 nautical miles. Where seas are less than 400 nautical miles wide, opposite states must partition the ocean and seabed between them. Many states are prepared to settle opposite boundaries by a median line, but they are not obliged to do so under existing international law or in the 1982 treaty, which permit all relevant circumstances to be considered in making an equitable solution. Thus, the peaceful resolution of maritime boundary disputes may take years, even where there is goodwill between the parties. The following sections briefly examine certain disputes to illustrate their variety and complexity. The selection is far from comprehensive.

Islands are the most frequent cause of offshore boundary disputes. Problems arise either when ownership is in dispute or because of differences over what weight to give to islands when drawing baselines. The attitude of states to the use of islands for baselines depends largely on what favors them most. Iran, with few islands, largely ignores them, the U.A.E., with hundreds of islands, regards certain islands, even beyond territorial water limits, as appropriate reference points for baselines. Saudi Arabia advocates the use of islands only when they are within the territorial waters of the mainland state. In some Mediterranean examples, boundaries have been fixed with reference to mainlands only, and the islands are given a share of continental shelf. Figure 5.5 illustrates one such solution. All habitable islands are eligible for territorial waters; with the coming of a standard 12-mile limit, this clearly gives ownership of islands added attraction because of possible access to offshore resources.

Most of the active disputes involving islands are in the Gulf. With huge reserves of oil and gas lying offshore beneath waters averaging less than 150 feet (46 meters) in depth, the incentives for boundary delimitation were powerful.[13] The task of partitioning the seabed between 13 political units was complicated by the physical characteristics of the Gulf. The Arabian side is quite shallow, with numerous small islands; at low tide, sand banks and coral reefs are exposed up to 20 miles offshore. The baseline from which the territorial sea is usually measured is the low watermark, so that the Arab states have an advantage over Iran, whose coastal waters are far deeper and relatively island free. History has further complicated matters. Most islands are sparsely populated or uninhabited, but throughout a long and turbulent history, they have been in the possession of various rulers and settled from time to time by fishermen and traders. It is, therefore, not difficult to claim sovereignty over even quite small islands on the basis of history.

Disputed Sovereignty over Islands

Bahrain claims the Hawar Islands—the largest of which is less than 1 mile (1.6 kilometers) from the west coast of Qatar—on historic grounds.

A small part of mainland Qatar around Zubarah is also claimed, though perhaps with less conviction. The islands are uninhabited apart from a token Bahraini presence. Qatar maintains that the islands are geographically and historically an integral part of the mainland. Geographically, there can be no doubt; the islands can be reached on foot at low tide. Historically, the case is more uncertain. Various compromise solutions have been proposed but so far without success. Meanwhile, the incentives to reach a solution grow stronger because the continental shelf boundary between Bahrain and Qatar remains undecided because of the dispute. As a result, a potentially rich oil field cannot be developed by either state, both of which are facing dwindling oil reserves.[14]

In 1971, the Iranian occupation of Abu Musa and the Tumb Islands at the entrance to the Gulf attracted worldwide interest, with strong reaction coming from the Arab world. The festering dispute could become the focus of a major flare up between Iran and the Arab Gulf states.

Abu Musa lies on the Arab side of the median line, 43 miles (69 kilometers) from Iran and 35 miles (56 kilometers) from the coast of Sharjah. It is about 3 miles (5 kilometers) wide and has some good deepwater anchorages. Iranian claims to the island are based on Persian occupation until the nineteenth century and the need to guard the entrance to the Gulf in the interests of national security. When the British withdrew in 1971, the ruler of Sharjah reluctantly agreed to joint occupation of Abu Musa, allowing an Iranian military presence and leaving Sharjah in control of the 800 or so inhabitants. Offshore oil revenues from Abu Musa's 12-mile limit were to be shared equally. Both states continue with this uneasy arrangement, but both still claim full sovereignty. It is doubtful how useful Abu Musa would be in the event of conflict at the southern end of the Gulf being about 100 miles (160 kilometers) from the Strait of Hormuz. On the other hand, when Iran declared a 12-mile exclusion zone in 1980, ships obeyed the orders of the Iranian navy and changed course when passing Abu Musa and the Tumbs. Arab forces, including those of Iraq, have never attempted to retake the islands by force, in spite of threatening to do so.

The Greater and Lesser Tumb Islands are both smaller than Abu Musa, lying about 8 miles (13 kilometers) apart. The nearest is only 15 miles (24 kilometers) from the Iranian island of Qeshm, and both are clearly on the Iranian side of the median line. The main tanker routes to and from Hormuz pass on either side of the islands. The British regarded the islands as belonging to the ruler of Ras al-Khaymah, but with scarcely any inhabitants and before the presence of oil was suspected, ownership was hardly a burning issue. In November 1971, the day before Britain was due to hand the islands over to Ras al-Khaymah, the Iranians took over the islands. Many Arabs accused Britain of complicity in the affair. There have been some hints from Iran since the Iranian revolution that the islands could be returned, but they still remained firmly in Iranian hands in 1985.

Qaru and Umm al-Maradim are tiny, low, scrub-covered islands located 25 and 15 miles (40 and 24 kilometers) respectively off the coast of the former Neutral Zone. The 1969 Kuwaiti-Saudi Arabian agreement to partition the Neutral Zone was not extended offshore because of disputed sovereignty over these islands. Saudi Arabia regards the islands as being under joint sovereignty as part of the former Neutral Zone; Kuwait claims absolute sovereignty. Accordingly, no adjacent boundary has been delimited between Kuwait and Saudi Arabia in an oil-rich sector of the Gulf. Delimitation of the opposite boundary with Iran is impeded for the same reason.

Disputes over Opposite Boundaries

The continental shelf dispute between Greece and Turkey in the Aegean Sea is perhaps the most serious maritime dispute in the region. The post–World War I Treaty of Lausanne gave Greece most of the Aegean Sea, with sovereignty over 3000 islands and islets compared with Turkey's 2 major islands. The 1923 international boundary, which defines sovereignty over islands, is not in question, but the continental shelf boundary is. Since islands are entitled to the resources of their continental shelf, Greece can claim most of the Aegean continental shelf. Turkey argues that the Aegean is a special case and seeks a continental shelf median line regardless of the islands. In 1973–74, concessions for oil exploration were made by Turkey as far as the median line.[15] The continental shelf dispute has been exacerbated by the proposed extension of territorial sea limits to 12 nautical miles, which would give Greece sovereignty over most of the Aegean. Apart from access to possible seabed resources, the Turks do not want the approaches to the Turkish Straits to be through Greek territorial seas.

Libya and Malta are over 220 miles (350 kilometers) apart in the central Mediterranean. Their continental shelf dispute flared up in 1980 when Libyan warships forced oil exploration to cease in a concession area granted by Malta, but it had gone on for at least a decade before that time. The Maltese seek a median line, whereas the Libyans argue for a division that more accurately reflects the relative lengths of their coastlines and the natural prolongation of Libya's landmass northwards. The dispute went to the International Court of Justice in 1982, and judgment was expected in 1985. Meanwhile, oil exploration is being delayed.

Another costly dispute over opposite boundaries is in the upper Gulf region where no boundaries have been agreed between Iran and Kuwait and between Iran and Iraq. After Iran and Kuwait granted overlapping oil concessions in the center of the Gulf in the 1950s, it was clear that there were differences over the role of the Iranian island of Kharg (nearly 20 miles, or 32 kilometers, offshore) and the Kuwaiti island of Faylakah (15 miles, or 24 kilometers, offshore). Both states take their own islands into account, but they disregard those of the other party.

The maritime boundary between Iran and the U.A.E. will extend some 200 miles (320 kilometers) when finally agreed to. The 45-mile (72-kilometer) section between Iran and Dubai was agreed to in 1974. This agreement is interesting because the Iranian island of Sirri was disregarded for the purpose of determining a median line, though the line was displaced southwards to accommodate Sirri's 12-mile territorial water limit (Figure 5.4). Iran has not reached agreement with the emirates east of Dubai, largely because of the dispute over Abu Musa and the Tumb Islands. No agreement between Iran and Abu Dhabi has yet been reached, possibly because of Iranian claims to Sir Bani Yas Island, lying less than 10 miles (16 kilometers) from Abu Dhabi's coast.

Disputes over Adjacent Boundaries

There is usually one fixed point in the delimitation of offshore boundaries between neighboring states, where the land boundary reaches the coast. If the boundary is in dispute, there is obviously no chance of delimiting an offshore boundary. For example, Egypt and Sudan will be unable to agree on their adjacent boundary in the Red Sea until there is agreement as to whether their de facto or de jure land boundaries are to be the starting point. The delimitation of adjacent offshore boundaries involves much the same principles as the delimitation of opposite boundaries. Should an equidistance line be devised, all points of which are equidistant from the coasts of the adjacent states? What weight should be given to islands and other physical features?

The potentially oil-rich continental shelf boundary between Tunisia and Libya was disputed for a number of years. Libya argued for a line roughly due north from the land boundary as representing the natural prolongation of its landmass northwards. Tunisia claimed a boundary line of about 45° as reflecting the configuration of the coastline. The dispute went to the International Court of Justice, which in a 1982 judgment recommended a line of 26°, and then 52° (Figure 5.5). The two angles were devised to take account of the difficulties created by Tunisia's Djerba and Kerkennah islands and the changes of direction taken by the Tunisian coastline.

Another actively disputed adjacent boundary is between Oman (Musundam) and the U.A.E. The discovery of offshore oil in 1977 revived an old quarrel about the location of the land boundary, with the Omanis claiming 10 miles (16 kilometers) of territory in Ras al-Khaymah. Troops and a warship were deployed by Oman in a show of force in the disputed areas. The dispute was reported to have been settled in 1979 but no details are available.

Agreement between states over boundaries does not preclude future disputes. Like land boundaries, maritime boundaries can be subject to

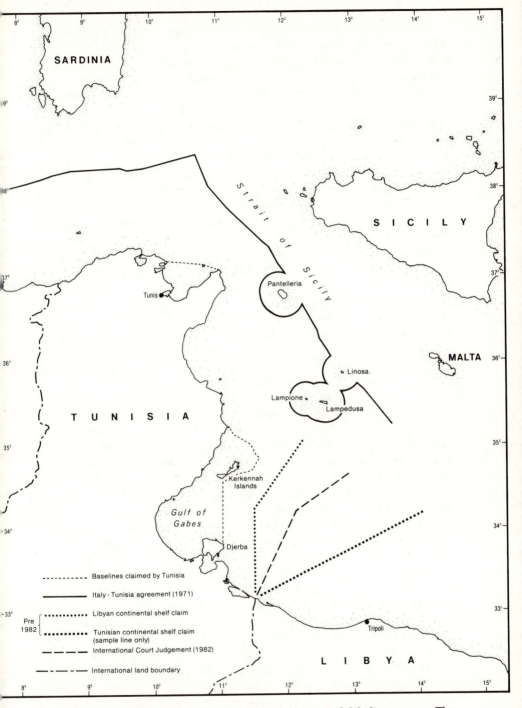

Figure 5.5 Continental shelf boundaries in the central Mediterranean: The
Italy-Tunisia and Libya-Tunisia agreements.

functional problems and wrangles over resource allocation. When an oil field lies close to, or under, an existing boundary, it can pose problems rather akin to having "two straws in one glass."[16] Such cases are not numerous, but many boundary agreements include clauses providing for the joint management and equal sharing of revenues accruing from any future discoveries of oil and gas divided by the boundary. An agreement reached between Qatar and Abu Dhabi in 1969 deliberately placed their common boundary in the center of the disputed Al-Bunduq oil field, and provided for sharing its income equally. An alternative approach was adopted by Saudi Arabia and Iran in 1968. Here, the vast Marjan-Fereydoon oil field at the center of the Gulf would have been affected by almost any reasonably equitable boundary agreement. The agreement took account of a median line solution (in which the Iranian Kharg Island was given half effect) that was combined with a partitioning of the oil field, which was designed to give a fair share of oil reserves to both parties. The resulting zigzag boundary does not show clearly on small-scale maps. Saudi Arabia and Bahrain reached an even more extraordinary solution in 1958 when the disputed Abu Safah oil field was ceded to Saudi Arabia in return for half the revenues from the field going to Bahrain in perpetuity.

Strategic Waterways

There are more than 100 interoceanic straits and waterways in the world less than 25 miles (40 kilometers) wide. If one could rank them on the basis of numbers of ships, volume of oil cargoes, alternative routes, intensity of military use, and geographic vulnerability (length, width, and depth), the result might highlight the extraordinary significance of the four waterways that act as natural gateways into the Middle East and North Africa. The Strait of Gibraltar, the Turkish Straits (Bosporus and Dardanelles), Bab al-Mandab, and Hormuz would probably all feature among the top half dozen waterways, with the straits of Dover and Malacca their closest rivals. In addition, the Suez Canal provides the key link on the sea route between the Atlantic and Indian oceans. Thus, five of the world's great strategic waterways are located in the region, powerfully influencing geopolitical thinking on both local and global scales. Wars have been fought in the past over the Turkish Straits and the Suez Canal, and there are fears that future conflicts might erupt over Hormuz or Bab al-Mandab. Significantly, U.S. military aid is heavily concentrated in states bordering or close to strategic waterways.

The new U.N. Treaty on the Law of the Sea sanctions territorial seas of up to 12 nautical miles. In practice, most coastal states adjoining strategic waterways have claimed 12 nautical miles for some time, though their claims were not internationally recognized.[17] Now all the region's waterways fall legally within the territorial seas of the coastal states.

The maritime powers have long feared that the extension of territorial seas into international waterways would result in increasing control by the coastal state. Article 38 of the U.N. Treaty on the Law of the Sea attempts to allay these fears by introducing the right of unimpeded transit passage for ships and aircraft. States with major trading interests, particularly oil-importing states, also fear that the passage of shipping might be more directly interrupted by physical blocking of navigation channels or by military threats from land or sea. Such fears have probably been greatly exaggerated, particularly in respect of Hormuz. Nevertheless, they continue to play an important part in the way in which strategic waterways are perceived.

The Strait of Gibraltar

The Strait of Gibraltar (Figure 5.6) is one of the busiest interoceanic waterways in the world, with about 150 ships a day passing through, excluding small boats and submarines. The traffic includes ships trading with Mediterranean and Black Sea ports, Suez Canal shipping, and movements of naval vessels, including nuclear submarines. Cargoes of particular strategic interest include South African coal bound for Israel and oil bound for Western Europe and the United States. There is considerable passenger and cargo traffic across the Strait of Gibraltar between Africa and Europe. Spain and Morocco are discussing the possibility of building a bridge or tunnel across the strait, which could be completed before the end of the century. Spain also wishes to regain control of Gibraltar, which has been in British hands since 1704. If this happens and Spain also retains Ceuta in North Africa, Spanish territorial waters (to 12 nautical miles) would cover the eastern approaches to the strait (Figure 5.6). This may explain why Morocco has threatened to raise the question of Ceuta and Melilla if Spain presses claims to Gibraltar. The U.S. has military facilities in both Spain and Morocco, although their purpose is not simply to watch over the strait.

The Turkish Straits

The Dardanelles and Bosporus (Table 5.5) are separated by the Sea of Marmara, so that ships in transit between the Black Sea and the Aegean must travel over 200 miles (320 kilometers) in Turkish waters. It is obviously a great asset to the North Atlantic Treaty Organization (NATO) to have a member state so well placed. The Turkish Straits (Figure 5.7) are the only outlet for ships of the Soviet Black Sea fleet, which primarily serve the Mediterranean.[18] On average, one Soviet warship transits the straits every 36 hours. Soviet merchant ships, on the other hand, average nearly 20 a day and account for over 40 percent of cargoes by weight.

Since the Russians expanded to the shores of the Black Sea in the

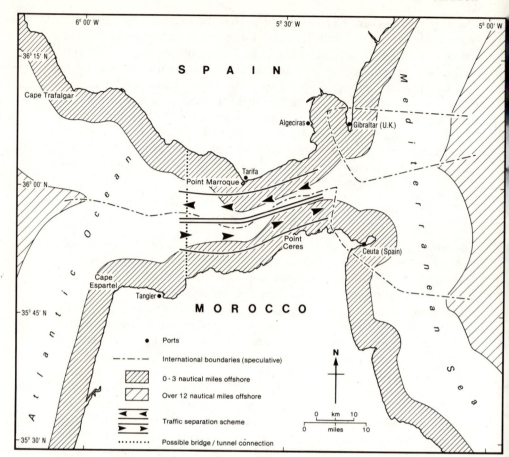

Figure 5.6 Gateway to the Mediterranean: The Strait of Gilbraltar, showing possible maritime bundaries. (After Gerald Blake, "Gateway to the Mediterranean," *Geographical Magazine* LV(5), 1983, p. 259.)

eighteenth century, they have sought control of the Turkish Straits or guarantees of freedom of navigation (Chapter 3). During World War I, the Russians came near to achieving absolute control under a secret agreement with Britain and France, which lapsed when Russia withdrew from the war in 1917. Under the Treaty of Lausanne in 1923, the straits were demilitarized and administered by an International Straits Commission. In 1936, at Turkey's request, the Treaty of Montreux changed these arrangements. Turkey took over administration of the straits and the straits zone was refortified, largely because the Great Powers feared German and Italian expansionism at the time. The Montreux Convention places constraints on the use of the straits by warships. All Black Sea navies must give eight days notice of passage and details of the vessels. Transit must be by day; no more than nine war-

Table 5.5
Characteristics of International Waterways

	Least Width (nautical miles)	Length (nautical miles)	Depth (feet)[a]	Approximate Number of Ships Daily	Coastal States
Strait of Gibraltar	10.0	35	270–2000 (80–600)	150	Spain, Morocco
Turkish Straits:					
Dardanelles	0.75	36	150–300 (46–91)	60	Turkey
Bosporus	0.33	17	160 (49)	50	Turkey
Bab al-Mandab	10.5	35	40–600 (12–183)	55	Yemen A.R., P.R.D. Yemen, Ethiopia, Djibouti
Strait of Hormuz	21.0	100	250–700 (76–213)	80	Iran, Oman
Suez Canal	584 feet (178 meters)[b]	287	53 (16)	60	Egypt
Strait of Tiran	3.0	7	240–600 (73–183)	<10	Egypt, Saudi Arabia

[a] Meters are given in parentheses.

[b] The width of the Suez Canal at water surface is about 930 feet (283 meters), but the deepest section (64 feet or 20 meters) is only 295 feet (90 meters) wide (see Figure 5.10).

Source: Based on data in Alastair Couper (ed.). The Times Atlas of the Oceans. London: Times Books, 1983; International Straits of the World series. The Hague: Martinus Nijhoff; and Ferenca Vali. The Turkish Straits and NATO. Stanford, Calif.: Hoover Institution Press, 1972.

ships may be in the waterway at the same time, and their aggregate displacement cannot exceed 15,000 tons. An exception is made for 'capital ships' of over 15,000 tons but by implication aircraft carriers are excluded. Submarines may transit the straits on the surface, but only to proceed to shipyards for repair. Moreover, Turkey also has the right to prevent passage of warships altogether if her security is deemed to be threatened. The Soviet Union would like to see revision of the Montreux Convention, but Turkey and her NATO allies clearly do not.

It is worth recalling in this context that none of the Soviet Union's four fleets enjoy unimpeded access to the open sea, and Soviet strategists are keenly aware of this geographic disadvantage. The northern fleet must pass close to the Norwegian coast and through the Iceland-Faroes gap to the North Atlantic. The Baltic fleet has to traverse the narrow Danish Straits into the North Sea. The Far East fleet, which provides units for the Indian and Pacific oceans, is ringed by the Japanese islands. The Turkish Straits are, thus, so vital to Soviet strategy that Russian forces would have to seize them in the event of war to

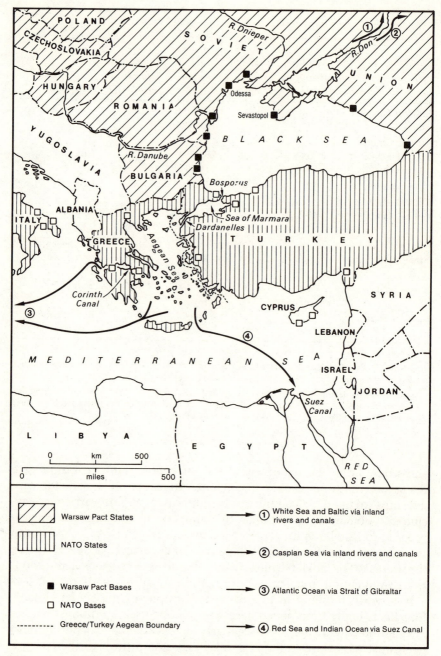

Figure 5.7 The regional setting of the Turkish Straits. (After Gerald Blake, "Turkish Guard on Russian Waters," *Geographical Magazine* LIII(15), 1981, p. 950.)

secure passage for the Soviet navy and prevent hostile forces from entering the Black Sea and threatening the Soviet industrial heartland. Short of all-out war, however, neither the superpowers nor Turkey have much to gain from closing the Turkish Straits[19] A high proportion of Turkey's maritime trade passes through the Dardanelles, including much oil. The straits region lies in Turkey's commercial heartland where intercontinental land routes between Europe and Asia intersect interoceanic sea routes. A bridge over the Bosporus was opened in 1973, and a second bridge is to be constructed.

Bab al-Mandab

A high proportion of the traffic that passes through the Suez Canal also passes Bab al-Mandab (Figure 5.8). To the extent, therefore, that the Suez Canal is important, so is Bab al-Mandab. Oil cargoes are not as vital as they were before 1967, and the trans-Arabian Petroline completed in 1981 has also diminished its role for oil transportation. Approximately 7 percent of Western Europe's oil imports pass through Bab al-Mandab, but the proportion could grow if plans to widen the Suez Canal still further come to fruition.

The Red Sea littoral states themselves have an obvious interest in Bab al-Mandab. Jordan, Yemen A.R., Ethiopia, and Sudan have no other outlets to the sea except via the Suez Canal. Saudi Arabia's chief commercial ports are at Yanbu and Jiddah. Egypt wants to maximize canal revenues by winning back oil cargoes, whereas Israel is anxious to preserve access to Eilat on the Gulf of Aqaba.

Bab al-Mandab is located in a region of political turmoil, where the superpowers are contending for influence both in the Horn of Africa and in the Arabian peninsula. In both regions, long-standing local rivalries have created opportunities for the promotion of their own geostrategic designs. Since the 1974 military takeover in Ethiopia, Soviet influence has grown in Ethiopia. The Soviet navy has facilities in the Dahlak Islands and at Assab. In 1978, the Ethiopians managed to recapture the Ogaden desert region from Somalia with strong Soviet and Cuban support. As a result, the Somalis allowed the U.S. Navy into the naval bases at Berbera and Mogadishu, formerly used by the Russians. Similarly, when Soviet-equipped forces from P.D.R. Yemen invaded part of Yemen A.R. in 1979, the United States rushed arms and advisers to assist the latter. The Soviet navy has naval facilities in P.D.R. Yemen at Aden, the Bay of Turbah, and on Socotra Island. Although Bab al-Mandab is too wide and deep to be physically blocked, the combination of superpower and local rivalries in the vicinity raises the remote but real possibility that shipping could be deterred from using the strait during some future conflict because of the risk of being caught up in a war zone. In July and August 1984, some 18 vessels were damaged by mines placed at the northern and southern ends of the Red

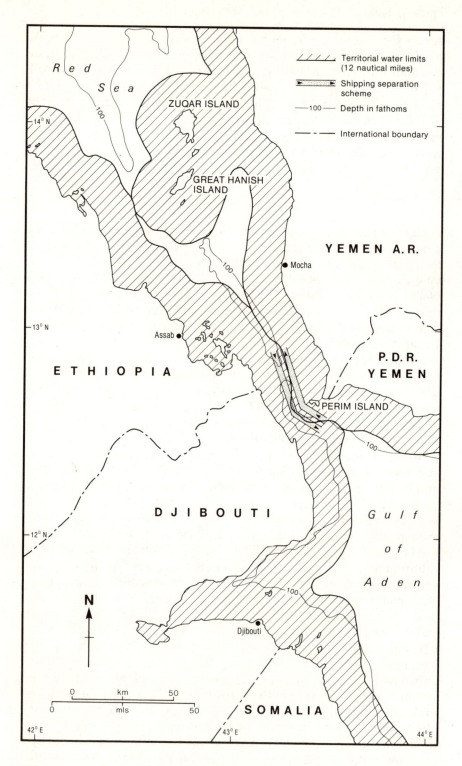

Territorial water limits (12 nautical miles)

Shipping separation scheme

100 — Depth in fathoms

International boundary

R e d
S e a

100

14° N

ZUQAR ISLAND

GREAT HANISH ISLAND

YEMEN A.R.

● Mocha

100

13° N

Assab ●

ETHIOPIA

P.D.R. YEMEN

PERIM ISLAND

100

DJIBOUTI

Gulf

of

Aden

12° N

100

N

100

Djibouti ●

| 0 | km | 50 |
| 0 | mls | 50 |

SOMALIA

42° E

43° E

44° E

Sea. Egypt requested U.S. and European assistance in minesweeping the sea lanes and in identifying who was responsible.

Great power involvement is not confined to the U.S.S.R. and the United States. The French maintain a military presence in Djibouti at the entrance to the Red Sea. The British have also played a major role in the region, especially in Oman and, in the past, Aden.

The Strait of Hormuz

The Strait of Hormuz is approximately 100 nautical miles long, bounded by Iran to the north and Oman's Musundam peninsula to the south (Figure 5.9). The narrowest part lies between the Iranian island of Jazirat Larak and the Omani islet of Great Quoin, a distance of 21 nautical miles. This is rather wider than a superficial glance at the map might suggest and wider than the English Channel at its narrowest point. Both Iran and Oman claim territorial waters of 12 nautical miles and there is, therefore, a stretch of about 15 nautical miles where their respective territorial waters are defined by an agreed median line. Until 1979, shipping generally took the shortest route, between Little Quoin and Musundam Island, a little over 5 nautical miles wide. Since 1979, Oman has insisted on the use of shipping lanes outside the Quoins, partly because of the difficulty of ensuring safe passage of ships so close to islands and the mainland. The new shipping lanes, which are about 1 mile wide and separated by safety zones of 1 mile, are within Oman's territorial waters and the government of Oman, therefore, undertakes responsibility for the safe passage of shipping through the strait. The Omani navy has half a dozen patrol boats that are responsible for patrolling a long coastline. In 1980, Sultan Qabus unsuccessfully appealed to other Gulf states for financial help to assist with the purchase of helicopters, minesweepers, and other equipment as well as the construction of a naval base on Goat Island to assist in policing the strait.

The Iranian revolution highlighted Oman's role as de facto sentinel of the Strait of Hormuz. One need only examine the sultanate's pivotal location to understand why it is caught in the vortex of superpower rivalries. The United States has acquired rights to use the ports of Muscat and Salalah and a former British airfield on the island of Masirah, some 500 (800 kilometers) miles from Hormuz. These facilities will be part of a network of American bases ringing the Indian Ocean designed to guard the main tanker routes. A large base has already been built on the island of Diego Garcia, 2500 (4000 kilometers) miles south-

Figure 5.8   Gateway to the Red Sea and Suez Canal: Bab al-Mandab. (After Gerald Blake, "Coveted Waterway of Bab al-Mandeb," *Geographical Magazine* LIII(4), 1981, p. 234.)

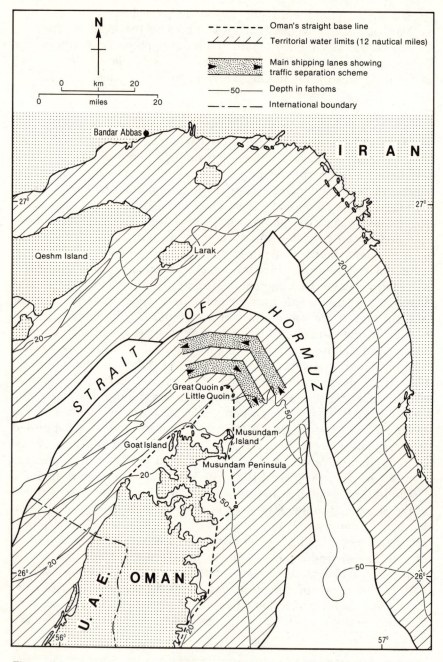

Figure 5.9   Gateway to the oil fields of the Gulf region: The Strait of Hormuz.

east of the Gulf, and Kenya has agreed to an expansion of U.S. naval facilities at Mombasa.

In the late 1970s, over half the oil involved in international trade and two thirds of the Organization of Petroleum Exporting Countries (OPEC) oil passed through Hormuz at the rate of approximately 18 million barrels daily. In a typical day, between 70 and 80 ships used the strait. About 38 percent of U.S., 60 percent of Western European, and 75 percent of Japanese oil imports were shipped via the strait. For reasons discussed in Chapter 10, Middle East oil exports generally have plunged since then. By early 1984, only 7.4 million barrels of oil left the Gulf by this route every day, and only 3 percent of North American and 28 percent of Western European oil supplies originated in the Gulf. Saudi Arabia has large quantities of oil stored outside the Gulf in surplus tankers and the United States has built up a strategic petroleum reserve. The industrial countries have stocks equal to 91 days of consumption. Some of the oil that leaves the Gulf via Hormuz could be diverted to Saudi Arabia's transpeninsular pipeline. In addition, oil-producing countries outside the Gulf have abundant spare oil-producing capacity. For all these reasons, the closure of the strait would not be as cataclysmic as sometimes portrayed. Nevertheless, when Iran threatened to block the strait in 1983 and 1984, the United States expressed its readiness to use force to keep it open. As with the Red Sea, the coastal states of the region also have an obvious interest in keeping Hormuz open, not only to ensure the flow of oil exports, but to protect imports. Iraq, Bahrain, Kuwait, and Qatar have no alternative outlets to the sea; several Gulf ports also conduct a profitable transit trade, primarily with Iran.

Blocking the strait by sinking a tanker or two would not be at all easy, despite popular fears to the contrary. The water depth in the main tanker channel varies between 250 and 700 feet (76 to 213 meters). Depths decrease towards the Iranian shore but there is still sufficient water for all the largest tankers to approach to within a few miles of the Iranian coast because a fully laden tanker draws only about 100 feet (30 meters). On the other hand, modern naval ships could mine the strait in a few hours, and aircraft could do the same in half an hour. The Omani navy is acquiring advanced equipment for the detection of mines, and there are enough minesweepers in the Gulf region to clear the straits in a short time.

There is also the fear that Hormuz might one day be controlled from one or both of its shores by a regime that, for political reasons, would interfere with the shipment of oil. The Soviet invasion of Afghanistan in December 1979, which brought the Soviet army to within 300 miles (480 kilometers) of the strait, added to these anxieties.

Between January and August 1984, 38 commercial vessels, including tankers, were intentionally sunk or hit by Iraq and Iran, causing mari-

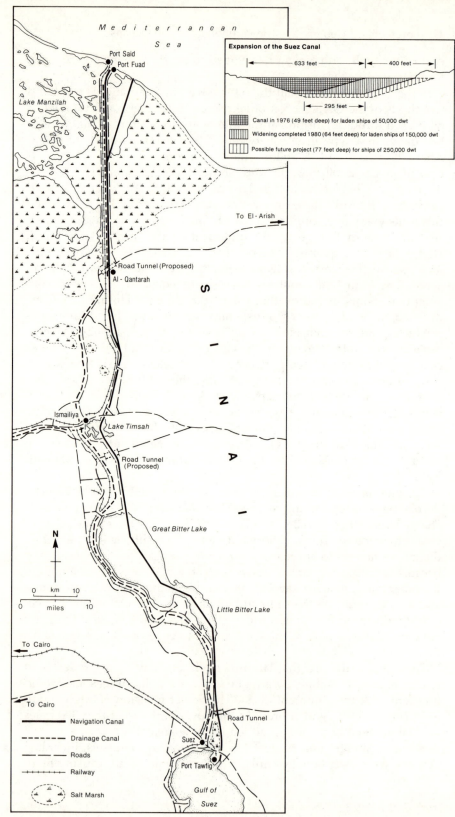

Figure 5.10   The Suez Canal, with widening schemes (insert), completed and proposed.

time insurance rates in the Gulf to climb. The perceived risks of being caught up in the fighting between Iran and Iraq may do more than anything else to discourage use of the Strait of Hormuz.

The Suez Canal

There is a tendency to undervalue the contemporary geopolitical significance of the Suez Canal. (Figure 5.10). Certainly, in the last full year before the canal closed as a result of Israel's occupation of Sinai in 1967, the amount of oil passing northbound via the canal was four-and-one-half times the present volume. In 1966, oil shipments accounted for 75 percent of tonnage through the canal. In 1984, such shipments represented only 37 percent of all traffic. Nevertheless, since its reopening in June 1975, the Suez Canal has gradually increased its share of the oil trade, particularly after a major widening project was completed in 1981 to enable passage of laden tankers of 150,000 tons. Approximately 10 percent of Gulf region oil exports to the United States and Western Europe now go through the Canal.[20] A second phase of widening could accommodate laden tankers of up to 270,000 tons in an attempt to recapture some of the Cape-route traffic. In the present economic climate, such an ambitious project seems unlikely, but it is still under discussion.

The relative decline in the importance of the Suez Canal for the movement of oil and petroleum products since 1966 also tends to obscure the fact that nonoil cargoes have more than doubled. Almost every maritime trading nation uses the canal, and the range of transiting goods is evidence of its key role in world trade. The traditional pattern of manufactured goods heading south and raw materials heading north still largely holds. Among the minerals northbound to Europe are a number of strategic importance, including chrome, manganese, tin, and nickel. If the Suez Canal was again closed to shipping, its effect on the movement of oil would be minimal, whereas general cargo trade would be seriously affected and transportation costs would increase at least 50 percent. On the other hand, no state is likely to go to war again over the canal as Britain and France did in 1956. In fact, there is no state that has a particularly large economic or strategic interest in the canal. Rather, a large number of states have some stake in the canal. It is notable in this connection that only 190 warships used the Suez Canal in 1981.

Egypt inevitably has a particularly keen interest in the security of the canal. Any repetition of the Israeli occupation of the east bank would be a national disaster, and effective defense of the Sinai Peninsula is an Egyptian priority. Three road tunnels are being or have been built under the canal to facilitate military movement into Sinai and promote development of the canal region.

The Strait of Tiran

The entrance to the Gulf of Aqaba is through the Strait of Tiran. Its importance is largely due to the access it gives to Israel's port at Eilat (see Chapter 9) and Jordan's only port at Aqaba. By world standards, it is not a strategic waterway. The number of ships using the Strait is only a fraction of the numbers shown for the straits in Table 5.5, probably fewer than 10 a day. Nor is it important as a passageway between major oceans of the world; the Gulf of Aqaba falls entirely within the territorial waters of Egypt, Saudi Arabia, Jordan, and Israel. On the other hand, this vulnerable strait has been the cause of international conflict in the past, and it could be again. The approaches to the strait are commanded by the islands of Tiran and Sanafir, and the main navigation channel is about 3 miles wide. Ownership of Tiran and Sanafir could be in contention between Saudi Arabia and Egypt. Saudi Arabia agreed that Egypt should occupy the islands in 1949 to control the Strait of Tiran in the struggle with Israel. Israel occupied the islands in 1967 to secure access to Eilat, but following Israeli withdrawal in 1982 from Sinai, the question of long-term sovereignty is a potential problem.

Conclusion

Chapter 3 outlined the historical background to the partitioning of the land areas of the Middle East and North Africa, and Chapter 4 discussed some characteristics of the partition lines. The resulting mosaic of states is already familiar, but familiarity should not lead us to assume that the pattern is either permanent or functionally efficient. Ocean space is now in the process of being partitioned among coastal states, and a new offshore political pattern is emerging that will no doubt become equally familiar in time. Although the political map of the land was taking shape for more than a century, the map of the oceans could be finalized in two or three decades, though how lasting this offshore map will prove to be is uncertain.

In many ways, offshore boundaries present at least as much potential for conflict among states as land boundaries, simply because they are invisible and present no physical barrier to movement. The right of ships of other states to pass through territorial waters on "innocent passage" can easily be abused and accusations of the unfriendly penetration of seaspace for illegal fishing or data collection are equally easy to make. Such incidents will multiply as states become more seaspace conscious and maritime boundaries begin to appear on charts and maps. Difficulties can also arise over fisheries, for example, when fish breed in the waters of one state and are caught in the waters of another. Both in the atmosphere and in the oceans, pollutants can move across international boundaries, bringing ecological damage and additional costs to states that had no part in their creation. Much Mediterranean chemical pollution, for example, is derived from the major rivers of Europe draining regions hundreds of miles inland and states suffering coastal oil pollution may be paying for the illegal behavior of foreign ships far out to sea. Thus, states may be subjected to costly "externalities" beyond their jurisdiction, regardless of the soundness of their boundaries.[21] In these circumstances, states may be driven to a recognition of the limitations of conventional boundary lines on land and sea and the adoption of a greater degree of regional cooperation, particularly with regard to environmental management. The states surrounding the semienclosed seas of the region have already made significant strides in this direction.

Notes

1. The first U.S. Conference on the Law of the Sea was held at Geneva in 1958; 60 states took part. Certain rules regarding territorial waters, continental shelves, and contiguous zones were drawn up, but no standard width was agreed for territorial waters. A second conference was convened at Geneva in 1960, but no progress was made on crucial questions, such as the width of the territorial sea. Accordingly, a third conference was convened in 1973, which subsequently held a series of tough negotiating sessions in Caracas, New York, and Geneva; some 150 states participated. By April 1982, a draft Treaty on the Law of the Sea had been agreed on; its 320 articles potentially represent one of the most significant international treaties of all time. Apart from proposing a standard 12-nautical-mile territorial sea and a 200-nautical-mile Exclusive Economic Zone, there is provision for environmental protection and guarantees of safe transit for ships through narrow waterways. The most controversial proposal is for an International Seabed Authority to be responsible for deep-sea mining beyond 200 miles. It was this idea, much favored by Third World states, that led the United States to refuse to sign the treaty when it opened for signature in December 1982. This extraordinary reversal of U.S. policy (which encouraged certain other industrial states, including the United Kingdom, to express doubts about the treaty) may not affect its long-term importance. Even nonsignatories of the treaty are likely to accept its main provisions as guidelines for national maritime claims and rights.

2. The number and size of commercial ports could also be taken as indicators of maritime interests. See *Ports of the World*. Benn Directories Series. (London: Benn Publications, 1981); also, Alastair D. Couper (ed.), *The Times Atlas of the Oceans* (London: Times Books, 1983).

3. Information on Mediterranean minerals is scarce. An excellent summary was supplied to the authors by Professor Antonio Brambati, "Some aspects of the mineral resources of the Mediterranean Sea," University of Trieste, 1983.(Unpublished paper)

4. Figures for oil transportation and loss are from "Toning Down the Mediterranean Blues", *Economist*, 11 June 1983, pp. 69–72. Both figures are substantially above those given a few years ago. See Philippe Le Lourd, "Oil pollution in the Mediterranean Sea," *Ambio* 6 (1977): 317–320.

5. Each year industrial effluents pour 5000 tonnes of zinc, 1400 tonnes of lead, 950 tonnes of chromium, and 10 tonnes of mercury into the Mediterranean. See Note 4 above; *Economist*, op. cit., p. 69.

6. See "Oil Slick Threatens Gulf Fishing industry," *Middle East Economic Digest*, 20 July 1983, pp. 12–14.

7. See "Gulf States Pool Resources to Combat Slick," *Middle East Economic Digest*, 20 May 1983, pp. 14–17.

8. The 1982 treaty will come into force one year after it has been ratified by 60 states. Although they may not feel bound by the treaty, nonsignatories are unlikely to fly in the face of its chief provisions.

9. The U.N. Convention on the Territorial Sea and the Contiguous Zone of 1958 specified that "a bay is a well-marked indentation whose penetration is in such proportion to the width of its mouth as to contain landlocked waters and constitute more than a mere curvature of the coast. An indentation shall not, however, be regarded as a bay unless its area is as large as, or larger than, that of the semicircle whose diameter is a line drawn across the mouth of that indentation." The closing line across the mouth of the bay (from which the territorial sea is measured) should not exceed 24 miles. See *Oceanography: Law of the Sea* (Milton Keynes, Eng.: Open University, 1978).

10. See J. R. V. Prescott, *The Political Geography of the Oceans* (Newton Abbott, Eng.: David and Charles, 1975).

11. Before 1979, the main tanker route through Hormuz actually passed inside Oman's straight baselines around the Musundam peninsula and, therefore, through Oman's *internal* waters.

12. There are at least six such territories in the Mediterranean Sea: the Spanish enclaves of Ceuta and Melilla, the two British sovereign bases in Cyprus, the Gaza Strip, and Turkish-occupied northern Cyprus. Between them these territories would require at least 18 maritime boundaries (all of which are counted in Table 5.4) Britain's Sovereign Bases have already delimited adjacent territorial sea boundaries with Cyprus. See Bureau of Intelligence and Research, *Territorial Sea Boundary: Cyprus-Sovereign Base Area (U.K.)* (Washington, D.C.: U.S. Department of State, May 1981).

13. There are a number of studies in the excellent U.S. Department of State *Limits in the Seas* series relating to agreed boundaries in the Gulf, including: *Bahrain-Saudi Arabia*, No. 12, 1970; *Abu Dhabi-Qatar*, No. 18, 1970; *Iran-Saudi Arabia*, No. 24, 1970; *Iran-Qatar*, No. 25, 1970; *Bahrain-Iran*, No. 58, 1974; *Iran-United Arab Emirates (Dubai)*, No. 63, 1975; and *Iran-Oman*, No. 67, 1976.

14. The dispute was rekindled in March 1982 when Bahrain named a new warship "Hawar," which Qatar regarded as highly provocative.

15. Legal aspects of the Aegean dispute are well summarized in Christos Rozakis, *The Greek-Turkish Dispute over the Aegean Continental Shelf* (Kingston, R.I.: Law of the Sea Institute, 1975).

16. Quoted by Will D. Swearingen, "Sources of Conflict over Oil in the Persian/Arabian Gulf," *Middle East Journal* 35 (1981): 327.

17. The United States has hitherto refused to recognize territorial sea claims beyond 3 nautical miles. Thus, in 1973, military supplies were ferried by air to Israel by U.S. aircraft flying through the Strait of Gibraltar against the wishes of Spain and Morocco.

18. The Black Sea is linked with a network of navigable waterways through which ships up to destroyer size can reach the Baltic Sea or Murmansk. Distances are great, however, and rivers and canals are often blocked by ice in winter.

19. There remains the remote possibility that conflict between Greece and Turkey in the Aegean could involve the Turkish Straits.

20. It is worth noting that in the same year (1981), the Suez-Mediterranean pipeline (SUMED) carried 572 million barrels of oil, more than twice as much as the Suez Canal. The overall importance of the Red Sea route for oil transportation is, thus, considerable.

21. Transnational pollution has been termed a "negative externality." The spread of acid rain from industrialized Western Europe over Scandinavia is given as an example by Kevin Cox in *Location and Public Problems* (Chicago: Maaroufa Press, 1979): 26.

Selected Bibliography

Amin, Sayed H. *International and Legal Problems of the Gulf.* London: Menas Press Ltd., 1981.

Bastianelli, Fabrizio. "Boundary Delimitation in the Mediterranean Sea." *Marine Policy Reports* 5 (1983): 1–6.

Blake, Gerald. *Maritime Aspects of Arabian Geopolitics.* Arab Papers No. 11. London: Arab Research Centre, 1982.

Bureau of Intelligence and Research. *Theoretical Allocations of Seabed to Coastal States.* Limits in the Seas Series A No. 14. Washington, D.C.: U.S. Department of State, 1972.

———. *Continental Shelf Boundary: Italy-Tunisia.* Limits in the Seas No. 89. Washington, D.C.: U.S. Department of State, 1980.

———. *Continental Shelf Boundaries: The Persian Gulf.* Limits in the Seas No. 94. Washington, D.C.: U.S. Department of State, 1981.

———. *National Claims to Maritime Jurisdictions.* Limits in the Seas No. 36. Washington, D.C.: U.S. Department of State, 1981.

Couper, Alastair D. (ed.). *The Times Atlas of the Oceans.* London: Times Books, 1983.

El-Hakim, Ali A. *The Middle Eastern States and the Law of the Sea.* Manchester, Eng.: Manchester University Press, 1979.

Farid, Abdel Majid (ed.). *The Red Sea: Prospects for Stability.* London: Croom Helm, 1984.

Glassner, Martin, and Unger, M. "Israel's Maritime Boundaries." *Ocean Development and International Law Journal* 1(1974): 303–313.

International Court of Justice. *Case Concerning the Continental Shelf Tunisia/Libyan Arab Jamahiriya,* Judgment of 24 February 1982. The Hague: I.C.J., 1982.

Khadduri, Majid, and Dixon, H. "Passage Through International Waterways," in Majid Khadduri (ed.), *Major Middle Eastern Problems in International Law.* Washington, D.C.: American Enterprise Institute for Public Policy Research, 1972.

Lapidoth-Eschelbacher, Ruth. *The Red Sea and the Gulf of Aden.* International Straits of the World, Vol. 5. The Hague: Martinus Nijhoff, 1982.

Litwak, Robert. *Security in the Persian Gulf: Sources of Inter-State Conflict.* London: International Institute for Strategic Studies, 1981.

Luciani, Giacomo (ed.). *The Mediterranean Region: Economic Interdependence and the Future of Society.* New York: St. Martin's Press, 1984.

MacDonald, C. G. *Iran, Saudi Arabia, and the Law of the Sea.* London: Greenwood Press, 1980.

———. "Iran's Strategic Interests and the Law of the Sea." *Middle East Journal* 34(1980): 302–322.

The Mitchell Beazley Atlas of the Oceans. London: Mitchell Beazley, 1977.

Ramazani, R. K. *The Persian Gulf and the Strait of Hormuz.* International Straits of the World, Vol. 3. The Hague: Martinus Nijhoff, 1979.

Suez Canal Authority. *Suez Canal Report.* Ismailiya: Suez Canal Authority Press, 1981.

Swearingen, Will D. "Sources of Conflict over Oil in the Persian/Arabian Gulf." *Middle East Journal* 35(1981): 315–330.

Truver, Scott C. *The Strait of Gibraltar and the Mediterranean,* International Staits of the World, Vol 4. The Hague: Martinus Nijhoff, 1980.

United Nations. *Draft Convention on the Law of the Sea.* Geneva: United Nations, August 1981.

Vali, Ferenc A. *The Turkish Staits and NATO.* Stanford, Calif.: Hoover Institution Press, 1972.

PART III

Integration

6

National Integration: Problems, Processes, and Prospects

Throughout much of the Middle East and North Africa, the partitioning of space in the last century or so created an entirely new political geographic template within which national and territorial allegiances could evolve or be cultivated. Boundaries, despite their apparent arbitrariness, have not withered away. On the contrary, they constitute a dominant feature of the political landscape. The political spaces they define have acquired a seeming permanence, and the state constitutes as basic, legitimate, and universal a unit of political geographic organization in the Middle East and North Africa as elsewhere. Given this reality, governments throughout the region recognize that one of their primary and immediate tasks is to unite the territories and peoples under their control, even if ultimately some of them seek broader regional or supranational unification. Integration processes, therefore, are the equilibrating corollary of partition processes: the two are part of a political geographic dialectic.

Few political geographers would still agree with the statement that their primary task is to analyze "the degree to which the diverse regions of the state constitute a unity."[1] Nevertheless, national integration problems remain a major focus of political geography, perhaps because they are a vital concern of virtually every state.[2] Integration is both a condition and a dynamic process. It refers both to the political unification of a region as a spatial entity and to the aggregation of disparate sectors of a population into a larger whole with a transcendent common identity. States exhibit various degrees of integration, so the term is relative. Here we use Muir and Paddison's definition of integration as "the process by which smaller political territories are subsumed into larger ones which are able to secure the loyalty and support of citizens."[3] This cementing of the state's varied territorial components into a single organized entity to which all inhabitants owe their ultimate allegiance can be one of the state's most difficult, yet urgent, tasks.

National integration depends on the relative strength of *centrifugal* forces, which divide a state and promote disunity, and *centripetal* forces, which unite and bind it together. From a political geographic standpoint, the three critical determinants of a state's integration are its cultural cohesiveness, the extent to which it is affected by political regionalism, and whether or not it has a raison d'être and distinctive national identity on which its citizens agree.

Cultural Cohesion

General Considerations

The most thoroughly integrated states in the world today are invariably *nation-states*, or ones inhabited by people with a strong awareness of their singularity and commonality. The terms *state* and *nation* are often wrongly used interchangeably. Strictly speaking, a state is a legal, political, and territorial entity—a place—whereas a nation is a social entity and refers to "a reasonably large group of people with a common culture, sharing one or more important culture traits such as religion, language, political institutions, values, and historical experience."[4] Language is usually the basis for national definition, but it is not always so. Multilingual nation-states, though unusual, do exist. Conversely, speakers of the same language can belong to different nations. The concept is, therefore, a complex one. Nations do not have a single diagnostic trait or defining attribute. Ultimately they are self-defined. From a political geographic viewpoint, the distinction between nation and state is fundamental because the two are rarely completely congruent spatially. Not all nations have their own state and, equally important, not all states are inhabited by one nation. States and nation-states are not synonymous. In a sense, the integration process involves building a nation within a state, or creating a nation-state.

There is no single greater obstacle to national integration in the Middle East and North Africa than the geographic mismatch between state and nation. Most states in the region are culturally diverse and, consequently, often have a weak sense of national community. However, the salience of cultural divisions is highly variable spatially. Not all heterogenous states are ipso facto disunited. Relations among subnational groups will partly depend on their numerical balance and relative political power. Rabushka and Shepsle have identified four types of multiethnic state: those with a dominant majority, those with a dominant minority, those with a balance between two groups, and those with extreme fragmentation.[5] The nation-building problems these multiethnic states experience may differ widely and, because too many other variables are involved, not necessarily in a predictable way. In a state with a dominant majority, for example, the minority may be spatially dispersed, which would reduce its chance of seceding and might weaken its individuality, or it may be geographically concentrated, which might encourage it to seek regional autonomy and reinforce its sense of cultural distinctiveness. The minority may be located centrally or peripherally, in an accessible area or in an inaccessible one. It may be relatively prosperous (therefore, resented) or disadvantaged and disenfranchised (therefore, aggrieved). It may be isolated and undivided or it may be part of a larger group in a neighboring state. The minority may or may not receive the support and backing of an outside power. It may or may not speak the language of the majority. If it does, this is no guarantee that tensions will be less. If it does not, this does not necessarily mean they will be more acute because there may be other countervailing centripetal forces. What is the central government's attitude to the minority? Does it try to suppress or assimilate it or does it tolerate and try to coexist with it? Does it share national power or decentralize it? For that matter, what are the minority's goals and aspirations? Does it simply seek a more equitable distribution of rewards, protection of its cultural individuality, and greater political participation in a state whose national identity and legitimacy it fundamentally accepts? Or does it wish to break away and form a state of its own?

It is often assumed that the growth of a capitalist economy, modernization, improved communications, and increased spatial and social interaction undermine subnational allegiances and replace them with class consciousness and a single national identity. The reality is usually far more complex. Increased interaction does not necessarily produce greater harmony or understanding. In fact, modernization may heighten group awareness and aggravate interethnic relations by intensifying competition over the allocation of scarce public goods.[6] The idea that modernization necessarily promotes unity is rooted in a belief that all subnational identitites are unimportant, ephemeral vestiges of a traditional way of life and incompatible with modernity and a national identity. An individual's ascriptive and nonascriptive cultural and social identities are actually numerous, multifaceted, and often ambiguous. They can all form foci for group solidarity and the salience of each is contextual. It would be more accurate to say that modernization supplements rather than supplants parochial identities with national ones. Hence, horizontal class cleavages may overlap with vertical language and religious ones. In such instances, they will invariably reinforce one another. The most serious integration problems have occurred where minority groups also have outstanding economic grievances and where lines of cultural and socioeconomic stratification coincide to some degree.

To discuss how cultural heterogeneity has affected integration experiences in the Middle East and North Africa, we have grouped countries according to the source rather than the seriousness of their principal cleavages. Our four main categories, therefore, are states that are linguistically diverse but religiously cohesive, religiously diverse but linguistically cohesive, both linguistically and religiously diverse, and divided between natives and nonnatives. Obviously, the scale of observation affects how states are classified because every country in the region has both linguistic and religious divisions to some extent. We are interested primarily in describing the major, politically salient cleavages—those that might have direct bearing on a country's national integration problems—and in examining the interplay between centrifugal and centripetal forces. Accordingly, we ignore many small minority communities.[7]

Linguistically Diverse but Religiously Cohesive States

Morocco, Algeria, and Iran are by no means the only countries in the Middle East and North Africa to exhibit language cleavages. They are the only ones, however, in which these divisions (in Iran's case most of them) are softened and mitigated by transcending religious ties.

Morocco and Algeria are both predominantly Arab countries with Berber-speaking minorities. Originally, the population in each was Berber. However, waves of Muslim Arabs arrived in the seventh and eleventh centuries. Their Semitic language and Islamic religion and culture gradually supplanted those of the Hamitic Berbers, even as they were modified by them. As a result, Morocco today is approximately 60 percent Arab and 40 percent Berber, whereas Algeria is 75 percent Arab and 25 percent Berber.

Differences between the two groups are complex. Whereas Arabs generally dominate the coastal plains and lowlands, the Berber strongholds are in the Rif, Middle Atlas, Kabylia, and Aurès mountains, where cultural assimilation has inevitably been slower. This spatial separation is breaking down with urbanization and considerable geographic mixing has occurred. Physically, Arabs and Berbers are more or less indistinguishable because most Moroccans and Algerians are of Berber stock, regardless of their spoken tongue. Arabic is generally the language of status as well as the official language. Consequently, a majority of all Berbers are now bilingual. Altogether, some 85 to 90 percent of all Moroccans and Algerians speak Arabic. Because the Berbers have no written language of their own, moreover, they use the Arabic script.

Outsiders have often exaggerated and misunderstood differences between Arabs and Berbers.[8] The French, who pursued a policy of divide and rule when they controlled the area, were especially guilty of reductionism, crudely stereotyping and dichotomizing the population into discrete polar ethnic categories that often bore little relationship to reality. Berbers actually have little sense of cultural or political cohesion. They speak at least three quite distinct dialects. Their communal allegiances are tribal or regional rather than to some hypothetical Berber nation. They lack any clear central authority and their nonauthoritarian political culture stresses representation, decentralization, and adaptability. Politically, they are fragmented. Paradoxically, this has helped them to survive; at the same time, it has precluded the development of a Berber national identity. Berbers participate fully in national life and do not threaten Morocco or Algeria with the kind of communal conflict that has occurred elsewhere in the Middle East. Any equation between them and the Kurds, whom they superficially resemble in being a non-Arab Muslim minority straddling an international boundary in a mountainous region, is false. Numerous ties cut across the Arab-Berber divide and greatly diminish its salience as a centrifugal force.

The balance between centripetal and centrifugal forces in Iran has always been uneasy because there is much that unites Iranians as well as divides them.[9] During the twentieth century, periods of tight central government control (such as from the mid-1920s to the early 1940s and between the mid-1950s and the late 1970s) have been punctuated with interludes of considerable national disunity and separatist ferment (such as in the early 1920s, at the end of World War II, and in the wake of the 1979 revolution that overthrew the monarchy).

Although Iran is over 90 percent Shi'i Muslim, it is without exception the most linguistically diverse country in the Middle East and North Africa. Only half of the population approximately speaks Persian as its first tongue. But Persians dominate the major cities and central plateau, provide most top religious officials, hold most senior government positions, and control most of the country's wealth. In addition, all educated Iranians speak and read Persian.

The most important linguistic minorities are the Turkish-speaking Azeris in the northwest, Turkomans in the northeast, Arabs in Khuzistan in the southwest and along the Gulf coastline, Kurds (whose language is a cousin of Persian) in the west and northwest, and Baluchis in the southeast (Figure 6.1). All straddle international boundaries, raising the possibility of external involvement. Not all present the same problem for the central government though. Separatist sentiment among Azeris, for instance, is weak because they are Shi'i. They are well integrated with the rest of the country politically, culturally, and economically, and they played a leading part in the early Iranian nationalist movement. Attempts were made by the Soviet Union after World War II to set up a puppet state, possibly as a first step to joining it with Azeri areas across the border.

The Kurds, by contrast, have frequently rebelled against the central government. Although many Kurds are Sunni Muslim, their separatism is not religious in origin. After World War II, Soviet occupying forces established a client Kurdish state called Mahabad, which collapsed when

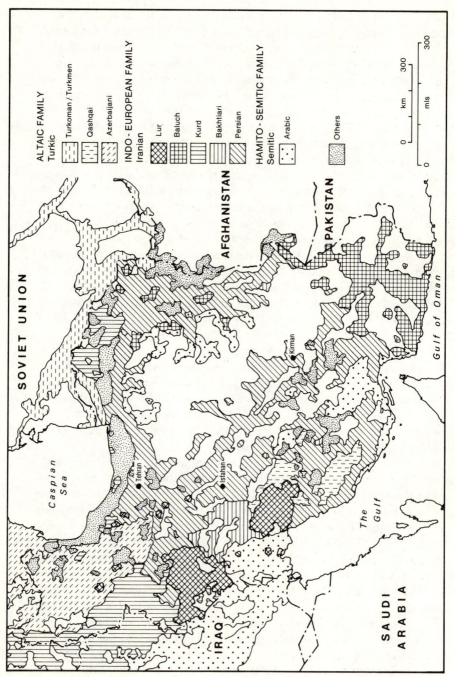

Figure 6.1 Ethnolinguistic groups in Iran.

they withdrew. Unlike their Azeri counterparts, Kurds generally supported this state's existence. Kurdish nationalism and separatism have invariably been met with repression. When the central government has been strong, the Kurds have been held in check. When it has been weak, they have seized the opportunity to assert their independence. After the overthrow of the Shah in 1979, the central government promised them autonomy. When this did not materialize, they took to arms.

Iran's Arabs are mostly Shi'i. Cut off from the rest of Iran by the Zagros mountains, many have been vaguely receptive to Arab nationalist ideas. In addition, they are concentrated in one of Iran's most oil-rich provinces and adjacent to the Shatt al-Arab waterway over which Iran and Iraq have been fighting since 1980. Fears about their loyalty after Iraq's invasion proved largely unfounded. The Baluchis live astride Iran's boundary with Pakistan, where there is a Baluchi separatist movement. As Sunnis, they have misgivings about the present regime. Living some 800 miles (1300 kilometers) from Tehran and isolated by desert and rugged terrain, they are in an excellent position to take advantage of the central government's weakness. However, the Baluchi community is small and relatively unimportant.

Religiously Diverse but Linguistically Cohesive States

At the regional scale, the Middle East and North Africa are overwhelmingly Muslim. At the national level, however, religious differences are common. The significance of these divisions varies, even among countries that are homogenous linguistically. States in this category can be classifed on the basis of whether their religious differences are *interfaith* or *intrafaith,* and *simple* or *multiple.* Only one linguistically cohesive country, Egypt, has a simple, interfaith division. States with simple, intrafaith cleavages include the Yemen Arab Republic (Yemen A.R.), many of the Gulf shaykhdoms, and Saudi Arabia. Syria and Lebanon both have multiple inter- and intra-faith religious divisions.

Egypt is, by most criteria, one of the most thoroughly integrated states in the Middle East and North Africa and centripetal forces far outweigh centrifugal ones. Nevertheless, it has experienced intermittent sectarian strife between its Sunni Muslim majority and its Coptic Christian minority.[10] The Copts account for only 10 percent of the population by most estimates, but this translates into 5 million people. Numerically, the Copts are, therefore, one of the largest minorities in any Middle Eastern country, outnumbering the Kurds in Iraq for example. About half of all Copts are concentrated in three provinces of Upper Egypt, which together have less than 20 percent of the total population. In the Nile Delta region, by contrast, there are relatively few Copts.

Differences between Egypt's Muslims and Copts should not be overstated. Besides speaking the same language, the two communities share many customs.[11] In addition, the Copts have played a conspicuous role in national life, especially before Nasir's 1952 revolution, and their loyalty to Egypt is not doubted. However, the resurgence of Islamic fundamentalism has caused apprehension. Many Copts feel that the more Egyptians define themselves in religious terms and identify with a broader Islamic as opposed to an Arab world, the more vulnerable and excluded they will be. Since the mid-1970s, serious sectarian clashes have taken many lives. In 1981, the late President Sadat accused the Coptic church of "sectarian sedition" and arrested the Coptic pope along with other opponents of his regime.

The populations of the Yemen A.R., many of the Gulf states, and Saudi Arabia are split between the Sunni and Shi'i branches of Islam. In the Yemen A.R., sectarian tensions contributed to a bloody civil war between 1962 and 1970, although they were by no means the sole cause of it. Even now, Yemen A.R., despite being totally Arab, is among the region's less well-integrated countries because of its communal structure. Shi'is are estimated to comprise up to 65 percent of the population, with Sunnis accounting for the remainder. The two communities differ in their geographic distribution and in several other important respects. The Sunnis (or Shafi'is) have traditionally been concentrated in the southern highlands and coastal areas. Part of this fertile region receives abundant orographic monsoon rainfall and, therefore, supports a dense sedentary farming population. The Shafi'is have tended to be outward-looking, with a high rate of emigration. Because most of the country's trade was historically channeled through the largely Shafi'i interior city of Ta'iz and Aden to the south, the community has a long commercial tradition. The Shi'i (or Zaydis) predominate in the mountainous northern and flatter eastern sections of the country. These more rugged and drier areas are better suited to pastoralism than farming so the Zaydis have generally been less sedentary and more tribally organized than the Shafi'is. Traditionally, the more remote, powerful tribes resisted the imposition of central governmental control. The Zaydis virtually excluded the Shafi'is from political power before the civil war.

Before 1962, a succession of Zaydi imams ruled the country. Yemen resembled a medieval theocracy, with no distinction between civil and religious matters. Top officials and administrators were selected from the 2 to 3 percent of the population who claimed descent from Ali, the Prophet Muhammad's son-in-law, and there was little to check the despotic tendencies of an imam. This anachronistic and often tyrannical system crumbled in 1962 when reform-minded Zaydi officers, with the backing of Shafi'i merchants, led a coup d'état, deposed the imam, and declared a republic. But the imam escaped and rallied many of the northern Zaydi tribes behind him in a "royalist" effort to regain power. The Sunni Shafi'is, who felt no particular loyalty to the Shi'i Zaydi imam and had much to gain form overturning the status quo, almost all supported the republican regime. Nevertheless, the ensuing civil war was not a simple sectarian power struggle and had numerous, complex causes. Certain Zaydi tribes with a grudge against the imam fought on the republican side for example. Suffice it to say that sectarian tensions were one exacerbating ingredient.

The war's outcome was somewhat indecisive. In 1970, with a clear victory for either side unattainable, a reconciliation was effected. Many royalist tribal leaders—though not the imam—returned and were given a share of power in a regime that remained moderately reformist and republican. Sectarian and tribal allegiances remain strong and the central government weak, especially in peripheral mountainous areas. However, the more equitable distribution of political power between the two main communities since the civil war has helped to alleviate communal tensions.[12]

Sunni-Shi'i tensions have been evident elsewhere in the Arabian peninsula, particularly since the 1979 Iranian revolution. Saudi Arabia is both united by religion and divided by it. Most native Saudis are Sunnis and belong to the strict fundamentalist Wahhabi movement, which helps to give the country its unique national identity. However, some 300,000 Shi'is live in eastern sections of the country, especially around Al-Qatif, where they may comprise one third of the total population. These Shi'is have never been able to participate fully or equally in a country whose religious leaders oppose aspects of their doctrine. Allegedly, Shi'i literature is proscribed and Shi'i history cannot be taught in local schools. Shi'is are admitted only to the lowest levels of the civil service and are shut out of the 30,000-man National Guard altogether. Although distinctly less well off than other Saudis, the Shi'is have prospered compared to Shi'is in neighboring countries because Saudi Arabia's oil fields are concentrated in the Eastern Province. Shi'is account for 35 to 50 percent of all oil workers. The Saudi government has been deeply concerned about the disruptive influence the Iranian revolution has had among these Shi'is, many of whom revere Ayatallah Khumayni. It had to call in the National Guard in 1979 and 1980 to squash large Shi'i demonstrations in the Eastern Province. The minister of interior pointedly noted that Saudi Shi'is "must be loyal to the homeland and not to their sect." He said: "Claiming that there is oppression [against the Shi'i] is mere talk propagated by Iran's radio and those who are after sedition." He explicitly drew attention to the geographical dimensions of the problem in noting that "service projects in the Shi'i regions are exactly the same as those in the Riyadh region and other regions of the Kingdom."[13]

Other countries in the Arabian peninsula with Sunni-Shi'i cleavages face slightly different problems. Kuwait and Dubai both have sizable Shi'i minorities, but not being Wahhabi, they have never had quite the same theological prejudice. More important, Sunni-Shi'i differences are relatively insignificant when compared with the cleavage between natives and nonnatives. Sunni-Shi'i relations are probably more tense and more complex in Bahrain than in any other Arabian peninsula state.

However, this particular problem cannot easily be divorced from Iranian territorial claims over the shaykhdom, so it is more appropriately examined when we discuss the role of external powers in aggravating national unity problems.

Lebanon and Syria are the Middle East's most religiously diverse states because their Christian and Muslim communities are themselves divided into numerous sects. Lebanon's acute integration problems are examined in the next chapter. Roughly 85 percent of Syria's population is Muslim and only 15 percent Christian. Sunnis account for about 60 to 65 percent of the total. The Muslim-Christian division has not presented Syria with a serious integration problem. In part, this is because the Christians are subdivided into numerous small sects—Greek, Armenian, and Syrian Orthodox and Catholic, Protestant, Nestorian, Chaldean, and Maronite—which are geographically dispersed, do not form a majority in any province, and have no separatist agendas. On the contrary, Syrian Christians played a crucial role in the development of Arab nationalism. Others were and are attracted to Syrian nationalist ideas, fearing that they would be overwhelmed if Syria merged with some other Arab state. Successive governments' secularist policies, for all their deficiencies and contradictions, have also generally ensured that Christians are not notably disadvantaged.

The Muslim population is not split just two ways as in the Arabian peninsula. Shi'i Islam is itself diverse, and there are certain splinter Shi'i sects that many Sunnis do not consider to be Muslim at all, so unorthodox are some of their doctrines and practices. The Alawis, Druzes, and Isma'ilis—all claim to be Shi'i and deny they are heretic—fit into this category. The Alawis (who make up perhaps 15 percent of Syria's population) and the Druzes (3 percent) have at various times and in different ways hindered Syria's national unity. Both are regionally compact and historically persecuted minorities who live in relatively inaccessible, peripheral areas. The Alawis, traditionally the most impoverished and disadvantaged community in Syria, are heavily concentrated in the mountains of Al-Ladhiqiyah and Tartus provinces, where they were able to resist the impostion of central governmental authority well into this century. They account for some two thirds of the population in these two provinces as a whole, but they account for a much higher proportion in their rural interiors. Alawis also live in adjacent regions of Turkey. They are subdivided into tribes. The Druzes are similarly concentrated in a marginal upland region in southwestern Syria where they make up 90 percent of the population. They were able to maintain a degree of independence until the 1950s and they, too, straddle international boundaries with Lebanon and Israel.

The French, who exploited communal and regional antagonisms and followed cynical divide-and-rule policies during their mandate over the country between the two world wars, created miniature Alawi and Druze states. These functioned as separate fledgling political entities during most of the colonial era. As a result, when independence came Syrians had little experience of living together under one government with a single set of laws. French rule seriously obstructed national integration by accentuating parochial ties and legitimizing and cultivating Alawi and Druze separatism. After independence, Sunnis, who led the nationalist struggle, remained mistrustful of Alawi and Druze intentions—and with good cause.

During the 1950s, Syria's peripheral minorities were gradually integrated with the rest of the state, although not as equals because the Sunnis dominated the national elite. In 1963, the communal balance of power took an unusual turn when the nominally secularist, socialist, and pan-Arabist Ba'th political party seized power in a military coup d'état. A disproportionate share of Syria's leaders since 1963 have been Alawis.[14] This sect has traditionally been overrepresented in the military, which offered it one of its few avenues of upward mobility, and in the Ba'th party, which promised to create a secular, egalitarian Syria in which Alawis (and other disadvantaged minorities) were not consigned to the bottom of the ladder by virtue of their identities.

The Ba'thi revolution initially aspired to be a nation-building one and succeeded in significantly strengthening the political center. In time, however, the regime degenerated and aggravated rather than muted communal tensions. Many Syrians resent what they perceive as the Alawi monopolization of power. President Hafiz al-Asad and most top officers and key political decision makers are from this sect, particularly certain tribes and villages. Alawi nepotism has become more open. The regime has lost considerable legitimacy because of its narrowing ethnic base. Numerous prominent Alawis have been assassinated and bombs have been exploded in every major city. Huge uprisings in Aleppo in 1980 and Hamah in 1982 had overt anti-Alawi themes and were suppressed only after much bloodshed. In Hamah, which was almost completely destroyed, the death toll may have exceeded 10,000. If the regime is overturned, Alawis could face reprisals. The most pessimistic view is that Syria could be rent by a civil war and fracture into Alawi and other small states. The chance of this happening is remote. Nevertheless, national unity is seriously threatened by continued sectarian strife, which can be fanned by Syria's many enemies in the region. The rapid growth of the Islamic fundamentalist movement has also accentuated sectarian polarization by depicting the war against the regime as a Muslim *jihad* (holy struggle) against heretics and, thus, sanctioned by God.

Both Linguistically and Religiously Diverse States

We have seen that in several states where language has a centrifugal effect, religion has a counterbalancing centripetal effect and that linguistic unity counteracts religious disunity to some extent in many others. But what of those states that have significant linguistic and religious divisions? There are five such countries: Turkey, Iraq, Cyprus, Sudan, and Israel. In Turkey and Iraq, language and intrafaith religious divisions crosscut, creating three main communities in each. In Cyprus and Israel, linguistic and interfaith religious cleavages coincide, producing a wide, possibly unbridgeable, chasm. Sudan's overlapping language and religious divisions are accentuated immeasurably by a racial fault line. Cyprus's cultural integration problems are most appropriately discussed in the context of outside interference; Israel and Sudan form case studies in our next chapter. Therefore, we will confine our discussion here to Iraq and Turkey.

The greatest obstacle to Iraq's unity has been the cleavage between the majority Arab and the minority Kurdish-speaking populations.[15] The Kurds number between 2.5 to 3 million, or 20 percent of the total population. This is a far higher proportion than in Iran and Turkey where Kurds are more numerous, and it helps to explain why Iraq's Kurds have been the most forceful in asserting what they feel are their national rights. The Kurds are concentrated in the relatively inaccessible, mountainous northern one third of the country, separated from Kurdish areas in Turkey, Iran, and Syria only by a permeable border. Weak central governments, thus, have had difficulty controlling them, let alone securing their political allegiance. Significantly, much of Iraq's oil is located within Kurdish areas, making national unity imperative for economic as well as political reasons.

Since their involuntary inclusion within Iraq, the Kurds have fought for autonomy or complete independence almost without interruption. Their protracted rebellions have seriously impeded nation-building efforts and diverted attention from other urgent national development tasks. Nevertheless, every Iraqi regime since the 1958 revolution has conceded that the country is made up of two peoples and tried to reach some accommodation. In a 1970 accord, the central government recognized Iraq's binational character and agreed to allow a measure of Kurdish political and cultural autonomy within an area to be delineated by a special census. This effort collapsed after Kurdish nationalists accused the government of delaying the tally so that it could transfer thousands of Arabs into the oil-rich Kirkuk area and, thus, exclude it from the autonomous region. In 1974, the government unilaterally created an autonomous region in an area one half the size demanded by the Kurds. This would have led to the establishment of an elected Kurdish legislative council and an executive council with authority over education, public works, housing, agriculture, transport, and communications, but sections of the Kurdish community rejected the scheme as a sham.

The round of fighting that followed exceeded all previous confrontations in its destructiveness and intensity. Some 45,000 Kurdish guerillas faced six Iraqi divisions totaling 84,000 soldiers. The rebellion ended abruptly in 1975 when Iraq agreed to move its Shatt al-Arab estuary boundary with Iran to midstream in return for an Iranian promise to cease aiding the Kurds. For the Kurds, the defeat was total. Some 100,000 fled temporarily to Iran. Another 30,000 were briefly imprisoned. To ensure its permanent control over Kurdish areas, the regime destroyed dozens of villages near the Iranian border, established non-Kurdish zones around the northern cities, and reportedly began settling Arabs in the north. Allegedly, the government also had plans to resettle 300,000 Kurds in southern Iraq, but these were eventually dropped. Meanwhile, the regime is unilaterally implementing past agreements. The Kurdish areas are nominally autonomous and have a representative government of sorts. Significantly, Kurdish is taught in schools and a university has been established in As-Sulaymaniyah. The government claims to be spending a disproportionate share of Iraq's oil revenues in the region. At a national level, special care is taken to ensure that Kurds play a prominent role in political life.

Iraq's population is also divided between Shi'is and Sunnis. There are actually three distinct large cultural groups: Kurdish Sunnis (20 percent), Arab Sunnis (25 percent), and Arab Shi'is (55 percent; see Figure 6.2). The Shi'is, although almost three quarters of all Iraqi Arabs, have historically been underrepresented politically. Conversely, the Sunni Arab minority has dominated Iraq's leadership since Ottoman times. The imbalance, which perpetuates as well as reflects class differences, is partly related to the geographic distribution of the two communities. Whereas the Shi'is have traditionally been concentrated in impoverished rural areas in southern Iraq, Sunni Arabs have been more numerous in the larger towns (particularly the capital) and consequently in a better position to take advantage of modern secular education. As a result, Sunni Arabs have enjoyed greater access to the modern professions from which the national elite is drawn.[16]

Iraq's rulers have been more committed than most in the region to creating a secular, egalitarian society because this is the only way in which sectarian differences can be dissolved or bridged. Since 1968, the Ba'thi regime has made serious attempts to lessen sectarian discontent by reducing urban-rural and interregional inequities. Nevertheless, some Shi'is still feel disadvantaged. Others are offended by the regime's secularism. Consequently, it is easy to understand why the government greeted the 1979 revolution in neighboring Shi'i Iran with apprehension.

Turkey's national unity has also been impeded by a serious Kurdish problem. Kurdish speakers make up perhaps 10 percent of the population but form a majority in the rugged, underdeveloped peripheral eastern and southeastern provinces where they are concentrated. They have rebelled on several occasions since the 1920s, necessitating the frequent imposition of martial law. The central government's authority in more remote Kurdish areas is still weak. Ankara has been unsym-

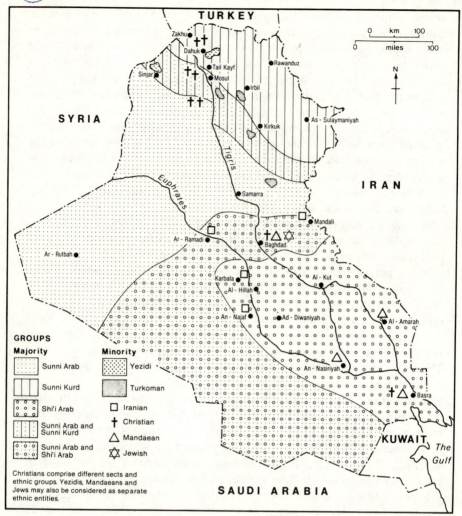

Figure 6.2 Ethnic and religious groups of Iraq.

pathetic to Kurdish grievances, which are fueled by the economic back-
wardness of Kurdish areas and by cultural suppression. It euphemisti-
cally calls all Kurds "mountain Turks" and has subjected them to a policy
of inexorable Turkification. Since 1924, the use of Kurdish has been
prohibited. It is an offense to teach it in the schools, and there are still
officially no Kurdish programs on the radio or on television. Kurdish
nationalist organizations are banned, as are Kurdish books and newspapers. Of all Middle Eastern states with a Kurdish minority, Turkey
has been the least tolerant, gambling that, in the long term, national

unity is best served by determined pursuit of a harsh assimilationist policy. As a result of this approach, a high proportion of young Kurdish men are now bilingual.

Turkey's population, like Iraq's, is split three ways because Turkish speakers are divided between Sunni and Alevi (Shi'i) Muslims. The Alevi minority is concentrated in south-central and eastern Anatolia and in the big city shantytowns. Alevis may comprise 20 percent of the total population. Historically, they have been victims of discrimation and governmental neglect. As a disadvantaged group, they have tended to favor reformist and secularist political parties. Clashes between supporters of different political factions or parties, therefore, have occasionally taken on a sectarian hue.

Turkey's population was significantly more variegated in the early 1900s. Some 1.5 million Christian Greeks lived scattered throughout western Anatolia, especially along the Mediterranean coast. After Turkey emerged out of the Ottoman Empire's ashes, it agreed with Greece in 1923 to exchange this population for the half-million Turkish Muslims living in Greece. The transfer of approximately 2 million people rid both countries of potentially troublesome minority problems but at a high human cost.

The fate of Turkey's Armenian population remains one of the Middle East's most tragic stories.[17] The Armenians, who speak a distinct Indo-European language and are Christian, once inhabited a large area of eastern Anatolia. During the ninteenth century, when Armenian nationalist ideas took root, they hoped that the Orthodox Russians would free them from Turkish rule as they expanded south. However, Russian subjugation and mistreatment of Muslim Circassians and Turkomans made the Armenians (and other Christians within the Ottoman Empire) an easy target for reprisals. In addition, the British opposed any Russian advance into Anatolia, which threatened their own interests. The Ottoman sultan increasingly viewed the Armenians and their growing demand for independence as a pretext for British and Russian intervention. This fear led to heightened repression of the minority, which began to arm in self-defense. Between 1894 and 1896, following an uprising, as many as 300,000 Armenians perished. The worst persecution occurred during World War I. The Turks, who were aligned with the Germans, feared the Armenians would act as a disloyal fifth column for the British and Russians and began expelling them from their strategically located homeland. During forced marches, starvation, disease, and massacres may have taken 600,000 to 1 million Armenian lives—no one knows precisely how many. Countless more were made homeless, fleeing north into the Soviet Union or south into Syria and Lebanon. Armenian nationalists today claim that the pre-war Armenian population of over 2 million fell to fewer than 100,000 within a few years. In 1918, following the Ottoman Empire's defeat, an independent Armenian republic was established in what is today eastern Turkey, as the Allies had promised. However, there were few Armenians left by then and the Turks and Russians crushed this state in 1920.

Irredentism and External Interference

Outside involvement can seriously aggravate national integration problems. Interference can range from verbal encouragement to covert support or even military backing for one particular community. In Yemen A.R.'s civil war, for example, Egypt dispatched 80,000 troops to help the republican side, whereas Saudi Arabia aided the "royalists." Occasionally, a country presses an *irredentist* claim, attempting to redeem or incorporate a portion (or all) of a neighbor's territory on ethnic or historical grounds, often with the support of the people living there.

There are several instances in which irredentism has accentuated internal cultural cleavages. One of the most notable examples is Cyprus, where linguistic and interfaith religious divisions perfectly overlap.[18] At root the conflict on this small, strategically located eastern Mediterranean island has been between Greek-speaking Orthodox Christians, who make up 81.9 percent of the population, and Turkish-speaking Muslims, who account for 18.1 percent. Greece has harbored an irredentist claim to the island, whereas Turkey has committed itself to defending the rights of the minority.

Cyprus was part of the mostly Muslim and Turkish-based Ottoman Empire for over three centuries. The Greek Cypriots, therefore, initially welcomed British control in 1878, which ended their minority status and which they wrongly believed would soon lead to the island's union *(enosis)* with mainland Greece. At the same time, the Turkish Cypriot minority looked to the British (and mainland Turkey ultimately) to protect it. In the 1950s, elements of the Greek Cypriot community waged a guerilla campaign to oust the British and unite the island with Greece. However, the British would only relinquish control if mainland Greece and Turkey agreed to guarantee Cyprus's independence. When the Republic of Cyprus was born in 1960, its constitution specified elaborate power-sharing arrangements. Turkish Cypriots were allocated the vice presidency, three of seven cabinet portfolios, 30 percent of seats in the House of Representatives, 40 percent of all army posts, and 30 percent of civil service positions. Nevertheless, Cyprus never really functioned as a united state, and the partnership between the two communities was always delicate. The Greeks resented Turkish quotas and soon sought drastic modifications of the constitution. The Turks resisted any change.

By 1963, the two communities were virtually at war and barbed wire laced the island. Nicosia, the capital, symbolized the cleavage, becoming a divided city. The population sorted itself out, with Greeks from mostly Turkish areas heading for Greek areas and vice versa. The United Nations dispatched a 7000-man peacekeeping force, but for the next 10 or so years, the island was effectively partitioned into two quasi-states. For a time, the Greek Cypriots controlled all ports of entry and the major roads, and they restricted the flow of gasoline, cement, and spare parts into the Turkish sector. Because virtually all of the island's booming tourist industry was located in the Greek areas, the Turks fell even further behind economically.

Archbishop Makarios, the Greek Cypriot leader, recognized that although sentiment in favor of *enosis* was strong, mainland Turkey, which was more powerful than Greece and much closer to boot, would not allow it. Soon a conflict developed between right-wing Greek Cypriots (backed by a chauvinist military junta in Athens) in favor of union with Greece and the Makarios regime, which saw that such a move might provoke a Turkish invasion. In 1974 pro-*enosis* forces staged a coup d'état and unilaterally united the island with mainland Greece. Within days, 30,000 Turkish troops invaded and seized control of the northern 40 percent of the island. Some 200,000 Greek Cypriots fled south, abandoning their homes, farms, and businesses. Several thousand mainland Turks have been settled in these vacated areas.

Turkey favors the creation of a federal bizonal state with a weak central government. The Greeks agree in principle to a federal solution but reject the division of territory sought by the Turkish side. The distribution of power is another contentious issue. Even if a federal solution is ultimately adopted and Turkish forces withdraw, Cyprus's national integration problems will remain formidable. If no settlement is forthcoming, the island's present division may become permanent, with the Turkish sector eventually being annexed to Turkey and the Greek sector to Greece. In November 1983, Turkish Cypriot leaders unilaterally proclaimed the birth of a new, independent state on the island, the Turkish Republic of Northern Cyprus. Strong international and especially Greek Cypriot opposition to the island's formal partition ensure that this state will not be recognized diplomatically by many countries. Nevertheless, the move reflected the depth of the chasm on the island.

In Bahrain, the cleavage between Sunni and Shi'i Muslims and Iranian irredentism are intertwined. Although no precise figures exist, 70 percent of Bahrainis are thought to be Shi'i. Significantly, vertical sectarian and horizontal class cleavages coincide. Although the peasantry and lower socioeconomic strata have been heavily Shi'i, the royal family and most top officials and merchants are Sunni. Despite nominal efforts to maintain political equilibrium between the two communities, Shi'i grievances are real.

The cleavage dates from the late eighteenth century, when clans of the Bani Utub tribe settled the area. At the time, Shi'i oasis farmers, fishermen, and pearl divers inhabited the archipelago. The newcomers, who were Sunni, formed a political aristocracy and merchant oligarchy over the indigenous population. The al-Khalifa family, which has ruled continuously for two centuries, formed the nucleus of this elite.

Sunni-Shi'i tensions are compounded by Iranian territorial claims. Ties between Bahrain and Iran have traditionally been strong and at various times in the past Iran controlled the archipelago, despite its proximity to the Arab side of the Gulf. Many Bahraini Shi'is are of Iranian descent. Although Arabic is the main language, Persian is widely spoken. Iran asserts that even Bahrain's Arabic speakers are of Iranian stock and referred to Bahrain as its "sixteenth province" until 1970, when it relinquished its claim after a U.N. commission reported that a majority of the population wanted to remain independent. In the past, Iran reserved a seat for a Bahraini representative in the Tehran parliament and refused entrance to travellers with Bahraini visas in their passports.

The antiroyalist revolution in Shi'i Iran reverberated in Bahrain. Ayatallah Khumayni has a large following among Bahrain's Shi'is. The revival of Iranian irredentism after the revolution and open appeals to Bahrain's Shi'is to overturn the monarchy seriously threatened national unity. The fears of Bahrain's rulers are not completely unjustified. In December 1981, an alleged Iranian-backed plot to topple the government was uncovered. The prime minister subsequently accused the Iranian regime of "instigating the Shi'is against the Sunnis and inciting sectarian sedition."[19]

Irredentist undertones complicate the current Iran-Iraq War. Both countries have openly tried to exploit one another's ethnic and sectarian divisions. When Iraq crossed the Shatt al-Arab into Iran's mostly Arab Khuzistan province, it asserted it had come to liberate what it calls "Arabistan." After its initial battlefield successes were reversed, Iraq dropped this irredentist claim. Nevertheless, its propaganda continues to focus on Iran's internal unity problems. The Baghdad government has also aided Iran's Kurds in their struggle for greater autonomy since the 1979 revolution.

Iraq has itself frequently been the victim of such interference. During the early 1970s, its own rebelling Kurds received substantial outside help. Iran, its archenemy and rival to become the dominant power in the Gulf, offered them arms and a sanctuary across the border. The United States also provided covert military assistance to destabilize a country it viewed as a strong ally of the Soviet Union. Finally, Israel helped the rebels in order to tie down a potentially formidable adversary. When Iran and by extension the United States withdrew their support in 1975 as part of an agreement between Tehran and Baghdad, the rebellion immediately collapsed. It seems likely that future opponents of the Iraqi regime will also attempt to weaken it by fanning the Kurds' grievances.

Like Bahrain, Iraq had good cause not to welcome Iran's revolution and its accompanying expressions of intense religiosity. Its politically and economically disadvantaged majority Shi'i population has always

had close links with Iran, notwithstanding linguistic differences. Before
the revolution, many Iranian clerics and religious dignitaries sought
refuge from the Pahlavi dynasty's repression and anticlericalism in Iraq,
where they often had high standing in the Shi'i community. Ayatallah
Khumayni himself lived there for a number of years. All devout Iranians, moreover, try to make a pilgrimage to the Shi'i sect's holy shrines
at Karbala and An-Najaf, both of which happen to be in Iraq. Many
Iraqi Shi'is, conversely, have visited Iranian cities like Mashhad and
Qum, which have a special religious significance. Because of this close
interaction, many Iraqi Shi'is initially welcomed the Iranian revolution
enthusiastically, falling under the spell of Khumayni's charisma. To make
matters worse, Iran's new religious leaders openly called for the overthrow of the "godless" secular Iraqi regime and backed a Shi'i opposition party. Iranian broadcasts promised to "liberate" Karbala and
An-Najaf. These seditious and sectional appeals contributed to Iraq's
decision in 1979 to execute a prominent Shi'i opposition leader and
expel 15,000 Shi'is (some say 100,000) it claimed were of Iranian origin.

Iraq's sectarian problems should not be exaggerated. In the current
Gulf war, Iran assumed Iraq's Shi'i population would rise up against
the Baghdad government and put its religious loyalties before its national or linguistic ones. This did not happen, which suggests that Iraq
may be somewhat better integrated than is sometimes assumed. Indeed, a majority of Iraq's frontline soldiers are Shi'i.[20]

States Divided Between Natives and Nonnatives

Many Middle Eastern countries cannot be described as well integrated
because of the presence of large nonnative populations within them.
These alien communities are made up, by and large, of involuntary political refugees or of immigrants attracted by economic opportunities.

In the past, the main refugee groups in the Middle East were the Circassians, who fled to Syria and Jordan from Russia in the late nineteenth
century, and the Armenians, who arrived in Lebanon and Syria from
Turkey early in the twentieth century. Both communities are fairly small
and do not threaten the cohesion of their host countries.

The 2.6 million Palestinian refugees living outside Israeli-controlled
territory are an altogether more serious matter. The origins of their dispossession and dispersal are examined in Chapter 9. Suffice it here to
say that Palestinians are scattered throughout the region but form especially large communities in Jordan, Lebanon, and—in proportional
terms—Kuwait. They have not been fully welcomed anywhere. In
Lebanon, they were catalysts to, and participants in, the civil war, as
we will see.

Jordan's nation-building experience in particular has been profoundly affected by the Palestinian presence. In 1950, Jordan's King
Abdallah unilaterally annexed those parts of Palestine that had not come

under Israeli control as a result of the U.N. partition plan or Israeli military victories in the 1948–49 Arab-Israeli War. This action, which was
condemned throughout the Arab world and resulted in Abdallah's assassination, both increased Jordan's size and added 400,000 Palestinians to the population. An additional 570,000 Palestinian refugees fled
into the country during the first Arab–Israeli War. Consequently, the
total population more than trebled from approximately 400,000 to about
1.37 million in only a few months, and native Jordanians living east of
the River Jordan suddenly found themselves heavily outnumbered.

The Palestinians were granted citizenship, but many felt little loyalty
to Jordan or to its conservative monarchy, and they hoped eventually
to return to a state of their own. As a whole, they were more urban-
ized, educated, politicized, and sophisticated than their Jordanian hosts,
whom they sometimes tended to look down on. Because of their skills,
they soon played a leading role in every sector of Jordan's life. Palestinians make up 60 percent of the population but account for perhaps
80 percent of Amman's residents. Some 90 percent of the country's
economic, financial, and commercial activities are reportedly in their
hands. Most of the teachers, lawyers, engineers, and architects are Palestinian. Significantly, they are excluded from many key political posts.
Tension between native Jordanians and nonnative Palestinians has remained a significant integrative problem, but it should not be exaggerated because the two communities have become increasingly intertwined through intermarriage, birth, and commerce. Ultimately,
however, they have differing political aspirations, and this has jeopar-
dized Jordan's very existence on occasion.

At no time was Jordan's ability to survive more in doubt than in the
three years after the 1967 Arab-Israeli War, when Israel annexed East
Jerusalem and occupied the West Bank. As a result of the war, some
400,000 additional Palestinian refugees fled east across the River Jordan, abruptly increasing the East Bank population by one third and
placing an added burden on already strained services. The 1967 war
also stimulated Palestinian nationalism. After the humiliating Arab defeat, Palestinians recognized they would never regain their homeland
if they relied solely on the Arab states. This led to a dramatic growth
in Palestinian guerilla organizations, which used Jordan as their main
base for operations against Israel. The guerillas openly defied the Jordanian authorities. By 1969, Palestinian refugee camps had, to all in-
tents and purposes, been extraterritorialized and ceased to be part of
Jordan. Native Jordanians resented this state within a state and the destructive Israeli retaliation raids that followed Palestinian attacks across
the border. Finally, King Husayn resolved to bring the guerillas under
control before he lost all authority. During the brief but intense civil
war that ensued, many thousands were killed and the guerillas driven
out of the country, principally into Lebanon.

If the Palestinians' national aspirations for a state of their own in a portion of Palestine are not met, the cleavage between natives and nonnatives will remain Jordan's outstanding nation-building problem. Native Jordanians are particularly nervous when some Israelis refer to Jordan as "the Palestinian state." They fear that Israel may one day simply annex the West Bank and Gaza Strip and expel their 1.3 million Palestinian residents to Jordan. The Reagan administration has suggested that Israel withdraw from the West Bank, which would then become a Palestinian "entity" confederated with the East Bank. Keeping such a binational state together would be exceedingly difficult.

Middle Eastern oil-producing countries with small indigenous populations have witnessed a massive influx of immigrant workers, especially since the price explosion of the early 1970s and its accompanying economic boom. In Saudi Arabia and Libya, natives still outnumber nonnatives. In several other countries, however, they have become a minority.

In Kuwait, the cleavage between those residents with citizenship and those without it is the greatest long-term obstacle to national unity. The shaykhdom's population has experienced phenomenal growth, mostly because of immigration, from only 70,000 to 100,000 in 1949 to 1.6 million in 1984. Non-Kuwaitis now comprise almost 60 percent of the population and a far higher proportion of the labor force. The country could not function without these workers, who are employed at all levels. Palestinians, the largest expatriate group, alone number approximately 300,000, or between 20 to 25 percent of the total population. Other Arabs include Egyptians, Jordanians, and Syrians. Among non-Arabs there are over 100,000 Indians and large Iranian and Pakistani communities.

Although aliens have access to social services and a few earn large incomes, they do not have equal political or economic rights. South Asian workers especially have been exploited. It is almost impossible to obtain citizenship, which greatly restricts business opportunities. Many immigrants have lived in Kuwait since the early 1950s and their children know no other home. Nevertheless, the government regards non-Kuwaitis with apprehension, questioning their loyalties and fearing that grievances about their inferior status might translate into serious unrest. The Palestinians, in particular, are carefully monitored because of their large number, relative political sophistication, and progressive and neutralist inclinations. Pressures to widen political participation—the franchise for National Assembly elections is currently restricted to 32,000 men who can trace their Kuwaiti ancestry to 1920 or earlier—will undoubtedly increase, especially as more Kuwaiti-born children of immigrants reach adulthood and refuse to accept second-class status as a result of their parents' origins.

Kuwait's problems are replicated elsewhere in the Gulf. In Qatar, expatriates, especially Indians, Iranians, and Pakistanis, make up an overwhelming share of the labor force. In the United Arab Emirates (U.A.E.) the numerical imbalance between natives and newcomers is even greater and poses a grave nation-building problem. In 1968, almost two thirds of the total population of 180,000 were local residents. By 1984, the population had climbed over sevenfold to 1.5 million, largely through immigration. Nonnatives now account for an astonishing 70 percent or more of the total. So far, immigrants have been quiet politically for fear of losing the opportunity to earn relatively high wages. As their roots become deeper, however, they may openly chafe at their inferior status. The difficulty of building a nation in a country almost completely run by foreigners may be insuperable if these outsiders are automatically excluded from full and equal membership of the society.

Regionalism

General Considerations

Almost all states with significant internal spatial variations in cultural identity, economic structure, historical experience, political culture, population density, and environmental makeup experience regional cleavages to some extent. Close identification with one region of the state does not ipso facto impede national integration. Attachment to place is universal and can be healthy as well as harmless. If regional consciousness translates into strong subnational political allegiances, however, it can adversely affect national unity. For this reason, most states try to undermine political regionalism as part of their nation-building process.[21]

Whether a state suffers from regionalism or not will depend on various factors. Size obviously affects a state's territorial integration prospects profoundly. Large states are usually more diverse geographically and culturally and are more likely to be poorly linked. Remote areas may perforce be relatively autarkic and retain a strong sense of their own territorial identity. Integration implies a high level of interaction and interconnection between places. However, spatial interaction and distance are usually inversely related. Consequently, a large state will be more difficult to bind together geographically than a small one, all things being equal. This was particularly true in the past when political power usually exhibited distance-decay characteristics, diminishing steadily away from the political center. Frequently, a central government's authority was absent altogether in peripheral zones, which enjoyed de facto independence and remained outside what Zaidi termed the "effective state area."[22] The gap between effective and actual state areas has narrowed as the bureaucratic and military power of central governments has grown. Nevertheless, the impress of state authority is still weak in peripheral regions of some of the largest states.

Measuring size or distance in miles can be deceptive. Travel time, cost, or effort, which are a function of transport technology and accessibility and connectivity within interaction networks, can be more relevant. By these standards of functional distance, Saudi Arabia and Libya are in a sense smaller than the Yemen A.R. Nor should the role of mass media and modern telecommunications in overcoming the frictional effects of distance and homogenizing and unifying a scattered population be forgotten. Everywhere, countries are, in effect, shrinking through what geographers call time-space convergence. A journey that might once have lasted days can now take hours or minutes. A piece of information, such as a governmental directive, can be transmitted instantaneously throughout a country, regardless of its size.[23]

Size, by itself, is often a poor predictor of territorial integration for yet another reason: it reveals nothing about how the space in question is enclosed and defined. A state's spatial configuration can affect its unity prospects. Political geographers have identified five state shape types: *elongated* (at least five times as long as wide), *compact* (nearly round or square), *prorupt* (almost compact but with a protruding peninsula or corridor), *fragmented* (consisting of two or more sections separated by land or international water), and *perforated* (containing part or all of another state). Various descriptive statistical measures of shape and compactness have also been widely used. States with a particular shape have certain theoretical advantages and disadvantages. Generally, elongated, prorupt, and fragmented states will be more difficult to administer and face higher transportation costs. Often, they are more prone to regionalism. Compact states are more efficient spatially: their boundaries are the shortest possible in relation to the area they enclose and communication lines are relatively short. Theoretically, small compact states are least likely to suffer regional cleavages and are easiest to integrate territorially. In practice, this is often not the case: one only has to think of Lebanon and Cyprus to recognize that shape, like size, means nothing if a population is culturally fragmented.

A state's surface configuration and settlement pattern may also affect its geographic unity. Obviously, the presence of physical geographic barriers, such as high mountain ranges, deserts, or swamps, can severely hamper communications—even in small compact states—and increase functional distances dramatically. In addition, the physical environment influences how people are distributed spatially. If the population is concentrated in one place, it may be easier to integrate. If it is widely scattered, it may be more susceptible to regionalism. But it is rarely this simple. The ecumene (the main settled area) may be central or peripheral, linear or compact. A country may have one dominant economic core or several competing ones. Discontinuities in a country's settlement pattern can have a pronounced centrifugal effect. Geographic concentrations of people separated by sparsely inhabited areas or physical barriers may develop a strong sense of regional distinctiveness, especially if no economic complementarities exist between them and they interact minimally.

Finally, spatial inequities in economic and social well-being, especially between center and periphery and between urban and rural areas, can aggravate political cleavages and feed regional discontent. Such inequities are present in all but the smallest and most prosperous Middle Eastern states.[24] According to one school of thought, uneven economic and social development is an inevitable but transitory by-product of modernization and growth. Eventually, as an articulated spatial hierarchy of urban central place settlements evolves and a national space economy emerges, wealth will trickle down and spread geographically from growth areas to underdeveloped ones and from center to periphery. Growth and development diffuse spatially. An alternative view is that geographic inequalities widen with time because growth in one region is parasitic in nature and depends on the simultaneous exploitation and underdevelopment of another. A process of backwash and agglomeration will increasingly concentrate wealth in primate capital cities, which through cumulative causation experience self-perpetuating growth. The periphery, far from catching up with the center, loses its talent and suffers a downward deprivation spiral. Either way, acute regional inequalities divide most Middle Eastern and North African states and impede their unity.

States with Significant Regional Cleavages

It is not practical to examine the extent to which every Middle Eastern and North African country suffers from political regionalism. Rather, we have selected four examples to highlight patterns and emphasize the wide range of states where geographic cleavages are politically salient.

Iran, it has been noted, is a "victim of a formidable geography."[25] Basically, the country consists of a vast central plateau framed by a triangle of the Elburz Mountains on the north, the Zagros Mountains in the west, and the Dasht-e Kavir and the Dasht-e Lut deserts in the east. These cut the central plateau off from the Caspian and Gulf coasts and from Khorasan, Sistan, and Baluchistan. Especially in the past, peripheral areas with strong local identities outside this triangle could ignore the central government with impunity. At the same time, the central plateau was reasonably well protected against invasion and somewhat isolated, which permitted a national identity to incubate. To some extent, this center-periphery difference coincides with cultural cleavages between Persians and non-Persians.

Iran's surface configuration and immense size hindered internal movement and fragmented the country until well into this century. Because the population is concentrated around Iran's western, northern, and southern margins in a fraction of the country's total area, overall population density is extremely uneven, amounting to fewer than five persons per square mile (2 per square kilometer) in over half the country. Even on the plateau, settlements are often far apart and separated by vast expanses of empty desert. It is easy to understand why Iranians have tended to identify strongly with their provinces or the widely spaced cities that dominate them, like Tabriz, Isfahan, Shiraz, Yazd, Kirman, and Mashhad.

Improved transportation and communication networks and the development of a national space economy have helped to undermine regional isolation and increase spatial interaction within an emerging national central place hierarchy. Development and modernization have had an uneven impact geographically, however, and the available evidence suggests that regional inequalities are both wide and increasing. Because of the way in which Iran's many cultural groups are distributed, regional disparities in living standard coincide to some extent with ethnic ones. In the mid-1970s, the literacy rate in the mostly Persian Central Province was 66.1 percent. In mostly Turkish West and East Azerbaijan provinces it was only 38.1 and 36.3 percent, respectively. In Kermanshehan and Kurdestan, where most of Iran's Kurds are located, it was 42.2 and 30.0 percent, respectively. In Sistan and Baluchestan, Baluchi areas, only 29.7 percent were literate. Inequalities were even more acute in other spheres. For example, whereas 80.7 percent of houses in the Central Province had electricity, in Sistan and Baluchestan only 12.4 percent had electricity. In most other provinces, roughly one third of the houses were so provided. As long as such inequalities persist, political regionalism will likely continue to be a potent political force.[26]

Regional political allegiances have also been most tenacious in Syria, where a national central place hierarchy, space economy, and communications infrastructure have been slow to develop. The French and British callously disrupted interaction patterns when they drew the region's political map, interposing political boundaries between Syria's main cities of Aleppo, Homs, and Damascus and the nearby Mediterranean ports of Haifa, Beirut, and Iskenderun, to which they were linked. The post-World War I political map also disrupted railway communications. The northern boundary was purposely drawn immediately south of the only west-east line, which passed just inside Turkey. Similarly, the line between Damascus and Homs (and, hence, Hamah and Aleppo) passed through Lebanon. Syria did not really begin to develop its own ports at Al-Ladhiqiyah and Tartus and to construct new, more appropriate railway lines or an adequate intercity road network until after the 1960s.

The lack of an obvious geographic focus has also hindered Syria's integration. Damascus and Aleppo, about equal in size until relatively recently, have traditionally been rivals. During the 1950s, political parties with strongholds in one or the other vied for national power. Whereas Damascus favored closer ties with Egypt and areas to the south, Aleppo wanted to orient Syria towards Iraq in view of its position on the main trade route between Asia Minor and the Tigris-Euphrates lowlands. These divergent spatial orientations contributed to the political instability that plagued Syria for years. Although Damascus, the capital, now outranks Aleppo in size and importance, the tension still exists. Other regional central places that have traditionally been foci for political loyalities include Al-Ladhiqiyah, Homs, and Hamah.[27]

For reasons already discussed, a high proportion of Syria's leaders have come from Al-Ladhiqiyah, Tartus, and other heavily rural and peripheral provinces since 1963. This has aroused resentment in Damascus, Aleppo, and Hamah particularly. Urban-rural and center-periphery political cleavages, which are fed by acute economic and social inequalities, have if anything widened. The Ba'thi regime has had only limited success in its efforts to lessen geographic disparities in social well-being. The uneven provision of health care and education illustrate the scope of these inequities. By the late 1970s, almost three quarters of all physicians were located in Damascus and Aleppo provinces. Damascus alone had roughly one half of Syria's total and 80 physicians for every 100,000 people. Several other provinces had fewer than 13 physicians per 100,000 people. Damascus had almost 70 percent of all dentists and roughly half of all nurses and pharmacists. Its share of hospital beds was likewise disproportionate. Although the distribution of schools and teachers is far more balanced now than 20 years ago, the gap in literacy rates is formidable, especially between urban men and rural women. According to the 1970 census, only 16.4 percent of men over 10 years of age in Damascus were illiterate. In every single province, by contrast, rural illiteracy for women exceeded 75 percent; in three provinces, it was greater than 95 percent. Syria will not be geographically integrated, in the full sense of the word, until such inequalities are substantially reduced.[28]

Geographic factors retard national integration in several Arabian peninsula countries. In Oman, there has always been a cleavage between the coastal plain and the interior.[29] The former has most of the population, the major city, and much of Oman's agriculture. Because of its location, it has traditionally been deeply involved in maritime trade and open to conquest and new cultural influences. This outward orientation is reflected in a relatively heterogenous, cosmopolitan population, especially in the Muscat-Matrah area, where sizable numbers of Iranians, Pakistanis, Indians, and Baluchis are engaged in commerce. Much of the population here is non-Ibadi Muslim and Hindu. The coastal plain is bordered by mountains that reach approximately 10,000 feet (3000 meters). Beyond them lies a fertile plateau where the oasis of Nizwa, Oman's historic political and spiritual core, is located. This interior region has traditionally been the stronghold of Ibadi Muslim orthodoxy and conservatism.

Until recently, a deep political cleavage paralleled these geographic and cultural differences. On the coast, power lay with the Muscat-based, secular Al bu Sa'id sultans, who through ocean trade built up a huge empire that included parts of coastal East Africa and Zanzibar. The sultanate's legitimacy and authority were not fully accepted in the interior where a politically autonomous, theocratic Ibadi imamate centered on Nizwa held sway. Periodically, an imam would challenge a sultan's power. After one almost successful such attempt, the Sultan agreed in 1920 not to interfere in the interior's affairs. This resulted in a 35-year peace between sultanate and imamate, but it also formalized the political dichotomy within the country without fully resolving the question of who had ultimate authority in the interior. This dualistic political structure found expression in the country's official name: the Sultanate of Muscat and Oman.

A Saudi-backed insurrection broke out in the interior in the mid-1950s, when the imam proclaimed an independent state and sought membership in the Arab League, with Arab nationalist encouragement. The rebels claimed the sultan had violated the agreement that recognized the interior's autonomy. The British consistently supported the sultans against the imams of the interior, seeing the dispute in simple terms of legitimate monarchs being threatened by tribal insurgents. Thus, they put down the rebellion and destroyed the imamate. Interestingly, the rebels, with some historical justification, viewed the sultanate as a politically autonomous entity within the larger geographic framework of the imamate rather than the other way around.

The sultanate was even more seriously threatened by a rebellion in the western Dhufar region in the 1960s and 1970s. This can only be understood in the context of Sultan bin Taymur's notoriously tyrannical rule, during which "medicines, radios, music, dancing, spectacles, trousers, cigarettes and books were all forbidden," and the most basic human rights did not exist.[30] The sultan took pains to keep out alien influences, himself issuing all visas. Women had to request (but rarely received) special permission to leave the country. Intercity travel was prohibited, except with special permission. Infrastructure was nonexistent and social services almost totally lacking. By the late 1960s, the country had only two elementary schools, and 85 percent of their students were not Omani Arabs.

Dhufar, with its mountainous terrain, thick monsoon-fed vegetation, and peripheral location, was ideal for guerilla warfare and the building of an insurgent state. However, the Marxist-Leninist rebels based there, with the assistance of the neighboring People's Democratic Republic of Yemen (P.D.R. Yemen), failed to overthrow the sultanate, which was supported by British and eventually Iranian and Jordanian forces. Recognizing that the old despotic sultan was a liability, the British engineered a palace coup in 1970 and brought his son to power. Significantly, one of his first actions was to rename the country the Sultanate of Oman and thereby indicate, if only symbolically, his determination to bridge the age-old cleavage between the coast and interior. At the same time, the discovery of oil permitted the initiation of government development plans. A combination of coercion and enticement brought the rebellion under control within a few years.

Geographically, P.D.R. Yemen's most serious national integration problem has been the acute economic, political, and social gap between Aden, the peripheral primate capital city, and the rest of the country. The dichotomy dates from the opening of the Suez Canal in 1869, after which Aden became a coaling station and vital link in Britain's imperial lifeline. The city soon developed into a thriving entrepôt for the immediate region, attracting banking, commerce, light industry, and oil refining and drawing immigrants from nearby countries. By the mid-twentieth century, native Adenis were a minority in what had become a booming, cosmopolitan port. This development was confined exclusively to a small coastal enclave because the British paid little attention to the backward and isolated interior, which had no mineral or agricultural resources of interest to them. At best, they saw the interior as a buffer zone between Aden and an irredentist North Yemen.

The chasm found expression in the territory's dualistic colonial political administration. Whereas the British tightly ruled Aden as a Crown Colony, they imposed only rudimentary, indirect control over tribal chiefs in the interior, which they divided into Western and Eastern Protectorates. In turn, the Western Protectorate consisted of 18 distinct and disparate units, varying from sultanates to shaykhdoms or other tribal entities, whereas the Eastern Protectorate was made up of 5 major and 2 minor entities. Not until the early 1960s when Britain created a loose Federation of South Arabia to strengthen its influence did it try to provide the region with a common political identity. After 1963, nationalists waged an increasingly effective rebellion against the British, who finally withdrew in 1967. Significantly, the victorious National Liberation Front immediately overthrew all the local Protectorate chiefs, replaced the old complex tribal divisions with 6 new governates, and proclaimed an independent and unitary republic.

States Without Significant Regional Cleavages

By no means all Middle Eastern and North African states suffer from regionalism. Kuwait, for example, is compact, flat, and smaller than New Jersey. The vast majority of its population lives in the capital. Territorial integration has, therefore, not been a problem. The same is true of other shaykhdoms along the eastern littoral of the Arabian peninsula. Bahrain is even smaller than Kuwait, measuring only 231 square miles (598 square kilometers), or about one fifth the size of Rhode Island. Although it is geographically fragmented and consists of an archipelago of some 30 islands, the population is agglomerated on a single island in the city of Manamah. Neighboring Qatar is also a small city-state, with 80 percent of its 400,000 people clustered in Doha, the capital. Most of the Qatar peninsula, which is approximately 100 miles (160 kilometers) from north to south and 50 miles (80 kilometers) from west to east, is a level, sparsely populated desert. The U.A.E., whose unity problems we examine in detail in our chapter on regional integration, is somewhat different. Although small, it is a loose federation of seven emirates. Three of its constituent city states in particular, Abu Dhabi, Dubai, and Sharjah, have a competitive and not always friendly relationship with one another.

In North Africa, Egypt, Tunisia, and Algeria have been relatively free of deep regional cleavages. Egypt's territorial cohesion and stability can be explained in part by geographical factors. The central fact of Egypt's existence is the River Nile. Without this lifeline, it would be almost uninhabited desert. The river serves as a natural focus for settlement. Some 99 percent of Egypt's 47 million people are concentrated in its fertile valley or delta on just 3.5 percent of the national territory—roughly equivalent to the area of Maryland. This densely settled and precisely defined ecumene, flanked to the west and east by protective desert buffers, has always been relatively easy to control, if not to defend. The Nile is a natural, efficient transportation artery that permits high levels of spatial interaction within the settled zone. Cairo, significantly, grew up where the valley and delta meet and their products could easily be exchanged. Because of its accessibility, it emerged as the state's political capital as well as a primate city. Even now, Egyptians call Cairo *Misr*, which is the Arabic for Egypt. If there is a regional cleavage, it is between Lower and Upper Egypt. Although Egypt is territorially compact, its ecumene has been likened to a lotus flower with a long, thin stem (the valley) and a small bud (the delta). For some 800 miles (1300 kilometers) south of Cairo, settlement does not extend more than a mile or two beyond the Nile River Valley. Functionally, therefore, Egypt is best thought of as having an elongated shape. The southern end of the settlement pole is somewhat remote.

Tunisia lacks many of the integration problems that plague other Middle Eastern and North African states, being small, compact, and relatively free of significant geographic, ethnic, religious, or tribal divisions. Approximately 90 percent of its 7 million people live in the moister north, and some two thirds are concentrated within a 100-mile (160-kilometer) radius of Tunis, the capital and primate city. Compared to other Maghreb countries, the terrain is not too rugged, and this has facilitated internal communications and the imposition of central government authority.

Neighboring Algeria is about one third the size of the coterminous United States and one of the region's largest states. Nevertheless, its size has not given rise to regional cleavages. Algerians are concentrated in a fraction of the national territory within a peripheral, narrow, well-watered band between the Atlas mountains and the Mediterranean coast. Algiers, the capital, may be over 1200 miles (1900 kilometers) from the country's southern extremities, but it is close to the population's center of gravity. The vast interior Sahara Desert is almost uninhabited outside of a few scattered oases.

In Jordan rainfall decreases sharply from west to east and north to south. Consequently, almost all the population hugs the northwestern corner or western edge of the country. Perhaps 90 percent live within 50 miles (80 kilometers) of Amman. The Amman-Zarqa metropolitan region alone has over half the population. Conversely, 80 percent of the country—roughly the area lying east of the Hijaz Railway—is uninhabited or sparsely populated steppe and desert. In these circumstances, regional political cleavages are unlikely to emerge.

The State-Idea and National Identity

General Considerations

The most closely integrated states are those with a raison d'être, or what Ratzel called a "political idea" and Hartshorne a "state-idea." According to Hartshorne, such an idea "convinces all the people in all the regions [of the state] that they belong together."[31] It can negate, or at least counteract, centrifugal forces and transcend cultural, geographic, or other divisions. The state-idea is the single most important centripetal force, a sine qua non of national integration. Nationalism offers the most potent state-idea, whether it is defined by language, religion, shared values, or a common historical experience, because it imbues the state with a unique national identity. Some Middle Eastern and North African states have no difficulty justifying their existence. Their political geographic identities are sharply defined and a consensus exists among their inhabitants that they belong together. Others have weak or recently confected state-ideas however. Usually, these states were unilaterally created by external powers. Because their initial raisons d'être were flimsy, at least in the eyes of their inhabitants, their national identities have been fragile and insecure.

The nation-building process is, in a sense, one of fashioning a state-idea. The degree to which this endeavor succeeds depends in part on the nature and goals of a country's political leadership. Some political elites are more highly motivated and able to articulate a state-idea and mobilize the population in support of it than others. A state led by a traditional hereditary monarch may have a very different nation-building experience from a state led by a charismatic populist or one led by an activist, ideologically based mass political party.

Political leaders, regardless of the source of their power and legitimacy, will attempt to develop and exploit what Gottmann termed the state's "iconography," or all those centripetal "symbols, references, and ideas which a people shares, and which lend a group some psychological cohesion or unity."[32] Icons objectify and emblematize national identity and, therefore, constitute an indispensable nation-building instrument. Obvious examples would include a national capital (with its governmental paraphernalia, monuments, and repositories of cherished artifacts) as well as a national anthem, flag, folklore, and mythology.

All states possess a number of instruments for diffusing their state-idea. A national school system, as Bergman notes, is an indispensable socialization tool that inculcates a sense of citizenship and performs the vital task of propagating and moulding a positive national self-image, especially through geography and history lessons. An army, which by definition has a strong, explicitly national ethos, can similarly promote integration by bringing together people from diverse geographic and ethnic backgrounds and instilling in them a sense of national community and pride. Access to mass media channels enables a central government to make its decisions and aims known in all parts of the state and to inform, persuade, galvanize, and lead its citizens. Political parties, especially activist mass ones, can also play a major and sometimes decisive nation-building role by mediating and aggregating separate geographic constituencies and disparate interest groups, mobilizing a population in support of specific development goals, widening political participation, and increasing the political center's legitimacy.[33]

Classifying Middle Eastern and North African states on the basis of their state-idea or the source of their national identity is no easy task, if only because these invariably have several components. Our categories are heuristic and seek to identify themes and patterns rather than to suggest a conceptual schema or to expound on every country's state-idea.

The Role of Territorial Continuity

The unique state-ideas and national identities of several Middle Eastern and North African countries derive in part from their historical continuity as distinct and relatively stable political geographic entities.

Morocco's territorial roots, for example, go back several centuries, even if its current boundaries are recent. Its people do not think of their country simply as a French creation. The present state has Almoravid, Almohad, Merinid, and other antecedents; the cities of Fez, Marrakesh, and Meknes have all, at one time or another, been political capitals of Moroccan-based empires. Morocco was the only North African state to escape Ottoman rule, which added to its distinctiveness. The current Alawite dynasty dates from 1666, making it among the oldest anywhere. Its claim to Sharifian status—that is, to have descended from Muhammad—enhances its legitimacy and power as a centripetal symbol among some sections of the population. Morocco's peripheral location within the Arab world—Rabat, the capital, is as close to London

as it is to Tripoli, Libya, and it is almost equidistant between Washington, D.C., and Mecca—and the heavy Berber imprint on Moroccan society have also favored the development of a local Moroccan nationalism.

Egypt, the Middle East's oldest and possibly best integrated state,
exhibits an even greater degree of spatial continuity and political geographic coherence. Whereas the history of many of its neighbors is
measured in centuries or even decades, Egypt's spans several millennia. To compare its nation-building experience with Libya's or Kuwait's
(or even that of the United States) seems impudent because it was first
united as a distinct political community under a single government in
3400 B.C. Egypt was the setting of one of the world's earliest civilizations. Not unexpectedly, Egyptians have a strong awareness of their
Pharaonic roots and continuity as a people with their own state. As a
result, local Egyptian nationalism has been a potent ideological force,
helping to differentiate the country from its Arab neighbors.[34]

Egypt, however, is also the Arab world's center of gravity, and this
complicates and blurs its identity somewhat. With twice as many people as the next largest Arab country, it is the political and cultural hub
of the Arab world. Consequently, Egyptians often disagree over whether
the country's Egyptian or Arab identity should take precedence. Until
the 1930s, Egypt involved itself relatively little in pan-Arab affairs and
the Egyptian component of its national identity was clearly dominant.
A period of active participation in the region's affairs followed: Egypt
played a leading part in the creation of the Arab League in 1945, for
instance, and in the 1948–49 Arab-Israeli War. This involvement reached
its zenith under President Nasir, who became the charismatic leader of
all Arabs, not just Egyptians. During this phase, from the mid-1950s to
Nasir's death in 1970, a conscious effort was made to downplay Egypt's
iconography and to emphasize its Arabism. Between 1958 and 1971, the
word Egypt was eliminated from the country's official name, which became the United Arab Republic. The flag was changed. Even postage
stamps no longer contained the word "Egypt." The country's Pharaonic past, which nourished Egypt's sense of uniqueness, was deem-
phasized in education and the media. President Sadat, after his accession to power, reverted to an Egypt-first approach. The pursuit of a
separate peace with Israel through the 1978 Camp David accords, which
led to Egypt's ostracism by the Arab world, epitomized the change of
emphasis. Symbolically, the country's name was changed to the Arab
Republic of Egypt, thereby combining the two elements of the country's identity. There is no necessary contradiction between Egyptian and
Arab identities. The problem comes when one is completely denied or
subordinated to the other.

Tunisia also boasts a long history as a separate entity, despite frequent conquests. It was a distinct state under the Hafsids from the thirteenth to the sixteenth centuries and was ruled continuously by the

Husayni dynasty between 1705 and 1957. Even when it was part of the Ottoman Empire, it enjoyed virtually complete autonomy. Significantly, President Habib Bourguiba, the "father" of modern Tunisia, and the neo-Destour party, which has ruled continuously since 1956, have eschewed pan-Arabism in favor of developing a local, secular Tunisian nationalism. To foster a sense of national identity, awareness of Tunisia's Carthaginian, Roman, Arab-Islamic, and Mediterranean-European heritage is carefully cultivated. Tunisia is depicted as unique because of its location as a bridge between the Maghreb and Mashreq and between Europe and Africa. This parochial focus, although often criticized by Arab nationalists and Islamic fundamentalists, has generally kept the country out of destabilizing inter-Arab disputes. Ironically, Tunisia's neutrality within the region and its low-key Arabism made it the most acceptable choice as a headquarters for the Arab League after Egypt's expulsion from the organization in 1979 and as the new home for the Palestine Liberation Organization (PLO) after its expulsion from Beirut in 1982.

The Role of Cultural Distinctiveness

The territorial identities of several countries are bound up with their linguistic or religious distinctiveness. Oman, for example, is unique in being largely Ibadi Muslim. Ibadis are part of the Kharijite schism and split from mainstream Islam during its early days. During the eighth century, they fled persecution in Iraq and settled in interior Oman, where they elected their own theocratic leader (imam) and established an imamate. Historically, Ibadism provided Oman with its political geographic raison d'être. It is still a distinctive, integral component of Omani national culture.

Zaydi Islam similarly has set the Yemen A.R. apart from other Arab countries, despite the presence of a large Sunni minority. Zaydis differ from the vast majority of Shi'is elsewhere in the Middle East over the line of succession to Ali, the Prophet Muhammad's son-in-law. Until 1962, the country was essentially an isolated Zaydi theocracy, which for centuries was able to enjoy a large measure of political geographic independence. Yemen A.R. is, therefore, distinctive without being integrated.

The predominance of the Persian and Turkish languages and cultures in Iran and Turkey, respectively, distinguish these two countries from all others in the region. In the case of Iran, Shi'i Islam, which has a close symbiotic relationship with Iranian nationalism, and a powerful sense of racial uniqueness—Iranians trace their ancestry to the eponymous Indo-European Aryans who settled the area approximately 3500 years ago—further reinforce the sense of national identity. Not surprisingly, for most of its long history Iran has been a distinct political entity, albeit one with fluid frontiers. Its political tradition dates back at least to the empire of Cyrus the Great and the Achaemenids in the sixth century B.C. Awareness of this historical continuity and pride in Persia's contributions to civilization over the centuries have had a cohesive effect.

The Role of Inertia

Certain Middle Eastern and North African states originated as colonial artifacts rather than through any felt need by those who lived in them. They had no satisfactory, indigenous state-ideas, and at first their national identities were ersatz or hastily concocted. Nevertheless, the passage of time has obscured their genesis somewhat and bestowed on them an air of permanence. Syria and Iraq are perhaps the best examples.

Syria, for a long time, had among the weakest state-ideas of any Middle Eastern country. Created by the colonial powers after World War I, its arbitrary boundaries ignored basic geographic, cultural, historical, and economic relationships within the general area. To the extent that its inhabitants identified with a space called Syria, this was a Greater Syria, *bilad al-Sham,* which included Palestine, Lebanon, and Jordan no less than those areas included within the state. President Asad reiterated a widely held view when he said, during a 1980 speech, that "in the recent past Arab Syria extended from Sinai to the Taurus Mountains. Who divided this Syria? Where is this Syria now? Why did they dismember Syria? Reaction, allied with colonialism, did all of this."[35]

Syrians initially viewed their state as an extemporaneous rump. From its inception, many of those responsible for nation building rejected its raison d'être. Thus, it had a fundamental political geographic flaw. Former President Shishakli once disparagingly defined Syria as "the current official name for that country which lies within the artificial frontiers [*sic*] drawn up by imperialism when it still had the power to write history."[36] The tendency of earlier rulers to avoid close identification with the state and their reluctance to cultivate a centripetal iconography were also exemplified in a communiqué issued after one of Syria's innumerable coups d'état: "Arab Syria and its people have never recognized the boundaries of its country and only acknowledge the frontiers of the greater Arab homeland. Even Syria's national anthem does not contain the word Syria but glorifies Arabism and the heroic war of all the Arabs."[37] Ambivalence about the state's identity is even reflected in the constitution, which observes that the "Syrian Arab *region*" (italics added) is a part of the Arab homeland and that its people "are a part of the Arab nation which strives . . . for . . . complete unity."[38]

The unusual strength of pan-Arabism hindered internal unity by equating Syrian national loyalties with betrayal of the larger supranational Arab state-idea and blurred the distinction between the foreign and domestic or the Arab and Syrian realms. Syria inevitably feels the Arab world's every twitch because it regards itself as Arabism's "beating heart" and as the progenitor and guardian of Arab nationalist ideas.

During the 1950s, Syria's survival as an independent entity was in doubt, so weak was its state-idea. Factions of the officer corps seeking to merge the country with Egypt or Iraq engineered frequent coups d'état. Egypt and Iraq, in turn, viewed Syria as a geopolitical prize and competed to gain its support in their respective quests to become the region's dominant power. In effect, Syria's leaders put the country up for adoption but squabbled about who the parents were to be. Eventually, they elected to erase Syria from the political map altogether, merging it with Egypt in 1958 to form the United Arab Republic. The union was a fiasco. Egypt's tendency to treat Syria as a minor, distant province rather than as an equal partner was deeply resented and led to rapid disillusionment and secession in 1961. Ironically, this failed experiment helped to define Syria's identity, making it more aware of its uniqueness and of the practical difficulties inherent in combining Arab countries. After 1961, Syria's leaders were far more cautious, and Syria has never surrendered its sovereignty again, even if regimes continue to exploit Arabism as a legitimating ideology.

It is not mere happenstance that the Ba'th party, which was founded specifically to bring about Arab unity, was born in Syria in the 1940s and has been continuously in power there since 1963. Ironically, Syria has gained a spatial coherence and independence under the Ba'th that it previously lacked. It is not easy to sustain an antistate idea. In time, states acquire their own justification. How many Syrians can remember a time when Syria did not exist? Forces of inertia alone favor Syria's continued existence.

Nevertheless, Syrians still have a blurred view of their political space, leading neighbors to fear irredentist efforts to create a Greater Syria. President Asad voices a common view (at least in Syria) when he asserts that Syrians and Lebanese "are one single people, one single nation. We may be divided into two independent states, but that does not mean that we are two different nations. . . . The feeling of kinship . . . runs deeper than it does between states in the United States."[39] Syrians do not necessarily think it odd when their president says, "we and Jordan are one country, one people and one thing"[40] or when a newspaper editorial claims that Jordan "is a natural part of Syria. History has never recognized the presence of an international, or even administrative, entity separate from Syria."[41] Many a time they have heard Syrian leaders claim that Palestine, too, is but southern Syria. For example, Asad once reportedly told Yasir Arafat, "There is no Palestinian entity. There is Syria. You are an integral part of the Syrian people. Palestine is an integral part of Syria."[42] It is telling that Syria's flag is almost indistinguishable from Iraq's to the east, despite the political antipathy between the two countries.

The idea of Iraq as a separate state originated with the British, who recognized Mesopotamia's strategic importance. Prior to its creation in what had been the Ottoman districts of Baghdad, Basra, and Mosul, "there had never been an independent Arab Iraq, nor was there any great demand among the local population for an Iraqi state."[43] Unlike in Egypt, where a highly agglomerated population had been linked together in a Nile-based state of one form or another for several millennia and where pride in an ancient Pharaonic ancestry served as a foundation for a modern, local Egyptian nationalism, few Iraqis saw the state that the British carved out for them as a natural outgrowth of, or successor to, the great Mesopotamian civilizations that had flourished in the Tigris and Euphrates river valleys. In part, this was a function of geography: neither of Iraq's main rivers provided as strong or dominant a focus for settlement as the Nile in Egypt, and many Iraqis lived as farmers in the rain-fed north or as tribally organized pastoral nomads in the desert margins and Zagros Mountains. Iraq's population, moreover, lacked the sort of cultural homogeneity that made the task of nation building in Egypt comparatively easy.

Initially, the process of fashioning a functioning state in this arbitrarily and artificially bounded space was largely the work of "a handful of British officials . . . acting with almost whimsical self-assurance."[44] One of their first tasks was to find a king to serve as a centripetal force in this fragmented society. After considering seven or eight candidates for the position, they selected Faysal, son of the Hashimite Husayn from the distant Hijaz, partly as a restitution for reneged wartime commitments. Because both the monarchy as an institution and the ruling Hashimite family were alien, Iraq's kings never united the country or became a focus for people's loyalties in the way that the British had hoped. Hence, they never played as crucial a nation-building or iconographic role as the Sa'uds, who were untainted by association with a colonial power and had deep roots in the society they governed. Few Iraqis felt a great sense of loss when the monarchy was overthrown in 1958.

As with Syria, the severing of Iraq from the rest of the Arab world rendered the newly born state illegitimate in the eyes of Arab nationalists. To accept the division of the Arab world and to recognize Iraq as a separate entity would have been a betrayal of pan-Arabist ideals as well as complicity with an imperialist fait accompli. Thus, not only did Iraq lack a convincing raison d'être, but also many of its early leaders actively sought to prevent the development of a distinct Iraqi national identity, preferring, instead, to emphasize its Arab heritage. During its formative years, many nationalists assumed that Iraq would eventually disappear and be submerged in some larger Arab entity. Significantly, the only country outside Syria where the Ba'th party has had any success is Iraq, where it has been in power since 1968. As in Syria, the Ba'thi regime has, paradoxically, greatly strengthened the political center and cultivated a local Iraqi nationalism. The country's Mesopotamian heritage is now being exploited to build up a sense of *wataniyyah* (patriotism).

The Role of Monarchies

A number of Middle Eastern states were created for, or by, royal families and continue to be closely identified with them. Until recently, citizens of these countries owed their allegiance to the monarch rather than to the territorial unit, which amounted to little more than the ruler's personal domain. In a sense, the raison d'être of these states was to preserve and perpetuate dynastic authority and define its geographic limits. Usually, a network of consanguinous tribal ties rather than a sense of citizenship bound these countries together. Eventually loyalties were transferred to the territory itself. Of course, many royal families have also been despised and rejected as alien, tyrannical, or corrupt; therefore, they were ultimately overthrown.

Of all the Middle Eastern states created after World War I, Jordan was probably the most geographically, politically, and economically artificial. During the Ottoman Empire, the northern part of present-day Jordan was a somewhat neglected subdivision of the *vilayet* of Syria. The south was part of the Hijaz Province in the Arabian peninsula. After World War I, Arabs considered the area to be part of Greater Syria, and the British and Zionists viewed it as part of Palestine. No one, certainly, thought of it as a separate entity, deserving of statehood. Nevertheless, the British created Transjordan, as it was originally called, to make amends for broken wartime promises to the Hashimite royal family, to dissuade Prince Abdallah from using the territory as a base for liberating Syria from French control, and to confine Jewish colonization to areas west of the River Jordan.

Jordan was a kind of consolation prize for the Hashimites, an imperial afterthought. From the start, its chances of surviving seemed remote. Well over one half of its tiny, tribally organized, and desparately poor Arab population of 200,000 was nomadic or seminomadic, and they had little or no sense of national identity—least of all a Jordanian one. Amman, the present capital, was little more than a village. There were hardly any roads, government services, or schools. Frequent bedouin raids went almost unchecked. Less than 3 percent of the territory was cultivated, and there was barely any economic base of which to speak. In these circumstances, Jordan's viability depended almost wholly on external subsidies. At independence in 1946, the British still supplied two thirds of all government revenue; even six years later, they contributed over half the budget. Now, Arab oil-producing states play a key role in keeping the country afloat.

Unlike in Iraq, the Hashimite monarchy took root in Jordan, where the settled population was considerably smaller and less sophisticated politically. Jordan's royal family had a vested interest in the state's survival and dominated the country's political life in a way that Iraq's did not or could not. King Abdallah, and after him King Husayn, cultivated the allegiance of the large bedouin population, which hardly distinguished between loyalty to the Hashimites and loyalty to Jordan as a territorial entity. The monarchy was, thus, a principal centripetal force in Jordan, at least among native Jordanians. Nonetheless, Jordan needs the Hashimites less than they need it because Jordan's raison d'être has become more multifaceted and complex and the allegiances of Jordanians have become more territorial and abstract.

Jordan's early experience is similar in certain respects to that of many of the small shaykhdoms along the eastern edge of the Arabian peninsula. Their state-ideas originally amounted to little more than the will of their rulers, to whom tribes owed their allegiance. Until recently, they did not really have a national identity. Peterson has suggested a simple model of sequent political development to describe how these states evolved.[45] In the first stage, certain cohesive tribes with strong leaders rose to political prominence and shifted from a seminomadic or nomadic existence to a sedentary one, creating nuclear coastal settlements in such places as Kuwait, Manamah, Doha, Abu Dhabi, and Dubai. This resulted in an identification between the tribe and its settlement. In time, the predominant clans evolved into aristocratic (ultimately ruling) families. The British reinforced this trend by assuming that the shaykhs of the coastal settlements exercised political authority over all residents, not simply members of their tribes. The discovery of oil required political boundaries to be delineated. The shaykhs, thus, became rulers of sovereign, territorial entities, not simply tribal patriarchs. Loyalties were owed to the ruling families rather than to the territory in which people lived. Hence, the phrase "L'état, c'est moi" accurately described the initial raisons d'être of these shaykhdoms. The ruling families were the glue that held each shaykhdom together. Even now, a strikingly high proportion of all top government positions are held by family members: al-Sabah in Kuwait, al-Thani in Qatar, al-Khalifah in Bahrain, and al-Nuhayyan, al-Maktum, and others in the U.A.E.

The Role of Charismatic Leadership

In certain states, a charismatic and dynamic leader has forcefully articulated a new state-idea or decisively shaped a nation-building experience by serving as a centripetal focus.

Turkey provides perhaps the best example. Turkey is the chief remnant of the multinational Ottoman Empire, which collapsed after being defeated in World War I. Had the victorious powers' plans been implemented, little of the empire would have been left for the emergence of a Turkish state: eastern Anatolia would have been divided into independent Armenian and Kurdish states, Smyrna and Thrace ceded to Greece, part of southwestern Anatolia given to Italy, and Cilicia left to the French. However, attempts to impose this humiliating peace settlement and an opportunistic Greek invasion of Anatolia prompted a dramatic, phoenixlike Turkish national revival. By 1923, the Turks had fought off their enemies and signed the far more favorable Treaty of Lausanne, which defined their national territory. The next task was to build a nation within this newly created space.

More than most states, Turkey bears the deep imprint of one individual, the authoritarian but charismatic Mustafa Kemal, who is also known as Ataturk, meaning "father of the Turks." Ataturk was truly Turkey's architect, rescuing it from total dismemberment and subsequently attempting to fashion a secular nation-state. His particular achievement was to provide Turkey with a powerful and unique centripetal stateidea and to sharply differentiate its people (with the notable exception of the Kurds) from all others. Specifically, he renounced and denounced lingering irredentist and atavistic pan-Turkish, pan-Ottoman, and pan-Islamic ideologies, all of which might diffuse loyalties and distract Turks from the difficult business of forging a modern state within its existing boundaries, no matter how flawed they might be.

The attempt to build a new, self-consciously Turkish state in a small part of what had been a vast empire required real and symbolic changes in its cultural and political geography. The capital was moved from cosmopolitan, "degenerate," and peripheral Constantinople—the capital of the Byzantine as well as Ottoman empires—to "pure" Ankara, which had a more central geographic location on the Anatolian Plateau, the Turkish heartland. This move had immense iconographic significance because it emphasized that the Ottoman past was being rejected for a new, Turkish beginning. In addition, many towns were renamed and Turkified: Constantinople was changed to Istanbul, Angora to Ankara, Smyrna to Izmir, and Adrianople to Edirne for example.

Ataturk's celebrated reforms were designed to place even greater distance between Turkey and the Arab-Islamic realm to which it had been linked for 400 years. For example, he introduced the Gregorian calendar and international time, replaced the Islamic *Shari'ah* law with secular western legal codes, and adopted the Roman script instead of the Arabic. He even outlawed the fez, encouraging men to wear the European wide-brimmed hat instead. His attempts to Turkify Islam by prohibiting the use of Arabic in mosques and by translating the Qur'an into Turkish were less successful. Although many reforms were never fully assimilated at the village level and traditional practices and values proved to be rather resilient, Ataturk unquestionably laid the foundations for the emergence of a relatively modern, cohesive state. His ideological influence was felt long after his death, and his successors continued to espouse his principles.[46]

The Role of External Stimuli

Real or imagined external threats can have a pronounced centripetal effect. Foreign domination invariably sharpens national self-awareness and may even unwittingly create it. The vigor of Iranian nationalism, for example, owes much to the country's bitter encounters with the Great Powers, which have been deeply involved in its affairs this century (see Chapter 3). Iran is by no means unique. As we have seen, the prospect of territorial dismemberment after World War I provoked a national revival in Turkey. Discontent with Turkish rule early this century nourished Arab self-awareness. The British and French kindled Egyptian and Moroccan nationalism. The Italians made the Libyans aware of their commonalities. Saudi and Egyptian interference helped to bring northern Yemenis together.

Algeria offers perhaps the best example. Its national identity was forged dialectically in opposition to the French. No other country in the Middle East and North Africa was so heavily colonized by Europeans or so traumatized, radicalized, and transformed by its encounter with foreigners. France took several decades to subjugate the territory completely after its initial conquest in 1830. By the end of the nineteenth century, an estimated 3 million Algerians had died. A massive colonial implantation followed this brutal pacification. France offered settlers free passage, land, seed, and animals. Virtually all the best land was seized from native Algerians and redistributed to European settlers, whose large farms grew citrus fruits and grape vines for the French market rather than food for Algerians. Almost the entire traditional economy was dislocated. Indigenous land-use patterns were altered and hundreds of thousands of people uprooted and put out of work. The French even tried to make the country an integral part of metropolitan France. By the mid-1950s, approximately 1 million European settlers comprised 10 percent of the total population. In the main cities, which were highly segregated, the proportion of Europeans was far higher.

Algeria's war of independence between 1954 and 1962 was among the bloodiest and most destructive anticolonial struggles anywhere.[47] An estimated 1 million Algerians—1 of every 10—lost their lives. An additional 2 million Algerians were displaced during the fighting, largely because of a French policy of moving people into "regroupment" villages. By 1961, perhaps one third of the rural population had been relocated in this manner. It is not difficult to understand how the Algerians came to think of themselves as one people. Collective memory of this intense experience cements Algerians together even now.

When Algeria finally won its independence, 800,000 Europeans abruptly fled the country. It is a measure of how little France did for the Algerians that this exodus deprived the country of most of its administrators, entrepreneurs, technicians, physicians, teachers, and skilled workers. Factories and shops were closed and farms abandoned, leaving over 70 percent of the population unemployed.

If the war had one positive outcome, it was that it created a powerful, triumphant sense of national solidarity and bestowed on post-independence nation builders a large reservoir of revolutionary legitimacy and goodwill, which made their difficult task easier. Nevertheless, the French cultural residue was substantial. At independence, most Algerians spoke French as well as Arabic or Berber. All but 1700 of 19,000 teachers were French. To create a sense of Arab-Muslim national identity, therefore, the educational system had to be Arabized. This was not easy; as recently as the early 1970s, teaching at all levels was still mainly in French. Even now, French is widely used at the university level and among educated Algerians.

Conclusion

The process of national integration involves adjusting to new spaces created by the partitioning of territory. Therefore, many unity problems of Middle Eastern and North African states are tractable and transitory, a product of youthfulness. National identities are being forged and territorial allegiances taking root, even in countries that once seemed hopelessly artificial. All but the most acute geographic cleavages seem destined to be bridged ultimately. National space economies are being developed, urban spatial hierarchies evolving, and improved transportation and communication networks breaking down geographic isolation and increasing spatial interaction virtually everywhere. In a purely geographic sense, the territories of all Middle Eastern and North African states are more thoroughly amalgamated today than a decade or two ago.

One cannot be so sanguine about the problem of cultural diversity. A strikingly large number of the region's states are divided linguistically, religiously, or between natives and nonnatives. Such differences do not ipso facto preclude national integration, but the evidence strongly suggests they often delay or impede it. It is important not to overgeneralize about the unity prospects of heterogenous states because the seriousness of their problems varies enormously. Most plural states will not disintegrate: they are searching for, or have found, formulas that allow their various communities to coexist reasonably peacefully. Certain others, by contrast, have suffered civil war, sectarian strife, or separatist rebellions. No additional formal, internationally recognized partitioning of space has occurred as a result of national integration problems, although Turkish Cypriots have proclaimed an independent state. No separatist movement has succeeded in redrawing the political map. That is not to say that this will never happen: as we will see in our next chapter, Lebanon, Israel, and Sudan could all conceivably face territorial redivision for very different reasons.

Notes

1. Richard Hartshorne, "The Functional Approach in Political Geography," *Annals of the Association of American Geographers* 40(1950): 117.

2. Two recent books by political geographers that deal with the subject are Colin H. Williams (ed.), *National Separatism* (Vancouver: University of British Columbia Press, 1982); and Nurit Kliot and Stanley Waterman (eds.), *Pluralism and Political Geography: People, Territory, and State* (New York: St. Martin's Press, 1983).

3. Richard Muir and Ronan Paddison, *Politics, Geography and Behaviour* (New York: Methuen, Inc., 1981): 156.

4. Martin Ira Glassner and Harm de Blij, *Systematic Political Geography*, 3rd ed. (New York: John Wiley & Sons, 1980): 46.

5. A. Rabushka and K. A. Shepsle, *Politics in Plural Societies* (Columbus, Ohio: Charles E. Merrill Publishing Co., 1972): 32.

6. For examples of this argument, see Clifford Geertz, "The Integrative Revolution: Primordial Sentiments and Civil Politics in New States," in Clifford Geertz (ed.), *Old Societies and New States: The Quest for Modernity in Asia and Africa*, pp. 105–157 (New York: Free Press, 1963); Robert Melson and Howard Wolpe, "Modernization and the Politics of Communalism," *American Political Science Review* 64(1970): 1112–1130; Walker Connor, "Nation-Building or Nation-Destroying," *World Politics* 24(1972): 319–335; and Ilya Harik, "The Ethnic Revolution and Political Integration in the Middle East," *International Journal of Middle East Studies* 3(1972): 303–323.

7. For example, we consider Syria essentially homogenous linguistically, despite small Kurdish and Armenian minorities, because its unity problems result from sectarian differences. Similarly, we classify Iran as religiously homogenous because it is over 90 percent Shi'i Muslim and the Sunni, Jewish, Zoroastrian, and Baha'i minorities are relatively small.

8. This point is emphasized repeatedly in Ernest Gellner and Charles Micaud (eds.), *Arabs and Berbers: From Tribe to Nation in North Africa* (Lexington, Mass.: Lexington Books, 1972).

9. See Richard W. Cottam, *Nationalism in Iran*, 2nd ed. (Pittsburgh: University of Pittsburgh Press, 1979).

10. E. Brodin, "The Christians in Egypt," *Plural Society* 9(1978): 75–84.

11. Rural Coptic women are often veiled, for example, and female circumcision or clitorodectomy is practiced by both communities. Marriage and funeral customs show certain resemblances.

12. For accounts of Yemen A.R.'s problems, see Robert W. Stookey, *Yemen: The Politics of the Yemen Arab Republic* (Boulder, Colo.: Westview Press, 1978); and J. E. Peterson, *Yemen: The Search for a Modern State* (Baltimore: Johns Hopkins University Press, 1982).

13. Foreign Broadcast Information Service (FBIS), *Daily Report, Middle East and Africa*, 1 April 1982, p. C4.

14. See Nikolaos van Dam, *The Struggle for Power in Syria: Sectarianism, Regionalism and Tribalism in Politics, 1961–1980* (New York: St. Martin's Press, 1981); and Alasdair Drysdale, "The Syrian Political Elite, 1966–1976: A Spatial and Social Analysis," *Middle Eastern Studies* 17(1981): 2–30.

15. The best account of this problem is Edmund Ghareeb, *The Kurdish Question in Iraq* (Syracuse: Syracuse University Press, 1981).

16. Today, a striking number of top elite members are Sunni Arabs from the small provincial town of Tikrit and owe their positions to the manipulation of kinship ties.

17. For a concise account, see David M. Lang and Christopher J. Walker, *The Armenians*, Report No. 32 (London: Minority Rights Group, 1977).

18. A brief, balanced description of the problem is contained in Peter Loizos, *Cyprus*, Report No. 30 (London: Minority Rights Group, 1976).

19. FBIS, *Daily Report, Middle East and Africa*, 28 January 1982, p. C2.

20. As we will see in the next chapter, Israel, Lebanon, and the Sudan must be added to the long list of countries in which national unity has been impeded by outside involvement or irredentism.

21. Two good discussions of regionalism are John A. Agnew, "Structural and Dialectical Theories of Political Regionalism," in Alan Burnett and Peter J. Taylor (eds.), *Political Studies from Spatial Perspectives*, pp. 275–289 (New York: John Wiley & Sons, 1981); and David B. Knight, "Identity and Territory: Geographical Perspectives on Nationalism and Regionalism," *Annals of the Association of American Geographers* 72(1982): 514–531.

22. I. H. Zaidi, "Towards a Measure of the Functional Effectiveness of a State: The Case of West Pakistan," *Annals of the Association of American Geographers* 56(1966): 24–40.

23. The United States offers a good example. The University of Chicago's National Opinion Research Center found that 68 percent of all adult Americans knew of President Kennedy's assassination within half an hour of the event.

24. There is now a vast and diverse literature on the whole problem. For representative contributions to, and summaries of, the debate, see especially Alan Gilbert and David Goodman, "Regional Income Disparities and Economic Development: A Critique," in Alan Gilbert (ed.), *Development Planning and Spatial Structure*, pp. 113–141 (New York: John Wiley & Sons, 1976); B. E. Coates, R. J. Johnston, and P. L. Knox, *Geography and Inequality* (London: Oxford University Press, 1977): 31–42, 111–134; D. R. Keeble, "Models of Economic Development," in Richard J. Chorley and Peter Haggett (eds.), *Socio-Economic Models in Geography*, pp. 257–266 (London: Methuen and Co., Ltd., 1967); John R. P. Friedmann, *Regional Development Policy: A Case Study of Venezuela* (Cambridge: MIT Press, 1966) and his "The Spatial Organization of Power in the Development of Urban Systems," *Development and Change* 4(1972–73): 12–50; Andre Gunder Frank, *Capitalism and Underdevelopment in Latin America* (New York: Monthly Review Press, 1969); Gunnar Myrdal, *Economic Theory and Underdeveloped Regions* (London: Duckworth, 1957); J. C. Williamson, "Regional Inequality and the Process of National Development: A Description of the Patterns," *Economic Development and Cultural Change* 13(1965): 3–43; Roland J. Fuchs and George J. Demko, "Geographic Inequality Under Socialism," *Annals of the Association of American Geographers* 69(1979): 304–318; and D. Slater, "Underdevelopment and Spatial Inequality: Approaches to the Problems of Regional Planning in the Third World," *Progress in Planning* 4(1975): 97–167.

25. See Note 9 above: Cottam, op. cit, p. 23.

26. Akbar Aghajanian, "Ethnic Inequality in Iran: An Overview," *International Journal of Middle East Studies* 15(1983): 211–242.

27. Michael H. Van Dusen, "Political Integration and Regionalism in Syria," *Middle East Journal* 26(1972): 123–136.

28. Alasdair Drysdale, "The Regional Equalization of Health Care and Education in Syria Since the Ba'thi Revolution," *International Journal of Middle East Studies* 13(1981): 93–111.

29. J. E. Peterson, *Oman in the Twentieth Century: Political Foundations of an Emerging State* (New York: Barnes & Noble Books, 1978).

30. Peter Mansfield, *The Arabs* (New York: Penguin Books, 1978): 386.

31. Friedrich Ratzel, *Politische Geographie*, 3rd ed. (Munich and Berlin: R. Oldenbourg, 1923); see Note 1 above: Hartshorne, op. cit., p. 116.

32. Jean Gottmann, *La politique des états et leur géographie* (Paris: Armand Colin, 1952); and Edward F. Bergman, *Modern Political Geography* (Dubuque, Iowa: William C. Brown, Co., 1975): 18–19.

33. See Note 32 above: Bergman, op. cit., pp. 263–287.

34. See Laila Shukri El-Hamamsy, "The Assertion of Egyptian Identity," in Saad Eddin Ibrahim and Nicholas S. Hopkins (eds.), *Arab Society in Transition*, pp. 276–306 (Cairo: American University in Cairo, 1977); and Mirrit Boutros Ghali, "The Egyptian National Consciousness," *Middle East Journal* 32(1978): 59–77.

35. FBIS, *Daily Report, Middle East and Africa*, 24 March 1980, p. H5.

36. Quoted in Patrick Seale, *The Struggle for Syria: A Study in Post-war Arab Politics, 1945–1958* (London: Oxford University Press, 1965): 130.

37. Quoted in Eliezer Be'eri, *Army Officers in Arab Politics and Society* (New York: Praeger Publishers, 1970): 151.

38. "The Permanent Syrian Constitution of March 13, 1973," *Middle East Journal* 28(1974): 55.

39. *New York Times*, 4 December 1983, p. A4.

40. FBIS, *Daily Report, Middle East and Africa*, 26 March 1981, p. H15.

41. FBIS, *Daily Report, Middle East and Africa*, 27 April 1981, p. H4.

42. *Nation*, 1 October 1983, p. 269.

43. Don Peretz, *The Middle East Today*, 3rd ed. (New York: Holt, Rinehart & Winston, 1978): 406.

44. Michael Hudson, *Arab Politics: The Search for Legitimacy* (New Haven, Conn.: Yale University Press, 1977): 272.

45. J. E. Peterson, "Tribes and Politics in Eastern Arabia," *Middle East Journal* 31(1977): 297–312.

46. See Bernard Lewis, *The Emergence of Modern Turkey*, 2nd ed. (London: Oxford University Press, 1969).

47. For a detailed account, see Alistair Horne, *A Savage War of Peace: Algeria, 1954–1962* (New York: Penguin Books, 1979).

Selected Bibliography

Agnew, John A. "Structural and Dialectical Theories of Political Regionalism," in Alan Burnett and Peter J. Taylor (eds.), *Political Studies from Spatial Perspectives*, pp. 275–289. New York: John Wiley & Sons, 1981.

Ahmed, Jamal M. *Intellectual Origins of Egyptian Nationalism*. London: Oxford University Press, 1960.

Anthony, John Duke. *Arab States of the Lower Gulf: People, Politics, Petroleum*. Washington, D.C.: Middle East Institute, 1975.

Batatu, Hanna. *The Old Social Classes and the Revolutionary Movements of Iraq*. Princeton, N.J.: Princeton University Press, 1979.

Bergman, Edward F. *Modern Political Geography*. Dubuque, Iowa: William C. Brown Co., 1975.

Betts, Robert Brenton. *Christians in the Arab East*. Atlanta, Ga.: John Knox Press, 1978.

Bonine, Michael, and Keddie, Nikki (eds.). *Continuity and Change in Modern Iran*. Albany: State University of New York Press, 1981.

Brodin, E. "The Christians in Egypt." *Plural Society* 9:1(1978): 75–84.

Chaliand, Gerard (ed.). *People Without a Country: The Kurds and Kurdistan*. London: Zed Press, 1980.

Cottam, Richard W. *Nationalism in Iran*, 2nd ed. Pittsburgh: University of Pittsburgh Press, 1979.

Deutsch, Karl W. *Nationalism and Social Communication: An Inquiry into the Foundations of Nationality*, 2nd ed. Cambridge: MIT Press, 1966.

———. "National Integration: A Summary of Some Concepts and Research Approaches," in Karl W. Deutsch (ed.), *Tides Among Nations*, pp. 269–294. New York: Free Press, 1979.

Douglas, J. Neville H. "Political Integration and Division in Plural Societies—Problems of Recognition, Measurement and Salience," in Nurit Kliot and Stanley Waterman (eds.), *Pluralism and Political Geography: People, Territory and State*, pp. 47–68. New York: St. Martin's Press, 1983.

El-Hamamsy, Laila Shukri. "The Assertion of Egyptian Identity," in Saad Eddin Ibrahim and Nicholas S. Hopkins (eds.), *Arab Society in Transition*, pp. 276–306. Cairo: American University in Cairo, 1977.

Gellner, Ernest, and Micaud, Charles (eds.). *Arabs and Berbers: From Tribe to Nation in North Africa*. Lexington, Mass.: Lexington Books, 1972.

Ghali, Mirrit Boutros. "The Egyptian National Consciousness." *Middle East Journal* 32(1978): 59–77.

Ghareeb, Edmund. *The Kurdish Question in Iraq*. Syracuse: Syracuse University Press, 1981.

Gottmann, Jean. *La politique des états et leur géographie*. Paris: Armand Colin, 1952.

Halliday, Fred. *Arabia Without Sultans*. New York: Vintage Books, 1975.

———. "Labor Migration in the Arab World." *MERIP Reports* 123(May 1984): 3–10.

Hartshorne, Richard. "The Functional Approach in Political Geography." *Annals of the Association of American Geographers* 40(1950): 95–130.

Horne, Alistair. *A Savage War of Peace: Algeria, 1954–1962*. New York: Penguin Books, 1979.

Hourani, Albert. *Minorities in the Arab World*. London: Oxford University Press, 1946.

Hudson, Michael. *Arab Politics: The Search for Legitimacy*. New Haven, Conn.: Yale University Press, 1977.

Johnston, R. J. *Geography and the State: An Essay in Political Geography*. London: Macmillan, 1982.

Joseph, Suad, and Pillsbury, Barbara L. K. (eds.). *Muslim-Christian Conflicts: Economic, Political, and Social Origins*. Boulder, Colo.: Westview Press, 1979.

Kaylani, Nabil M. "Politics and Religion in Uman: A Historical Overview." *International Journal of Middle East Studies* 10(1979): 567–579.

Kelidar, Abbas (ed.). *The Integration of Modern Iraq*. New York: St. Martin's Press, 1979.

Khalifa, Ali Mohammed. *The United Arab Emirates: Unity in Fragmentation*. London: Croom Helm, 1980.

Khuri, Fuad I. *Tribe and State in Bahrain: The Transformation of Social and Political Authority in an Arab State*. Chicago: University of Chicago Press, 1980.

Knight, David B. "Identity and Territory: Geographical Perspectives on Nationalism and Regionalism." *Annals of the Association of American Geographers* 72(1982): 514–531.

Lang, David M., and Walker, Christopher J. *The Armenians*. Report No. 32. London: Minority Rights Group, 1977.

Lewis, Bernard. *The Emergence of Modern Turkey*, 2nd ed. London: Oxford University Press, 1969.

Loizos, Peter. *Cyprus*. Report No. 30. London: Minority Rights Group, 1976.

Long, David. *The Persian Gulf: An Introduction to Its Peoples, Politics, and Economy*. Boulder, Colo.: Westview Press, 1978.

Long, David, and Reich, Bernard (eds.). *The Government and Politics of the Middle East and North Africa*. Boulder, Colo.: Westview Press, 1980.

McLaurin, R. D. (ed.). *The Political Role of Minority Groups in the Middle East*. New York: Praeger Publishers, 1979.

Merritt, Richard L. "Locational Aspects of Political Integration," in Kevin R. Cox, David R. Reynolds, and Stein, Rokkan (eds.), *Locational Approaches to Power and Conflict*, pp. 187–211. New York: John Wiley & Sons, 1974.

Muir, Richard. *Modern Political Geography*. London: Macmillan, 1975.

Muir, Richard, and Paddison, Ronan. *Politics, Geography and Behaviour*. New York: Methuen, Inc., 1981.

Peterson, J. E. *Oman in the Twentieth Century: Political Foundations of an Emerging State*. New York: Barnes & Noble Books, 1978.

———. *Yemen: The Search for a Modern State*. Baltimore: Johns Hopkins University Press, 1982.

Seale, Patrick. *The Struggle for Syria: A Study in Post-war Arab Politics, 1945–1958*. London: Oxford University Press, 1965.

Shaw, Stanford H., and Shaw, Ezel Kural. *History of the Ottoman Empire and Modern Turkey, vol. 2, Reform, Revolution, and Republic: The Rise of Modern Turkey, 1808–1975*. London: Cambridge University Press, 1977.

Stookey, Robert W. *Yemen: The Politics of the Yemen Arab Republic*. Boulder, Colo.: Westview Press, 1978.

van Dam, Nikolaos. *The Struggle for Power in Syria: Sectarianism, Regionalism and Tribalism in Politics, 1961–1980*. New York: St. Martin's Press, 1981.

Wilkinson, John C. "The Oman Question: The Background to the Political Geography of South-East Arabia." *Geographical Journal* 137(1971): 361–371.

7

National Integration:
Five Case Studies

In the previous chapter, we identified some of the main political geographic factors that promote or impede national unity and drew cross-national comparisons in the process. Ultimately, however, no country is affected by the same constellation of centripetal and centrifugal forces. It can be misleading to isolate and discuss these forces separately because they interact with one another in complex and sometimes synergistic ways. The integration equations of the various Middle Eastern and North African states are unique and often different. Each state has its own peculiar combination of integrative assets and liabilities. Case studies are, therefore, an invaluable tool to understanding integrative problems and processes. We have selected five disparate countries for detailed discussion: Lebanon, Israel, Saudi Arabia, Sudan, and Libya. These well illustrate the range of integrative problems the region's countries face.

Lebanon

The Middle East and North Africa can provide no better example of a country without an effective state-idea than Lebanon. During its 1975–76 civil war, some 60,000 to 100,000 out of a total population of approximately 3 million lost their lives—more than the combined deaths in all four Arab-Israeli wars. An additional 200,000 were wounded. Some 250,000 fled the country. The war's economic cost was put as high as $25 billion by some experts. Large areas, including much of Beirut and the country's infrastructure, lay in ruins. Quite simply, Lebanon disintegrated as a functioning political entity. It has yet to recover. In June 1982, Israel launched a massive invasion, occupying virtually the entire southern half of the country. West Beirut, the capital, was heavily bombarded and tens of thousands killed or made homeless. The Lebanese government's authority did not extend much beyond Beirut in early 1985. Outside the capital lay a patchwork of fiefdoms controlled by assorted warlords and militias and zones policed or occupied by non-Lebanese troops. By one estimate there were 179 cease-fires between 1975 and 1983. All of this occurred in a country about the size of Connecticut.

Lebanon's Origins

Although Lebanon's roots are Phoenician, the state itself is a relatively recent creation. Its historical and cultural geography is complex. The Lebanese mountains, which reach roughly 10,000 feet (3000 meters) within 15 miles (25 kilometers) of the Mediterranean coastline, have always offered refuge to dissident religious minority groups fleeing persecution. After conquering Muslim armies spread into the region from the Arabian peninsula in the seventh century and established control of the coastal plain, Maronite Christians, and ultimately Druze and Shi'i Muslim minorities, were left to dominate the mountainous interior. This dichotomy was formalized by the Ottoman authorities, who created a special semiautonomous entity in the interior during the nineteenth century to avert further sectarian strife. The *mutasarrifiyyah* of Mount Lebanon had a Christian governor appointed in consultation with five European powers. Its unique status lasted until the Ottoman Empire's collapse during World War I. The French, who received a League of Nations mandate over the Levant, created in its place a far larger state of Greater Lebanon. This combined Mount Lebanon with the coastal plain to the west, the Biqa' Valley to the east, Akkar plain to the north, and some territory to the south. The demographic and political ramifications of this gerrymander were profound, because the newly added areas were overwhelmingly Sunni and Shi'i Muslim. Not only were many Christians unhappy about becoming part of a state in which their proportional strength was greatly diluted, but also Muslims objected to being unilaterally severed from their compatriots in Syria and shunted into a state in which Christians played a dominant role.[1]

A Fragmented Population

Lebanon's population is the most religiously diverse in the region. Officially, 17 sects, or "confessions," are recognized. The current population's exact composition is not known because no national census has been conducted since 1932, when Christians supposedly outnumbered Muslims six to five. Today, at least 60 percent of all Lebanese are probably Muslim. Significantly, because Christians and Muslims are both subdivided, no sect comes close to forming a majority (Table 7.1).[2]

To accommodate the various sects politically and find a modus vivendi among them an elaborate system of power sharing was agreed on in the 1943 National Pact. All cabinet portfolios, parliamentary seats, and government or other official positions were allocated to the communities on a fixed proportional basis. The presidency was always reserved for a Maronite, the prime ministership for a Sunni, and the parliamentary speakership for a Shi'i. Maronites monopolized sensitive military and internal security posts however; on balance, they were by far the most powerful group. To give Lebanon a chance of surviving, the Christians agreed not to tie Lebanon too closely to France and the West and the Muslims not to seek Lebanon's unity with other Arab states, particularly Syria. These compromises seemed to work for a while. Lebanese had access to a vigorous free press and could express political opinions openly. Indeed, for many years, Lebanon was admired as the most tolerant country in the Arab world. Somewhat conceitedly, it characterized itself as the Switzerland of the Middle East. The calm was deceptive. The political system was inflexible and functioned well only as long as it was not confronted with new demands and problems.

From its inception, Lebanon has been "a precarious republic,"[3] largely because parochial and communal identifications are often stronger than national ones. Primary loyalties are to family, village, and especially sect. Lebanon is a mosaic society, a patchwork of loosely associated com-

Table 7.1
Religious Communities in Lebanon

Community	Estimated Percentage of Population
Total Muslim	(60)%
Sunni	26
Shi'i[a]	27
Druze	7
Total Christian	(40)
Maronite	23
Greek Orthodox	7
Greek Catholic	5
Other Christian[b]	5
Total	100

[a]Includes Alawis and Isma'ilis.

[b]Includes Armenian Catholic and Orthodox, Syrian Catholic and Orthodox, Chaldean, and Protestant.

Source: Fiches du monde Arabe, No. 1699, 24 September 1980; reprinted in *Christian Science Monitor,* 2 December 1982, p. B22.

munities to whom being Lebanese is often an irrelevant abstraction.[4] The religious community is also often a geographic, social, cultural, political, and even economic unit. Most of the institutions that build national identity and inculcate a sense of citizenship elsewhere are absent or weak. The central government has always adopted an extreme non-interventionist laissez-faire approach, providing minimal services and offering little direction. The various sects have, therefore, provided their own education, welfare, and even internal security through their armed militias.

Because over half of all children attend private confessional schools, the national educational system is fragmented and curricula varied. Children often grow up without much contact with Lebanese from other sects and learn different histories and values.[5] The right of each religious community to handle marriage, divorce, inheritance, and other matters of personal status in its own courts further deepens social and cultural cleavages by reducing interaction across sectarian lines. Not surprisingly, intermarriage is almost nonexistent.[6]

The political and judicial system permitted Lebanon's confessional groups to coexist, but it also kept them apart by formalizing, legitimizing, and politicizing sectarian differences. Fixed proportional representation and the peculiarities of the electoral system also greatly retarded the development of modern, secular, ideologically based political parties with a national constituency. Instead, the leading parties had a narrow sectarian base, their fortunes rising and falling with those of the individual politicians of which they were really an extension. Lebanon never enjoyed truly national leadership.

The various sects' geographic separation impeded national unity by reinforcing differences and nourishing stereotypes. Outside the capital—which had a mixed though loosely segregated population, with Muslims in West Beirut and Christians in East Beirut—most Maronites and Druzes lived around Mount Lebanon or the Shuf Mountains, most Sunnis on the coastal plain, and most Shi'is in southern Lebanon, the Biqa' Valley, and after the late 1960s, Beirut's peripheral squatter settlements.[7] In addition, 84 percent of all Sunnis lived in towns over 10,000, compared to only 45 percent of Maronites, 55 percent of Shi'is, and 46 percent of Druzes. Regional inequalities have, therefore, had sectarian dimensions. The Shi'i community has been the poorest in part because it is concentrated in southern Lebanon, the most underdeveloped part of the country. The overlapping of vertical sectarian and geographic cleavages with horizontal class cleavages is crucial to understanding Lebanon's integrative problems because the civil war was as much one between haves and have nots as between Christians and Muslims. Sectarian differences would not have mattered as much had they not been broadly congruent with acute socioeconomic disparities. In a 1971 survey of Lebanese couples, the average annual income of husbands showed a wide range by sect, with Catholics (mostly Maronites) on average earning 7173 Lebanese pounds (LL), Druzes LL 6180, Sunnis LL 5771, and Shi'is only LL 4532. Whereas Catholic wives typically had had 4.4 years of schooling and non-Catholic wives 5.2 years, Shi'i women in the survey on average had only 1.6 years of education. Among Christian wives, only 20 to 29 percent (depending on the sect) had no schooling, whereas 70 percent of Shi'i women fit in this category. Occupational differences were also pronounced. Christians tended to be in professional, technical, business, or managerial occupations to a far higher degree; Shi'is especially tended to be laborers or unskilled.[8]

The various communities have never been able to agree over Lebanon's fundamental identity and orientation and have had a tendency to look to conflicting reference groups outside Lebanon for political support and cultural sustenance. Before the civil war, the Maronites favored the status quo, emphasizing that Lebanon's unique identity stemmed from its pre-Arab Phoenecian roots. Traditionally, their external ties have been with Christian European states, particularly France and the Vatican. Although Arab speaking, many do not identify strongly with the Arab world and educated Maronites often prefer to converse in French. The Maronite sense of cultural separateness constitutes a kind of protonationalism. The fact that after the mid-1970s some sections of the Maronite community formed an alliance with the Israelis, whom other Lebanese view as their archenemy, is a good measure of their sense of isolation within the region.

Sunnis, by contrast, never fully acquiesced to their inclusion within Lebanon by the French. Their nationalism is as likely to be Arab as Lebanese. Culturally and politically, they traditionally looked to Damascus and Cairo, not Paris and Rome. These ties, and the Sunni desire to involve Lebanon more fully in the Arab world's affairs—particularly its conflict with Israel—provoked anxiety among the Maronites. The growing influence of President Nasir of Egypt among Lebanon's Muslims and his call for closer Arab unity was one of the contributing factors to Lebanon's brief 1958 civil war. Similarly, Maronites saw the Sunni alliance with the Palestinians after the late 1960s as a serious threat to the status quo. The Shi'i, Druze, Greek Orthodox, Armenian, and other communities likewise have different conceptions of what Lebanon is and should be.[9]

Muslim dissatisfaction with the maldistribution of national political power in the Maronites' favor became an increasing problem in the 1960s and was perhaps the single most important cause of the civil war. Despite the elaborate quota system for all public positions, Maronites clearly dominated Lebanon. Naturally, they were not enthusiastic about changing the system because they would be the principal losers. Shi'i discontent was particularly well founded because the 1943 National Pact was essentially an agreement between the traditional leaders of the Maronite and Sunni communities. Shi'is, now the single largest sect, are seriously underrepresented, which reinforces their disadvantaged economic and social position. The Muslims, in general, base their case for redistributing power in their favor on demographic change. The 1932 census, the base of the system, is hopelessly outdated in view of the Muslims' far higher birth rates and heavy Christian emigration. The Christians oppose taking a census for this very reason. Their demand that Lebanese émigrés be included in any count is rejected by the Muslims.

The Palestinians as a Catalyst

The presence of 400,000 to 600,000 Palestinians in Lebanon was probably the 1975–76 civil war's catalyst. These predominantly Muslim refugees, who make up 15 to 20 percent of the population and are, thus, one of the largest communities, came in three waves: after the establishment of Israel in 1948, the 1967 war, and the 1970 Jordanian civil war. At first, they remained quiet politically. The traumatic Arab defeat in 1967, however, prompted a rapid growth of Palestinian guerilla organizations, many of which used southern Lebanon as a base for attacks against Israel. The weak central government seemed powerless to control them (which angered the Maronites) or to prevent massive Israeli retaliation raids (which annoyed the Shi'is in the south, the main victims). The problem intensified after most of the Palestinian guerillas expelled from Jordan in 1970 came to Lebanon, where no one could prevent them from operating freely. The Muslims generally supported the Palestinians and welcomed them as potential allies in their struggle to gain more power. The Maronites, therefore, viewed them as disruptive and likely to upset the precarious balance on which Lebanon's continued existence depended. By the early 1970s, the Palestinian refugee camps were a virtual state within a state, and heavily armed guerillas openly flouted the central government's authority. The Maronites nervously responded by strengthening their own paramilitary organizations.

The 1975–76 Civil War

The conflict, when it finally erupted, was not simply one of Christian against Muslim. It was also between haves and have nots; between those who wanted to keep the political system intact and those who wanted to reform and secularize it; between those who favored a laissez-faire capitalist approach to economic development and a minimal role for government and those who felt Lebanon's problems required socialist solutions and a strong political center; between Lebanese and Arab nationalists; and even between different political generations. The simple, shorthand description of the two main camps as Christian rightists and Muslim and Palestinian leftists does not convey how complex and multidimensional the divisions were. For example, there were three important Maronite militias: one associated with Pierre Jamayyil's Kata'ib party (a Phalangist movement inspired by European fascist parties in the 1930s), another with Camille Sham'un's Liberals, and a third with Sulayman Franjiyah. These were by no means on good terms and much blood was shed before the Phalange emerged as the dominant Maronite faction. Nor were all Christians equally committed to the rightist camp. The Greek Orthodox and non-Arab Armenians tried to stay out of the war altogether, not always successfully because of Maronite pressure. The leftist alliance, or National Movement, consisted of about 50 often feuding organizations with disparate goals and ideologies. If most of these happened to be Sunni, Shi'i or Druze, this was less because of theology than their shared desire for change and secular reform. Sections of the traditional Muslim elite felt threatened by the National Movement and opposed it. Some Christian leftists, on the other hand, backed it. Within the leftist alliance, there were often tensions between Sunnis, Druzes, and Shi'is.

The civil war was greatly complicated and prolonged by extensive outside interference. Neighboring Syria has never fully accepted France's division of the Levant and harbors an irredentist claim to Lebanon. Significantly, it has never established an embassy in Beirut. Geographic, historic, cultural, economic, and even familial links between the two countries are close. It was perhaps inevitable that the Damascus government would become entangled in Lebanon's problems. It sent in 30,000 soldiers in 1976, at first to prevent victory by the leftist-Palestinian Muslim alliance, which might have provoked Israeli intervention and a war for which Syria was not ready, and then later to bring to heel the rightist-Christians, who formed an open alliance with Israel and thereby radically altered the region's strategic map. The Israelis involved themselves both to tie down the Syrians and to goad the Christians and Shi'is into fighting the Palestinians. In particular, they formed a close alliance with the Phalangist Maronite militias, providing them with money, arms, and training. With the collapse of the central government's authority and the rapid disintegration of the Lebanese army, Lebanon became a regional battleground. Pro-Iraqi and pro-Syrian Ba'thists attacked one another. Iraq and Iran conducted a surrogate miniwar. They, along with the Saudis, Egyptians, Jordanians, and Libyans, to name only a few, funneled an estimated $300 million annually to the 40 or so militias operating in the country. Even the various Palestinian guerilla organizations clashed.

The civil war resulted in Lebanon's de facto division into several quasi-autonomous microstates and fiefdoms (Figure 7.1). By early 1982, most of the country's northern and eastern sections had fallen under the nominal control of Syrian soldiers attached to the peacekeeping Arab Deterrent Force. The Maronite Christians controlled a tiny enclave extending from the coastal ports of Junieh and Byblos to a high mountain ridge in the interior. This zone functioned as a Maronite protostate,

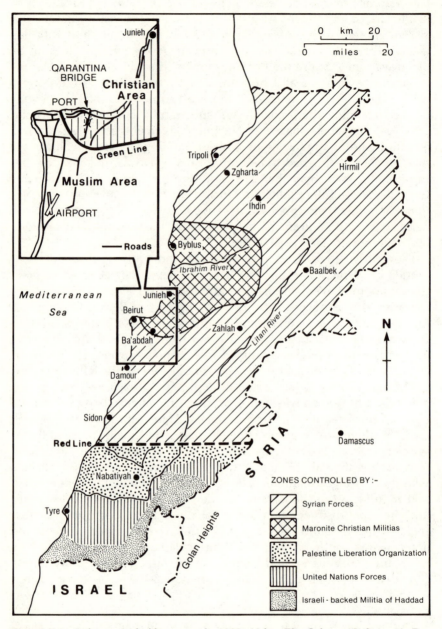

Figure 7.1 Lebanon's fiefdoms, early 1982. (After Elie Salem, "Lebanon's Political Maze: The Search for Peace in a Turbulent Land," *Middle East Journal* 33 (1979), p. 456.)

dubbed Marounistan, with its own taxes on movie tickets, restaurant checks, gasoline sales, business profits, property, and rents as well as its own infrastructure and administration. Immediately to the south of the so-called Red Line, beyond which Syrian forces could not go without risking Israeli intervention, the Palestine Liberation Organization (PLO) held sway. To its south, U.N. troops patrolled a thin strip of territory. Finally, along the southern border there was an Israeli-supported Christian buffer zone, controlled by a renegade Lebanese officer, Major Haddad. Beirut itself was divided by a Green Line into a western Muslim-leftist half and a Christian-rightist half. Interaction between the two sectors was minimal and dangerous. The Lebanese central government did not really control anywhere.

Israel's invasion of Lebanon in June 1982 to destroy the PLO, to create a "security zone" in the south, and to impose a strong Maronite central government with which it could have peaceful relations dramatically altered the situation in certain respects but changed nothing in other respects. By early 1984, the Palestinian and Syrian military presence was confined to northern and eastern Lebanon, with Israeli-backed Christian militias or the central government attempting to move into areas they had vacated. American, British, French, and Italian troops from a multinational peacekeeping force were stationed in and around Beirut in accordance with the Palestinian withdrawal agreement. However, the United States committed itself to backing the central government, which many Lebanese saw as being Maronite-dominated and hence illegitimate. Repeated attacks eventually forced the multinational forces to withdraw. In a sense, Israel, in invading Lebanon, temporarily decided the civil war in the Maronites' favor.[10] Not only were Palestinian guerillas forced to withdraw from Beirut and southern Lebanon, their leftist Lebanese allies ware temporarily disarmed. After the assassination of Lebanon's new president, Bashir Jamayyil, Israeli forces stood by while their Phalangist Christian allies went into the unprotected Sabra and Shatila Palestinian refugee camps, where they massacred 400 to 1200 Palestinians and Lebanese Shi'is.[11]

Far from solving Lebanon's problems, the Israeli invasion added to them. An astonishing 16 foreign armies and 60,000 troops were stationed in or occupied 80 percent of the country by 1983. Although Lebanese of most political persuasions and religious affiliations are exhausted by several years of fighting and many seem prepared to find common ground and rebuild the country, the central government is still weak and many scores remain to be settled. Despite the desire for peace and reconciliation—as manifested in talks among the main factions in Geneva in late 1983 and early 1984—and a new sense of Lebanese nationalism among both Christians and Muslims as a result of so much foreign involvement, Lebanon's integration prospects do not look good. Many fear that Lebanon may be partitioned between Israel and Syria, although Israel's phased withdrawal, which began in early 1985, made this less likely.

What Future?

To state that there is no easy solution is as true as it is platitudinous. A return to the pre-civil war status quo is out of the question. The ideal solution, the creation of a secular state in which religious identity is just that, seems unachievable. A few Maronites still favor partition and the establishment of their own state as the only hope for peace. Most Christians oppose this however. Such a state would most probably be an ally of Israel and, therefore, ostracized by the Arab world. Because Lebanon earns its living as an emporium and regional banking center, the loss of Arab investments could be devastating. Lebanese Muslims oppose partition both on principle and because they fear their areas would be incorporated within a Syria whose repressive government many of them have come to dislike. Partition is also opposed by Christians elsewhere in the Middle East, both because their national identity is defined by their Arabic language and culture and because the establishment of a Christian state might make their own position more precarious. The logistical and geographic problems in partitioning Lebanon would be awesome. One possible solution is the establishment of a federal state with Swiss-style cantons. This idea has some Christian and (possibly) Druze support, but it has been rejected by many Muslims as a first step to, or thinly disguised form of, partition. Any long-term solution must include a redistribution of power that takes account of demographic realities, particularly the growth of the radicalized Shi'i community. The Shi'i Amal militia is now far and away the most powerful Muslim militia in the country. The Sunnis, especially, worry about the growing role of the Shi'is. The complete withdrawal of Syrian and Israeli troops from all of Lebanon must also be engineered. Lebanon's neutralization might help assuage the security fears of its two neighbors. Finally, Lebanon's problems cannot realistically be separated from the broader question of the Arab-Israeli conflict. If there is one thing that almost all Lebanese, regardless of their religious affiliations, agree on, it is that there must be a solution to the problem of the Palestinians' statelessness—but not at Lebanon's expense.

Israel

Israel's nation-building experience cannot easily be compared with that of any other country in the area. Israel itself is a paradox. From one perspective, its national identity is the most sharply defined and assertive in the area. Israel is the political geographic incarnation and fruition of Zionist ideology, whose cardinal aim was to reconstitute the

Jewish people as an independent sovereign nation in Palestine. To a greater degree than in most Middle Eastern and North African countries, a potent state-idea preceded rather than followed the establishment of the state. There is among Israeli Jews overwhelming consensus about the state's raison d'être, if not about where its boundaries should be or about the degree to which it should be secular or theocratic. Only a tiny proportion of ultra-Orthodox Jews reject the state-idea. Israeli Jews also share an ancient common religion, Judaism, a revived national language, Hebrew, and a powerful sense of collective suffering and persecution as a people. The hostility of Israel's neighbors and periodic wars have had a pronounced centripetal effect, cementing the population together and enhancing its sense of national community.

From another perspective, Israel has formidable integrative problems. The realization of the Zionist dream depended not only on the exodus of the original Arab population, but also on massive Jewish immigration. Israel's Jewish population hails from 102 different countries. The modernization, secularization, and revival of Hebrew as a lingua franca was, therefore, a matter of necessity, not just a symbol of national reawakening. Even now, Israel's population is polygot and Hebrew is spoken with Arabic, German, Polish, English, and many other inflections. Absorbing the various *aliyas* (sequent waves of immigrants) and acculturating new arrivals has not been easy. A process that occurred over two centuries in the United States has been telescoped into less than four decades.

The Western-Oriental Division

The cleavage between Western (mostly Ashkenazi) Jews from Europe and the Americas and Oriental (mostly Sephardic) Jews from Asian and African countries, especially Arab ones, has been a major integrative problem.[12] Israel's pioneers and founders were overwhelmingly Eastern European. The second and third *aliyas* (1904–23) particularly left an indelible imprint on Israeli society. These early waves for the most part consisted of committed, idealistic Zionists who built most of Israel's characteristic institutions (e.g., the kibbutzim collective agricultural settlements and the Histadrut trade union) and infused it with their spirit and ideology. Until recently, they also dominated the national elite.[13]

At the state's establishment in 1948, almost 90 percent of all Jewish immigrants were from Europe and the Americas. Since then, there has been a massive influx of Jews from the Middle East and North Africa. In the process, Israel's character has been fundamentally altered and many of the bonds that tied the early European arrivals into a highly motivated and tightly integrated prestate national community (*yishuv*) have been loosened. Now, over half of Israel's Jews either originally came from Asia and Africa or they have parents who did. Moreover, Oriental Jewish immigrants, who had no experience of the late nineteenth-century Eastern and Central European pogroms, the holocaust, or even (strictly speaking) of classic antisemitism, conceived Israel differently from European Jews. Modern political Zionism was a product of the tragic Jewish experience in Europe. Oriental Jews felt no mission to create a model socialist society or to reestablish links with the land. In the Arab countries they left, those who worked the land were the lowliest; unlike Israel's Ashkenazi founders, they could not idealize or comprehend any ideological justification for agricultural work. No less patriotic than those who came before, they, nevertheless, lacked the same excited sense of ideological mission and social experimentation.

Culturally, socially, and economically, the Oriental Jews also differed significantly from their Western counterparts. The early European *aliyas* generally consisted of well-educated, secular, urban Jews. Many had professional backgrounds and a progressive political bent. Oriental immigrants, by contrast, were generally much poorer, less educated, less skilled, and more socially conservative. Even their food and musical tastes differed.

Differences between the two groups have persisted.[14] By the late 1960s, whereas 1 of every 6 Oriental families still had 7 or more members, only 1 of every 100 European families was of this size. Differences in educational attainment are also acute. For many years, Oriental children comprised 60 percent of all pupils at kindergarten (which is free and compulsory) but only 5 percent of secondary-school graduates and 2 percent of university graduates. Affirmative action has narrowed, but not closed, the gap. In 1977–78, of Western Jews, 70.7 percent attended secondary school compared to only 56.4 percent of Oriental Jews. Whereas 22.4 percent of Western Jews enrolled in universities, only 5.1 percent of Orientals did. Oriental Jews comprised only 17.6 percent of B.A. and 10.7 percent of M.A. and Ph.D. students, with Western Jews accounting for 70.8 percent and 82.1 percent, respectively.

Not unexpectedly, Oriental Jews generally have poorer jobs and lower incomes. By 1981, an average urban Oriental family's income was 80 percent of a Western family's income. Because of larger family size though, per capita income among Orientals was only 50 percent that of Western Jews. Some 85 percent of Israeli Jews in the poorest 20 percent of the population are Sephardic. In employment, only 12.9 percent of Israeli Jews born in Asia or Africa were in the professional category in 1977. Even among *sabras* (native-born Israelis) with Oriental parents, only 14.6 percent were classified in the professional category, suggesting that inequalities have internal structural roots no less than external causes. By contrast, 30.9 percent of Israelis born in Europe and America and 45.6 percent of native-born Israelis with European parents were professionals. Oriental Jews suffer disproportionately from poor housing and unemployment. They are more likely to be both the perpetrators and the victims of crime (reportedly some 95 percent of Jews in Israeli prisons are Sephardic).

The Ashkenazi-Sephardic cleavage is also partly geographic. The earliest, overwhelmingly European Zionist settlers concentrated on the narrow coastal plain around Tel Aviv. This posed economic as well as strategic problems. After Israel's birth, the government adopted a policy of dispersing the population into sparsely inhabited peripheral areas, where so-called new development towns were established. New immigrants, who were overwhelmingly Sephardic, thus, often found themselves steered into relatively remote regions. Some 80 percent of Jews living in towns located in the Negev and Galilee are of non-European descent. In certain towns, like Hazor, Shelomi, and Netivot, over 95 percent of the residents are Sephardic in origin. The dispersal of many Oriental immigrants to peripheral areas helped to build a sense of "ethnic peripheral solidarity against the central, European origin core."[15] Moreover, many residents of these towns still entertain a deep resentment against the Ashkenazi establishment for having "dumped" them in remote settlements, where the standard of living is lower and opportunities fewer, and for having neglected them.

Because ethnic, class, and geographic cleavages overlap and reinforce one another, the problem has a political dimension. At the elite level, inequalities are highly conspicuous. Of 277 members of the Knesset (parliament) between 1949 and 1970, 74 percent were born in Eastern or Central Europe. In the 1969–74 parliament, 80 percent of Jewish Knesset members were born in Eastern Europe or were *sabras* with European parents. Until recently, the typical cabinet might have only 2 Oriental ministers and 16 Western ones. Complaints about such imbalances have resulted in greater Oriental representation. Nevertheless, a large majority of top civil servants, judges, officers, academics, and professionals are still of European origin.

Oriental grievances culminated in a spate of demonstrations in the early 1970s led by the so-called Black Panther protest movement. A more lasting consequence, however, has been the increasing ethnic polarization of politics. In the 1969 election, 51 percent of Israelis born in Africa or Asia voted for the moderately socialist Labor Alignment and only 32 percent for the right wing Likud bloc. In subsequent elections, Oriental Jews steadily deserted Labor in favor of Likud; thus, in the 1981 contest, Labor's share of the Oriental-born vote was only 25 percent, whereas Likud won 60 percent. *Sabras* with Oriental-born parents defected to an even greater extent. The trend continued in the 1984 election, when Labor got 21.5 percent of the Oriental vote. Labor is now seen as the "establishment" party—despite its leftist orientation—with a white-collar, better educated, more affluent Western Jewish constituency. Likud's supporters, conversely, are mainly Oriental, younger, less educated, blue collar, more religious, and poorer, notwithstanding the party's commitment to laissez-faire capitalism and its close links to business interests. Ironically, whereas 14 of 47 Labor Knesset members elected to parliament in 1981 were Oriental, only 6 of Likud's 48 members were. Obviously, if the two main parties increasingly have ethnically based constituencies, this will have adverse consequences for national integration.[16]

Political polarization has been reflected in, as well as stimulated by, differing views about critical issues. Insofar as one can generalize, Sephardic Jews have been far less receptive to Israel withdrawing from territories it occupied in 1967 and far more supportive of its invasion of Lebanon in 1982 than the Ashkenazis. The implications are serious: a highly charged debate over national policy has acquired an ethnic dimension. The use of racist epithets has become increasingly common.

This fault line should be kept in perspective. Some 20 percent of all marriages are between Oriental and Western Jews. As proportionately more Israelis are native-born, differences should gradually lessen. The army, in which all Israelis have to serve, has been an effective integration instrument. Israel is not in danger of falling apart because of this particular cleavage. The ties that bind Israeli Jews far outweigh the differences that pull them apart.

The Jewish-Arab Division

Ultimately, Israel's most serious integrative problem is the division of the population into Jews and Arabs (Muslim, Christian, and Druze). Although almost 800,000 Palestinian Arabs were expelled or fled from what became Israel in 1948, some 156,000 stayed behind, mostly in the northern Galilee region. Although they were granted Israeli citizenship and voting rights, in fact they became second-class citizens in what had just been their own homeland. Zionism, like most other nationalisms, is implicitly exclusivist. Its cardinal aim is to create a Jewish state. Israel's Arabs by definition can never be full and equal members of that society, except in a narrow, nominal sense. Nor can they be expected to subscribe to the Zionist state-idea, especially because Israel was created at their expense. Israeli Jews, in turn, suspect this residual Arab population's loyalties, viewing it as a potential fifth column. A 1981 opinion poll conducted for the *Ha'aretz* newspaper indicated the depth of Jewish mistrust. To the question: "Do you think that Israel's Arabs are loyal or disloyal to Israel?" 50.8 percent of respondents answered disloyal and only 10.6 percent answered loyal.

Israel has developed an elaborate and effective system to control its Arab minority. According to Lustick, this system rests on three, interrelated mechanisms: *segmentation*, which fragments the minority internally and isolates it from the majority; *dependence*, which forces the minority to rely on the majority for resources; and *co-optation*, whereby selected minority group members are rewarded for their cooperative behavior with the provision of benefits.[17] Until 1966, Arab villages and towns in Galilee and elsewhere were declared special security zones and placed under military government for almost 20 years. As a result, the military governor could prohibit travel into or out of these areas without a written permit, banish or deport residents, and impose curfews. Under military government regulations, Arabs could be searched, seized, and detained if this was deemed necessary for security reasons, and they could be tried in closed military courts. In addition, Muslim and Christian (but not bedouin or Druze) Arabs were, and still are, exempt from military service, a principal national socialization instrument. Consequently, they are ineligible for veteran benefits (such as low interest mortgages) and excluded from jobs where security clearance is required.[18]

If Israel's Sephardic Jews have grounds to complain about discrimination, its Arabs have even more grounds. In 1982, the income of an average Arab urban household was only 70 percent of its Jewish counterpart. If rural families were compared, the gap would be far wider. Arabs also suffer from poor housing. In 1982, 32.9 percent of Arab homes had more than three people per room compared to only 1.3 percent of Jewish homes. Only 12.7 percent of Arab households had telephones compared to 65.6 percent of all households nationally. Whereas 33.5 percent of all Israeli families owned private cars, only 13.3 percent of Arab families did. The gap extends to education. In Israeli universities, Jews hold about 6000 academic positions, Arabs only about 20 (or 1 of 300, despite being one sixth of the population). The central government, which pays for most municipal services, provides Arab municipalities with smaller budgets than Jewish ones. For example, in the 1983 budget, the Arab city of Nazareth got $629 per capita. Upper Nazareth, the mainly Jewish city next door, got $1688 per capita.

In recent years, Israel has sought to alter the mostly Arab Galilee's cultural geographic complexion through the expropriation of Arab land and the settlement of Jews. A confidential 1976 report to the Israeli Ministry of Interior noted that Galilee's Arabs had become increasingly nationalistic; it suggested that Israel "expand and deepen Jewish settlement in areas where the contiguity of the Arab population is prominent" and "examine the possibility of diluting existing Arab population concentrations."[19] In 1976, opposition to Galilee's Judaization prompted the first violent mass demonstrations by Israel's Arabs since the state's creation.

For Israel the problem has worsened with time. The Arab fertility rate is 6.1, the Jewish only 2.8 and falling. Because of high birth rates, Israel's Arab population had increased by 1981 to 657,000, or 16.5 percent of the total population. Whereas the Arab population's doubling time is only eighteen years, without further immigration the Jewish population will double in forty-one years. By 2000, Israeli Arabs could account for 25 percent of the total population. Significantly, in 1981, for the first time since the state's creation, more Jews emigrated (26,000) than immigrated (15,000). The only large remaining reservoirs from which Israel could attract large numbers of immigrants in the future are the Soviet Union and the United States. Since 1970, about 260,000 Jews have left the Soviet Union (the 1.8 million remaining account for 0.7 percent of the population). However, two thirds of these ended up in the United States, not Israel. Of 9400 Jews who left the U.S.S.R. in 1981, only 1820 chose to go to Israel. Nor can Israel look to the United States as a large source of immigrants. Only 2200 U.S. Jews emigrated to Israel in 1981. Altogether, less than 1 percent of all American Jews have moved to Israel. Moreover, an estimated 250,000 to 300,000 Israelis were thought to be living in the United States in the early 1980s; the flow is opposite to what Israel would like. Some 10 percent of Israelis now live outside Israel and continued high emigration in response to Israel's chronic economic problems is a serious concern.

Israel's Arabs have traditionally voted for the small Rakka Communist party, only because Arab nationalist organizations have been suppressed. However, this pattern may change. The Arab vote for Rakka declined from 51 percent in 1977 to 33 percent in 1984. Had Arabs voted as an organized bloc in the 1981 election, they would have received 11 of the 120 seats in the Knesset and formed the third largest faction after Likud and Labor.

Israel's occupation of additional Arab territories in 1967 has aggravated its integrative problems and brought them into sharper focus. As a result of the occupation, Israel's Arab citizens, who had been cut off geographically from the Arab world, suddenly found themselves reunited, in a manner of speaking, with Palestinians in the West Bank and the Gaza Strip. These Arabs were more assertive and politicized. Contact with them and indirectly with Arabs elsewhere because of Israel's "open bridges" policy heightened Israeli Arabs' identification with the Palestinian nationalist cause and widened the chasm between them and Israeli Jews.

As will be discussed more fully in a later chapter, the inclusion of 1.3 million additional West Bank and Gaza Arabs under Israeli control has profound demographic implications. If Israel annexed the West Bank and Gaza and granted citizenship to their inhabitants, Arabs would make up 36 percent of the total population. Given high Arab birth rates and declining Jewish immigration, Arabs could be a majority by 2000. Israel cannot annex these territories and continue to function as both a democracy and a Zionist state. However, the continuation of the status quo also present a dilemma. Are the Arabs in the occupied territories forever to be deprived of the right of free and open political expression and controlled ultimately through force? Even if Israel does not annex these territories, Arabs will soon be a majority in Israeli-ruled areas. If Arabs from the occupied areas are allowed to work in Israel proper, but not to live there, as at present, will this not amount to the Bantustanization of the West Bank and Gaza? Israel will face monumental integration problems in the near future unless it surrenders areas it occupied in 1967 or expels its Arab inhabitants. The fear among Arabs that they might be driven out is very real, particularly in light of what happened in 1948–49. The question of what to do with the occupied territories has increasingly polarized Israelis.

Saudi Arabia

Saudi Arabia ranks among the better integrated countries in the region, despite its vast size, its relatively sparse and widely scattered population, and the persistence of tribal allegiances. In part, this cohesion results from the kingdom's linguistic and racial homogeneity: Saudi Arabians are profoundly conscious and proud of their "pure" Arab ancestry and have few doubts about their cultural identity. An even greater binding agent, however, is religion.

Islam as a Centripetal Force

Saudi Arabia's distinctive identity partly derives from the preeminent position accorded to Islam in the country. This finds iconographic expression in the Saudi Arabian flag, which is inscribed with the *shahada*—"There is no deity but God and Muhammad is his Messenger." Islam enjoys its high status for two reasons. First, Saudi Arabia bears the imprint of the eighteenth-century Muslim reformer, Muhammad Ibn Abdul-Wahhab, who advocated the moral and spiritual regeneration of Arabian society according to fundamental Islamic principles.[20] Wahhab followed Hanbali Sunni jurisprudence, the strictest of the four classical legal schools. Wahhabism does not reject change or innovation, but it is ultrastrict and conservative. Although Saudi Arabia is not a theocracy, the *ulama* (Islamic scholars) do play a more important role in shaping Saudi society than in most other Middle Eastern countries. Certainly, Wahhabism is a key element of the country's state-idea and clearly distinguishes it from its neighbors.

The Wahhabi movement was in a sense also a nation-building one and played a crucial role in Saudi Arabia's political geographic evolution. The mutually beneficial alliance of the ruling Sa'ud family with the movement's founder in 1744 enabled both to expand their power beyond their bases in Najd in the heart of the peninsula and to consolidate their influence and control over other tribes. Still intact, this marriage has also given the royal family formidable political legitimacy.

Islam enjoys an especially elevated status for a second reason: Saudi Arabia is the birthplace of the Prophet Muhammad and the guardian of Islam's most holy cities of Mecca and Medina. Each year, 2 million Muslims from every corner of the world perform the pilgrimage to Mecca, one of their five major religious obligations. As the spiritual and geographic center of the Islamic world, Saudi Arabia feels a special responsibility to uphold and promote Islamic values.

The Sa'ud Dynasty

The Sa'ud family has itself been a major instrument of national integration. Its contribution to the state's formation and national identity is suggested in the country's name: alone in the world, Saudi Arabia is named after the clan that founded it. King Ibn Sa'ud, the charismatic founder of modern Saudi Arabia, united the country in part through the force of his personality and in part through judicious alliance building.[21] Sa'ud's many wives and dozens of children linked the ruling family to potentially troublesome tribes, who were co-opted or neutralized. Hudson points out that the dynasty includes between 2000 and 3000 men, who occupy most of the crucial positions, and that it is "in itself an effective and elaborate political organization." Indeed, the dynasty "appears to be no less effective than the ruling single parties of neighboring revolutionary regimes. Kinship seems quite as cohesive an organizing bond as ideology. . . . It links the still-distinct regions of the country with a network of marriage and patronage connections."[22]

Regionalism

Saudi Arabia is three times the size of France but has roughly only 10 million people living in discrete clusters separated by hundreds of miles of empty desert. The kingdom lacks either a primate city, such as Cairo or Baghdad, or an obvious single core region. Moreover, regional differences are still marked. Najd, the Sa'ud family's domain, was the state's nucleus and is today its political heartland with Riyadh, the capital. This area was never controlled by the colonial powers. Surrounded on all sides by desert, it has historically been insular in outlook. To its east, across the Nafud desert, is the oil-producing Al-Hasa region, renamed the Eastern Province to lessen its sense of regional distinctiveness. Historically, this coastal area was more closely linked with Iraq, Bahrain, and even Iran than with Najd and its people lived by fishing and maritime trade as well as by oasis agriculture. In part, this orientation resulted from the presence here of an estimated 300,000 Shi'i Muslims. The Shi'is have little affinity for Wahhabi Islam (which in 1802 destroyed the tomb of their martyr, Husayn, in Karbala) and, thus, have not fully subscribed to the Saudi state-idea. The cities of Mecca, Medina, and Jiddah have always given the western Hijaz region, which was not fully incorporated within Saudi Arabia until the 1930s, a distinct identity. Unlike Najd, Hijaz has traditionally been cosmopolitan because of the annual influx of pilgrims from all over the world. In the past, many of these stayed on, making the area a melting pot. Over many centuries the pilgrimage gave Hijazi merchants an unequaled opportunity to develop commercial and trading links with distant lands. Exposed to varied cultural, intellectual, and economic influences, Hijazis have prided themselves on their sophistication and looked down somewhat at the relatively insular, ascetic, and often nomadic Najdis. Although Riyadh has now emerged as the kingdom's banking and financial as well as political capital—because this is where the oil revenues are concentrated—merchants from Hijaz, particularly Jiddah, dominate commerce. The Hijaz also provides a disproportionate share of the country's diplomats, bureaucrats, and technocrats. Not unexpectedly, a rivalry of sorts exists between the two regions.

Infrastructural Development

Massive oil revenues—some $112.6 billion in 1981 alone—have facilitated national integration by greatly strengthening the central government and by making possible ambitious development projects. In the 1981–86 five-year plan, total expenditures are projected to reach $235 billion, or well in excess of $20,000 per capita. Sigificantly, a high proportion of all government investment has gone towards tying the kingdom together. Particular attention has been given to building an extensive air transportation network. Saudia, the national airline, regularly flies to virtually every town of any size, giving the country one of the best air route systems of any developing country. Its fleet of 50 aircraft is more than twice the size of any other airline in the region. Since 1970, a total of 29 airports have been constructed. A basic road grid linking all the major cities is also under construction. Whereas in 1960 there were fewer than 2500 miles (4000 kilometers) of paved road, in 1981 there were almost 14,000 (22,400 kilometers). A 875-mile (1400-kilometer), six-lane transpeninsular highway is currently being laid and will be completed by 1986. In the 1981–86 development plan, almost 4000 miles (6400 kilometers) of additional paved road will be built.

Saudi Arabia's oil revenues have helped to unite the country in other ways too. First, they have permitted a dramatic expansion of public education. Between 1975 and 1980, an estimated $22.7 billion was spent in this sector, with the result that primary-school enrollment doubled to 1.3 million and secondary-school enrollment rose to 40,000. Although up to 80 percent of the adult population may still be illiterate, slightly under one half of children between the ages of 6 and 11 now attend school, and the enrollment ratio is expected to approach 75 percent by the end of the decade. Clearly, this expansion and the development of a national curriculum will help to promote a sense of citizenship. In addition, the kingdom's oil wealth has underwritten a variety of schemes to sedentarize nomads, who traditionally have had strong tribal but relatively weak national allegiances.

Oil has enabled Saudi Arabia to spend lavishly on national defense and internal security. During the 1970s, the country purchased $18.7 billion worth of American military equipment (opening itself to charges of dependence on the United States as well as of wastefulness). In 1980, Saudi Arabia spent more per capita on defense than any other country in the world. Obviously, this cannot guarantee the kingdom's unity, safety, or stability. But it has enhanced the power and coercive capabilities of the central government to a degree that would have been unthinkable even a decade ago.

Natives Versus Nonnatives

Perhaps the greatest threat to Saudi Arabia's unity and long-term stability has paradoxically also been created by oil. Like most oil-producing countries in the region, Saudi Arabia suffers a chronic shortage of both skilled and unskilled labor. As a result, there has been a huge influx of foreign workers. There are no reliable statistics on just how many. The government estimated that in 1975 there were 314,000, but it noted that this number was growing by 21 percent annually and would exceed 800,000 by 1980. This was probably a serious underestimate. Some experts believed there were at least 2 million foreign workers by 1983. Yemenis, who could enter the country without a passport until 1972, alone may have accounted for 500,000 to 1 million of these workers. There are said to be more Yemenis in Jiddah than in any city in Yemen. Indigenous Saudis comprise only 18.6 percent of manufacturing workers, 15.0 percent of construction workers, and 31.5 percent of those engaged in wholesale and retail trade. According to official statistics, Saudis make up only 57 percent of the labor force. In reality, they probably make up even less than this. The presence of so many aliens is changing the country's character, diluting its cultural homogeneity and exposing Saudis to new ideas. Saudi Arabia's greatest challenge in the future may be to survive in its present form when an increasing proportion of the population neither subscribes to Wahhabi Islam nor feels any particular allegiance to the Sa'ud family.

Sudan

Not even Lebanon's civil war was as bloody as Sudan's, which over 17 years took the lives of possibly 500,000 to 1.5 million people. Sudan is Africa's largest state, sharing land boundaries with eight other countries and covering an area equivalent to one third of the contiguous United States. Yet it only has a population of 20 million. Inevitably, the impress of state authority is weak, even absent, over vast areas. Because Sudan extends some 1000 miles (1600 kilometers) from north to south, it encompasses a wide range of physical environments (from desert to tropical rain forest) and modes of existence (from sedentary irrigated farming to pastoral nomadism, hunting and gathering, and slash-and-burn cultivation).

North and South

Sudan's chief integration problem results from its racial and cultural heterogeneity. Although the north is essentially Arab, the south lies within black Africa. Moreover, the population is divided into 572 tribes, who speak 26 major and dozens of minor languages. Arabs, the largest group, account for only 40 percent of the total. Racial and linguistic differences are compounded by a deep religious cleavage: whereas the north is Muslim, the south is part Christian and part animistic.[23] Significantly, Sudan's population lacks any of the bonds that attenuate and crosscut communal divisions in most other Middle Eastern and North African states.

With minor exceptions, virtually all of Sudan is part of the Nile River basin. However, between Malakal and Juba, the White Nile flows through the Sudd, an almost impenetrable swamp covering several thousand square miles. Even today, it is a buffer between north and south and makes communication arduous. Partly because of physical geography, northern and southern Sudan experienced separate histories and had different spatial orientations. Whereas the north's political, economic, and cultural contacts were with the Middle East and the Mediterranean, the south's were with black Africa. Interaction between the two was negligible until Arabs and other outsiders bent on exploitation penetrated the Sudd in the 1840s and began taking out slaves and ivory.[24]

The British, who controlled the country from 1899 until 1956, favored a system of indirect rule and treated north and south as entirely different entities until 1947. For many years, they actively discouraged interaction between the two regions. They also widened cultural and social distances among Sudanese by encouraging Christian missionary efforts and the adoption of English as a lingua franca in the south.

The British did little to develop the south economically or socially. By the mid-1940s, 483 of the 514 students in Sudan's secondary schools came from the three northernmost provinces. Even at independence in 1956, 88 percent of all secondary-school graduates were northerners. This had two important consequences. First, few southerners could be employed in local administration, so that, after independence, Arabs filled posts vacated by the British. Second, the south had no indigenous modern elite, so that at the national level Arabs were able to monopolize the country's political, economic, military, and cultural life. Black southerners felt underrepresented and neglected.

The central government's postindependence development plans concentrated all investment in the north, thus widening regional disparities and fueling black resentment. By the mid-1960s, per capita GNP was ten times higher in the north than in the south.[25] There were still virtually no tarmac roads in the south, so that tracks became impassable during the rainy season.

The Civil War

The civil war might have been averted had Sudan adopted a federal system of government. It did not because the south was deemed incapable of managing its own affairs and because northerners feared that granting the south regional autonomy might ultimately lead to Sudan's disintegration. Between 1958 and 1964 the country lived under a military regime, whose heavy-handed approach to national integration was to Arabize and Islamicize the south. It changed the south's weekly holiday from Sunday to Friday, for example, and it expelled 600 Christian missionaries, accusing them of subversion. Arabic became the south's official language, although almost no one could understand it.

By the mid-1960s, the south was in open rebellion against the Arab central government. The so-called Anya-Nya rebels received some outside assistance. Within a few years, an estimated 250,000 southern refugees had fled to Uganda and other neighboring black African states. In 1969, Ja'far al-Numayri seized power in a military coup d'état and, recognizing that neither side could win, sought a reconciliation with the south. Three years later, an agreement ending the war granted numerous concessions to the south. The Anya-Nya rebels won amnesty and were incorporated into the Sudanese armed forces. The refugees were repatriated and resettled and a commitment made to reconstruct and develop the south. English became a "working language" in the south. Most important, the south was given regional autonomy in everything except defense, foreign affairs, communications, economic and social planning, and finance. Recognizing Sudan's biracial and binational nature appeared to heal some wounds and enhanced the country's viability. Nevertheless, cleavages are deep and memories of the war so recent and bitter that national unity will necessarily be precarious for years to come. Geographic inequalities are still acute and many in the south feel the central government has done little at all to develop the region. Moreover, the imposition of Islamic law throughout the country in 1983 and an administrative reorganization of the south that suggested the central government was pursuing a divide-and-rule strategy provoked widespread black opposition. By 1984, there were reports of serious new fighting.

Libya

Libya is overwhelmingly Sunni Arab. Nevertheless, until recently, it suffered acute integrative problems. Libya is over three times the size of France but has only 3.7 million people, so population density is among the world's lowest, 4 persons per square mile (1.5 per square kilometer). Even this figure is misleading because over 90 percent of the country is virtually uninhabited desert. Almost all Libyans are concentrated on the coast around Tripoli and Benghazi, 700 miles (1100 kilometers) to the east. The remaining few live in desert oases to the south. As a result of this archipelago-like population distribution, geographic cleavages have been uncommonly strong.

Regionalism

Libya can be divided into three major regions: Tripolitania, Cyrenaica, and the far less important Fezzan in the desert south. Historically, these developed as separate geographic and political entities with their own distinct identities, political cultures, and spatial orientations. Tripolitania, with approximately two thirds of the population and the largest city, is Libya's most economically developed, socially modernized, and politically sophisticated region. Geographically, culturally, and historically, it has always been considered part of the Maghreb to the west. By contrast, eastward-looking Cyrenaica has traditionally been more conservative, in part because its largely tribal population was influenced by the fundamentalist Sanussiyyah Muslim brotherhood. The separation between Tripolitania and Cyrenaica is far greater than distance alone would suggest because desert extends to the coastline for 300 miles (480 kilometers) along the Gulf of Sirte. This desert separates not only the Tripolitanian and Cyrenaican cores, but also the Maghreb from the Mashreq, with the unfortunate result that the western margins of many maps of the Middle East—even some definitions of the Middle East—bisect Libya. Significantly, whereas Tripolitanians speak a Maghrebi Arabic dialect, Cyrenaican Arabic resembles the Egyptian variant. The west-east division was compounded in the past by the north-south orientation of trans-Saharan trade routes and by nomadic seasonal migration patterns, which exploit ecological differences between steppe and interior desert regions. For centuries, spatial interaction between western and eastern Libya was minimal, certainly less than between Tripolitania and Tunisia or Cyrenaica and Egypt.[26]

The Italians, who began their conquest in 1911, treated Tripolitania and Cyrenaica as separate colonies until 1934, when they formally combined them into Libya. Because Italy's subjugation was particularly brutal, it provoked a nationalist response and, thus, helped to define Libya's national identity as well as its political geography. After Italy's defeat in World War II, Libya's future disposition was referred to Britain, the United States, the Soviet Union, and France, but they could not agree what to do with the territory. Finally, the matter was handed to the United Nations. In the absence of any other widely supported plan, it voted in favor of Libya's independence in 1951. Libya, therefore became independent not as the culmination of a nationalist struggle, but because none of the allies knew what to do with it.

Internal regional divisions were evident from the start. Tripolitania, with its larger and more modern population, favored the establishment of a unitary state, which it would inevitably dominate. Precisely for this reason, Cyrenaica and Fezzan preferred a loose federal system of government in which all three regions had equal status and representation. Some Cyrenaicans, in fact, wanted a separate state altogether. Another problem was the location of the capital. Whereas westerners viewed Tripoli as the obvious choice, easterners insisted Benghazi be selected. So great were centrifugal forces that a loose federation seemed to offer the only prospect for long-term national unity of the three disparate regions. This arrangement lasted until 1963, when Libya became a unitary state comprised of 10 provinces. The dispute over the capital ended with a novel compromise: it would rotate between Tripoli and Benghazi. This simply drew attention to Libya's geographic disunity. The inconvenience and expense of a movable capital subsequently prompted an unsuccessful attempt to develop a compromise third permanent capital in Al-Bayda.

Infrastructural Development

Libya's nation-building problems at independence were formidable. The country was destitute and ravaged by war. Its population lacked much sense of nationhood and was overwhelmingly illiterate and uneducated as a result of Italian neglect. King Idris, who was supposed to be a symbol of national unity, was ultimately viewed as a Cyrenaican by Tripolitanians. Salvaging scrap metal from World War II battlefields was the biggest nonagricultural source of income. There were no telephone, telegraph, or radio communications between Tripoli and Fezzan's main town and a trip between the two involved five days of difficult driving across a mine-littered desert. Three currencies were in use.

The discovery of oil in the mid-1950s provided the central government with enormous revenues to lavish on economic and social development. The 1981–85 five-year plan projected investments of $62.4 billion, or $20,000 per capita. However, actual expenditures have been less because of falling oil revenues, which were more than $22 billion in 1980 but less than $10 billion in 1982. A vast road-building program has helped to break down regional isolation and encourage greater spatial interaction. Libyan Arab Airlines, which carried 259,000 passengers in 1970, transported over 1 million by 1980. Education for all children between 6 and 15 is now free and compulsory, and the number of pupils climbed from 360,000 in 1969 to 780,000 in 1977. As in several other Middle Eastern and North African countries, the oil bonanza did much to tie Libya and its people together. Simultaneously, however, the oil boom also led to an influx of foreign workers, especially Egyptians. By the mid-1970s, these made up one third (possibly more) of the total labor force, 40 percent of the unskilled workers, 65 percent of those in construction, and 90 percent of all doctors and dentists.

The Imprint of Qadhafi's State-Idea

In 1969, Mu'ammar al-Qadhafi and a group of other young officers overthrew the monarchy. In one sense, Qadhafi complicated and blurred Libya's national identity by stressing his commitment to pan-Islamic goals and by his repeated attempts to merge the country with other Arab states. However, his neighbors viewed his activist foreign policy as meddling and increasingly isolated the country. In addition, Qadhafi set Libya apart from all other Middle Eastern and North African states by attempting to fashion a society whose values, precepts, and institutions are based on his particular interpretation of Islam. His "Third International Theory," as expounded in the *Green Book*, provides a blueprint for Libya that rejects both capitalism and communism in favor of an unabashedly populist, participatory, egalitarian Islam. Libya has become a laboratory of sorts for Qadhafi's eclectic ideas. Conventional political institutions have been dismantled or modified. Embassies, for example, have become "people's bureaus" and government cabinets renamed "people's committees." Libya itself has been renamed the Libyan Arab Jamahiriyyah. This last word has no exact English equivalent, but it broadly means state of the masses and it emphasizes the populist, experimental nature of Libya's political organization. Nationalization of industry and commerce, restrictions on property ownership, and workers' control have radically transformed the economy. Factories, workplaces, businesses, schools, and government offices are all run by elected people's committees. Among the many measures designed to foster national unity have been the abolition of the regional terms Tripolitania, Cyrenaica, and Fezzan and the requirement that all street signs, shop-window notices, and the like be exclusively in Arabic. Even if many of Qadhafi's unconventional policies are reversed when he is eventually replaced, there can be little doubt that he has emphatically placed Libya on the political map—both for people inside and outside the country.

Conclusion

Of the five countries we have discussed, Saudi Arabia and Libya have the least serious unity problems. Both are well on their way to becoming reasonably well integrated. Oil revenues have enabled them to build comprehensive national communications infrastructures and to undermine regionalism. Their central governments are infinitely stronger today than two decades ago. So, too, are their national identities. If they have a nagging integrative problem in common—and it is not an unsurmountable one—it is the cleavage that has arisen between natives and nonnatives as a result of oil-boom related immigration. Saudi Arabia and Libya are typical of most Middle Eastern and North African states in the sense that their disintegration is now inconceivable.

One cannot be so sanguine about Lebanon, the Sudan, and Israel. Lebanon's civil war seems destined to simmer, if only because of outside interference from Syria, Israel, and others. Paradoxically, there is widespread recognition within Lebanon that a new modus vivendi and power-sharing arrangement must be worked out. Most Lebanese now support Lebanon's continued existence and separatist or partitionist solutions would be strongly opposed. This could change however. In addition, Lebanon could be unilaterally partitioned by external powers, namely Syria and Israel.

Certainly, objective cultural differences among the Lebanese are far narrower than those among the Sudanese, who differ in race and language as well as religion. Sudan's integration problems seem intractable. A recrudescence of the civil conflict in 1984 suggested the depth of the problem.

Israel's integrative problems are potentially explosive. The Ashkenazi-Sephardic split, though serious, does not endanger Israel's existence. But the Jewish-Arab cleavage is so profound as to be unbridgeable. Israel's current policies of colonizing and purchasing or seizing land in Arab areas it occupied in 1967 and denying fundamental rights to the politically impotent and increasingly frustrated Arabs living in these regions is a sure recipe for disaster. One can confidently predict that barring any significant territorial or policy changes, the conflict between Israeli Jews and Palestinian Arabs under their control will intensify dramatically in coming years. Numayri's overthrow in April 1985, however, revived hopes for north-south reconciliation.

Notes

1. Sa'ab Salam, a prominent Sunni politician, tells of how as a child he would write in his schoolbook, "Beirut, Syria."

2. Lebanon's ethnic arithmetic is an extraordinarily sensitive issue because so much depends on it (hence, the lack of a recent census). Estimates of community size vary widely. Many Christians still claim they make up 50 percent of the population. Other Lebanese would say that the Shi'is are more numerous than the figures in Table 7.1 suggest.

3. Michael Hudson, *The Precarious Republic: Political Modernization in Lebanon* (New York: Random House, 1968).

4. See Halim Barakat, "Social and Political Integration in Lebanon: A Case of Social Mosaic," *Middle East Journal* 27(1973): 301–318.

5. This segregation exists even at the university level. Although the American University of Beirut and Lebanese University have balanced enrollment, the University of St. Joseph was 85 percent Christian and Beirut Arab University 93 percent Muslim before the civil war. See Halim Barakat, *Lebanon in Strife: Student Preludes to the Civil War* (Austin: University of Texas Press, 1977).

6. Joseph Chamie, "Religious Groups in Lebanon: A Descriptive Investigation," *International Journal of Middle East Studies* 11(1980): 178.

7. It must be emphasized that there is still considerable local mixing. In the Shuf Mountains, for example, many villages have Druzes, Maronites, and Greek Orthodox Christians.

8. See Note 6 above: Chamie, *op. cit.*, for other details.

9. Ayatallah Khumayni has attracted a wide following among sections of Lebanon's Shi'i community for example. In poor Shi'i neighborhoods of Beirut, like Burj al-Barajnah, Khumayni posters abound.

10. In a sense, Israel has been attempting to create the kind of Lebanon for which it has long wished. The diary of Moshe Sharett—Israel's foreign minister under David Ben-Gurion and prime minister between 1953 and 1955—contains some fascinating insights into Israeli plans for Lebanon, which look extraordinarily prescient over 30 years after the fact. On 27 February 1954, Prime Minister Ben-Gurion sent Sharett a letter saying: "It is clear that Lebanon is the weakest link in the Arab League. . . . Perhaps . . . now is the time to bring about the creation of a Christian state in our neighborhood. Without our initiative and our vigorous aid this will not be done. . . . If money is necessary, no amount of dollars should be spared. . . . We must concentrate all our efforts on this issue." In an entry for 16 May 1954, Sharett recounted a meeting at which Moshe Dayan had said something to the effect that "the only thing that's necessary is to find an officer, even just a Major. We should either win his heart or buy him with money, to make him agree to declare himself the savior of the Maronite population. Then the Israeli army will enter Lebanon, will occupy the necessary territory, and will create a Christian regime which will ally itself with Israel. The territory from the Litani [River] southward will be totally annexed to Israel." See Livia Rokach, *Israel's Sacred Terrorism* (Belmont, Mass.: Association of Arab-American University Graduates, Inc., 1980): 24–29. Many Arabs fear that Israel aims to Balkanize the region into sectarian ministates that would present less of a threat to its security. In February 1982, Oded Yinon, a former senior Israeli Foreign Affairs Ministry official, argued in *Kivunim* magazine that Egypt could be divided into Coptic Christian and Muslim states; Syria into Alawi, Sunni, and Druze states; Iraq into Kurdish, Sunni and Shi'i states; and Lebanon into five parts. See Michael Jansen, *The Battle of Beirut: Why Israel Invaded Lebanon* (London: Zed Press, 1982) for details.

11. Many of those massacred were actually Lebanese Shi'is who had fled from southern Lebanon after previous Israeli raids there. The massacre was by no means unique in Lebanon's history. In the nineteenth century, Druzes massacred Maronites in the Shuf Mountains. During the civil war, Phalangists massacred thousands of Palestinians at Tal Za'tar refugee camp; Christians were the victims at Damour. Phalangist militias massacred Druze villagers in the Shuf region in 1983 after Israel withdrew.

12. See Nadav Safran, *Israel: The Embattled Ally* (Cambridge: Harvard University Press, 1981): 83–106, for a good discussion of the problem.

13. See Amos Elon, *The Israelis: Founders and Sons* (New York: Holt, Rinehart & Winston, 1971).

14. It might be noted that Israel is unique within the region in publishing statistical data on ethnic inequalities, despite their sensitivity. In most countries in the area, communal differences are simply explained away as irrelevant.

15. Yehuda Gradus, "The Role of Politics in Regional Inequality: The Israeli Case," *Annals of the Association of American Geographers* 73(1983): 396.

16. See Don Peretz and Sammy Smooha, "Israel's Eleventh Knesset Elections," *Middle East Journal* 39(1985): 86–103.

17. Ian Lustick, *Arabs in the Jewish State: Israel's Control of a National Minority* (Austin: University of Texas Press, 1980).

18. See Sabri Jiryis, *The Arabs in Israel* (New York: Monthly Review Press, 1976).

19. Reprinted in *MERIP Reports*, No. 51, October 1976, p. 12. The idea of Judaization seems to have originated with Joseph Nahman, head of Keren Keymeth (Jewish National Fund) from 1935 to 1965. In a 1953 memorandum to the Israeli minister of defense, he noted that Western Galilee "still has not been freed [*sic*] of its Arab population, as happened in other parts of the country. . . . The Arab minority centered here presents a continual threat to the security of the nation. . . . When the time comes, it will play the part played by the Germans in Czechoslovakia at the beginning of World War II" (see Note 18 above: cited in Jiryis, op. cit., p. 105).

20. See Edward Mortimer, *Faith and Power: The Politics of Islam* (New York: Vintage Books, 1982): 60–64, 159–184 on the role of Islam and Wahhabism in Saudi Arabia.

21. See Ghassane Salameh, "Political Power and the Saudi State," *MERIP Reports*, No. 91, October 1980, pp. 5–22; and Christine Moss Helms, *The Cohesion of Saudi Arabia: Evolution of Political Identity* (Baltimore: Johns Hopkins University Press, 1980).

22. Michael Hudson, *Arab Politics: The Search for Legitimacy* (New Haven, Conn.: Yale University Press, 1977): 179.

23. Edward Hoagland has jested that as a result of this fracture, Sudan is one of the few countries in the world where "you may see women veiled to the eyes and women naked to the waist in the same village." *African Calliope: A Journey to the Sudan* (New York: Penguin Books, 1981): 15.

24. See K. M. Barbour, "North and South in Sudan, A Study in Human Contrasts," *Annals of the Association of American Geographers* 54(1964): 209–226; El-Sayed El-Bushra, "Regional Inequalities in the Sudan," *Focus* 24(September–October 1975): 1–8; and Godfrey Morrison, *The Southern Sudan and Eritrea*, Report No. 5 (London: Minority Rights Group, 1973).

25. David Roden, "Regional Inequality and Rebellion in the Sudan," *Geographical Review* 64(1974): 498–516.

26. See Frank Ralph Golino, "Patterns of Libyan National Identity," *Middle East Journal* 24(1970): 338–352.

Selected Bibliography

Allen, J. A. *Libya: The Experience of Oil.* Boulder, Colo.: Westview Press, 1981.

Barakat, Halim. *Lebanon in Strife: Student Preludes to the Civil War.* Austin: University of Texas Press, 1977.

Barbour, K. M. "North and South in Sudan, A Study in Human Contrasts." *Annals of the Association of American Geographers* 54(1964): 209–226.

Cabib, Amalia. "Israel's Demographic 'Cabala'." *Intercom* (October 1981): 8–9.

Chamie, Joseph. "Religious Groups in Lebanon: A Descriptive Investigation." *International Journal of Middle East Studies* 11(1980): 175–187.

Deeb, Marius. *The Lebanese Civil War.* New York: Praeger Publishers, 1980.

El-Bushra, El-Sayed. "Regional Inequalities in the Sudan." *Focus* 24(September–October 1975): 1–8.

Entelis, J. "Ethnic Conflict and the Reemergence of Radical Christian Nationalism in Lebanon." *Journal of South Asian and Middle Eastern Studies* 2:3(1979): 6–25.

First, Ruth. *Libya: The Elusive Revolution.* Harmondsworth, England: Penguin Books, 1974.

Friedlander, Dov, and Goldscheider, Calvin. *The Population of Israel.* New York: Columbia University Press, 1979.

———. "Israel's Population: The Challenge of Pluralism." *Population Bulletin* 39:2(1984): 1–39.

Friendly, Alfred. *Israel's Oriental Immigrants and Druzes.* Report No. 12. London: Minority Rights Group, 1972.

Golino, Frank Ralph. "Patterns of Libyan National Identity." *Middle East Journal* 24(1970): 338–352.

Gordon, David C. *Lebanon: The Fragmented Nation.* Stanford, Calif.: Hoover Institution Press, 1980.

Haley, P. Edward, and Snider, Lewis W. (eds.). *Lebanon in Crisis.* Syracuse, N.Y.: Syracuse University Press, 1979.

Helms, Christine Moss. *The Cohesion of Saudi Arabia: Evolution of Political Identity.* Baltimore: Johns Hopkins University Press, 1980.

Jiryis, Sabri. *The Arabs in Israel.* New York: Monthly Review Press, 1976.

Khalidi, Walid. *Conflict and Violence in Lebanon: Confrontation in the Middle East.* Cambridge: Harvard University Press, 1980.

Lustick, Ian. *Arabs in the Jewish State: Israel's Control of a National Minority.* Austin: University of Texas Press, 1980.

Morrison, Godfrey. *The Southern Sudan and Eritrea.* Report No. 5. London: Minority Rights Group, 1973.

Owen, Roger (ed.). *Essays on the Crisis in Lebanon.* London: Ithaca Press, 1976.

Oz, Amos. *In the Land of Israel.* New York: Vintage Books, 1984.

Randal, Jonathan C. *Going All the Way: Christian Warlords, Israeli Adventurers, and the War in Lebanon.* New York: Viking Press, 1983.

Roden, David. "Regional Inequality and Rebellion in the Sudan." *Geographical Review* 64(1974): 498–516.

Roumani, Jacques. "From Republic to Jamahiriya: Libya's Search for Political Community." *Middle East Journal* 37(1983): 151–168.

Salameh, Ghassane. "Political Power and the Saudi State." *MERIP Reports* 91(October 1980): 5–22.

Salem, Elie A. "Lebanon's Political Maze: The Search for Peace in a Turbulent Land." *Middle East Journal* 33(1979): 444–463.

Salibi, Kamal S. *Crossroads to Civil War: Lebanon 1958–1976.* London: Ithaca Press, 1976.

Soffer, Arnon. "The changing situation of majority and minority and its spatial expression—The case of the Arab minority in Israel," in Nurit Kliot and Stanley Waterman (eds.), *Pluralism and Political Geography: People, Territory and State,* pp. 80–99. New York: St. Martin's Press, 1983.

Wright, John. *Libya: A Modern History.* Baltimore: Johns Hopkins University Press, 1982.

8

Regional Integration: Prospects for Arab Unity

Spatial integrative processes, like centripetal and centrifugal forces, occur at a variety of scales. In much the same way that individual states are being tied together, regional links are also gradually being forged. These range from simple bilateral or multilateral cooperation in specific spheres to functional economic integration and even occasionally complete political amalgamation. Potentially, regional integrative processes could redraw the political map in Arab sections of the Middle East and North Africa. The partitioning of political space could yet be reversed.

We confine ourselves here to examining prospects for regional integration within the Arab world. Although Iran, Turkey, and Cyprus do have important ties with other Middle Eastern and North African countries and participate in various minor regional cooperation schemes, there is no possibility that they will surrender their sovereignty and unite with their Arab neighbors. Israel is virtually isolated within the region. Among many Arabs, by contrast, there is still a nagging sense that the political map is a capricious colonial artifact that reflects the interests of the outside powers who drew it, not the aspirations of those who inherited it, and that its drafting is neither final nor complete. Pan-Arabism—the belief that the Arabs could surmount the artificial boundaries separating them—was one of the chief ideological currents in the region during the 1950s and early 1960s. However, many Arabs have been disillusioned by their lack of success in achieving unity. Attachments to the individual 21 Arab states are now openly cultivated by their governments. The difficulties of merging Arab countries is universally recognized. The dream of joining the Arabs together into one nation-state is today largely seen as unrealistic. But the desire for closer cooperation and, among some states, for loose confederation is very much alive.

The prospect of unity tantalizes all Arabs to some degree. Arabic is the world's fifth most commonly spoken language after Chinese, English, Spanish, and Russian. Were the Arab countries to merge, the resulting state would extend almost 5000 miles (8000 kilometers) from west to east, or one fifth of the way round the globe. Its total area, 5.3 million square miles (13.7 million square kilometers), would be second only to the Soviet Union and considerably larger than Europe, Canada, China, or the United States. Such a state would have had a population in 1984 of roughly 180 million, a figure exceeded only by China, India, the Soviet Union, and the United States. By 2000, it would have more people than either of the two major superpowers. This state would contain almost two thirds of the world's proven oil reserves. It would also have enough capital to finance its own economic and social development. Conceivably, it could feed itself if Sudan's vast agricultural potential were tapped. Access to a huge market could stimulate rapid industrial growth, especially in countries like Egypt. Present regional inequalities could ultimately be lessened and the mismatch between labor-surplus and labor-short areas corrected. The aggregate military strength and political influence of this strategically located state would be formidable and possibly qualify it as a second-tier world power. It is easy to comprehend why this dream has long intoxicated Arab nationalists.

Unfortunately, the discrepancy between hope and reality is immense and a source of anguish to all Arabs. Even those who favor the loosest form of political association among the existing states can claim only modest successes. The Arab world's political disunity has generally been far more apparent than its unity. In focusing attention exclusively on political relations among Arab states, however, one may make unduly pessimistic predictions about the region's integration prospects and neglect the numerous small, less obvious ways in which they have grown closer together since the mid-1940s. Because inter-Arab conflict seems endemic, it is easy to forget that there is also a great deal of cooperation. As spatial interaction multiplies and infrastructural links are forged, a regional system is gradually emerging. This incremental, functional integration may be more important than what happens in the political realm in the long term because it is less easily reversed. In the future, subregional groups of Arab countries may find themselves so closely tied together that political disagreements among them become irrelevant or unaffordable.

In this chapter, we examine what impels Arabs to seek unity, what obstacles stand in their way, and how effective various integration schemes have been.

The Bases of Arab Unity

Issawi has succinctly characterized the unity of the Arabs as that of a people "inhabiting a definite stretch of territory, bound by ties of kinship, speaking a common language, sharing common historical memories, and practicing a common way of life, expressed in the form of religion and other cultural traits."[1] Because Arabs share many attributes besides language, they believe they belong to one nation *(qawm)*, despite being distributed among many states. This belief has sustained Arab nationalism and pan-Arabism, but it has not precluded growing attachment to the individual Arab states.[2]

Some have equated the Arabs' current fragmentation with that of the Germans and Italians before their respective political unifications in the nineteenth century. Others have drawn an analogy with the Anglo and New World Hispanic realms. In reality, the Arabs' situation falls somewhere in between and has no counterpart elsewhere. The kinship Arabs feel is far stronger than that among English speakers of North America, Britain, Australia, and New Zealand or Spanish speakers of Middle and South America. At the same time, their bonds are somewhat less than would be found among people within one nation-state. Consequently, Arabs themselves disagree about the meaning and relevance of pan-Arabism.

Language

Language is the glue that binds all Arabs together, transcending religious, tribal, and regional differences. Arabic, in its written and classical forms, does not vary geographically. The Qur'an, whose Arabic cannot be changed, ensures uniformity and standardization. Thus, literate Arabs from Morocco to Oman can all read the same newspapers, classic works of literature, and history books. Colloquial Arabic, however, does differ geographically, especially among the less educated. Although a Moroccan intellectual could converse with a Syrian intellectual if they used the classical form, peasants from these two countries would have serious difficulties communicating because of pronunciation and idiomatic differences. Nevertheless, the rapid spread of literacy has expanded the number of Arabs familiar with the classical form, which is a kind of lingua franca. News broadcasts from any Arab capital would be equally easily understood anywhere in the Arab world. The diffusion of radio, television, and cinema have exposed Arabs to one another's dialects, particularly Egyptian Arabic. The Maghrebi dialects are most difficult for other Arabs to comprehend.

Religion

Religion is one of the most important of the many bonds among Arabs. Islam is explicitly a universal religion and strives to appeal to all races and peoples. Not all Arabs are Muslim and most Muslims are not Arab. The terms Arab and Muslim, therefore, cannot in any sense be equated. Nevertheless, the nexus between the two is central to understanding the Arab national identity. Islam is an integral component of Arabism. Even Christian Arabs recognize how profoundly Islam has shaped their cultural identity. God chose to transmit His message through an Arab, Muhammad. Because His words were perfect, they cannot be changed, so translations of the Qur'an are not permissible substitutes for the original Arabic version, even among non-Arabs. The Arabs were responsible for diffusing Islam spatially, carrying it well beyond the confines of its Arabian peninsula hearth. Conversely, Arabs occupy a vast area largely because of religious expansion. Prior to the seventh century, they were restricted largely to the Arabian peninsula.[3]

Islam integrates the Arabs in the sense that it affects virtually every sphere of life and prescribes a code of behavior that binds all Muslims, regardless of race or language, into a spiritual community (*ummah*). Throughout the *Dar al-Islam* (Islamic domain), Muslims are obliged to honor the so-called five pillars (or basic duties), which provide most of the region's inhabitants with common experiences. One of the pillars is prayer at five appointed times each day. The form and content of these prayers vary little geographically. Significantly, all Muslims pray facing Mecca, which emphasizes their oneness and Islam's centripetal role. All Muslims are also supposed to profess their faith, repeating the phrase "There is no deity but God and Muhammad is his Messenger," give alms to the needy, fast totally during the daylight hours for the 28 days of the Ramadan lunar month, and make a pilgrimage (*hajj*) to Mecca at least once in their lifetime. The *hajj* serves especially to reinforce a profound sense of belonging to the Islamic community. In recent years, over 2 million Muslims have made the trip to Mecca during the appointed week. The *hajj* is one of the principal forms of spatial interaction among Muslims and one way in which Islam's unity has been preserved over the centuries. A high proportion of pilgrims are Arab. In 1982, for instance, of 853,555 foreign (non-Saudi) pilgrims, 396,882 (46 percent) came from Arab countries (see Table 8.1).

Arab societies show their Islamic heritage in numerous other ways, too. Education and religious instruction were, until recently, virtually synonymous because secular schools did not exist. Islam, therefore, moulded intellectual and scholastic traditions. The Islamic heritage also pervades political life, explicitly shaping the institutional and ideological development of such disparate states as Saudi Arabia and Libya. Even in relatively secular, progressive states, leaders must appear to be devout or have a modicum of legitimacy among those who are. Fundamentalists have been a strong and growing political force almost everywhere in the region. For centuries, a common Islamic legal code, the *shari'ah*, linked the Arabs. Although modern secular codes have largely replaced it, Islamic courts are often still responsible for marriage, divorce, inheritance, and other matters of personal status. The *shari'ah*'s legacy and influence are considerable. Throughout the Arab world, Islam has etched the cultural landscape and graced it with its ubiquitous

Table 8.1

Pilgrims Arriving from Foreign Countries by Nationality and Mode of Arrival, 1982 (A.H. 1402)

Nationality	Total	By Land	By Sea	By Air
Arab Countries				
Egypt	98,408	3,542	24,403	70,463
Yemen Arab Republic	63,241	50,528	4	12,709
Algeria	40,400	271	—	40,129
Sudan	26,983	222	355	26,406
Jordan	25,429	23,056	2	2,317
Iraq	23,179	21,849	—	1,330
Morocco	18,686	339	1	18,346
Libya	17,787	6	1,844	15,937
Tunisia	9,645	204	3	9,438
Oman	9,473	8,657	18	800
People's Democratic Republic of Yemen	9,085	116	—	8,969
Kuwait	6,558	4,955	—	1,603
United Arab Emirates	5,812	1,298	15	4,499
Palestine	3,680	1,600	6	2,074
Bahrain	3,109	22	2,307	780
Somalia	2,483	71	528	1,884
Lebanon	1,723	1,480	—	243
Mauritania	1,559	2	—	1,557
Qatar	1,118	1,020	2	96
Djibouti	632	—	—	632
Total Arab Countries	396,882	120,090	29,491	247,301
Non-Arab Asian Countries	341,159	53,637	26,144	261,378
Non-Arab African Countries	110,390	36	99	110,255
European Countries	4,220	597	1	3,622
American Countries	700	30	—	670
Australia	71	2	—	69
Miscellaneous Nationalities	133	3	—	130
Total	853,555	174,395	55,735	623,425

Source: Adapted from *Statistical Yearbook 1402 A.H.—1982 A.D.* Riyadh: Kingdom of Saudi Arabia, Ministry of Finance and National Economy, Central Department of Statistics, 1982, pp. 206–208.

symbols, notably the mosque. Even gardens, conceived as earthly models of paradise, show a religious inspiration. Art and architecture, with their emphasis on Qur'anic calligraphy, avoidance of depicting human forms, and widespread use of arabesque ornamentation suggest how Islam traditionally defined aesthetic tastes. Finally, Islam has fortified the Arabs' sense of unity by providing them with shared historical memories. Pride in the achievements of the early Islamic Umayyad and Abbasid empires serves to remind them of their past glory and unity. The Ottoman Empire, which nominally united most of the Arab world for the four centuries preceeding its twentieth-century fragmentation, was at root an Islamic one.

The geographic, cultural, and historical ties that bind Arabs together are, therefore, many. The failure of the Arabs to create a state encompassing this "nation" can only be understood by reference to a multiplicity of centrifugal forces.

Obstacles to Regional Integration

Geographical Factors

Geography divides as well as unites the Arabs. The Arab world's immense size, which makes the prospect of unity so enticing, is in itself an obstacle to regional integration. Until well into this century, travel from one end to the other took weeks. The advent of modern air transportation and mass communications have resulted in significant time-space convergence, but they can never wholly negate the centrifugal effects of distance. The settlement pattern compounds the problem. Because of pronounced geographic variations in precipitation and water availability, settlement is discontinuous and clustered in narrow coastal bands, in uplands exposed to moisture-bearing winds, along river valleys, and around oases. Vast empty arid spaces typically separate these concentrations (see Figure 8.1).

This discontinuous settlement pattern encouraged subregional particularism because, until recently, transportation links among population clusters were absent or deficient. The colonial powers built transportation networks geared to exporting raw materials rather than to serving regional or even local needs.[4] Improvements in the regional grid were delayed by the area's political fragmentation and by the feeling that traffic levels did not justify the enormous expense they would entail. Since independence, national planners have devoted most of their attention to upgrading transportation links within their countries. Unfortunately, insufficient attention has been paid to the interrelationships between adjacent national transportation systems and to the coordination of plans; some sections of international routes, therefore, suffer chronic congestion, whereas others have a wasteful overcapacity. Because regional transportation planning is still in its infancy, international links are still generally inadequate and often made in an ad hoc, haphazard manner.[5]

There has been substantial progress in improving road and rail links within the Arab world since the 1960s, especially between the Mediterranean and the Gulf and within the Arabian peninsula. Before the end of this century, the international road network may be essentially complete. The rail system might also be expanded to provide a more direct connection between Syria and Iraq. The former Hijaz line between Jor-

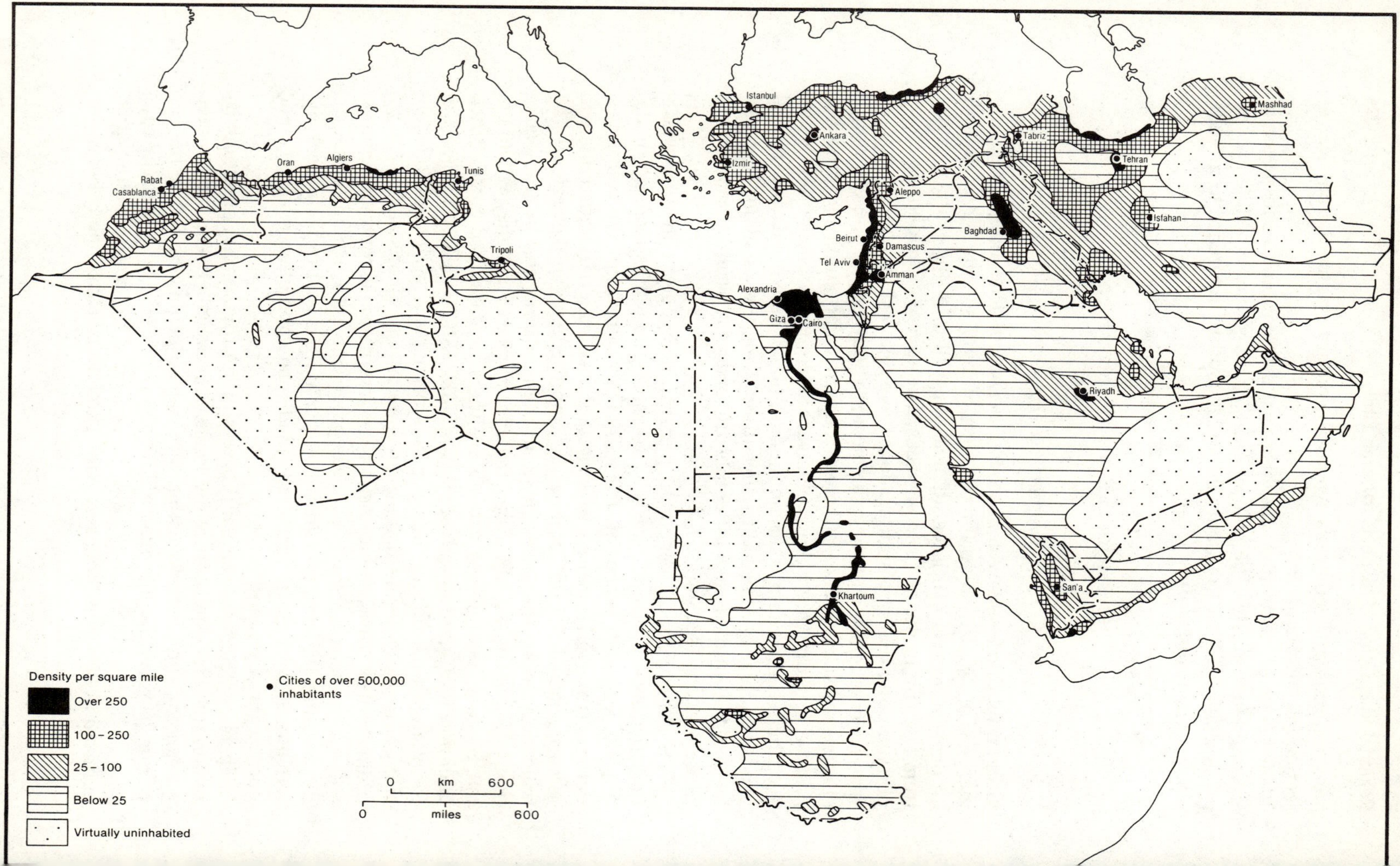

Density per square mile

	Over 250
	100 – 250
	25 – 100
	Below 25
	Virtually uninhabited

• Cities of over 500,000 inhabitants

Mashhad
Tehran
Isfahan
Tabriz
Riyadh
San'a
Baghdad
Aleppo
Damascus
Amman
Ankara
Beirut
Tel Aviv
Izmir
Istanbul
Cairo
Guiza
Alexandria
Khartoum
Tripoli
Tunis
Algiers
Oran
Rabat
Casablanca

0   600
km

0   600
miles

dan and Medina or Jiddah in western Saudi Arabia might be rebuilt. Preliminary plans exist to construct a new line from Basra along the eastern edge of the Arabian peninsula to Oman and to extend Saudi Arabia's line between Damman and Riyadh across the peninsula to the Red Sea. If all these lines are built, the Middle East will have a reasonably complete network (Figure 8.2).

Adequate transportation links are a precondition but not a guarantee of greater integration within the Arab world. Time-consuming, cumbersome, and arbitrary border-crossing formalities still often impede interaction. Crossing the Syrian-Jordanian border, for example, took 3 or 4 hours in 1984. Immigration and customs procedures need to be standardized and simplified considerably if Arab unity is to mean anything. More important, borders have to be kept open. Too frequently they have been closed altogether during political disputes between neighboring regimes. This can obviously have an impact beyond the parties immediately involved. For over three decades, Israel has severed all overland connections between Egypt and the Arab countries to its east. Recent hostility between Egypt and Libya has similarly affected links between the Maghreb and the Mashreq. One of the main offenders has been Syria, which has closed its borders and airspace to Jordanian and Iraqi traffic on several occasions. The most recent closure of its border with Iraq in 1982 disrupted both the movement of Iraqi oil to the Mediterranean and trade between Europe and the entire Gulf region.

Historical Factors

Partly because of the Arab world's areal extent and discontinuous settlement pattern, the historical experiences of its constituent parts have frequently diverged. Consequently, Moroccans, Tunisians, and Egyptians, among others, often have a strong sense of *wataniyyah* (patriotism for their respective countries) as well as of *qawmiyyah* (Arab nationalism). In the past, these local nationalisms were ignored or belittled as unacceptable manifestations of *iqlimiyyah* (regionalism). Failure to make allowances for countries' different historical experiences doomed many a unity scheme by creating unrealistic expectations. There is a far greater willingness now to recognize that the Arab world's diversity does not necessarily preclude its unity.

One of the more important historical differences among the Arab countries is the degree to which they were affected by Western colonial intrusion. Some, like Algeria and Libya, were brutally subjugated and experienced large-scale colonization by European settlers. Others escaped direct colonial control altogether (Yemen Arab Republic [Yemen

---

Figure 8.1 Population distribution.

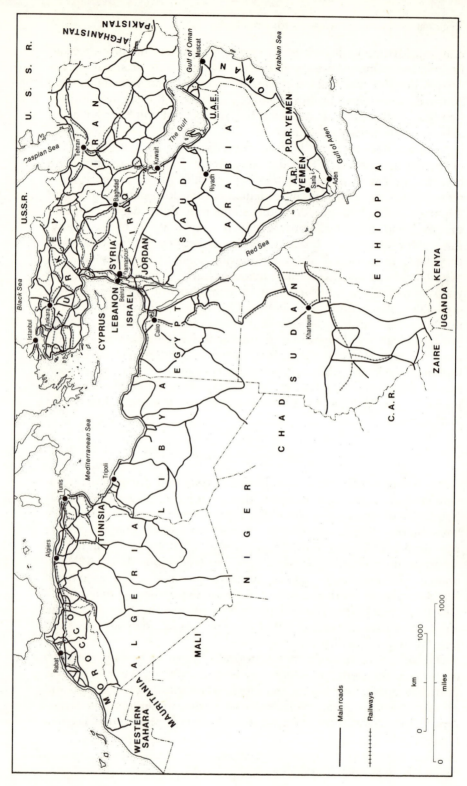

Figure 8.2 Major roads and railways in the Middle East and North Africa.

A.R.] and Saudi Arabia) or had relatively superficial and limited treaty relationships with a colonial power (Kuwait, the former Trucial shaykhdoms, and Oman). In countries like Egypt, Lebanon, and Syria, substantial Western capitalist penetration resulted in major economic transformation and altered class relationships. Elsewhere it was insignificant and the traditional subsistence economy and social structure were left almost intact.

The European colonial powers used different methods and had diverse objectives. The French considered Algeria an integral component of metropolitan France and tenaciously clung to it until 1962, when they were compelled to relinquish it after a bloody struggle. By contrast, they ruled Morocco as a mere protectorate and granted it independence after less than 50 years. Tunisia, too, did not suffer the radical dislocation experienced by Algeria as a result of French colonialism. France's imprint was least discernible in Syria and Lebanon, which it controlled as League of Nations mandated territories only between the two world wars. The similarities among these countries as a result of their French colonial heritage are, thus, rather superficial. The British generally favored indirect rule through traditional local elites. Their involvement was considerably deeper in places like Egypt and Aden, which had an economic or strategic significance, than in countries like Iraq and Jordan, which they abandoned quickly and relatively uneventfully. Their mark on the Gulf shaykhdoms was relatively shallow, with the exception of Bahrain. Italy's only interest was in Libya, which it viewed in much the same way France regarded Algeria, except on a smaller scale. Unlike the French, the Italians made no attempt to assimilate Arabs into their culture, with the result that Libya's Italian legacy is today somewhat meager. Libya's independence also came serendipitously as a result of Italy's defeat in World War II and not as the culmination of a protracted war on national liberation. Spain's colonial interests in the Middle East and North Africa were confined to relatively small parts of Morocco, some of which to this day have a distinct personality.

Colonial rule heightened differences among Arab countries by imposing institutions and traditions patterned after those of the colonial power. In areas controlled by France a Francophone and Francophile elite usually emerged. Even now the political, administrative, and educational apparatus of these states show French influences. In British-held territories, English acquired a special status and national institutions often reflected the tastes and prejudices of British officials. Whereas the French bequeathed republicanism, the British favored monarchies. The cleavage between former French and British colonies is not of great significance today, even though it has not been completely surmounted. In the early postindependence era, however, it hampered regional integration efforts among the Fertile Crescent countries, which might otherwise have formed the nucleus of a larger pan-Arab state.

The colonial powers, when they created new states, bolstered traditional local ruling classes, which quickly developed vested interests in perpetuating the Arab world's political fragmentation. After independence, few were willing to dissolve their states and sacrifice their power in the name of Arab unity. The colonial powers' role in dividing the Arabs, therefore, goes far beyond mere boundary drawing. Indeed, boundaries were probably the least of their legacies and simply symbolized other deeper divisions the colonial powers had purposely or unwittingly fostered.

National Integration Problems

Acute national integration problems within individual countries have also impeded Arab unity. Although the vast majority of the Arab world's population is Arabic speaking and Muslim, there are, as we have seen, significant linguistic and religious minorities in certain countries. These groups have generally viewed Arab unity with apprehension or hostility. Lebanon's Christians secured from their Muslim compatriots a commitment to uphold the country's independence and not seek its unification with Syria or any other Arab state for this very reason. Egypt's Coptic Christian minority has similarly preferred to stress the country's Egyptian, as opposed to Arab, identity. In Iraq, any government seeking Arab unity must heed the concerns of the large Kurdish-speaking population. In Morocco and Algeria, many Berbers are not enthusiastic about being incorporated within a larger Arab state. Sudanese regimes have learned that unity schemes antagonize the large black minority.[6] Syria's Sunni Arabs have generally been more receptive to Arab unity than its Alawis, Druzes, Christians, and Kurds. No country with acute internal problems can realistically entertain hopes of successfully participating in a far-reaching regional integration scheme without aggravating intercommunal relations. Merging two poorly integrated states together is more likely to compound their problems than to produce one well-integrated state.

Political Factors

It was observed in the early 1960s that if one was "to measure the density of national tensions and stresses in terms of unit areas, the Middle East would lead all other regions."[7] This is no less true today. Syria's foreign minister, Abd al-Halim Khaddam, in a 1980 speech, lamented that "if we look at the map of the Arab homeland, we can hardly find two countries without conflicts."[8] Political differences among the Arab states are by far the single greatest obstacle to their unification. The differences, which stem in part from locational and historical factors, are both structural and ideological. Until the late 1960s, a chasm separated the Arab world's traditional, conservative, capitalist, and Western-oriented monarchical regimes and its modernizing, reformist, socialist, and neutralist or Eastern-leaning republican ones. This dichotomy resulted in what was aptly termed the Arab Cold War.[9] Saudi Arabia, Jordan, Morocco, the Gulf shaykhdoms, Oman, Iraq (until 1958), and Libya (until 1969) belonged in the conservative category. The radical camp's main members were Egypt, Syria, Algeria, People's Democratic Republic of Yemen (P.D.R. Yemen) and, after their monarchies were overthrown, Iraq and Libya. Countries like Tunisia, Lebanon, and Sudan did not fit neatly into either group. Unity between countries belonging to the two camps was inconceivable, so fundamental were the differences. The categorization of states as radical or conservative is crude and does not adequately convey the scope and complexity of inter-Arab political differences before the late 1960s. Neither camp was itself united. Numerous dynastic rivalries and personal squabbles divided the monarchical regimes for instance. Until the 1958 Iraqi revolution, the closely related Iraqi and Jordanian kings remained united in their antagonism towards the Saudi dynasty, which had expelled the Hashimite royal family from its base in the Arabian peninsula earlier in the century. The royal families of the Arabian peninsula also had numerous disagreements. Although the various monarchies would occasionally stick together for mutual protection, they were unwilling to surrender their power in the interests of Arab unity. Kingdoms, by their very nature, are not amenable to thorough political integration with one another. To the extent that Arab monarchs have sought unity, it has been of the most limited, loose variety.

The republics have been the main proponents of pan-Arabism. Nevertheless, their record is no better than that of the monarchies. Even when regimes seem compatible, integration eludes them because of rivalries and jealousies. Some of the most bitter disputes in the Arab world have been between ostensibly like-minded radical regimes. Iraq and Syria, although both ruled by the Ba'th party, whose original raison d'être was to unite all Arabs, have had an epic feud for example. The last three decades are littered with the remains of failed or stillborn unity schemes between broadly similar regimes, most prominently Egypt and Syria (1958–61); Egypt, Syria, and Iraq (1963); Egypt, Sudan, Libya, and Syria (assorted schemes in various combinations between 1969–73); and Syria and Iraq (1978–79).

The gap between the republics and monarchies has narrowed since the late 1960s, when Egypt and Saudi Arabia, traditionally the leaders of the two camps, mended relations following the solution of the Yemeni civil war and the 1967 Arab-Israeli War. The accession to power of Anwar al-Sadat as president of Egypt strengthened the rapprochement and resulted in a measurable relaxation of tensions within the region since Nasir, the former charismatic Egyptian leader, had been the monarchies' nemesis. The massive infusion of petrodollars into the region after the oil-price explosion of the early 1970s also moderated the conflict between the monarchies (many of which became fabulously rich) and the republics (which, with the exception of Iraq and Libya, remained poor). After the 1967 Arab-Israeli War, but especially after the early 1970s, Saudi Arabia, Kuwait, the Gulf shaykhdoms, and other oil producers began making large payments to the frontline states of Egypt, Syria, and Jordan. This mutually convenient arrangement softened antagonisms and gave the traditional monarchies a new influence within the region. Significantly, conservative regimes were far more secure in the 1970s than in previous years, when countries like Egypt and Syria had openly agitated for their overthrow.

Nevertheless, acute political differences remain. Occasionally these still have an ideological basis. Libya's vitriolic attacks on Egypt because of its separate peace treaty with Israel and on Saudi Arabia, whose rulers it depicts as U.S. stooges, are an example. Frequently, enmity between countries stems from historic rivalries or regional power struggles. The river-based civilizations of Egypt and Iraq have traditionally aspired to become the Arab world's center of political gravity, for instance; at times, this has resulted in tension between these two countries. Similarly, Iraq and Saudi Arabia, although not on bad terms, are today competing to become the dominant Arab power in the Gulf region. As we have seen, boundary and territorial disputes can poison neighborly relations. President Hafiz al-Asad of Syria, in a 1980 speech, asked in frustration: "Where are the Arab states that have no border disputes? If we take a look at the Arab homeland, form the exteme east to the extreme west, we can hardly find an Arab state with no border disputes."[10]

In a few instances, political tensions result from a small and relatively weak state's apprehensions that a more powerful, sometimes bullying, neighbor is constraining its freedom of action. Many of the Gulf shaykhdoms and the Yemen A.R., for example, fear Saudi Arabia.[11] More generally, a great many states have at one time accused neighbors of interfering in their internal affairs. Oman, for instance, has repeatedly charged the P.D.R. Yemen of providing a sanctuary for guerillas seeking to overthrow the sultanate. The two Yemens, in turn, have blamed one another for fomenting internal disturbances and have clashed along their common border. A striking number of neighbors are, or have been, political antagonists: Syria versus Jordan, Lebanon, and Iraq; Libya versus Egypt, Sudan, and Tunisia; and Morocco versus Algeria—to name but a few.

Political instability has also impeded regional integration. Unity schemes usually tie authoritarian regimes, not states and peoples, together; thus, they are poorly equipped to withstand political change. Successive governments typically exhibit little continuity in their foreign policies. Military coups d'état have aborted many a proposed integration plan.

Differing views about how to solve the dispute with Israel have been another major source of political cleavage within the Arab world. Although all Arabs agree that Israel should withdraw from the territories it occupied in 1967, including East Jerusalem, and that the Palestinians must have a state of their own, they have disagreed about how to achieve these goals. Prior to the adoption of a common position at the 1982 Fez summit of Arab heads of state, the Arab world was split at least three ways: (1) the maximalist "Steadfast and Confrontation Front," consisting of Syria, Algeria, Libya, P.D.R. Yemen, and the Palestine Liberation Organization (PLO); (2) those regimes favoring the moderate Saudi Fahd peace plan; and (3) the few countries, like Morocco, Sudan, and Oman, that implicitly agreed with Egypt's approach and the Camp David framework. The Arab-Israeli conflict has exacerbated all other differences within the Arab world.

The Middle East's vast oil resources and location at the junction of three continents immediately south of the Soviet Union ensure it will be the object of superpower rivalries. The Arab-Israeli dispute widened outside involvement by providing opportunities to project the Cold War into the area and to win friends and clients through large arms sales and economic assistance programs. This has seriously impeded regional integration by accentuating differences within the Arab world. On occasion, the superpowers have seemed to treat the area as a playground, obsessively searching for military bases and using states as their surrogates. Any unity scheme that seems to extend one superpower's influence is immediately met with suspicion by the other. The United States opposed the Egyptian-Syrian union of 1958–61 and the proposed Syrian-Iraqi merger of 1978, for instance, whereas the Soviet Union today depicts the efforts of several Arabian peninsula countries to create a Gulf Cooperation Council, which the United States supports, as a thinly disguised way of consolidating American control of the region. This pattern is not new. Until the late 1940s, the French were hostile to any Arab unity scheme that appeared to further the position of Egypt, Iraq, or Jordan (and, thus, Britain), whereas the British were chary of any unity talk that emanated from Syria (and, thus, might expand French influence). Pan-Arabists often assert that throughout the twentieth century outside powers have followed a policy of divide and rule in the region. Although there is an element of truth in the charge, the failure of Arab unity cannot be ascribed solely to external factors.

Economic Integration

A growing number of Arabs argue that political unity cannot be achieved unless solid foundations are first built through incremental functional cooperation, particularly in the economic sphere, as in Europe. Theoretically, the advantages of economic integration are considerable. An enlarged market of 180 million would permit economies of scale and broaden and diversify the agricultural and industrial production base. Closer economic cooperation and coordination could also encourage greater functional specialization by maximizing comparative advantages associated with spatial variations in resource endowment and factors of production. Other advantages might include increased trade through the reduction or elimination of tariff and nontariff barriers, expanded investment opportunities as a result of the elimination of restraints on capital mobility, and improved efficiency and equitability in the allocation and distribution of resources. In sum, economic integration could accelerate the region's development as a whole.

Economic Disparities: Capital Rich and Capital Poor States

The numerous obstacles to economic integration are, unfortunately, often no more easily surmounted than those to political integration. It is axiomatic that if two countries are to unite, they must both believe that the advantages outweigh the disadvantages. Few Arab countries have reached this point, except in the most abstract sense, because the asymmetries among them are too glaring. Arab countries differ enormously in their population size, resource endowment, economic structure, labor force, development orientation, trade patterns, and living standards. Smaller states invariably fear being overwhelmed by larger ones, less developed by the more developed, and richer by the poorer.

Waterbury has suggested a useful, if imperfect, fivefold classification of Arab states based mostly on economic considerations.[12] This typology underlines why economic unity may be difficult to achieve. His first category includes the states of Algeria, Iraq, and (less convincingly) Morocco. These depend heavily on raw material exports of oil, gas, or phosphates; are big; have relatively large populations of 14 to 22 million; and have good agricultural bases, reasonably well-developed transportation and communications infrastructures, and sizable skilled labor forces, as well as growing technocratic and managerial elites, expanding industrial bases, and a capacity to absorb export revenues productively. As a result, their long-term development prospects are reasonably good, even if in 1982 per capita incomes were still comparatively low ($860 to $3000).

The second group includes Saudi Arabia, the United Arab Emirates (U.A.E.), Kuwait, Libya, Oman, and Qatar, whose economies are artifacts of the oil boom. Without oil, they would be among the world's very poorest states instead of its most prosperous. In 1982, per capita GNP was $23,770 in the U.A.E. and $21,880 in Qatar compared to only $13,160 in the United States. Generally, these countries have small populations (only Saudi Arabia has significantly more than 3 million); a small, if affluent and increasingly saturated, local market; little or no agriculture; a narrow, although growing industrial base; an immature infrastructure; a tiny skilled indigenous labor force; and an acute shortage of homegrown technocrats and managers. Many of their fundamental weaknesses are disguised by their ability to purchase and import wholesale the paraphenalia of development. Without foreign workers, their economies would grind to a halt. Even after lavish expenditures on arms and ambitious social and infrastructural development, these countries still accumulate huge capital surpluses that cannot be productively absorbed locally. Other poorer Arab countries have sought access to this pool of capital to finance their own development and to promote the region's integration. Whether these oil-producing states can use the few years they have left before their oil runs out to build self-sustaining economies remains uncertain. Saudi Arabia probably has the best prospects.

Egypt, Syria, Tunisia, and Sudan fall into Waterbury's third category, although some might question Sudan's inclusion. Despite major differences among them, these states have typically begun industrializing and have a solid agricultural base; good road, rail, and port facilities; an adequate skilled and unskilled labor force; and a sizable domestic market. Generally, their growth potential is good, but unlike states in the first category, they do not have the means to finance it. As a result, they have chronic external debt problems or depend heavily on aid. Because some of their export earnings go to servicing these debts or to pay for food purchases, they cannot afford to import as many capital goods as they would like. These countries have an aggregate population perhaps five times greater than the previous category. Nevertheless, their combined GNP is substantially less. Egypt, with almost one quarter of all Arabs, had a per capita GNP of only $690 in 1982. A more dramatic way of expressing this is that Egypt's total GNP is less than the amount Saudi Arabia—with one fifth to one quarter of Egypt's population—earned from oil exports in 1982 and less than it invests annually on development. This typology understates differences among countries within categories and exaggerates them between countries in different categories. Egypt's industrial structure is far more advanced than that of Sudan for example. At the same time, Egypt's economic and demographic problems greatly exceed those of Syria or Tunisia, countries which in certain respects have more in common with Morocco (in the first category).

The widest disparity within the Arab world is between the small oil-producing states and members of the fourth category: both Yemens, Somalia, and Mauritania (the last two being Arab League states beyond the scope of this book). Per capita annual incomes in these peripheral, heavily rural, underdeveloped states are only $300 to $400. Paradoxically, the countries in the second group would probably have the same standard of living if they had no oil. Waterbury's fifth category includes Jordan and Lebanon, whose economic characteristics are inseparable from their special political status. Since Israel's occupation of the West Bank and Jerusalem in 1967, Jordan's economy has been severely truncated. Consequently, Jordan is highly dependent on foreign, especially Arab, aid. Despite these liabilities, it has achieved a certain prosperity as a result of phosphate exports, large foreign investment, and remittances from workers in the Gulf. Its per capita income is similar to that of Syria. Were the West Bank to be returned, Jordan's growth prospects would be dramatically improved. Lebanon, before its civil war, was one of the most prosperous and economically advanced countries in the Middle East, acting as the region's clearinghouse, emporium, and banking center. This role can probably be recaptured quickly, but it depends on Lebanon avoiding regional entanglements.

Although one can easily disagree with aspects of the schema, it has the advantage of not reducing economic differences among Arab countries to whether or not they produce oil. More important, it helps to identify the divergent economic interests of the region's states and suggests why they view integration in significantly different ways. The richer oil states, with the exception of Libya, have little enthusiasm for unity with poorer states because this would diminish and dilute their wealth and power. Indeed, their influence derives in part from the imbalance between rich and poor states and the latter's recurring need to "drink from the trough of the rich." Waterbury has summarized the dilemma: "The superrich neither need nor promote integration, yet they would be indispensable to any plan for unity. The poor both need and occasionally promote integration, but they lack the leverage to bargain for it on their own terms." [13]

Differences in Political Economy

One of the more obvious weaknesses of the preceding classification is that it does not classify states according to their political economic philosophies. These run the gamut from P.D.R. Yemen's austere and somewhat doctrinaire socialism to the almost untrammeled laissez-faire capitalism of the Gulf shaykhdoms and Lebanon. Syria, with its mixed public-private sector approach, and Libya, with its emphasis on revolutionary Islamic egalitarianism and worker control, would, along with most other Arab states, fit somewhere in between. There are major and possibly insurmountable obstacles to merging states with incompatible ideas about how wealth should be generated and distributed or about the appropriate roles to be played by the public and private sectors. No discussion about economic integration can ignore the fact that Arab countries have widely differing fiscal policies, tax structures, exchange and monetary controls, and attitudes to private or foreign investment. Arab oil states with surplus capital long avoided investing in countries like Egypt and Syria because they feared their assets would be expropriated or because discriminatory legislation concerning business ownership and profit repatriation made it unattractive. Generally, states with mixed or quasi-socialist economies have liberalized investment laws since the early 1970s to attract Arab petrodollars. In Syria and Egypt, this policy of *infitah* (opening) resulted in a significant influx of outside capital. The old distinction between capitalist and socialist countries has, therefore, blurred since the early 1970s. Nonetheless, the bulk of surplus oil earnings are invested outside the Middle East, where opportunities are wider, returns higher, and risks fewer.

Labor Flows: The Tie That Binds

Although differences in the economic structures and development goals of the Arab countries seem to militate against their integration, the emergence of a regional labor market has promoted irreversible interdependence among them. Perhaps no single development has bound the Arab countries so closely together since the early 1970s as the extraordinary flow of migrant workers from labor-surplus to labor-deficit Arab countries. The interests of the rich and poor are wedded whether they like it or not. The same phenomenon that has been responsible for causing national integration problems in certain countries in the Arabian peninsula has paradoxically advanced regional integration. Accurate statistics concerning the flow of Arab labor are impossible to obtain. However, Birks and Sinclair estimate (conservatively in our judgment) that 1.76 million Arabs worked in other Arab countries in 1980. Flow patterns are exceedingly complex but strongly suggest that no country could easily disentangle itself from the regional matrix (Table 8.2).

Other intraregional movements of people have also grown spectacularly and helped to break down national barriers. Easier and cheaper travel, for instance, has encouraged tremendous expansion of inter-Arab tourism.

Inter-Arab Trade

Regional economic integration cannot proceed far when levels of inter-Arab trade remain as low as they do. Trade is one of the principal forms of international spatial interaction. If one excludes North Africa, Arab countries with relatively little or no oil sent less than one third of their exports to, and received only one fifth of their imports from, other Arab countries in the early 1980s. The developed industrial world is by far their largest market and supplier. Furthermore, countries that depend most heavily on Arab trade, like Lebanon, are often the least likely to seek regional economic integration. Among the oil producers, only 3.6 percent of exports and 5 percent of imports went to, or came from, other Arab countries in 1979.

Such trade patterns reflect most countries' narrow industrial base and overdependence on a few raw material exports, like oil, cotton, and phosphates, which are needed primarily by developed industrial countries. Arab states tend to export the same items and to duplicate their efforts and compete rather than to promote functional specialization and

Table 8.2

Migrant Workers in the Arab World by Sending Country and by Country of Employment, 1980

Sending Country					Country of Employment						
	Saudi Arabia	Libya	United Arab Emirates (U.A.E.)	Kuwait	Qatar	Bahrain	Jordan (East Bank)	Oman	Yemen A.R.	Iraq	Total
All Arab	820,550	377,300	89,700	243,800	20,200	9,010	68,500	12,500	10,250	112,500	1,763,840
Egypt	155,100	250,000	18,200	85,000	5,750	2,800	68,500	6,300	4,000	100,000	695,650
Yemen A.R.	325,000	—	5,400	3,000	1,500	1,125	—	120	—	—	336,145
Jordan and Palestine	140,000	15,000	19,400	55,000	7,800	1,400	—	2,250	2,000	7,500	250,350
P.D.R. Yemen	65,000	—	6,600	9,500	1,500	1,125	—	120	—	—	83,845
Syria	24,600	15,000	5,800	35,000	1,000	150	—	600	1,000	—	83,150
Lebanon	33,200	5,700	6,600	8,000	750	300	—	1,500	500	4,500	61,050
Sudan	55,600	21,000	2,100	5,500	750	900	—	620	2,250	500	89,220
Maghreb	500	65,600	—	300	—	—	—	120	—	—	66,520
Oman	10,000	—	19,400	2,000	1,150	900	—	—	—	—	33,450
Iraq	3,250	—	1,200	40,000	—	310	—	—	—	—	44,760
Somalia	8,300	5,000	5,000	500	—	—	—	400	500	—	19,700
Non-Arab	202,700	168,200	321,300	134,900	60,050	58,710	7,500	84,770	6,750	13,000	1,057,880
Total	1,023,250	545,500	411,000	378,700	80,250	67,720	76,000	96,800	17,000	125,500	2,821,720

Source: J. S. Birks and C. A. Sinclair, "The Socio-Economic Determinants of Intra-Regional Migration." Paper presented to the Economic Commission for Western Asia (ECWA) Conference on International Migration to the Arab World, Nicosia, Cyprus, May 1981: Appendix A.

geographic complementarities. Opportunities for exchange simply do not exist much of the time. With the notable exception of the growing market for agricultural products from the Levant in the food-short, oil-producing states of the Arabian peninsula, the import needs of most Arab states are not met within the region. Capital and consumer goods, which together account for most imports, are invariably obtained from industrialized countries. Even when such products are available within the region, a strong preference is often shown for similar items imported from the developed world because these are thought to be of higher quality.

Low levels of inter-Arab trade result, to some extent, from quantitative and qualitative tariff and nontariff barriers, despite repeated efforts to reduce or eliminate these bilaterally or multilaterally. The nonoil producing but industrializing states especially have strong protectionist inclinations and often restrict or ban imports of products that directly compete with locally manufactured ones. In addition, customs duties constitute a major source of government revenue in countries, like Jordan, that lack oil, public sector industries, or a well-developed internal sales and income tax system. States with chronic balance of payments deficits, like Egypt and Syria, may also limit or prohibit the importation of specific items to conserve scarce foreign currency reserves. Alternatively, they may permit certain of their products to be sold only for hard, convertible currencies, which can be used to pay for vital imports. Much inter-Arab trade, therefore, is in the form of agricultural products. This is unlikely to promote significant regional development or cooperation.

Commercial transactions within the region have been hindered in other ways too. In nominally socialist countries, trade is conducted through state importing and exporting companies. Often these develop into huge, inefficient, and centralized bureaucracies that are best equipped to negotiate large barter deals with similar agencies in other countries. Elsewhere, trade may be in the hands of thousands of private sector merchants, big and small. These organizational and institutional differences can retard trade between countries. Until the creation in 1977 of the Arab Monetary Fund, trade also suffered from the lack of standard procedures and permanent regionwide mechanisms for settling payments efficiently. The region's traditionally poor transportation network further discouraged economic interaction.

Inter-Arab trade has frequently been governed by politics, not economics, and it has as a result acquired a peculiar symbolism. Trade is both a tool and a barometer. When two countries reestablish ties or announce their intention to unite, one of their first steps will be to cement their friendship by increasing trade, often dramatically. Conversely, trade is one of the first things to suffer when political relations sour.[14]

The predilection for closing boundaries during disputes is especially detrimental to trade, destroying long-term confidence and dislocating trade patterns even between innocent parties. Jordanian-Iraqi-Syrian relations illustrate the problem well. In the early 1970s, Syria and Iraq briefly closed their borders with Jordan to protest King Husayn's suppression of the Palestinian guerillas. As a result, the value of trade between Jordan and Iraq dropped by 46 percent between 1970 and 1971. Jordan's imports from Syria fell by 28 percent in the same period. The closure of the Syrian border affected Jordan's extraregional trade too. With the Suez Canal blocked and Israel lying astride Jordan's natural outlet to the Mediterranean, about three quarters of Jordan's principal export, phosphates, and over half its imports, including oil, had been passing through Syria. The Damascus regime, thus, had considerable leverage and maximized it to the full by also closing its airspace, which meant that the flying time between Amman and Beirut increased from its normal 45 minutes to 4 hours, with planes rerouted over Saudi Arabia and Egypt. Early in 1972, Egypt also briefly considered closing its airspace after King Husayn suggested that the West Bank be confederated with Jordan should Israel withdraw from the territory. The Syrian-Jordanian rift eventually healed, and trade and cooperation between the two increased throughout the decade. However, Syria briefly closed its border again in 1980.

Meanwhile, trade between Iraq and Jordan grew significantly as a result of their new friendship, which owed much to geography. During its war with Iran, Iraq's traditional Gulf outlets were closed. In addition, Syria, in order to help its Iranian ally, would not allow Iraqi imports or exports to cross its territory. Iraq, therefore, regarded its overland route to the Jordanian port of Aqaba as its lifeline. Syria has exploited its pivotal location with respect to Lebanon as well as to Jordan and Iraq. Lebanon, more than most states in the area, prospers from commerce with other Arab countries. However, all of its overland trade must pass through Syria. If the Asad regime wants to apply pressure on the Lebanese government, it can simply impede this transit trade. Inter-Arab trade must be uncoupled from politics and the vicissitudes of interstate relations if regional economic integration is to progress.

National Versus Regional Planning: The Example of Port Development

The economies of the Arab states still function largely independently of one another. National development plans are drawn up without reference to regional needs or even to what neighbors are doing. Much wasteful duplication and destructive competition could be avoided by coordinating development projects. An attempt is currently underway to calibrate and harmonize national five-year plans, but one should not expect too much success.

The proliferation of ports in the region illustrates how short-sighted beggar-thy-neighbor policies can be. After the oil-price explosion in the early 1970s, imports into the region grew exponentially, straining handling facilities severely. At the same time, several countries were still in the process of developing their own transportation infrastructures and outlets. Syria, for example, was building or expanding ports at Al-Ladhiqiyah and Tartus. Because of the Suez Canal's closure and then the Lebanese civil war, these ports became a vital link in trade between Europe and many of the Arab countries to the east and south. Whereas in 1974 these ports handled 40 percent of the dry cargo landed at non-Israeli eastern Mediterranean ports, by 1976 they offloaded 70 percent. This caused serious congestion. When the Suez Canal reopened, Jordan seized the opportunity to siphon off some of this cargo through Aqaba. However, Saudi Arabia is building a new Red Sea port at Yanbu and has greatly expanded Jiddah's capacity. These will compete to some degree with Aqaba and divert some traffic away from the eastern Mediterranean ports. Once Lebanon's problems have been resolved, Beirut and Tripoli can also be expected to recapture some of their former traffic. It is quite probable, therefore, that the combined capacity of ports along the eastern Mediterranean and Red Sea will exceed demand and that yesteryear's congestion will give way to empty or underused berths.

The situation is even worse in the Gulf where, partly because of the area's political fragmentation, there are eight major and nine secondary ports. Each state, no matter how small, has developed its own facilities, for reasons of national prestige as much as any economic benefit. The surfeit in the lower Gulf is particularly marked. Unfortunately, many of the Gulf's general cargo berths were planned or expanded before the implications of containerization were fully apparent. Quicker turnaround has significantly reduced congestion, obviating (but not stopping) port expansion. By one estimate, Gulf port capacity in 1982 exceeded requirements by 50 percent. In the U.A.E., 70 percent of all existing or planned berthage was unlikely to be needed. There is no question that regional planning or at least closer consultation would have resulted in a more rational spatial allocation of resources. Such duplication of efforts underlines both the need for, and the obstacles to, greater regional cooperation. Unfortunately, many other examples could be cited.

Regional Institutions

It would be easy to enumerate the many failed Arab unity schemes and to use this as a measure of how unsuccessful and ephemeral regional integration efforts have been. But it would be misleading to do so because, in the last four decades, a network of regional institutions have been established to promote cooperation and integration. Most of these have survived and constitute a framework on which Arab unity can be built.

The Arab League

The League of Arab States has been the chief vehicle for institutionalized regional cooperation since 1945. Initially, only 7 states signed the organization's founding charter, but others joined as they won their independence. The most recent admissions have been Mauritania (1973), Somalia (1974), and Djibouti (1977). Egypt was expelled in 1979 after signing a peace treaty with Israel but will likely be readmitted eventually. Currently there are 22 members, including the PLO. Paradoxically, the association has survived because of its looseness. Its constitution explicitly pledges to uphold each member's independence and sovereignty. Some pan-Arabists view it as an obstacle rather than a means to unity precisely because it recognizes the region's political fragmentation.

The League was created to promote voluntary cooperation and coordination. Its powers are limited, and the implementation of its policies and resolutions depends entirely on its members' consent. Decisions of the League's Council, its supreme organ, are binding only on states that accept them. As with the United Nations, a distinction must be made between the League's political and nonpolitical accomplishments. In the political sphere, its main achievement—besides surviving at all—has been to provide a forum for consultation and conflict resolution. Many important regional policy decisions since the mid-1960s have been made at summit meetings of League heads of state.[15]

Although many of these conferences forged a consensus, others brought Arab divisions into sharp focus and set back the cause of unity. Dissident states have often boycotted or sabotaged meetings. On balance, though, Arab League summits have contributed positively to the elaboration of a common strategy, especially with respect to Israel. In addition, although the League has no collective security system, it has played an active role in resolving inter-Arab disputes.[16]

The League's role in encouraging economic, social, and cultural cooperation among its members may be of more lasting significance. The League has created a huge bureaucracy. Within its General Secretariat, individual departments promote closer regional coordination in economic, financial, health, information, legal, social, labor, communications, petroleum, and other affairs. All League members also belong to its numerous specialized autonomous agencies. Among these are the Tunis-based Arab League Educational, Cultural, and Scientific Organization (ALECSO), the Baghdad-based Arab Labor Organization, and the Amman-based Arab Organization for Standardization and Metrology. Other specialized agencies include an Arab Postal Union (Tunis based), an Arab Satellite Communications Organization (Riyadh based), an Arab States Broadcasting Union (Tunis based), an Arab Telecommunications Union (Baghdad based), and a Civil Aviation Council of Arab States (Rabat based)—to mention only a few. Unfortunately, it is difficult to evaluate the effectiveness of these bodies. Their mere existence should not be used to measure regional cooperation.

The expulsion of Egypt following its separate peace treaty with Israel seriously hurt the League. Egypt, besides being by far the leading Arab country, was the organization's principal sponsor and founder. Moreover, the League's headquarters was in Cairo. Many Egyptians joked that they had expelled the Arab League, not the other way around. The relocation of the General Secretariat to Tunis disrupted operations. Egypt refused to cooperate, so many vital documents remain in Cairo. The League also lost many of its top employees. The temporary headquarters in Tunis has proved inadequate.

The Council of Arab Economic Unity (CAEU) and Arab Common Market (ACM)

The Council of Arab Economic Unity (CAEU) was established in 1964 to promote full economic integration among Arab states. Currently, it has 13 members.[17] Its ultimate goal is to create a region within which capital, people, and goods can move freely and reciprocal rights of residence, employment, ownership, and transit are guaranteed. One of its first steps was to create an Arab Common Market (ACM) in 1965, consisting of Egypt, Jordan, Syria and Iraq. Subsequently, Egypt was expelled, but Libya and Mauritania joined. Sudan was to have belonged but did not ratify all the membership formalities. The two Yemens and Somalia have expressed an interest in being admitted if membership conditions are relaxed.

The ACM hoped to decrease gradually and eventually eliminate tariff and nontariff barriers to trade among its members, who would adopt a common external tariff. The European Economic Community (EEC) served as a model for this proposed customs union. However, member states did not eliminate tariffs on their imports of locally produced animal, mineral, and agricultural products from one another until 1971. Manufactured goods were not freed until 1973. Even now numerous nontariff barriers survive and members can and do use an escape clause that allows them to impose import levies on particular products or to ban them altogether. Although the ACM is open to any state that signed the 1957 Arab Economic Unity Agreement, it has not grown as anticipated. Many potential members fear local producers will be undermined or customs revenues drastically reduced if they join. The ACM has failed resoundingly to increase trade among its members. In the late 1970s, approximately only 2 percent of the four original members' trade was with each other, and much of this consisted of minor agricultural products. All the obstacles to economic integration and inter-Arab trade discussed earlier apply with particular force to the ACM. Acute political differences among its members, culminating with Egypt's expulsion, have made the ACM a salutory lesson in Arab unity's elusiveness rather than a catalyst to more ambitious schemes. Two decades after its founding, it still has no common external tariff.

One of the CAEU's greatest accomplishments may have been its authorship or sponsorship of several multilateral agreements that, on paper, significantly enhance functional economic integration. Many of these agreements were designed to improve the interstate investment climate: the Investment and Transfer of Arab Capital (1970), the Avoidance of Double Taxation and Tax Evasion (1973), Cooperation in Tax Collection (1973), and Investment Guarantees Against Non-Commercial Risks in Host Countries (1973). Other agreements facilitate transit trade and labor mobility and ensure that social insurance systems are reciprocal. The great majority were signed in the early to mid-1970s. Once again, these agreements must be interpreted cautiously—making them is the easy part. They are not always honored, even minimally.

Despite their deficiencies, these and similar agreements, in aggregate, are beginning to make many of the Arab world's political boundaries more permeable, a prerequisite to lasting regional integration.

Functional Service Federations and Producers' Associations

National professional, business, trade, and producers' organizations have traditionally tried to maintain links with their counterparts in other Arab countries. For example, Arab Chambers of Commerce, Industry, and Agriculture have been joined in a General Federation since 1951; Arab trade unions in an International Confederation since 1956; and even Arab airlines in an Air Carriers Organization for many years. Since the 1970s, the number of functional service federations and producers' associations has exploded, largely under the CAEU's auspices. These include a Federation of Arab Banks, an Arab Seaports Union, and regional associations for producers of iron and steel, chemical fertilizers, textiles, engineering and electrical goods, food, leather, cement, and numerous other goods. The Organization of Arab Petroleum Exporting Countries (OAPEC) is the most successful and best known. If these organizations facilitate the coordination of production, marketing, and pricing policies, as intended, they should enhance the long-term prospects for regional integration. But it cannot be too strongly stressed that these bodies are only what their members make of them. Life has to be breathed into them if they are to advance the cause of Arab unity.

Joint Ventures

The Middle East and North Africa are unique in being probably the only underdeveloped region with enough capital to finance their own development. The region as a whole also has a varied resource base and an adequate labor force. Since the mid-1970s, a large number of transnational joint ventures have been established to combine these spatially variable factors of production. Most are profit-seeking autonomous holding companies established through public financing and provide capital to worthwhile projects or engage in equity financing. Membership is typically open to all Arab states or to private Arab investors from several countries. Potentially, joint ventures are among the most significant forms of regional economic cooperation because their composition or operations transcend national boundaries. Because they are designed to function at a regional scale and to pool efforts, theoretically they have greater resources and opportunities available to them and can reduce unit costs and rationalize production. By their very nature, they should encourage regional cooperation.

The CAEU in particular has sponsored a plethora of joint ventures since the early 1970s. Often these prevent wasteful competition. Syria and Jordan established a joint textiles venture rather than each building their own mills for example. Other CAEU-inspired joint ventures include the Arab Company for Pharmaceuticals and Medical Supplies, the Arab Livestock Company, and the Arab Mining Company, among many others. OAPEC has also established several petroleum-related joint ventures, such as the Arab Maritime Petroleum Transport Co., which has its own tankers; the Arab Shipbuilding and Repairs Yard, which has a drydock in Bahrain, and the Arab Petroleum Services Co., which has subsidiary exploration and drilling divisions.

Joint ventures, whether intergovernmental, mixed public-private, or totally private, have proliferated to the point that listing them all would be pointless as well as difficult. They encompass virtually every type of commercial and industrial activity. Not all have succeeded. Overall, they have contributed to the region's integration by multiplying transnational, infrastructural links, nurturing geographic complementarities, and creating communities of shared interest. Equally important, they have proved their ability to survive ephemeral political disputes, the rock upon which Arab cooperation schemes have invariably floundered in the past.[18]

Development Funds, Financial Institutions, and Aid

As a result of the post-1973 oil-price explosion, several oil-producing states accumulated massive capital surpluses. Because of their inability to absorb these by themselves, there has been a tremendous spillover to non-oil-producing states. This dramatic increase in capital flows since the early 1970s has lubricated economic cooperation and bound Arab states more closely together.

The Arab League, CAEU, and especially individual countries have established a variety of regional institutions to recycle surplus petrodollars, aid development in non-oil-producing states, and promote financial cooperation. In 1977, an Arab Monetary Fund was created for example. The proliferation of development funds has been especially striking. The Kuwait Fund for Arab Economic Development (KFAED) established by the Kuwaiti government in 1961 to provide soft (long-term low-interest) development loans to Arab countries was the earliest of these. In the mid-1970s, it widened its mandate and began offering loans to all developing countries. Typically, KFAED loans finance industrial, power, irrigation, agricultural, and infrastructural projects within individual countries. A measure of the Fund's global importance is that its lending capacity ranks not far behind the International Bank for Reconstruction and Development. By 1978 it had approved 124 loans worth $1.6 billion to 46 countries.

The KFAED was the model for the Abu Dhabi Fund for Arab Economic Development, the Iraqi Fund for External Development, and the Saudi Fund for Development—all established in the early 1970s. Their soft loans have also financed a wide range of projects. Strictly speaking these funds do not promote regional integration in the sense that their loans are for national projects. Nevertheless, they have reduced the region's need to seek external assistance and, hence, increased its self-sufficiency. In 1980, the four main national funds together committed $1.055 billion in loans and grants, with the Abu Dhabi Fund accounting for $203 million, the Iraqi for $253 million, the Kuwaiti for $268 million, and the Saudi for $331 million.

The most important multinational fund is the Arab Fund for Economic and Social Development (AFESD), which began operations in 1974 and includes all 22 members of the Arab League. The oil-producing states are by far its greatest capital subscribers. The AFESD makes loans and grants only to its members. Its principal goal is to advance Arab economic integration rather than to finance limited national projects; approximately one third of the $1.1 billion it awarded up to 1978 went for transportation and communications schemes. AFESD has also financed numerous Arab joint ventures. One of its more ambitious plans is to develop Sudan into the Middle East's breadbasket. Two additional multinational funds with mostly Arab participation are the Islamic Development Bank and the Organization of Petroleum Exporting Countries (OPEC) Special Fund. Whereas AFESD in 1980 committed $107 million in loans, the Islamic fund allocated $429 million and the OPEC Special Fund $251 million.

Not all Arab aid is channeled through the preceding national and multilateral institutions. Most aid takes the form of bilateral government-to-government grants. These usually go to reduce budgetary or balance-of-payments deficits or for arms purchases rather than to finance specific development projects. From the perspective of both the donor and the recipient, this is the most convenient form of assistance. Unfortunately, almost none of it goes towards tying economies together, except in dependency relationships.

The amount of Arab aid dispensed since the early 1970s has been staggering. The United Nations urges developed countries to give 0.70 percent of their GNP in foreign aid annually. Most typically give only about half that amount, with the United States, which in the early 1980s gave about only 0.22 percent of its GNP, consistently near the bottom of the list. By contrast, Saudi Arabia, the U.A.E., and Qatar have regularly given more—sometimes considerably so—than 5 percent of their GNP in foreign assistance each year. Kuwait has usually given more than 3 percent. Obviously figures vary from year to year: in 1979, for instance, Saudi Arabia gave 3.13 percent of its GNP as official development assistance, whereas Kuwait gave over 5 percent. In some years, Saudi Arabia has given the equivalent of $800 per capita in aid.

As recently as 1975, approximately 60 percent of all Arab aid went to other Arab countries. This proportion had declined to about 51 percent in 1983. Nonetheless, the non-oil-producing Arab states, as a group, have been the primary beneficiaries of this largesse. By one estimate, Egypt received $17 billion from Arab oil producers between 1973 and 1978 alone, with $7 billion from Saudi Arabia and $5.5 billion from Kuwait. During that period Egypt got approximately half of all bilateral Arab aid. Syria, Jordan, and the Yemen A.R. were the other main recipients. In the early 1980s, Syria was supposed to receive $1.85 billion annually in Arab aid, which would amount to about one fifth of its budget or enough to cover 80 percent of its trade deficit.

The sharing of oil wealth has not promoted regional integration to the extent one might expect. Very little has been explicitly used for that purpose. On the contrary, it has fostered patron-client relationships. An aid recipient may resent its benefactors, alternately ingratiating itself and going out of its way to prove that its ability to act independently has not been compromised. It may even threaten to "misbehave" unless subventions are increased. Conversely, a donor may give aid to co-opt or pacify a recalcitrant neighbor. Far from being a token of a close, friendly relationship between countries, aid can become a subtle, but sophisticated, form of extortion and protection. Syria has been especially adept at playing the Arab aid game, demanding payment for its services to the Arab cause in Lebanon and against Israel.

Subregional Integration

The most realistic way to integrate the Arab world may be in stages, first forging links among subregional blocs of countries. The Maghreb, Nile Valley, Fertile Crescent, and Arabian peninsula countries come to mind as natural groupings. Unfortunately, what geography and economic logic would put together, "politics and long historical memories keep apart."[19]

The Maghreb

The Maghreb countries, despite their common French colonial heritage and contiguity, have been singularly unable to create lasting subre-

gional integrative links. Numerous bilateral and multilateral cooperation agreements have not amounted to much. During their independence struggle, Moroccan, Algerian, and Tunisian nationalists were much
interested in the idea of Maghreb unity. The three major nationalist
parties, meeting in Tangier in April 1958, expressed their determination to build a united Maghreb. But events since then have "made a
mockery of the 1958 Tangier declaration."[20] Periods of détente have alternated with ones of strained and occasionally antagonistic relations.
The cleavage between radicals (Algeria and Libya) and moderates (Morocco and Tunisia) accounts for some of the tension. Boundary disputes, particularly between Morocco and Algeria and between Tunisia
and Libya, have not helped. The tendency to meddle in one another's
internal affairs and even to engage in subversive activities has further
clouded the atmosphere. The long-standing power rivalry between Algeria and Morocco, the leading states, is yet another serious obstacle to
Maghrebi unity. Finally, the Western Sahara dispute, in which Algeria
and Libya have supported Polisario guerillas against an irredentist
Morocco's attempts to annex the territory, has polarized the region. The
sudden, unexpected union between Libya and Morocco in 1984 has little chance of long-term success.

Northeastern Africa

Egypt and the Sudan are both dependent on the Nile; have close historical, political, and military ties; and naturally complement one another. Overpopulated Egypt faces growing problems feeding itself. But
it has a skilled labor force and expanding industrial base. Relatively underpopulated Sudan has enormous agricultural potential but little industry. Egyptians have often assumed that marriage between the two
countries makes such excellent sense that it is inevitable. This feeling
is not reciprocated, however, and many Sudanese fear being overwhelmed and exploited. They are especially nervous about Egypt's dream
of easing demographic pressures by resettling peasants in the Sudan.
Sudan's black population also strongly opposes unification with Egypt.
Nevertheless, the two countries have cooperated closely, especially since
1974. Egypt has provided the Sudanese regime with vital backing against
attempted coups d'état. In 1982, the two countries signed a wide-ranging
charter to strengthen ties over a 10-year transitional period. Nationals
of both countries are now theoretically accorded equal treatment. Customs duties will ultimately be abolished. The agreement also provided
for the creation of an appointed joint Egyptian-Sudanese parliament,
whose biannual meetings will alternate between the two capitals. It is
not realistic to expect full union though. A large, unpopulated area
separates the two countries and land links between Cairo and Khartoum are poor. Even telephone and telex communications have to go
through a third country. The fact that Egypt and Sudan share the Nile

may even be a source of conflict rather than cooperation in the future if they have to compete for its water as some predict.

Egypt may have the technical skills Sudan needs to develop its agriculture, but it lacks the capital. The addition of oil-rich Libya would theoretically strengthen any Nile Valley unity scheme. In 1969, the three countries announced their intention to create a tripartite federation. Syria subsequently joined this so-called Federation of Arab Republics (FAR). Like so many other schemes, the FAR failed despite its auspicious beginnings. From a strictly geographic point of view, the plan had much to commend itself. Politically, however, it had serious shortcomings. Sudan, preoccupied with its own national unity problems, soon withdrew. Libya felt that the federation was too loose and sought full union with Egypt. Egypt, despite reservations stemming from its failed merger with Syria between 1958 and 1961, pledged in August 1972 to unite with Libya within a year. In September 1973, the two countries agreed to draft a new constitution, adopt a common currency, and take other steps to promote integration. Egypt benefited from this relationship because it enabled it to export some of its surplus labor to Libya. However, many Egyptians were disturbed by Colonel Qadhafi's austere ideas and radical social and political experimentation, and they had little enthusiasm for the proposed merger. Libya's population, it should be noted, is only one third of Cairo's. When Egypt and Syria launched the October 1973 war against Israel, they did not even consult Libya. After that, relations deteriorated. An irate Qadhafi expelled Egyptian workers from Libya. After Sadat's trip to Jerusalem, the two countries even had a border clash. Libya is on no better terms with Sudan, its other original federation partner, having participated in plots to overthrow the Numayri regime. But it has maintained links with Syria. In 1980, these two countries announced their intention to create a "single identity" and "complete political, economic, military, and cultural unity." Given that Damascus and Tripoli are 1400 miles (2250 kilometers) apart, the scheme had almost no chance of succeeding.

Fertile Crescent

Unity among the Fertile Crescent countries of Iraq, Syria, and Jordan has a compelling geographic logic. Historically, political and economic ties within this subregion, which the colonial powers artificially divided not much more than 60 years ago, have been intimate. The dissolution of boundaries would greatly improve transit between the Mediterranean and the Gulf. If Iraq could trade through Jordanian and Syrian ports without repeated interruptions, its locational disadvantages would be significantly ameliorated. A state that extended from the Mediterranean to the Gulf would possess immense strategic leverage. Unity would also enable more efficient use of the Euphrates River, which passes through Syria and Iraq and from which water could also be diverted to arid Jordan. Syria and Jordan's development prospects would be improved by access to Iraq's oil wealth.

Since the late 1940s, there have been frequent attempts to unite the Fertile Crescent. In 1958, the Hashimite Iraqi and Jordanian monarchies briefly merged to counteract Syria's unification with Egypt, which they considered threatening. Syria, Iraq, and Egypt attempted to federate in 1963 when they had broadly similar radical nationalist regimes. This came to nought. In 1978 Syria and Iraq, which are both ruled by the Ba'th political party, tried to unite, again without much success. More recently, Jordan and Iraq, without formally uniting, have fashioned a strong friendship, based essentially on Iraq's dependence on the Jordanian port of Aqaba during its war with Iran. Nevertheless, the Fertile Crescent countries have little of lasting consequence to show for all these efforts because political rivalries have been too deeply rooted.

Arabian Peninsula

The best prospects for subregional integration are probably among the Arabian peninsula oil-producing kingdoms. This is paradoxical because traditionally it has been assumed that Arab unity would be achieved by republican regimes. Some pan-Arabists have argued that unity was impeded by the very existence of the conservative monarchies, which generally avoided integration schemes in the past and jealously guarded their independence. Yet the U.A.E., for all its faults, is still the most successful—indeed, the only—example of subregional integration. The U.A.E. is a federation of seven emirates formed in 1971 following Britain's withdrawal from the Gulf. It is very much a state in the making, and the federation's individual members retain considerable independence.

One of the U.A.E.'s basic integrative problems is that its members differ greatly in area, population, resources, level of development, and commitment to the federal state-idea. Oil-rich Abu Dhabi, covering 86.7 percent of the total area and with at least 40 percent of the total population, is unquestionably the federation's core. Its emir has been the president and principal backer of the U.A.E. since its inception. Abu Dhabi's large oil revenues finance most of the U.A.E.'s budget—over 90 percent in the late 1970s—and most development projects in the poorer emirates. Inevitably, some have seen the U.A.E. principally as a vehicle for Abu Dhabi to expand its influence.

The rival city-state of Dubai is the sole counterweight to Abu Dhabi's domination of the federation. Although tiny in area, Dubai has about one third of the U.A.E.'s population. It does not have as much oil as its larger neighbor, but it has thrived economically because of its port and long mercantile tradition, which have attracted a heterogeneous and cosmopolitan population. Dubai has been less enthusiastic about the federation, periodically threatening to withdraw altogether. Its financial contributions to the federal budget have been meager, and it jealously defends its local autonomy. Nevertheless, the emir has been the U.A.E.'s vice president and three of his sons have variously been prime minister, minister of defense, and minister of finance.

With the possible exception of Sharjah, none of the other emirates compares in importance with Abu Dhabi or Dubai. Umm al-Qaywayn, Ajman, and Fujayrah were political geographic oddities, originally amounting to little more than fishing villages with fewer than 30,000 people each in the mid-1970s. Their prospects for surviving as independent entities outside the U.A.E. were remote, although Ras al-Khaymah delayed joining until 1972.

If the U.A.E. fails—and this seems unlikely—it will be because it could not withstand the many complex rivalries among its members. Throughout the Gulf these have a clear geographic pattern: typically, emirates are at loggerheads with their immediate neighbors but on good terms with their neighbors' neighbors. For example, Qatar's rulers have traditionally been on poor terms with those of Bahrain and Abu Dhabi, partly because of territorial disputes. Dubai has customarily quarreled with Abu Dhabi and Sharjah. And Sharjah has been rivals with Dubai and Umm al-Qaywayn. Conversely, Abu Dhabi has cultivated cordial relations with Bahrain and Sharjah, Dubai with Qatar (they once even shared their currency), and Sharjah with Ras al-Kaymah.

The single greatest threat to the U.A.E.'s continued existence is probably the rivalry between Abu Dhabi and Dubai, which fought a boundary war as recently as the 1940s, despite the fact that their ruling families come from two branches of the Bani Yas tribal confederation. Each tries to line up support among the smaller emirates, aggravating the cleavage. Another inveterate feud is between Dubai and Sharjah. Historically, these two emirates, though only 10 miles (16 kilometers) apart, competed to capture the lower Gulf's entrepôt trade. In the 1940s, however, the creek on which Sharjah's port was situated silted up, whereas Dubai dredged its estuary and eventually completely eclipsed its erstwhile challenger. A long-standing boundary dispute compounded the problem, even though adding light relief for those not involved in it (the disagreement involved ownership of a shopping center site).

Lethargic federal institution building has also hindered integration. In theory the federal government is responsible for foreign affairs, defense, and finance, and the individual emirates for everything else. In practice, the emirates have almost as much latitude as they want to conduct their affairs as they see fit. They have surrendered their powers to the federal government begrudgingly. Each emirate retains the right to grant oil concessions independently. Until 1976, when an attempt was made to merge all internal and external armed forces and place them under one command, virtually each emirate had its own army.

The weakness of central planning agencies or other coordinating bodies has allowed much needless duplication. For example, Abu Dhabi, Dubai, Sharjah, and Ras al-Khaymah have all developed "international" airports within 125 miles of one another. Sharjah's is 20 minutes by car from Dubai's and only 25 miles from Ras al-Khaymah's. These also compete with nearby airports in Bahrain and Qatar, which once considered joining the U.A.E. Similar wasteful competition has given the U.A.E. several large ports.

A potentially far more consequential unity experiment than the U.A.E. is currently underway among six peninsula states. In March 1981, Bahrain, Kuwait, Oman, Qatar, Saudi Arabia, and the U.A.E. established the Gulf Cooperation Council (GCC) "to realize coordination, integration, and closer relations in all spheres." These geographically contiguous states have similar economic systems and political orientations. On balance, they probably agree on more issues than they disagree. Their problems are also alike: all are trying to cope with extraordinary economic growth, rapid social change, a large foreign labor force, and perceived external threats, notably from Iran. By Middle Eastern standards, they are all rich and, therefore, do not fear that unity will necessitate sharing and diluting their wealth.

Even before the GCC's creation, several of its members cooperated closely, sharing an airline (Gulf Air), a news agency, and numerous other joint ventures. The Iranian revolution and the Soviet Union's invasion of Afghanistan brought them closer together and prompted discussion over common security concerns. The GCC's gradual functional approach to integration is explicitly modeled on the EEC. All heads of member states belong to a Supreme Council, which meets twice annually but can be convened if requested by two members. The presidency rotates among member states in alphabetical order. In addition, a Ministerial Council consisting of the six foreign ministers meets regularly. A permanent Secretariat General has been established in Riyadh. Close consultation among the GCC states has enabled them to adopt joint foreign policy positions on many issues. Rules have been, or will be, drawn up to standardize and coordinate internal security, economic and financial affairs, education, cultural and social matters, health, transportation and communications, and customs and immigration. As in the EEC, citizens of GCC states will ultimately have the right to live and work in any member state. A joint investment and foreign aid policy and a unified currency are planned. In May 1981, the GCC announced it would set up a $6 billion common fund to finance joint venture projects in the region. GCC defense ministers have also discussed the creation of a joint air defense system.

It would be premature by far to call the GCC a success. Many problems still exist. Several other Arab countries object to the GCC's creation outside the Arab League framework. Political tensions among GCC members have not been eliminated; some of the smaller states fear Saudi domination. The exclusion of Iraq and the two Yemens has been somewhat controversial. The organization is still extremely loose. Many a promising Arab integration scheme has withered, its good intentions never being translated from rhetoric to action. Nevertheless, the GCC may, in time, prove to be the most effective subregional integration scheme attempted in the Arab world. Much depends on the political environment. Time and again, political events have interfered with integration efforts.

Conclusion

Although a variety of centripetal forces work to bind the Arabs together, they have not been able to counteract the centrifugal forces keeping them apart to the degree that states have withered away and been replaced by a larger pan-Arab entity. Arab unity has proved to be more difficult to achieve than any of its early proponents imagined. There have been repeated setbacks, which have sometimes seemed to call into question the very idea of regional integration. With these failures and frustrations, however, pan-Arabism has matured. Its goals have become less ambitious and more realistic. Genuine differences among the Arab states are no longer being ignored or wished away. Obstacles to unity are no longer automatically assumed to be easily surmountable just because Arabs share a common language and culture. The states themselves (or at any rate most of them) are here to stay, imperialist creations or not. Their boundaries may become more permeable with time, but they are unlikely to dissolve. In a revealing 1982 speech, Iraq's President Saddam Husayn captured the significant change of attitude that has occurred in the Arab world:

> Arab unity can only take place after a clear demarcation of borders between all countries. . . . Arab unity must not take place through the elimination of the local and national characteristics of any Arab country. . . . The question of linking unity to the removal of boundaries is no longer acceptable to present Arab mentality. It could have been acceptable 10 or 20 years ago. We have to take into consideration the change which the Arab mind and psyche have undergone. We must see the world as it is. Any Arab would have wished to see the Arab nation as one state. . . . But these are sheer dreams. The Arab reality is that the Arabs are now 22 states, and we have to behave accordingly. Therefore unity must not be imposed, but must be achieved through common fraternal opinion. Unity must give strength to its partners, not cancel their national identity.[21]

Although a cursory glance at the current state of inter-Arab relations would give few grounds for being optimistic about the future, it would be premature to conclude that pan-Arabism had failed utterly and for all time. Paradoxically, recognition of the Arab world's diversity may be the best starting point for achieving unity. Even the most hopeful pan-Arabists are no longer certain that one Arab state will eventually emerge. But whether it is 50 or 500 years from now, the Arab world is likely to grow closer together in a functional sense. It is quite possible that in the distant future the Arab states will establish federal arrangements among one another, either subregionally or regionally. Such a happy medium would allow centripetal and centrifugal forces to coexist comfortably.

Notes

1 Charles Issawi, "The Bases of Arab Unity," *International Affairs* 31(1955): 36.

2. See Stewart Reiser, "Pan-Arabism Revisited," *Middle East Journal* 37(1983): 218–233. Other studies, by contrast, describe the "demise" of pan-Arabism and suggest that the vacuum it has left is being filled by the growth of religious and state identification: see Fouad Ajami, "The End of Pan-Arabism," *Foreign Affairs* 57(1978–79): 355–373.

3. Maxime Rodinson, *The Arabs* (Chicago: University of Chicago Press, 1981): 26–35. Rodinson tries in his book to answer the question: "Who are the Arabs?"

4. This is, of course, true of most underdeveloped regions of the world. Regional cooperation in Africa and South America has been seriously hampered by segmented transportation systems.

5. See United Nations, Economic Commission for Western Asia, "Development of an Integrated Transport System for Western Asia," *Studies on Development Problems in Countries of Western Asia, 1980* (New York: United Nations, 1981) for a detailed description of the problem.

6. Sudan withdrew from the Federation of Arab Republics (FAR) (Egypt and Libya were the other members) partly because of its black minority's opposition. One of the conditions of the 1972 settlement that ended the civil war was that Sudan not involve itself too deeply in any Arab unity scheme.

7. Saul Cohen, *Geography and Politics in a Divided World* (London: Methuen and Co., Ltd., 1964): 231.

8. Foreign Broadcast Information Service (FBIS), *Daily Report, Middle East and Africa*, 24 November 1980, p. A2.

9. See Malcolm H. Kerr, *The Arab Cold War: Gamel Abd al-Nasir and His Rivals, 1958–1970* (London: Oxford University Press, 1970).

10. FBIS, *Daily Report, Middle East and Africa*, 12 November 1980, p. H4.

11. This helps to explain Bahrain's ambivalent feelings about the causeway that will link it to the mainland.

12. John Waterbury, *The Middle East in the Coming Decade: From the Wellhead to Wellbeing?* (New York: McGraw-Hill, 1978).

13. Ibid., pp. 50, 53.

14. For example, Egypt's imports from Syria, before the two countries merged, amounted to 3.46 million Egyptian pounds (LE) in 1957. In 1959, during their union, Egypt's imports increased to LE 7.74 million. Egyptian exports to Syria totaled LE 1.41 million and LE 6.09 million in the same years. Even at their peak, these are astonishingly low figures, given that the two countries were supposed to be united.

15. At the 1967 Khartoum conference, for instance, it was decided that oil-producing states would bankroll Egypt, Syria, and Jordan for their war efforts. At Rabat, in 1974, the Arab states recognized the PLO as the sole, legitimate representative of the Palestin-

ians. As a result of the 1979 Baghdad meeting, they expelled Egypt from the organization. The 11th Arab summit in Amman, in 1980, endorsed a Strategy for Joint Arab Economic Action until the year 2000. It declared the 1980s the First Arab Development Decade and allocated $5 billion to finance projects that would strengthen ties and increase economic integration within the region. The 1982 Fez summit adopted a joint Arab peace plan that implicitly accepted Israel's right to exist.

16. For example, the League helped to solve disputes between Iraq and Kuwait (1961), Oman and the P.D.R. Yemen (1972–76), Egypt and Libya (1977), and countless others. It has also acted as a mediator during civil wars in Yemen A.R. (1962–67), Jordan (1970), and Lebanon (1975–76).

17. Egypt, Iraq, Jordan, Kuwait, Libya, Mauritania, P.D.R. Yemen, PLO, Somalia, Sudan, Syria, UAE, and Yemen A.R.

18. The serious political rift between Syria and Jordan after 1978, for example, does not seem to have impaired the operation of several joint companies established by the two countries after the formation of a Joint Syrian-Jordanian Higher Coordination Committee in 1975 when relations were excellent.

19. See Note 12 above: Waterbury, op. cit., p. 54.

20. John Damis, "Prospects for Unity/Disunity in North Africa," *American-Arab Affairs* No. 6 (Fall 1983): 35.

21. FBIS, *Daily Report, Middle East and Africa*, 14 September 1982, p. E5.

Selected Bibliography

Ajami, Fouad. "The End of Pan-Arabism." *Foreign Affairs* 57(1978–79): 355–373.

Albar, Ahmad. *Le marché Arabe*. Cairo: ALECSO, 1978.

Askari, Hossein, and Cummings, John Thomas. "The Future of Economic Integration Within the Arab World." *International Journal of Middle East Studies* 8(1977): 289–315.

Demir, Soliman. *The Kuwait Fund and the Political Economy of Arab Regional Development*. New York: Praeger Publishers, 1976.

———. *Arab Development Funds in the Middle East*. Elmsford, N.Y.: Pergamon Press Inc., 1979.

El-Mallakh, Ragei, and Kadhim, Mihssen. "Arab Institutionalized Development Aid: An Evaluation." *Middle East Journal* 30(1976): 471–484.

Ghantus, Elias. *Possibilities for Industrial Integration in the Arab Middle East*. Economic Research Paper No. 7. Durham, Eng.: Centre for Middle Eastern and Islamic Studies, University of Durham, 1980.

———. *Arab Industrial Integration*. London: Croom Helm, 1982.

Hassounna, Hussein A. *The League of Arab States and Regional Disputes*. Dobbs Ferry, N.Y.: Oceana Publications Inc., 1975.

Hudson, Michael C. "The Integration Puzzle in Arab Regional Politics," in Michael Hudson (ed.), *The Arab Future: Critical Issues*, pp. 81–94. Washington, D.C.: Center for Contemporary Arab Studies, Georgetown University, 1979.

Kerr, Malcolm H. *The Arab Cold War: Gamel Abd al-Nasir and His Rivals, 1958–1970*. London: Oxford University Press, 1970.

Kerr, Malcolm H., and Yassin, El Sayed (eds.). *Rich and Poor Nations in the Middle East*. Boulder, Colo.: Westview Press, 1982.

Khalifa, Ali Mohammed. *The United Arab Emirates: Unity in Fragmentation*. London: Croom Helm, 1980.

Macdonald, Robert W. *The League of Arab States: A Study in the Dynamics of Regional Organization*. Princeton, N.J.: Princeton University Press, 1965.

Makdisi, Samir A. "Arab Economic Cooperation," in Roberto Aliboni (ed.), *Arab Industrialization and Economic Integration*. London: Croom Helm, 1979.

Musrey, Alfred G. *An Arab Common Market*. New York: Praeger Publishers, 1969.

Niblock, Tim. "The Prospects for Integration in the Arab Gulf," in Tim Niblock (ed.), *Social and Economic Development in the Arab Gulf*, pp. 187–209. New York: St. Martin's Press, 1980.

Poulson, Barry W., and Wallace, Myles. "Regional Integration in the Middle East: The Evidence for Trade and Capital Flows." *Middle East Journal* 33(1979): 464–478.

Reiser, Stewart. "Pan-Arabism Revisited." *Middle East Journal* 37(1983): 218–233.

Rodison, Maxime. *The Arabs*. Chicago: University of Chicago Press, 1981.

Saqr, Naomi. "Federalism in the United Arab Emirates: Prospects and Regional Implications," in Tim Niblock (ed.), *Social and Economic Development in the Arab Gulf*, pp. 177–186. New York: St. Martin's Press, 1980.

Stevens, Robert. *The Arabs' New Frontier*. Boulder, Colo.: Westview Press, 1976.

United Nations. Economic Commission for Western Asia. "Economic Cooperation and Integration Efforts in Selected Countries of Western Asia." *Studies on Development Problems in Countries of Western Asia, 1974*. New York: United Nations, 1975.

———. "Development of an Integrated Transport System for Western Asia." *Studies on Development Problems in Countries of Western Asia, 1980*. New York: United Nations, 1981.

———. "Evolution of Economic Cooperation and Integration in Western Asia." *Studies on Development Problems in Countries of Western Asia, 1980*. New York: United Nations, 1981.

Zahlan, Rosemarie Said. *The Origins of the United Arab Emirates: A Political and Social History of the Trucial States*. New York: St. Martin's Press, 1978.

Critical Issues

9

The Arab-Israeli Conflict:
The Control of Territory

Few twentieth-century disputes have proved to be as intractable as the one between the Arabs and the Israelis, who have fought wars in 1948–49, 1956, 1967, 1973, and 1982. The conflict has contributed significantly to the region's accelerating militarization and could spark a confrontation between the superpowers.

In a sense, the dispute is simple: there are two peoples, Israeli Jews and Palestinian Arabs, who both claim the same territory, variously called Palestine or Israel, as their own. At the beginning of this century, Palestine was overwhelmingly Arab, as it had been for well over 1000 years. During the next half century or so, the Jews, who had been expelled almost 2000 years previously and had lived as a scattered, and often persecuted people, wrested control of the territory away from the Arabs, who were then expelled or fled to the surrounding countries. In the process, the Jews found a national home, which they called Israel, but the Palestinian Arabs lost their national home and formed a new diaspora. Each people insists on its right of national self-determination and statehood but, by and large, denies the same to the other. It follows that for there to be a reasonable chance of peace, the national aspirations of both peoples have to be at least partially satisfied.

In almost every other sense, the dispute is exceedingly complex. Few residents of the region see the conflict in the simple terms we have outlined in the previous paragraph. This chapter traces the conflict from its origins to the present day. As we will see, the topic lends itself well to political geographic analysis because the dispute is above all else about the control of territory. So much can be understood (and misunderstood) by simply looking at a map.

Early History: Pre-1914 Palestine

The Jewish and Arab Connections

The Jewish connection with Palestine, depending on one's perspective, is almost 4000 years or only a century old. According to the Bible, God commanded Abraham and his followers to leave Mesopotamia for Canaan (or Palestine), which He promised would belong to them after a period of persecution in a strange land. A famine forced these Hebrews (Israelites) to Egypt, from where they were eventually expelled and led by Moses in the twelfth century B.C. to Palestine, the "Promised Land." The Hebrews remained divided into separate warring tribes until Saul united them into one Kingdom, which was expanded and strengthened by David, his successor. Solomon, David's son, built the first Temple in Jerusalem in the tenth century B.C. This Kingdom, the only united Jewish state to exist in Palestine before 1948, lasted just 200 years, splitting into the kingdoms of Israel and Judah after Solomon's death. In 721 B.C., the Assyrians conquered and destroyed Israel. The same fate befell Judah in 586 B.C., when the Babylonians destroyed the first Temple and deported many of the kingdom's inhabitants to Babylonia. However, the Persians conquered Babylonia a few decades later and let some 40,000 Judeans return home, where they constructed a second Temple. In the next few centuries, Palestine was variously ruled by the Persians, Macedonians, Ptolemies, Seleucids, and finally after 63 B.C. by the Romans. As a result of three Jewish revolts between A.D. 64 and A.D. 135, the Romans destroyed the Temple and killed, enslaved, or expelled the Jews. From the time of this scattering until the twentieth century—about 1800 years—very few Jews lived in Palestine. As recently as 1914 they accounted for less than 10 percent of the population and not until 1949, after the expulsion or flight of 700,000 Arabs, were they a majority.

Palestine became part of the Byzantine Empire when the Roman Empire split in A.D. 395. At the time, its population, which was largely descended from the original Canaanites, was Christian. In A.D. 634, however, Arabs carrying the infant Muslim faith from its Arabian peninsula hearth invaded the area. In A.D. 691 they built the Mosque of the Dome of the Rock in Jerusalem where Muhammad, the Prophet, is believed to have ascended briefly into heaven. Jerusalem, thus, became one of Islam's most sacred cities, along with Mecca and Medina. This particular conquest had lasting consequences because Palestine's inhabitants were gradually Arabized and, with few exceptions, converted to Islam. Palestine's population remained overwhelmingly Arab and Muslim until the mid-twentieth century. Nevertheless, Arab rule lasted only until 1071, when Seljuk Turks took over the region. In subsequent centuries, the Crusaders, Tatars, Mongols, Egyptian Mameluks, and—from 1517 until World War I—the Ottoman Turks controlled Palestine. However, regardless of who ruled, the population remained largely Arab and Muslim. In addition, from the thirteenth century on, Palestine's rulers were always Muslim, which mattered far more than being Arab until the growth of nationalism in the late nineteenth and early twentieth centuries.

The Growth of Political Zionism

The scattered Jews of the diaspora settled mainly in Europe and elsewhere in the Middle East and North Africa. Those in Christian areas were generally persecuted. Originally, the breach between Christianity and Judaism was theological. The division quickly acquired a deeper character however. European Jews could not own land and often had to live apart, usually in urban ghettoes. Excluded from certain occupations, many became middlemen, merchants and, because the Catholic Church proscribed usury, moneylenders. Often, they were singled out as scapegoats during times of economic or other difficulty. In virtually every European country, they suffered violence and expulsion, especially during the Crusades. The situation reached its worst in Spain, where in 1391 over 70,000 Jews, faced with a choice of baptism or death, were killed. By 1500 most professing Western European Jews had fled east.

The plight of European Jews remained harsh until the French Revolution and the Napoleonic wars guaranteed them full equality under the law. With the growth of liberal democracy and reduced official discrimination, assimilation for the first time became a possibility. Had Eastern Europe's Jews also been emancipated, modern political Zionism, which sought to reconstitute the Jews as a nation in Palestine, might never have gained the force it did. But from the 1880s onwards, Russia's tyrannical Tsarist regime imposed new restrictions on Jewish geographic mobility and employment. Pogroms resulted in thousands of Jewish deaths and a massive exodus. As estimated 2.5 million Jews fled Eastern and Central Europe between 1880 and 1914, with the vast majority going to the United States.

For almost 2000 years, diaspora Jews never completely surrendered the hope of being delivered from exile and returning eventually to Zion, the Promised Land. If the Jews did not live in it, it lived in them. Numerous rituals and prayers expressed this attachment. Jews commemorated the exodus from Egypt, the destruction of the Temple and, tellingly, the agricultural seasons of Palestine, not Russia or Poland. Passover ends with a prayer whose geographic iconography is explicit: "Next year in Jerusalem." Rabbinate literature was full of similar place imagery: "It is better to dwell in the deserts of Palestine than in palaces abroad" and "The air of Palestine makes one wise." The term "Jew" originally denoted a geographic rather than a religious identity; it described a person from Judea, within which Jerusalem was the main city.

Jews believed throughout most of their history that the Return would follow the Messiah's arrival and could only be effected through divine

intervention. In the nineteenth century, however, the growth of nationalist ideas throughout Europe and renewed persecution in Russia
gave birth to modern secular political Zionism, which was essentially a
Jewish nationalist movement. One of its founders was Leo Pinsker, a
Russian physician, whose pamphlet "Self-Emancipation" (1882) argued
that assimilation was impossible and that anti-semitism would exist until Jews were able to establish their own state and become a normal nation. Interestingly, he mentioned Palestine as only one of several possible locations for such a state. Theodor Herzl, whose *The Jewish State*
(1895) reiterated many of Pinsker's points, was far more influential
however. The Jewish problem, Herzl argued, was a national one, not
religious or social, and Jews would forever be considered aliens in their
respective countries. "The idea I have developed," he said, "is a very
old one: it is the restoration of the Jewish state." He urged that "sovereignty be granted us over a portion of the globe large enough to satisfy the rightful requirements of a nation, the rest we shall manage ourselves." He called the Jews "a people without land" and described
Palestine, incorrectly, as "a land without people." Herzl was instrumental in convening the first World Zionist Congress in Switzerland in
1897, whose final resolution reaffirmed that "the goal of Zionism is the
establishment for the Jewish people of a home in Palestine."[1]

The Growth of Arab Nationalism

At precisely the same time, the Arabs were also becoming increasingly
conscious of their national identity for reasons discussed in Chapter 3.
Much of the Arab world lay within the Ottoman Empire after the early
sixteenth century. Until the late nineteenth century, though, most of
the empire's inhabitants were far more aware of their religious affiliations than their linguistic ones. The growth of Arab nationalism, which
stressed the commonalities among all those who spoke Arabic and were
steeped in Arab culture, regardless of religious denomination, was the
product of contact with European political ideas, the expansion of secular education, the spread of the printing press and its accompanying
literary revival, and the rising discontent with Turkish rule. At first, Arab
nationalists hoped that the Turks and Arabs could coexist within the
empire, possibly through as Austro-Hungarian style joint monarchy or
political decentralization. But Turkish repression precluded these op-
tions, and Arabs seriously began to consider breaking away altogether
and forming their own independent Arab state.

World War I and Its Aftermath

World War I was a major turning point for the Arab world generally
and Palestine in particular. For various reasons, the Ottoman Empire

joined the war on Germany's side and declared a *jihad* (holy struggle) against Britain, France, and Russia, which all had millions of Muslim subjects. Ottoman tyranny impelled the Arabs to side with Britain and its allies and to seize the opportunity to win complete independence. Britain was not blind to the benefits of an alliance with the Arabs, whose revolt would complicate Turkey's war effort considerably and undermine its summons to *jihad*.

The McMahon Correspondence

Between 1915 and 1917, the British made a series of conflicting promises and agreements that profoundly shaped the area's political map and set the stage for the current Arab-Israeli dispute. The first of these came during 1915 in an exchange of 10 letters between Sir Henry McMahon, Britain's high commissioner in Egypt, and Sharif Husayn of Mecca, the Prophet Muhammad's most prominent living descendant and the guardian of Islam's most holy sites. Essentially, Britain pledged in the McMahon correspondence to support Arab independence if Husayn's forces revolted against the Turks. But it excluded three areas: the *vilayets* (Ottoman provinces) of Basra and Baghdad, the Turkish districts of Mersin and Alexandretta, and most importantly, "portions of Syria lying to the west of the districts of Damascus, Homs, Hama, and Aleppo." What Britain meant by the last exclusion remains highly controversial to this day. In later years, Britain asserted it meant to exclude Palestine from the area in which it would recognize Arab independence. For obvious reasons, Zionists have taken the same position. The Arabs interpreted the letter as it reads: Lebanon, not Palestine, is to the west of Damascus and the other cities or districts mentioned. In any case, Britain justified the exclusion on the basis of French interests, which were strong in Lebanon but not in Palestine. Tellingly, Lebanon, not Palestine, came under French control at the war's end. The issue is complicated by the fact that Palestine did not exist as a separate administrative entity at the time of the correspondence but was split between the independent *sanjak* of Jerusalem and the two *vilayets* of Beirut and Syria (Figure 9.1). Britain later claimed it used the term "district" synonymously with *vilayet* and noted that because Damascus was part of the *vilayet* of Syria, which covered much of present-day Jordan, the excluded area encompassed Palestine. The Arabs reject this explanation, noting that there was no such thing as a *vilayet* of Damascus, Homs, or Hama. If the British meant areas to the west of the *vilayets* of Aleppo and Syria, why didn't they say so? In one letter, McMahon explicitly recognized Arab objections to the exclusion of "the *vilayets* of Aleppo and Beirut" without correcting Husayn's interpretation. It hardly seems believable that in a matter of such importance Britain would not carefully consider the words it used in advance. If Britain meant to exclude Palestine, why didn't it at least refer to the *sanjak* of Jerusalem, within

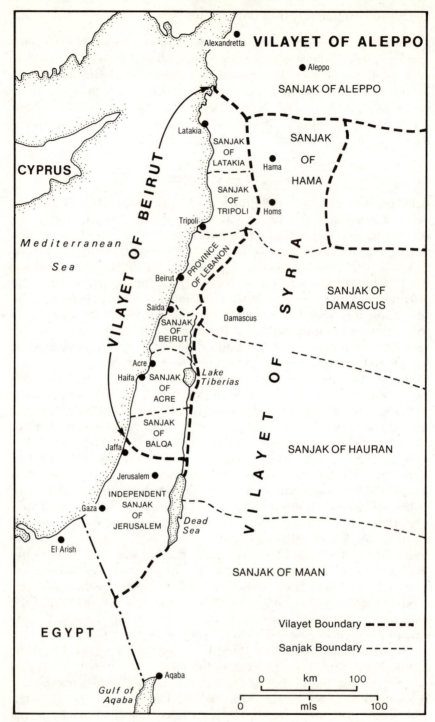

Figure 9.1 Early twentieth-century Ottoman administrative divisions. (After United Nations, *The Origins and Evolution of the Palestine Problem, Part 1: 1917–1947.* New York: United Nations, 1978, p. 97.)

which much of it lay? Whatever the truth of the matter, the Arabs began their revolt against the Turks with the understanding that Palestine would become part of an independent Arab state and the British did not dispel them of that notion.

Sykes-Picot Agreement

As we saw in Chapter 3, in May 1916 Britain, France, and Russia signed the secret Sykes-Picot agreement, which provided for the division of Anatolia and the Fertile Crescent into European spheres of influence and control after the Ottoman Empire's defeat (Figure 3.8). According to this plan, an international administration was to rule most of Palestine. The agreement clearly contradicted the McMahon correspondence. After the Bolshevik Revolution in 1917, Russia's new rulers disavowed the pact and publicized it to discredit the former Tsarist regime. The Turks and Germans were quick to tell the Arabs that they had been the victims of imperialist chicanery, while the British attempted to reassure them.

Balfour Declaration

The most momentous wartime agreement concerning Palestine was the Balfour Declaration of November 1917, in which the British government stated that it viewed favorably "the establishment in Palestine of a national home for the Jewish people" and would use "its best endeavours to facilitate the achievement of this object." However, nothing would be done that would "prejudice the civil and religious rights of existing non-Jewish communities in Palestine."[2] The British issued the Balfour Declaration in part because of a large reservoir of sympathy for the Zionist cause, nourished both by the Bible and by recent pogroms in Eastern Europe. Humanitarian concerns were only part of the reason however. Some British politicians felt that a friendly Jewish presence in Palestine close to the Suez Canal, an imperial lifeline, would have strategic benefits. At the time, few Europeans doubted their right, even obligation, to colonize and, as they believed, civilize non-western regions. Herzl urged that the Jews should, in Palestine, "form a portion of the ramparts of Europe against Asia, an outpost of civilization as opposed to barbarism." He called Palestine "a plague-ridden, blighted corner of the Orient" to which Jews, "as representatives of Western civilization," would "bring cleanliness, order, and the well-distilled customs of the Occident."[3]

However, Palestine was still formally a part of the Ottoman Empire; Britain had no rights over the territory and no authority to dispose of it as it saw fit. The native Palestinian Arabs were never seriously consulted; had they been, they would have opposed large-scale Jewish colonization. Palestine was not, in Herzl's words, "a land without people" or a backward corner of the Orient. It was inevitable, therefore, that any attempt to establish a large, permanent Jewish presence against the will of the people who lived in Palestine would lead to an anti-colonial struggle.

The British Mandate over Palestine (1920–48)

The 1920 San Remo Conference, at which it was agreed that Britain would control what later became Palestine, Transjordan, and Iraq and that France would control what became Syria and Lebanon, dashed Arab hopes of establishing an independent state in areas liberated from Turkish rule. The League of Nations sanctioned this division, granting Britain and France mandates to govern these territories and prepare them for independence. The Palestine mandate, which was officially awarded in 1922, specifically charged Britain with establishing a Jewish national home, facilitating Zionist immigration, and encouraging "close settlement by Jews on the land" in areas to the west of the River Jordan—in other words, with implementing the Balfour Declaration, which now acquired the imprimatur of international law. Hebrew was to become an official language along with Arabic and English, and Jewish immigrants were to receive Palestinian citizenship.

From the start, the Arabs bitterly opposed British control and Zionist colonization plans, which they correctly believed would ultimately result in the creation of a Jewish state and their dispossession. Throughout the mandate, they expressed frustration over their inability to control events. Their fear was that Britain would relinquish control only once Jews were a majority and could form their own state. These anxieties were not unjustified. Weizmann himself had said that the Zionist intention was to make Palestine as Jewish as England was English.

Jewish Immigration

Because Arabs constituted 90 percent of Palestine's population at the end of World War I, the realization of Zionist goals depended on large-scale immigration, which was consequently among the main points of contention between Arabs and Jews. Palestine underwent a radical demographic transformation during the mandate. Initially, Jewish immigration remained relatively light. In most years between 1920 and 1929, for example, fewer than 10,000 Jews arrived; in 1928, barely 1000 entered the territory. According to the 1922 census, Palestine's 84,000 Jews comprised 11 percent of the population. By the 1931 census, their number had doubled to 174,000, but they still constituted only 16 percent of the population. There was a massive influx of Jews into Palestine during the 1930s, however, as a result of Hitler's rise to power in Germany and growing restrictions on immigration into the United States.

Whereas only 4075 arrived in 1931, 30,327 came in 1933, 42,359 in 1934, and 61,854 in 1935. Altogether, some 174,000 Jewish immigrants entered Palestine between 1932 and 1936, by which time they made up 28 percent of the total population. These settlers accounted for only a tiny fraction of world Jewry. Palestine had little appeal to most Jews and attracted only 15 percent of those who left Europe between 1920 and 1936. After peaking in 1935, immigration declined sharply, both because the British imposed quotas and because of World War II, which reduced the flow to a trickle of 3000 to 4000 annually. By 1946—two years before Israel's birth—there were 583,000 Jews in Palestine, or about 500,000 more than in 1922, a sevenfold increase. Because of a high rate of natural growth among Arabs, however, they made up only 31 percent of the total.

The Zionist Spatial Imprint

The Zionist spatial imprint was not uniform and must be seen in the context of Palestine's physical geography. Mandatory Palestine measured only 16,450 square miles (26,320 square kilometers)—roughly 140 miles (225 kilometers) at its longest and 45 miles (75 kilometers) between the Mediterranean and the Jordan Valley. By no means all of this area was equally attractive for settlement. Palestine can be crudely divided into the coastal plain, the interior uplands, the Negev Desert, and the Jordan rift valley (Figures 9.2 and 9.3). The mostly well-watered, fertile, and densely populated coastal lowlands vary in width between 4 and 20 miles (6 and 32 kilometers). To their east lie the Galilean Mountains, which reach 4000 feet (1200 meters) in the north, and the slightly lower and drier hills of Judea and Samaria in the south. The Plain of Esdraelon (Jezreel Valley), which separates these uplands, is an important corridor that connects the coastal plain with the Jordan rift valley. The Judean and Samarian massif has a steep, barren, east-facing escarpment overlooking the Jordan Valley and more thickly settled, gentler western slopes. The thin, long, and (as one goes south) progressively hot and arid Jordan Valley contains Lake Galilee, the River Jordan, and the Dead Sea. The sparsely populated Negev Desert lies to the south of these regions.

Had the Jewish settlers been inspired by purely religious motives and wanted to reposses the territory of their ancient homeland, they would have focused their attention on the upland interior. Instead, they colonized the lowland coastal plain, the Jezreel corridor, and the upper Jordan Valley, where the agricultural potential was greatest and land most readily available for purchase or reclamation; they virtually ignored the rest of Palestine (Figure 9.4). In addition, the vast majority of Jews settled in urban areas, despite the Zionist goal of creating a peasantry and establishing links with the land. According to the 1922 census, some three quarters of all Jews were concentrated in a small

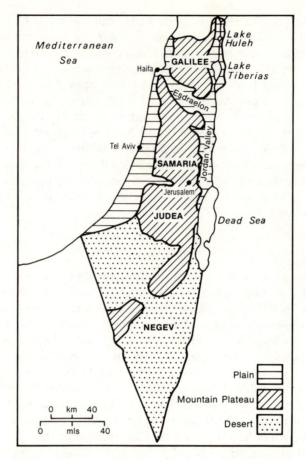

Figure 9.2   Palestine: Physical subdivisions. (After Fawzi Asadi, "Some Geographic Elements in the Arab-Israeli Conflict," *Journal of Palestine Studies* 4(1976), p. 83.)

zone between Jerusalem and Jaffa-Tel Aviv. This spatial distribution had changed little by the 1931 census: many subdistricts had almost no Jewish settlers (Figure 9.5). By 1946, approximately 70 percent of all Jews were urban. Some 66 percent resided in Jaffa-Tel Aviv, Jerusalem, and Haifa; another 19 percent lived in their rural environs. About 36 percent dwelled in Jaffa-Tel Aviv, which two years before statehood was the only subdistrict of Palestine with a Jewish majority (70 percent).

Zionist Land Acquisition

Jewish land purchases were foremost a means of establishing a permanent physical presence, of possessing Palestine. However, they had an important ideological motivation, too. For centuries, European Jews

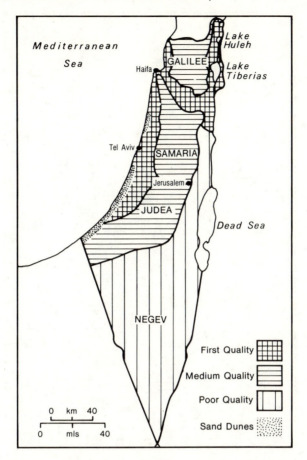

Figure 9.3   Palestine: Soil quality. (After Fawzi Asadi, "Some Geographic Elements in the Arab-Israeli Conflict," *Journal of Palestine Studies* 4(1976), p. 83.)

had been barred from owning land and compelled to live in urban
ghettoes, where they specialized in a limited range of occupations. Zionists believed this distorted occupational structure and uneven geographic distribution had prevented Jews from becoming a normal society.

To a people whose history was marked by rootlessness, buying land
had a symbolic, almost spiritual connotation. Particularly for the many
early Zionist settlers who were socialists, the experimental kibbutzim
(collective rural settlements) depended on being able to purchase land.
The Jewish National Fund (JNF) was established in 1901 to buy, improve, and colonize land in Palestine. In 1920, Jews owned some 2.5
percent of Palestine. By 1946 they owned only 6 to 7 percent. Their impact was far greater than these figures would suggest however.

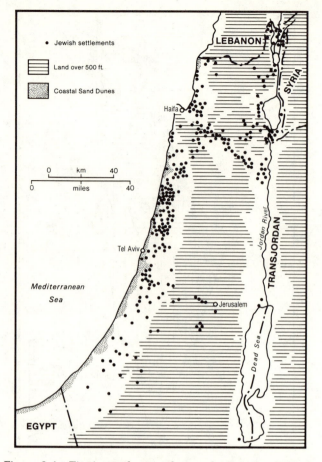

Figure 9.4   Zionist settlement during the British mandate.

As a result of capitalist penetration of the countryside and deeply flawed Ottoman land-registration attempts, most farmland in Palestine was, by the late nineteenth century, owned by a limited number of large landlords—who often lived in Beirut or Damascus—and worked by sharecroppers. This ownership pattern facilitated JNF purchases of large blocs of Arab land. Arab landowners, in turn, often could not resist the high prices being offered, although the overwhelming majority of Arabs did not sell their land.

Jews owned only 12 percent of Palestine's arable land by the end of the mandate. Most of this, however, was in prime agricultural areas and resulted in large Arab displacements. The constitution of the Jewish Agency, which acted as a quasi-government for the settlers, specified not only that all land acquired by the JNF was the inalienable property of the Jewish population (and, therefore, could never be sold back or otherwise transferred to Arabs), but also that "it shall be deemed

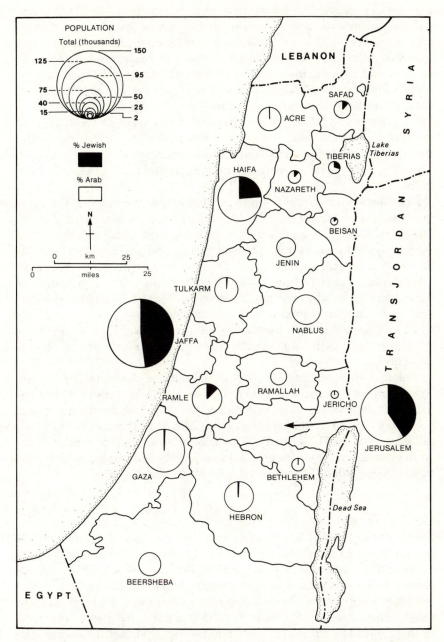

Figure 9.5   Population of Palestine by subdistrict, 1931. (After Janet Abu Lughod, "The Demographic Transformation of Palestine," in Ibrahim Abu Lughod, ed., *The Transformation of Palestine*. Evanston, Ill.: Northwestern University Press, 1971, p. 148.)

a matter of principle that Jewish labor shall be employed" on these lands. JNF leases prescribed fines and even eviction of Jewish farmers who employed Arabs. This discrimination was rationalized on the grounds that Jewish immigrants needed work and that reliance on cheap Arab labor would prevent the creation of a normal society with a balanced occupational profile. Arabs, naturally, saw only the fact that once Jews bought the land, they were expelled from it.[4] The British authorities' timid attempts to protect the rights of tenants were to no avail, and thousands of Arab peasants were forced from the land. Eventually, Britain attempted to restrict Jewish land purchases to certain areas, so explosive did the issue become, especially during the depression in the 1930s.

Palestine's Arabs could not remain oblivious to the fact that the ever-growing Jewish population slowly built up an elaborate shadow state. The settlers established their own factories and trade unions, social welfare system and schools, political parties and governmental institutions—in short, the infrastructure for a future Jewish state. The cleavage between Arabs and Jews was exacerbated by the fact that most of the settlers were educated and relatively affluent Europeans who had little or nothing in common with the mostly illiterate, poor, rural Palestinian Arabs. Zionism, from the Arab perspective, was at root a colonial intrusion with which there could be no compromise or accommodation.

Violence erupted sporadically throughout the mandate. By far the worst outbreak occurred between 1936 and 1939 as a result of the cumulative effects of economic depression, growing Arab landlessness, and pressures created by the sudden arrival of tens of thousands of Jewish refugees from Nazi Germany. This conflation of factors produced an Arab general strike, which escalated into a rebellion during which 3000 to 5000 were killed, 110 executed, and 6000 imprisoned.

British Policy

Britain found itself in a mess of its own making, having made conflicting promises to both Arabs and Jews. It could not satisfy both sides because their claims were incompatible. British rule was, thus, characterized by indecisiveness as each attempt to soothe one party aroused the other's apprehensions and necessitated yet more counterbalancing reassurances. Arabs and Jews both quickly realized that the British stood in their way. The British, in turn, soon recognized that they were sailing between Scylla and Charybdis.

Britain's vacillation was evident in the numerous White Papers (policy statements) that punctuated the mandate. The 1922 Churchill White Paper, for instance, dismissed Arab fears as the result of "exaggerated interpretations" of the Balfour Declaration and affirmed that Britain did not contemplate "the disappearance or the subordination of the Arabic population, language, or culture in Palestine." Simultaneously, though, it reassured the Jews that their fears that Britain would deviate from the Balfour Declaration were unfounded. In 1929–30, Britain dispatched the Shaw and Hope-Simpson commissions of inquiry to Palestine to investigate the causes of recent Arab riots. The resulting Passfield White Paper concluded that Arab grievances had some validity and blamed the disturbances on Jewish land purchases, employment practices, and excessive immigration. Recommendations that these be restricted or modified aroused the ire of the Zionists, who succeeded in pressuring Prime Minister Ramsay MacDonald to repudiate much of the White Paper. This retreat seriously damaged already poor Anglo-Arab relations because the Arabs felt that even when the justness of their case was admitted, it made no difference. Their confidence in Britain's claim to be impartial evaporated altogether.

After renewed Arab rioting in 1936, Britain appointed the Peel Royal Commission to investigate the situation in Palestine. It concluded that the conflict between Arabs and Jews was one of "right against right" and that the problem could never be solved by "giving either [side] . . . all they want." It asserted the mandate was unworkable and should be ended. Jewish immigration should not exceed 12,000 annually over the following five years. From a political geographic standpoint its most significant recommendation was that Palestine be partitioned into Arab and Jewish states (Figure 9.6). The initial partition plan would have been a disaster had it been implemented. Sir Herbert Samuel, one of Palestine's high commissioners, showed a keen political geographic sense when he observed that the Peel Commission "seemed to have picked out all the most awkward provisions of the Peace Treaty of Versailles, and to have put a Saar, a Polish corridor and a half dozen Danzigs and Memels into a country the size of Wales."[5] Most Zionists were pleased that the plan explicitly offered them sovereignty over a portion of Palestine. But there were several aspects of the plan that made them unhappy. The Jewish state would have been fragmented and encompass only 20 percent of Palestine. Because it included Galilee, it would have been half Arab. Jerusalem, Zionism's iconographic territorial center, would have been left out. The Arab section, covering much of the present day West Bank, Gaza Strip, and Negev Desert, would have been linked to Transjordan. The Arabs rejected this idea outright, both on principle and on the practical grounds that they would have been allocated the least productive and most rugged, arid areas. A third zone, encompassing an enclave around Jerusalem and Bethlehem linked by a corridor to the Mediterranean and another enclave around Nazareth, would remain under Britain's control to ensure equal access to holy places. However, with growing awareness of the enormous practical difficulties involved in partitioning Palestine and with an Arab rebellion raging, Britain quietly abandoned the plan.[6]

As World War II approached, British policy took yet another turn.

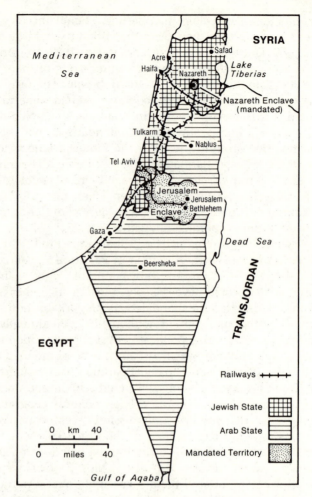

Figure 9.6   The Peel partition plan for Palestine, 1937.

No doubt recollecting how they had courted the Arabs against the Turks
with promises of independence in World War I, the British grew concerned that the Axis powers would use similar enticements and that
they would lose control of the Suez Canal and access to the region's
oil. They, therefore, tilted to the Arab side. The 1939 White Paper reflected this shift. Britain declared unequivocally that it was not its intention to make Palestine a Jewish state and that the Arabs should not
be made the subjects of such a state against their will. Essentially, Britain now opted for a binational, one-state solution. Palestine would gain
independence within ten years and Arabs and Jews would share power.
Significantly, Jewish immigration would be limited to 75,000 over the
following five years, bringing the Jewish population to one third of

the total population. After that, immigration would only be allowed if the Arabs agreed—in other words, there would be no more immigration.

The Birth of Israel

The Holocaust

World War II gave irreversible momentum to the creation of a Jewish state. Zionists had always argued that Jews would be persecuted unless they formed a majority in a territory they themselves controlled. The holocaust, during which the Nazis exterminated 6 million Jews in the most brutal manner imaginable, tragically confirmed these fears. The magnitude of this genocide was almost incomprehensible. A wave of sympathy for the Zionist cause swept through Europe and America. The voices of Palestine's Arabs, who argued that they should not have to pay the price for Europe's sins, went unnoticed or were dismissed as irrelevant in view of what had befallen the Jews.

In this charged atmosphere, Britain nevertheless lamely tried to fulfill its obligation to the Palestinian Arabs, maintaining quotas on Jewish immigration and frustrating attempts to create a Jewish state immediately. As a result, it faced mounting terrorist attacks, initially by such extreme Zionist organizations as Stern and Irgun, but eventually also from mainstream groups fighting for independence and statehood. Despairing it would ever be able to solve the problem, it decided in 1947 to refer the entire issue to the newly formed United Nations.

The U.N. Partition Plan

The General Assembly promptly charged an 11-member U.N. Special Committee on Palestine (UNSCOP) with examining possible solutions. UNSCOP recommended that Palestine receive its independence from Britain immediately. However, its members disagreed about the precise form the entity should take. The minority proposed the creation of a federation of autonomous Arab and Jewish states. The majority recommended that Palestine be partitioned into a Jewish state (with approximately 500,000 Jews and an equal number of Arabs), an Arab state (with 725,000 Arabs and 10,000 Jews), and an independent Jerusalem under U.N. trusteeship. After making minor adjustments to the majority plan, the General Assembly voted, in November 1947, to partition the territory (Figure 9.7). The plan was deeply flawed from a political geographic standpoint, given the deep antagonisms between the two communities. No map could have heightened each side's sense of vulnerability more successfully. Both territories were fragmented and had highly irregular, interdigitated shapes and long sinuous boundaries.

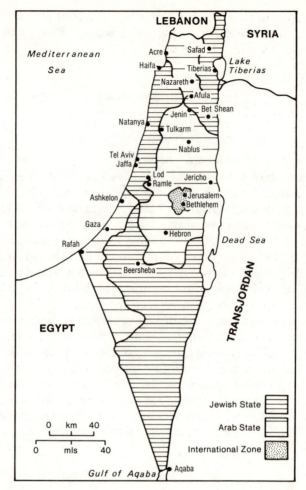

Figure 9.7   The U.N. partition plan for Palestine, 1947.

The 1948–49 War

Fighting between Arabs and Jews intensified after the U.N. partition resolution and Britain's announcement that it would withdraw its forces by 15 May 1948. Zionist groups, following the Plan Dalet, tried to secure more territory for the future Jewish state by occupying areas allotted to the Arabs. Arabs, in turn, attacked Jewish settlements.

On 14 May 1948, Israel declared its existence as a sovereign, independent Jewish state. The following day disorganized, badly trained, and poorly equipped armies from neighboring Arab countries attacked, marking the beginning of the first Arab-Israeli war. By the time the fighting had ended, Israel had seized control of 77 percent of Palestine, greatly reduced the length of its land boundaries, and improved its

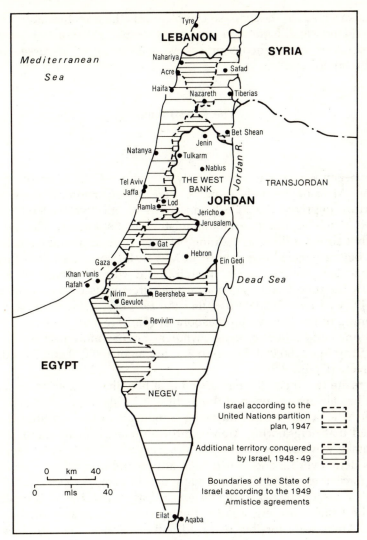

Figure 9.8   Post-1949 Israel.

shape. Israel also gained access to the Gulf of Aqaba, providing it with an alternate ocean outlet while effectively cutting the Arab world in two by severing direct land links between Egypt and all Arab countries to its east (Figure 9.8). No independent Palestinian Arab state came into existence in those areas not taken by Israel owing to Egypt's takeover of the Gaza Strip and Jordan's annexation of the West Bank in 1950. Those parts of Palestine that became Israel were virtually cleared of their Arab population. Entire Arab villages were abandoned or razed and their lands redistributed to incoming Jewish settlers. Usually not even their names survived on the map, so complete was the transformation of the cultural landscape. Israel's creation and Palestine's destruction were interdependent, simultaneous processes: one cannot be discussed without the other.[7]

The Palestinians

The Refugee Problem

Arabs began fleeing Palestine shortly after the 1947 U.N. partition resolution. Most of the early refugees were upper or middle class; their departure deprived the Palestinian Arabs of effective leadership and caused much economic and administrative dislocation. The exodus quickly became a flood as fighting between Jews and Arabs escalated. Even before Israel's formal birth in May 1948, some 200,000 Palestinians had left. Most refugees, though, left during the first Arab-Israeli war. By the time Israel signed armistice agreements with its neighbors in 1949, well over 700,000 had fled the territory. This, then, was the beginning of the Palestinian diaspora or *ghurba* (exile). Jordan received about one half of these refugees, whereas Egypt—more particularly the Gaza Strip—got 200,000. Lebanon and Syria got 100,000 and 75,000, respectively (Figure 9.9).

There are two quite different accounts of how the problem came about. Israel has always maintained the flight was partly a normal reaction of people who wanted to avoid being caught up in the fighting. It also claimed that neighboring Arab countries broadcast instructions to flee and make way for the Arab armies that would liberate Palestine. The Arabs deny ever having issued such advice and insist the Palestinians were forcibly expelled. Certainly many fled in panic, especially after the Irgun's massacre of 254 Arab villagers at Dayr Yasin. There is evidence that the Israelis also encouraged this reaction by planting rumors.[8] In places Arabs were forcibly removed, either because the land they occupied was wanted by Israel or because the advance of the Arab armies would be halted or slowed by a mass of refugees coming the other way.[9] Unquestionably, Palestinians who fled in 1948–49 believed their move was temporary.

Whatever the truth of the matter, Israel was the direct beneficiary of the Arab departure. War and the scattering of the Palestinians accomplished what three decades of immigration could not: the creation of an overwhelming Jewish majority. The presence of several hundred thousand Arabs obviously threatened the Zionist goal of creating a Jewish state.[10]

One of Israel's first actions was to pass the Law of Return, which granted full citizenship to any Jew who immigrated. In 1949 alone, some 250,000 Jews, mostly survivors of the holocaust, entered the country.

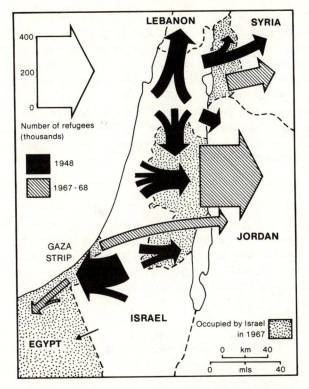

Figure 9.9   Palestinian refugee movements in 1948 and 1967. (After Gerald Blake, "The Wandering Arabs," *Geographical Magazine* XLV(3), 1972, p. 180.)

In the first three years of statehood, 680,000 immigrants—remarkably close to the number of Arabs who left—more than doubled the Jewish population. The property of the Arabs who fled was taken over and ultimately redistributed without compensation. In addition, Israel refused any significant repatriation of Palestinians. The dispossession of the Palestinians was evident in other ways too. Israel, since 1948, has steadfastly denied the existence of a distinct Palestinian Arab people with its own national identity and legitimate national aspirations in much the same way that many Palestinians for long were or still are unable to accept Israel's existence in any form. Golda Meir, when she was prime minister, once remarked: "It was not as though there was a Palestinian people . . . and we came and threw them out and took their country away from them. They did not exist." [11]

Israel's occupation in 1967 of the remainder of what had been Palestine as well as portions of Syria and Egypt compounded the refugee problem. The fighting displaced an additional 500,000 Arabs. About one half of these were already refugees from the 1948–49 war who had settled in the Gaza Strip or the West Bank. By far the largest flow, about

350,000 people, was from the newly occupied West Bank to a truncated Jordan to the east. The 1967 war also resulted in the displacement of significant numbers of non-Palestinian Arabs for the first time. An estimated 100,000 Syrians fled the Golan Heights, leaving it almost empty. An additional 350,000 Egyptians left the badly damaged cities along the Suez Canal. Parenthetically, Israeli shelling in 1968 temporarily caused the almost complete abandonment of the eastern Jordan River Valley. In recent years, southern Lebanon has also been substantially depopulated as a result of both Israeli incursions and bombardment and internecine fighting.

Geographic Distribution

Because of a high rate of natural increase, the number of Palestinians has almost trebled since 1948 to an estimated 4.4 million by 1982 (Table 9.1). Not only is this more than Israel's Jewish population, it is larger than the populations of 74 states in the world. The popular image of Palestinians is of a people living in tents in squalid refugee camps. In

Table 9.1
Geographic Distribution of the Palestinians, 1982

Country	Total	Percentage Local Population	Percentage Total
Israel and occupied territories:	1,834,800	47.0	41.2
Israel	550,800	14.0	—
West Bank	833,000	—	—
Gaza	451,000	—	—
Jordan	1,148,334	53.3	25.8
Lebanon	358,207	11.5	8.0
Syria	222,525	2.5	5.0
Iraq	20,604	0.2	0.5
Egypt	45,605	0.1	1.0
Libya	23,759	0.7	0.5
Saudi Arabia	136,779	1.6	3.0
Kuwait	299,710	22.0	6.7
U.A.E.	36,504	3.5	0.8
Bahrain	2,100	0.6	—
Qatar	24,233	9.7	0.5
Oman	50,706	6.0	1.1
U.S.	104,856	—	2.3
Other	140,116	—	3.1
Total	4,448,838		100.0[a]

[a]Because of rounding, does not add up to 100.0 percent.

Source: *Middle East* (July 1982), p. 10.

fact, the Palestinian experience is diverse and complex. Fewer than one half of all Palestinians are registered U.N. Relief and Works Agency (UNRWA) refugees. Only 36 percent of these, in turn, actually live in camps, some of which in any case have taken on an air of permanence. The largest concentration of Palestinians lies within the borders of pre–1948 Palestine. A distinction should be made between Palestinian Arabs who never fled in 1948–49 and subsequently received Israeli citizenship and those who came under Israeli control only as a result of the occupation of the West Bank and Gaza in 1967. The next largest concentration is in Jordan, where Palestinians make up over half the total population. The Palestinian communities of Lebanon and Syria have also grown enormously since 1948. Outside of this core, the *ghurba* has scattered Palestinians over an ever-wider area. Many countries of the Arabian peninsula, especially Kuwait, have large Palestinian communities. Farther afield, many have emigrated to the United States and Canada. Nevertheless, probably over 80 percent of all Palestinians live within a 200-mile (320-kilometer) radius of Tel Aviv.

Palestinian Nationalism

The Palestinians have not been fully welcome in any Arab country. Their activities are restricted and their rights usually circumscribed. No Arab country came to the Palestinians' defense when Israel attacked Lebanon in 1982. Their status as outsiders has sharpened a sense of national identity and a desire to establish a state of their own. The idea of returning to Palestine is as strong, if not stronger, today as three decades ago. Geographic imagery pervades poetry, literature, painting, and songs of exiled Palestinian artists. Palestinians note that they have all the prerequisites of nationhood—except territory. They boast that on a per capita basis they produce more university graduates than Israel. Because of the tremendous emphasis placed on acquiring education, Palestinians are among the most literate peoples in the region. In many Arab countries, they account for a disproportionate share of all doctors, academics, lawyers, and other professionals. They play a crucial role in the region's business and commerce.

It is often assumed that Palestinian nationalism sprang from, and is nourished by, the refugee camps and that if those living in camps were to be resettled in the Arab countries this nationalism would lose much of its force. In reality, the most articulate proponents of the Palestinian state-idea are usually from the professional class, from people who have never lived in a camp. The problem, therefore, is not simply one of refugees, even if the camps are a potent iconographic symbol. The Palestinians assert the problem is one of national self-determination. They ask: How can Jews reasonably expect us to forget our homeland in only 30 years when they kept alive their desire to return to Palestine for 2000 years?

The Palestine Liberation Organization (PLO) and Palestinian Institutions

In the early days of their exile, the Palestinians remained politically disorganized and hoped other Arab governments would win back Palestine for them. Since the early 1960s, they have developed a number of
political, military, social, and other institutions. The foremost of these
is the Palestine Liberation Organization (PLO), which was established
in 1964 and serves as an umbrella for eight guerilla organizations and
numerous nonmilitary organizations concerned with educational, social, medical, cultural, and financial affairs. Before the 1982 war, the PLO
was one of Lebanon's largest employers, with 6500 full-time industrial
workers and 4000 part-time staffers in addition to its 15,000 or so guerillas. Because it ran enterprises producing "religious articles, hand-
embroidered dresses, kitchen utensils, safari suits, Louis XIV chairs, high-
heeled shoes, shoulder bags, lace tablecloths, butter, poultry, and candy"
some Lebanese referred to it facetiously as "PLO Inc."[12] The organization also operated a news agency and radio station, published a daily
newspaper and several magazines, ran some 100 schools and eight
hospitals, and even had a garbage collection service. The PLO budget
reputedly depended on income from Wall Street investments, American money markets, and donations from the increasingly prosperous
Palestinian diaspora, as well as contributions from certain Arab countries.

Al-Fatah, with about 10,000 members, is the dominant and most
moderate element within the PLO. Increasingly, the PLO has become
the de facto Palestinian government in exile. Since 1974, it has had ob-
server status at the United Nations and been recognized by all other
Arab countries as the sole legitimate representative of the Palestinians.
By 1982, it had 83 offices throughout the world and official relations
with over 100 countries. Another important forum is the Palestine National Council (PNC), a quasi-parliament whose members include a broad
spectrum of occupational and ideological groups. In essence, the Palestinians have developed the paraphernalia and infrastructure of statehood.

The presence of thousands of armed Palestinian fighters has caused
apprehension, if not turmoil, in several Arab countries, notably Jordan
(from which they were expelled in 1970) and Lebanon (from which they
were partially expelled in 1982). Paradoxically, their military successes
against Israel, or within Israel, have been modest, especially compared
to those of national liberation movements elsewhere. Between 1967 and
1982, an estimated 282 Israeli civilians were killed in Palestinian terrorist attacks. Certainly, the Israeli military threat to the Palestinians is infinitely greater than the other way around.

The PLO charter calls for Israel's destruction and the establishment
of a secular, democratic state in any part of Palestine freed from Israeli
control. The Palestinians themselves disagree about possible solutions

to the problem. Moderates seem resigned to accepting a ministate on the West Bank and Gaza, whereas maximalist factions seek the complete liberation of Palestine. These differences contributed to bitter intra-PLO fighting in Lebanon in 1983.

The Changing Political Map

Israel and its neighbors have undergone several territorial adjustments since 1949 as a direct or indirect result of wars in 1956, 1967, and 1973. Israel's invasion of Lebanon in 1982 also led to a lengthy occupation of Arab territory.

The 1956 War

The 1956 war had the least far-reaching political geographic consequences, resulting mainly in Israel's brief occupation of the Gaza Strip and the Sinai peninsula. The war itself was the product of a constellation of factors. In 1952, Jamal Abd al-Nasir and a group of nationalist officers overthrew King Faruq of Egypt. The United States misconstrued Nasir's nonalignment policy and withdrew its offer to aid in the construction of the vital High Dam at Aswan. Egypt responded by nationalizing the Anglo-French Suez Canal Company, hoping to use canal tolls to finance the dam's construction. This caused much anxiety to Britain and France, who decided to seize the canal and topple Nasir.

Israel quickly recognized an opportunity to address some of its own concerns by launching a strike against Egypt. First, it wished to stop Palestinian guerilla attacks from the Gaza Strip. Second, it sought to destroy or capture arms recently acquired by Egypt from the Soviet Union before they posed a threat. Finally, it hoped to open up the Suez Canal and Gulf of Aqaba to Israeli shipping. Because Egypt had closed the canal to Israeli vessels since 1949, the southern port of Eilat at the head of the Gulf of Aqaba had a particular strategic significance. Without it, Israeli ships trading with Asian countries would have to circumnavigate Africa. However, Egypt claimed that Israel had illegally occupied Eilat after the 1949 armistice. In addition, it argued that because most of the Gulf fell within territorial waters, the narrow Strait of Tiran through which all vessels entering or leaving it had to pass was not technically an international strait but rather wholly under Egypt's jurisdiction. Egypt, therefore, installed gun batteries at Sharm al-Shaykh and asserted it had the right to visit and search all ships entering the Gulf. During Israel's early years, Eilat was little used and remained undeveloped. Egypt searched only 3 of 267 vessels going through the strait between 1951 and 1955. In 1955, however, it required all ships to obtain permits before entering the Gulf. Israel claimed its right of innocent passage to the high seas was being infringed and sought U.N. support for its case.

Finally, it decided to solve the problem through military means. Britain, France, and Israel devised a secret plan whereby Israel would invade the Sinai peninsula and Britain and France would subsequently occupy the canal zone under the pretext of protecting it from the fighting. In reality, Israel wanted to take over the Sinai and Britain and France to take back control of the canal and oust Nasir.

The tripartite invasion of Egypt in November 1956 provoked strong United States and international condemnation and failed ignominiously to achieve its aims. Not only did the canal remain in Egyptian hands, Nasir's position was greatly strengthened, Britain and France suffered an immense loss of prestige, and Israel was pressured to withdraw from the Sinai after four months. However, as a result of the war, the United Nations created a special Emergency Force (UNEF), which was stationed along the Egyptian-Israeli boundary and at Sharm al-Shaykh, with the result that the Gulf of Aqaba was opened to Israeli shipping.

Israel's Strategic Concerns

Many Israelis were dissatisfied with their post-1949 boundaries. The more ardent ones complained that the state encompassed only a small part of Eretz Israel, the historic Jewish homeland, and that all of pre-1948 Palestine, at least, rightfully belonged to the Jews. An even more widespread sentiment, though, was that Israel's boundaries left the country vulnerable militarily. Pre-1967 Israel measured 7992 square miles (20,699 square kilometers), slightly larger than New Jersey. Despite its small size, it had uncommonly long sinuous boundaries of 613 miles (981 kilometers) and a highly irregular shape.

To Israel, the political map had a number of specific defects. First, some 80 percent of Israel's population is concentrated on the coastal plain, especially around Tel Aviv, where the country measures only 10 to 16 miles across. Many Israelis felt vulnerable squeezed into this narrow strip between the Mediterranean and Jordan, with hostile Arabs overlooking them. Second, Jerusalem was rigidly divided, with many important Jewish holy sites in the Jordanian sector and, thus, inaccessible. Access to the city was via a protruding corridor. For about 20 miles (32 kilometers), the main road from Tel Aviv passed within 2 or 3 miles (3 to 5 kilometers) of the Jordanian boundary. Third, Syria occasionally shelled northeastern Israel from the commanding Golan Heights. Israelis living here were also cut off to some degree from the rest of the country because the West Bank's northern margins almost meet the southern edge of the Galilee hills, where many of Israel's Arabs live. Fourth, Eilat, some 175 miles (280 kilometers) south of Tel Aviv, was situated on a narrow sliver of territory within 5 miles (8 kilometers) of both Egypt and Jordan. Access by sea was not secure because Israeli vessels had to pass between Egypt and Saudi Arabia. Finally, the Egyptian-administered Gaza Strip, with its several hundred thousand

Palestinians, penetrated to within 35 miles (56 kilometers) of Tel Aviv along the coastal highway. In sum, Israel's spatial morphology produced a deep sense of insecurity and encirclement. Israelis were keenly aware of the close proximity of their opponents. Flying time between Cairo, Amman, or Damascus and Israel's heartland was minutes, leaving little warning in any attack.

Israeli perceptions of spatial relationships within the area obviously differed from those of the Arabs, who felt threatened by what they considered to be Israeli expansionism. Whereas Israel saw itself as surrounded, Arabs saw it as a beachhead, ready to push out in all directions. Whereas Israelis thought of the Gaza Strip and the West Bank, respectively, as a pointing finger and clenched hand prodding their belly, Arabs looked at the same map and noted how these territories were almost encircled, with Israel poised to snap off the finger at its base and to amputate the hand at its wrist (as it ultimately did). Israel's Arab neighbors, too, were conscious of the proximity of their own cities to the confrontation zone. After all, planes and shells can cross political boundaries in two directions. The fact is that both sides mistrusted and feared one another, not without good reason.

The 1967 War

The immediate causes of the 1967 war are of minor importance. In May, President Nasir placed Egyptian forces on alert after receiving reports that Israel had built up its troops along its boundary with Syria, to which Egypt was linked by a military alliance. In addition, he asked the United Nations to remove its force from the Sinai Peninsula, including Sharm al-Shaykh at the entrance to the Gulf of Aqaba. There is evidence that Egypt neither wanted nor was prepared for war and expected the United Nations to reject the request. But the U.N. Secretary General quickly acceded, an egregious error because it removed the only buffer between the two sides. If Nasir did not want war, his behavior did not suggest it because he then closed the Gulf of Aqaba, the passageway for 10 percent of Israel's imports, to Israeli shipping. At the end of May, he signed a mutual defense pact with Jordan, which exacerbated Israeli fears. Meanwhile, several Arab countries were making excessively bellicose broadcasts. By this time, Israel was ready to fight. On June 5, it attacked airfields in Egypt, Syria, Jordan, and Iraq, virtually destroying these countries' forces and gaining complete air superiority within a few hours.

The Territorial Consequences

After six days of fighting, Israel had more than trebled the territory it controlled by occupying the Sinai Peninsula, the Gaza Strip, the West Bank, the Golan Heights, and all of Jerusalem (Figure 9.10). These areas contained approximately 1 million Arabs. The new political map seemed

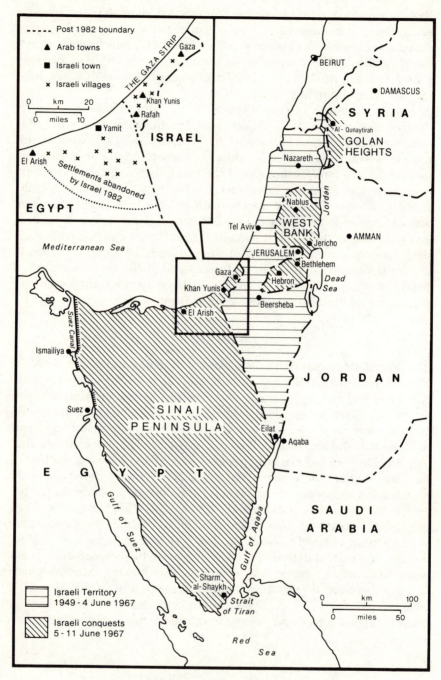

Figure 9.10   Post-1967 Israel and the occupied territories.

to be a dramatic strategic improvement for Israel. Paradoxically, its land boundaries shrank by about 25 percent to only 471 miles (754 kilometers). Its shoreline, by contrast, more than doubled to 564 miles (902 kilometers). Egyptian forces were pushed back across 120 miles (190 kilometers) of desert to behind the Suez Canal, a moat of sorts. The Gulf of Suez separated the two where the Suez Canal did not. Because Israel controlled Sharm al-Shaykh and the Strait of Tiran, access to Eilat was not impeded. In the north, Israel gained the high ground over Syria and controlled Al-Qunaytirah, an important route center. Occupation of the Golan Heights advanced Israeli forces to within 15 miles (24 kilometers) of the main Damascus-Amman road. The area seized from Syria also contained a section of the trans-Arabian oil pipeline (Tapline) and a significant part of the River Jordan's watershed. In the center of the country, the cease-fire line was pushed back to the River Jordan. Now any attacking force from the east, after crossing the river, would be confronted with the steep, east-facing escarpment of the West Bank mountains, through which there are only a few easily defended passes.

Israel clearly sought to establish physiographic (or what it erroneously termed "natural") boundaries and to secure whatever topographical advantages it could. From a political geographic standpoint, Israel had a precise idea of what it was doing. However, Israel's vulnerability ultimately stems not from its spatial configuration or from "bad" boundaries but from the hostility of its Arab neighbors—a hostility that the continued occupation of territory acquired in 1967 has only increased. This is not to deny the undoubted psychological benefits Israelis enjoyed as a result of having trebled the area they controlled. It should be pointed out that Israel is now the world's fourth power militarily. Realistically, it is not likely to be wiped off the face of the map, as it might have been in 1948–49, no matter what its boundaries.

The Economic Consequences

As a result of the 1967 war, Egypt lost $200 million in revenues annually from the closed Suez Canal, two oil refineries that provided 90 percent of its needs, and the Sinai oil fields. Although few Egyptians lived in the Sinai Peninsula and, hence, there were few refugees from Israeli-occupied zones, the cities of Port Said, Ismailiya, and Suez in the canal zone were destroyed and virtually abandoned. Israeli forces were poised only 75 miles (120 kilometers) from Cairo, not almost 200 miles (320 kilometers) as before.

Jordan's economy was devastated. The West Bank had 60 to 80 percent of its agricultural land and produced 60 to 65 percent of its fruit and vegetables. The loss of Jerusalem and Bethlehem ravaged the tourist industry. Altogether, areas occupied by Israel accounted for 38 percent of its gross domestic product. To make matters worse, it had to cope with an influx of several hundred thousand additional refugees.

Israel's advance to the River Jordan also brought its forces to within 20 miles (32 kilometers) of Amman, completely reversing the pre-1967 situation. Syria's loss was the least hard to bear probably because the Golan's contribution to the national economy was relatively small. Nevertheless, 100,000 Syrian refugees flooded Damascus, which was less than 30 miles (48 kilometers) from the war zone.

The 1973 War

The October 1973 war resulted largely from Arab frustration over the lack of progress in winning back territories Israel occupied in 1967. This time there was no prior indication that fighting might erupt and Egypt and Syria, respectively, launched a surprise attack across the Suez Canal and the Golan Heights. Israel, in the midst of Yom Kippur, was unprepared. Initially, the Arab armies made quick gains, winning back some of the territory lost in 1967. However, Israel soon mobilized and reversed these early defeats, pushing beyond the Golan Heights and crossing west of the Suez Canal.

The minor territorial changes that followed this war accompanied disengagement agreements negotiated through U.S. mediation. In the first agreement, signed in January 1974, Israeli troops pulled back from the canal, allowing Egypt to regain control of the waterway and a small sliver of territory in the Sinai. After a similar agreement with Syria in May 1974, Israel withdrew from all Syrian territory occupied in the recent war and from a small portion of the Golan Heights, including its main town, Al-Qunaytirah. In each instance, U.N. forces policed neutral zones between the parties. Egypt and Israel signed a second disengagement agreement in September 1975. This led to Israel's withdrawal east of the strategic Gidi and Mitla passes and from a strip of territory along the Gulf of Suez coastline containing the Abu Rudais oil field.

The 1973 war enabled all sides to claim one sort of victory or another. In strictly military terms, Israel repelled a massive, surprise attack. Had a cease-fire not been declared, damage to the Arab forces would certainly have been greater. The Arab victory, though, was no less significant. Egypt and Syria regained territory. More important, they destroyed the myth of Israeli invincibility and exonerated themselves of the 1967 defeat. The fighting tipped in Israel's favor only after a vast U.S. aerial resupply of weapons that left North Atlantic Treaty Organization (NATO) forces in Europe much weakened. The simultaneous use of the oil weapon—an embargo on the United States and the Netherlands—also underlined the growing global power of the Arabs.

Each of the Arab-Israeli wars has been progressively more destructive and fought with ever-more sophisticated and plentiful weaponry. In the wars of 1956, 1967, and 1973, Egypt had respectively 205, 431, and 620 jet combat aircraft and Israel had 110, 290, and 488. Whereas

Egypt had 430, 1300, and 1955 tanks in the three wars, Israel had 400, 800, and 1700. Syrian, Iraqi, and Jordanian forces grew by proportionately similar amounts. The rising number of casualties reflects this escalation. In 1967, 690 Israeli soldiers were killed. In the October 1973 war, the figure reached 2552, or proportionately two-and-a-half times American losses during the several-year-long Vietnam War. Arab casualties have always been far higher, although not relative to total population. Some 7700 Egyptians and 3500 Syrians were killed in the 1973 war. Perhaps the scale of the 1973 warfare can be comprehended by comparing it to other battles. More tanks were engaged on the Golan Heights and in the Sinai in 1973 than in any other battle in history, except the World War II confrontation between the Germans and Russians at Kursk. The three combatants lost approximately 2800 tanks and 614 aircraft between them—in just three weeks. The total cost of the war, by one estimate, may have exceeded $15 billion.

Camp David and the Israeli-Egyptian Peace Treaty

In November 1977, President Sadat of Egypt, which had borne the brunt of the fighting on the Arab side, made an historic trip to Jerusalem to argue for peace before the Israeli parliament. Subsequent negotiations at Camp David in September 1978 led to agreement over two frameworks for peace. One described the main elements of a peace treaty to be signed within three months. The other specified guidelines for granting the West Bank and Gaza limited autonomy. Little has become of the latter. The Israeli-Egyptian accord was finally signed in March 1979, notwithstanding vehement Arab opposition and threats that Egypt would be ostracized and expelled from the Arab League. Essentially, this agreement provided for Israel's phased withdrawal from the Sinai, which would revert to Egyptian sovereignty, in return for the establishment of diplomatic, economic, and cultural relations between the two countries. The parties agreed to "recognize . . . and respect each other's sovereignty, territorial integrity and political independence." They also pledged to recognize "each other's right to live in peace with their secure and recognized boundaries" and to "refrain from the threat or use of force." The number of Egyptian troops in the Sinai was to be strictly limited and an international peacekeeping force to be stationed in a demilitarized buffer zone extending from the Mediterranean to Sharm al-Shaykh. Significantly, Israel's right of free passage through the Suez Canal was reaffirmed and the Strait of Tiran and Gulf of Aqaba formally pronounced "international waterways open to all nations." Israel officially withdrew from all of the Sinai Peninsula in April 1982, a little more than six months after Sadat's assassination (Figure 9.11).

The Egyptian-Israeli peace treaty was, at best, partial both because all the other major Arab states opposed it and because it ignored Palestinian national aspirations and left uncertain the future status of the

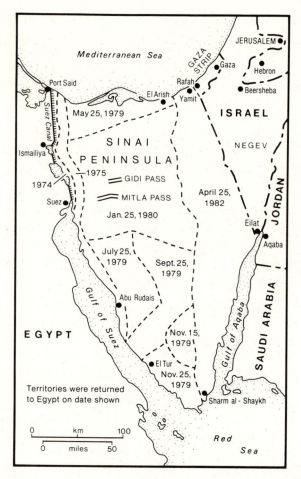

Figure 9.11   Arrangements for Israel's withdrawal from Sinai.

West Bank, Gaza Strip, and the Golan Heights. Without a solution to these problems, there is unlikely to be genuine peace between Arabs and Israelis. The outbreak of war again in 1982 emphasized that fundamental questions remained unresolved.

The 1982 War

The 1982 confrontation differed from all the others in being essentially a massive Israeli onslaught against the Palestinians in Lebanon. Many Israelis opposed the attack since the country was not directly threatened. As we have seen, the Palestinians had made Lebanon, which virtually lacked a central government, their main political and military base, creating a state within a state in the south. Periodically, the Israelis un-

leashed attacks against these Palestinian strongholds, which were occasionally used for launching small raids across the border. Palestinian
guerilla attacks on northern Israel ended after a July 1981 cease-fire
agreement however. The PLO, recognizing its military weakness, increasingly pursued its goals by political means in order to win international support. It was the PLO's growing international legitimacy that
concerned Israel, not its military might, which paled in comparison to
Israel's. On 6 June 1982, 40,000 Israeli troops poured into Lebanon, with
implicit U.S. support. Their announced goal was to push Palestinian
guerilas 25 miles (40 kilometers) north of the border and create a security zone. In reality, they aimed to crush the PLO altogether, to expel
the Syrians from Lebanon, and to install a strong but compliant Christian central government on which Israel could impose a peace treaty.
Israel sought to destroy the PLO in part so that it could strengthen its
hold over the West Bank and Gaza Strip. In a sense, it aimed to extin-
guish forever the possibility of creating an independent Palestinian state.

Israeli forces rapidly advanced north to Beirut. After a brief but intense confrontation, the Syrians, who lost one third of their air force,
agreed to a cease-fire. Because not one other Arab government came to
their assistance, the Palestinians were left to fight one of the world's
best equipped military forces alone. The war differed from all previous
ones in two other respects. First, for the first time ever, an Arab capital
city, Beirut, was beseiged and heavily bombarded from land, air, and
sea. Second, and concomitantly, civilian casualties were massive. The
Lebanese government put the death toll at almost 20,000, with approximately 7000 of these in Beirut. The Israeli death toll exceeded 620 by
February 1985. This is not to mention the displacement of 600,000 civilians. Southern Lebanon especially was devastated. Of all the wars,
this one was the most tragic in human terms. Eventually, the Palestinian guerilas were forced to withdraw from Beirut.

In 1983, Israel and Lebanon signed an agreement whereby Israel would
withdraw its forces in return for significant Lebanese concessions, including the establishment of an Israeli security zone in the south. This
withdrawal would only proceed, however, if Syria simultaneously pulled
out its troops. Syria, and many Lebanese, bitterly denounced the accord as an unacceptable infringement of Lebanon's sovereignty. As a
result, in 1984 the Lebanese government canceled the agreement. In early
1985, Israel began a three-stage withdrawal of its forces, which were
suffering heavy casualties as a result of Shi'i attacks. Syrian and Palestinian forces continued to occupy eastern and northern Lebanon.

The Occupied Territories

It was clear soon after the 1967 war that some Israelis envisioned a long,
even permanent, stay in the occupied territories, whether because of

their strategic significance, their likely usefulness as a bargaining chip in future peace negotiations, or their historic significance to the Jewish people.[13] To be sure, there were many Israelis at that stage who would have been willing to withdraw in exchange for a peace treaty. With the passage of time, however, more Israelis favored retaining the occupied territories permanently in some form.

Israeli Settlements

From the early days of Jewish colonization of Palestine, Zionists viewed rural settlements as a means not only of reestablishing links with the land and normalizing their occupational structure, but also of reappropriating Eretz Israel, of expanding the *yishuv* spatially, and of establishing a line of defense outposts. The establishment of Jewish settlements in the occupied territories, far from being a new and different process, was a continuation of the very colonial settler policies that gave birth to Israel in the first place (Figure 9.12).

Within weeks of the 1967 war Prime Minister Levi Eshkol had appointed an official planning committee for the occupied territories' development and entrusted a study group with "preparing comprehensive settlement plans for these areas." As early as July 1967 Yigal Allon, the deputy prime minister, presented his plan for the territories to the Israeli cabinet. Although never formally accepted, a modified version of this plan guided the spatial distribution of settlements for almost a decade. Like many Israelis, Allon's premise was that "the land belongs to the people who live on it—territories will be ours if Jews settle them."[14] His plan was a compromise between the maximalists' proposals to incorporate all of the occupied territories permanently and those of the minimalists, who advocated only minor territorial adjustments and were conscious of the political risks of absorbing several hundred thousand Arabs. Essentially, Allon sought to enhance Israel's security without upsetting its demographic structure. Throughout the 1967–77 period, when Israel was ruled by the Labor Alignment, settlements were, thus, generally located in peripheral regions where there were fewer Arabs.

After the 1977 electoral victory of the Likud Bloc, Jewish colonization of all the occupied territories was deemed a matter of historic right more than strategic necessity. Former Prime Minister Menachem Begin and his supporters believe that if Jews have a right to settle on the coastal plain, their claims to "Judea and Samaria," as Israel now officially describes the West Bank, are still more valid because this was where the ancient Jewish kingdoms were located. It should be noted that even with this expansion, Israel's boundaries do not conform with those of Eretz Israel, a source of considerable Arab apprehension. Begin pointedly refers to the occupied territories as being part of "western Eretz Israel," with the clear implication that Jordan and parts of other Arab countries

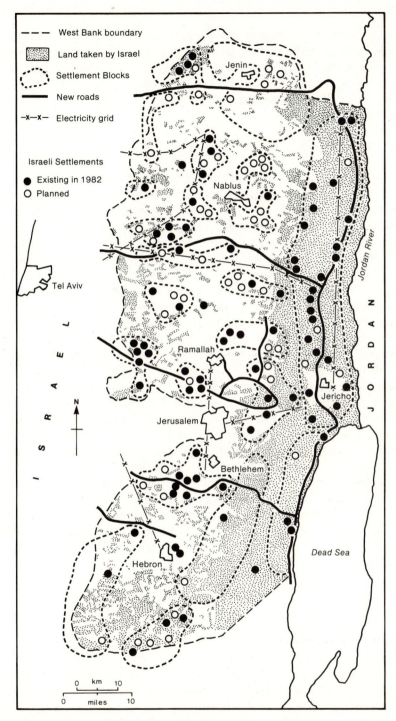

Figure 9.12   Jewish settlements and land acquisition in the West Bank. (After
New York Times, September 11, 1982, p. 14. Copyright © 1982 by the New York
Times Company. Reprinted by permission.)

are also part of the historic Jewish homeland. The Likud government made itself absolutely clear: it would never withdraw from the Golan Heights or the West Bank, few parts of which have escaped heavy Jewish settlement since 1977. The Labor-led coalition government that came to power in 1984 has placed less emphasis on colonization of the West Bank.

The Golan Heights

The settlement experiences of each of the occupied territories has been different. The Golan Heights were colonized first because almost all Israelis agreed that their strategic significance required their retention. The exodus of 100,000 Syrians, which virtually depopulated the region, also made the Israeli task considerably easier here. By November 1967, the Settlement Department had presented a detailed plan advocating the establishment of 20 settlements with 7000 people within 15 years. Subsequently, even more ambitious plans—one in 1969 foresaw 50,000 settlers in 10 years—were aired. By 1973, almost all the settlements were concentrated around Al-Qunaytirah or in southern peripheral parts of the Golan Heights where no land improvement was needed for agriculture. Central Golan, the most important section strategically, was not settled partly because of its poor soil. It was here that Syrian forces penetrated the Heights during the 1973 war. Not unexpectedly, after the fighting, the focus of Israeli settlement activities shifted to this area.

Heavy settlement of the Golan began really only after the 1973 war. Whereas in 1972 there were only 600 settlers, by 1974 there were 1800. Israel's withdrawal from Al-Qunaytirah and from the eastern portions of the Golan as a result of the 1974 disengagement agreement did not slow the settlement drive. The current plan is to construct a network of agricultural and industrial villages oriented towards the new urban center of Qatzrin, which was begun in 1976 and is projected to have 20,000 residents eventually. The expansion of settlement after the Likud victory was dramatic. By 1980, there were almost 7000 settlers. The region's formal annexation in December 1981 was the logical outcome of 14 years of Israeli policy.

The West Bank

The West Bank presented an entirely different situation. Although some 350,000 Arabs fled this Delaware-sized territory, over 700,000 remained. Conveniently for Israel, most of those who left were from the Jordan rift valley and the Jericho region, precisely the areas the Allon plan considered most vital strategically. The Allon plan sought to incorporate into Israel a north-south strip of territory 10 to 15 miles (16 to 24 kilometers) wide along the Dead Sea shoreline, the Jordan rift valley, and the eastern margins of the adjacent uplands. Such a buffer would encircle almost all the West Bank's Arabs. Most Israeli settlements on the West Bank until the mid-1970s were located around Hebron or in this strip, either in a line along the valley floor or in another parallel line in the nearby uplands at 2000 to 3000 feet (600 to 900 meters) above sea level. The latter were linked by the new, paved Allon road completed by the mid-1970s. By 1975, there were 15 Jewish settlements in the strip with 1800 inhabitants. This had increased to 25 settlements with 3300 settlers by 1977, although 1400 of these lived in the town of Qiryat Arba, adjacent to Hebron. The relatively small population of the rift settlements was partly a function of the region's hot, dry climate, which settlers found relatively unattractive compared to other parts of the occupied territories. Significantly, the Allon plan did not completely surround the West Bank with Jewish settlements but left a narrow corridor between the West Bank and Jordan around Jericho. The Labor government did not exclude the possibility of a peace settlement in which the Arab core of the West Bank would be returned to Jordan.

For almost all Israeli Jews, the 1967 war's greatest prize was the Old City of Jerusalem, with the Western Wall and numerous other sacred sites. Israel annexed East Jerusalem and a large surrounding area immediately after the war, taking care to draw the new municipal boundary to exclude several large Arab villages but to include high areas overlooking the city's Arab suburbs. It also demolished the Arab Maghrebi quarter of the Old City to facilitate access to the Western Wall and expropriated considerable amounts of Arab land. The Jerusalem area has received by far the most attention of any part of the occupied territories, both under Labor and Likud. An estimated 90,000 Jews—some 70 percent of the total in the occupied territories—have settled there since 1967. Many of these live in a ring of new ridge-top satellite towns, which have grown up on all sides of the city, encircling Arab areas and forming a kind of outer wall. In the early 1970s, a second outer ring of industrial satellite towns was begun. Many of these were located beyond the original annexed area, giving rise to Arab fears that eventually the intervening areas would also be annexed (Figure 9.13). The Allon plan also envisioned widening the narrow, exposed corridor that connected Jerusalem with the coastal plain. Four Arab villages in the Latrun area were completely razed soon after the 1967 war and a settlement established in their place at Mevo Horon. The Etzion Bloc of settlements similarly fattened the corridor to the south.

Few Jewish settlements were built in the West Bank's rural, densely populated Arab heartland until the mid-1970s when the ultranationalist Gush Emunim movement attempted to settle it unilaterally. Initially, the government declared these footholds unauthorized and evicted the squatters. Before long, however, it tacitly supported the settlers in founding permanent settlements.

After the 1977 Likud victory, any restraints on settling heavily populated areas of the West Bank ended abruptly and a crash program of

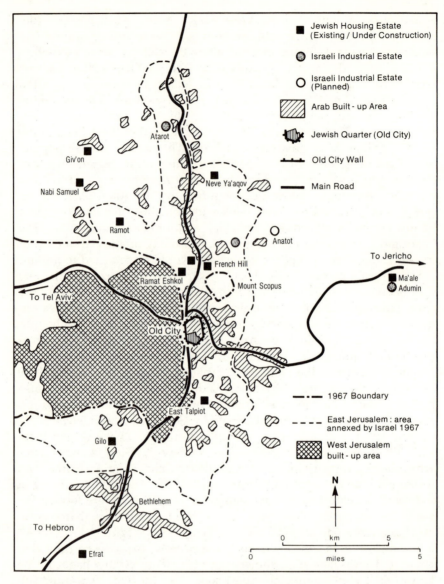

Figure 9.13   Jerusalem since 1967. (After William Harris, *Taking Root*. New York: Wiley, 1980, p. 54. Copyright © 1980 by John Wiley & Sons, Inc. Reprinted by permission.)

colonization began. All prohibitions against private land purchases by Israelis were removed. Between 1978 and 1985 the number of West Bank settlements outside annexed Jerusalem increased from approximately 24 (most of which were in the rift valley) to 114 (most of which were in the Arab highlands). The number of settlers lept from 3200 to 42,500.

The chief architects of settlement policy after 1977 were Matityahu

Drobles, head of the World Zionist Organization's Settlement Department, and Ariel Sharon, former minister of defense. Drobles's 1978 plan merits special attention. Its premise was that "the best and most effective way to remove even the slightest doubt of the intention to hold Judea and Samaria [the West Bank] forever is enhanced settlement in these areas." He observed that "it is incumbent upon us to run a race against time" for "it may be too late tomorrow to do what is not done today." The plan envisioned "the dispersion of the [Jewish] population from the densely populated urban strip of the coastal plain eastward to the presently empty *[sic]* areas of Judea and Samaria." Significantly, it recommended the location of colonies "not only around the settlements of the [Arab] minorities *[sic]*, but also in between them." [15] Specifically, it advocated the development of settlement blocs surrounding the main Arab towns, which would obviously have the practical effect of fragmenting and compartmentalizing Arab areas into small isolated cells.

Ariel Sharon has been one of the leading proponents of building a north-south strip of hilltop settlements between Nablus and Tulkarm through the heart of the West Bank. This will be crossed by a west-east strip extending from Israel proper to the rift valley's regional center. Where the two axes intersect, the new urban center of Ariel, projected to have over 50,000 residents eventually, is being developed. A new 35-mile (56-kilometer) west-east Trans-Samaria Highway was completed in 1982 to link many of these settlements and to reduce travel time between the rift valley and Tel Aviv to one hour only. Two more west-east roads are planned or under construction. One crosses the northern part of the West Bank to the rift valley, the other connects the Dead Sea with Israel proper. These highways will integrate the West Bank even more closely with Israel and greatly facilitate Jewish settlement by allowing settlers to commute to work in Tel Aviv and other major employment centers.

Early Israeli settlement plans for the occupied territories all failed to measure up to expectations because few Israelis were willing to move into these areas as pioneer farmers. The Likud government introduced incentives to encourage broad based settlement of the West Bank, where the overall costs of settling each family in 1982 were estimated at roughly $225,000 to $300,000. Cheap land and generous building subsidies have made housing costs a relative bargain. [16] This has opened up a much larger reservoir of potential settlers. Plans to settle 100,000 by 1990 no longer seem unrealistic. Most of the growth will come through the expansion of existing settlements rather than the establishment of new ones. Increasingly, settlers commute to work in Israel proper from what amount to dormitory towns. Some 80 percent of the Jewish population in the occupied territories will ultimately live in urban settlements. The plan to settle 100,000 by 1990 is part of a more ambitious 30-year Jewish Agency Settlement Department plan to populate the West Bank with

1.2 million Jews by the year 2010. By then, only 1.3 million Arabs will be living in the area.

Jewish settlers in the occupied territories are segregated from the Arabs in more than just a geographic sense. Administratively, the areas they inhabit are treated as if they were integral parts of Israel. All are organized into regional councils, similar to counties in Israel. Jewish settlers pay the same taxes; are subject to the same laws, police, and courts; and vote in the same elections as Jews living within Israel proper. While Arab-owned cars on the West Bank have blue license plates, those of Israeli settlers are yellow and identical to ones within Israel.

The segmentation and integration of the West Bank is clearly designed to forestall any meaningful Arab regional autonomy. When the plan is complete, the West Bank's Arabs will be divided from one another by an Israeli grid of highways and settlement nodes. The Allon plan's concept of an unsettled corridor linking the West Bank to Jordan through Jericho has been completely abandoned. Hence, Jerusalem and the settlements to its east will cut the northern and southern parts of the West Bank off from one another, whereas the West Bank generally will be a buffer cut off from Arab areas east of the River Jordan. Interestingly, 52.5 percent of West Bank settlers outside Jerusalem live in only eight settlements and 25 percent live in just one, Maale Adumin, east of Jerusalem (as of January 1985).

The Gaza Strip and Sinai

The Gaza Strip offered few opportunities for Jewish settlement. In 1967, some 300,000 Arabs were crowded into this 139-square-mile (360-square-kilometer) area. Moreover, very few fled as a result of the fighting, mostly because there was no escape route. By 1976, there were only five Jewish settlements in the strip itself. The Israeli approach here was to encircle the territory with a cluster of a dozen or so settlements to the southwest, astride the main route from Egypt. These settlements were demolished and vacated prior to Israel's withdrawal from Sinai. The only other Israeli outposts in the mostly mountainous desert Sinai Peninsula were a line of five settlements along the Gulf of Aqaba. Although these acquired some economic importance through tourism, their real import was obviously strategic. They, too, were abandoned in the withdrawal.

Land Acquisition

Because world attention has focused on the spread of settlements, which are generally recognized as directly contravening the Fourth Geneva Convention of 1949 on behavior in occupied areas, other equally profound geographic changes have often gone relatively unnoticed. It is sometimes pointed out that the number of Jewish settlers in the occupied territories is still comparatively small. This ignores the fact that Israel, especially since 1977, has been trying to take the land, not necessarily to outnumber the Palestinians.[17] The means that Israel has used to take possession of Arab land merits discussion. In 1950, Israel passed the Absentee Property Law, which enabled the government to confiscate the property of Palestinian Arabs who were not present or had absented themselves even temporarily since November 1947. In this manner, it dispossessed literally thousands of Arab refugees who were absent precisely because Israel would not allow them to return. This method of land seizure was used after 1967 in the Golan Heights and Jordan rift valley particularly. Israel has also made use of laws, introduced originally by the British, that allow private land to be "closed off" from its owner for "security" or other reasons. This was used to prevent Arabs from returning to their properties after the 1948–49 war. Israeli military authorities have "closed off" large areas in the West Bank. According to customary law, communal or unclearly titled land must be used continuously if usufruct rights are to be kept. If Israeli authorities "close off" an area or prohibit entry into it for security reasons, the land may be deemed "abandoned" or uncultivated, in which case control will revert to the state. A 1949 Israeli ordinance vests the Ministry of Agriculture with the power to seize land to ensure its cultivation. Military authorities in the West Bank have used this to expropriate marginal lands that are cultivated only in years with good rainfall. Another 1949 Israeli law permits the government to take property declared necessary for security and settling immigrants, among other reasons.

Most of the land transfers have been in the state land category. State lands were formerly controlled nominally by the Jordanian government but used as commons land by Arab villagers. Israel has interpreted state land in the most literal, legalistic, and exclusive way. Because establishing settlements on sequestrated state lands circumvents court challenges, it is by far the most attractive land category for colonization. After Likud's victory, Israel embarked on a crash program to unilaterally convert as much West Bank land as possible into state land, using obscure Ottoman statutes. For instance, it can simply declare that a piece of land is state owned, which puts the burden of proving the contrary on the occupant or owner. Most West Bank lands have not been properly surveyed. Only a fraction are registered and have titles with clear ownership because, as in most Arab societies, land rights are traditionally derived from customary usage rather than a western-type registration system. Israel has exploited this informal and somewhat haphazard approach to the utmost. Military Decree No. 59 states that land with "no ownership claims" is to be considered state land. Given that West Bank land registration procedures fall short of Israeli standards of acceptability, Israel can easily dispossess Arabs of their land by simply refusing to accept the validity of their ownership claims. In addition, Military Decree No. 291 of 1968 stopped the issuing of new title deeds to Arabs on "unsettled" land, which accounted for about two thirds of the total at the time. This also paved the way for large-scale conversion to Israeli-controlled state land. It is conservatively estimated that by 1982 Israel had appropriated 395,000 to 410,000 acres (160,000 to 166,000 hectares) of the West Bank's total 1.45 million acres (587,000 hectares)—almost 30 percent. Moreover, the Israeli government directly controls 797,000 to 942,000 acres (322,000 to 381,000 hectares), or 55 to 65 percent of the entire West Bank.

Water

Israel has also exploited the West Bank's water resources. Before 1967, wells inside Israel tapped approximately 15.7 billion cubic feet (450 million cubic meters) of water annually from aquifers under the West Bank. This amounted to approximately one third of total Israeli water consumption. Only 4 percent of Arab cultivated land on the West Bank was irrigated, however, and there were comparatively few deep wells. Israel, with its heavy water demands and projections of imminent serious shortages, was concerned that if more deep Arab wells were dug into the West Bank aquifers and if local consumption increased substantially, this would directly threaten its own water supply. The occupation of the West Bank placed all the territory's water resources under Israeli control. All wells were metered and consumption limited to 1967 levels. The occupation authorities also banned the drilling of any more wells, except in rare instances where this was vital to provide drinking water for domestic use. What is more, Israeli settlers on the West Bank have been allowed to drill wells. Many of these, especially in the Jordan Valley, are deep and use efficient, modern pumps, with the result that a relatively small number extract a disproportionate share of the region's ground water. Several Arab villages have complained that their own wells have dried up because of deep Israeli ones nearby. Many Palestinians suspect that Israel is trying to strangle Arab agriculture to encourage emigration and accelerate land transfers.

Economic Integration

The occupied territories have been thoroughly integrated with Israel economically. As a captive market, they have been flooded with Israeli products. In fact, they get some 90 percent of their imports from Israel and are its second largest export market after the United States. Trade with the rest of the Arab world is severely hampered by Arab boycott laws and Israeli barriers. The trade between Israel and the occupied areas is asymmetrical, however, because with the exception of a few agricultural products and construction materials, the Israeli market is almost closed to the West Bank and Gaza's products. Agricultural goods have been increasingly shut out to protect local Israeli producers. The occupied territories, thus, suffer from a chronic, large trade deficit with Israel that is lessened only by remittances from workers overseas and a surplus in agricultural exports to Jordan.

About 60,000 Arabs now commute to work in Israel every day. This amounts to one third of the West Bank's nonagricultural labor force and almost one half that of Gaza. Such workers are strictly prohibited from spending the night in Israel. Perhaps an additional 10,000 to 20,000 workers are not recruited through the official Israeli labor exchange offices. A high proportion of workers from the occupied territories hold unskilled or menial jobs, especially in construction, and they are the first to feel the effects of recession.[18] Certain sectors of the Israeli economy have become quite dependent on this large reservoir of cheap, nonunion labor. The wages these workers earn are recycled back into the Israeli economy to some degree by the purchase of Israeli products in the occupied territories.

The Israeli military occupation is deeply unpopular, as frequent disturbances testify. To maintain control, Israel has had to resort to repression: the repeated closure of universities and schools, censorship, the ousting of elected mayors, the cultivation of a more pliant local Arab leadership, and lengthy curfews of entire villages and towns. In recent years, Amnesty International, the U.S. State Department, and numerous independent organizations have documented Israeli violations of human rights, including deportation, collective punishment, the demolition of houses, administrative detention, and even torture. So bad is the economic and political climate that an estimated 20,000 Arabs, many of them professionals, leave the West Bank annually. Between 1968 and 1980, an estimated 100,000 emigrated. Some Palestinians fear that this is precisely what Israel hopes. Drobles, the architect of settlement policies in the occupied territories, has said as much: "When we clarify that this [West Bank] is an integral part of Israel, some will leave to other Arab states."[19]

Most serious proposals for solving the Arab-Israeli dispute envision an Israeli withdrawal from the occupied territories, with perhaps minor territorial adjustments, and the creation of a self-governing Palestinian entity in the West Bank and Gaza. Although some would prefer this entity to be linked to Jordan and to have little autonomy, others feel only an independent Palestinian state will suffice. It seems clear, though, that Israel, at least under the Likud government, did not plan any territorial concessions in the West Bank and Gaza. The so-called Green Line that marks Israel's pre-1967 boundaries is not shown on Israeli maps.[20] The Likud government interpreted the provisions of the Camp David accords dealing with West Bank and Gaza autonomy in the most restrictive possible sense, that is, to mean autonomy for people, not territory. Clearly this was not how the United States or Egypt understood the agreement. The most explicit statement of Israel's intentions was provided by Begin, who in 1982 remarked: "As soon as, one day, our national sovereignty is applied to Judea, Samaria, and the Gaza district, we will maintain and observe full autonomy for the Arab inhabitants of these parts of Eretz Israel."[21] In other words, Israel wants the land without the people. Israel has annexed the occupied territories in all but name already. Nevertheless, Israelis are themselves divided about the future of these territories. The Labor Alignment, which won most seats in the Knesset in the July 1984 election, has expressed a greater willingness than the Likud to make territorial concessions.

Conclusion

The risk of another general Arab-Israeli war is ever present. Such a war could be even more destructive than the last one. Between 1977 and 1980, data show that 7 of the 10 largest Third World weapons-importing states were in the Middle East and North Africa. The region spent $4.5 billion on imported conventional armaments in 1982. The United States, which accounts for 40 to 50 percent of world arms transfers, sends about 60 percent of its weapons exports to this region. Between 1971 and 1978, the United States sold $47.7 billion worth of military equipment to the area. By no means all of this was destined to frontline states in the Arab-Israeli conflict; both Saudi Arabia, which purchased $18.7 billion of U.S. arms, and Iran, which got $13.5 billion worth, received more than Israel ($8.6 billion) and Egypt ($3 billion). How or where weapons will be used cannot be controlled, however, and even sales to countries not directly involved in the dispute contribute to the arms race in the region. Reliable figures on Soviet military sales to the region are not easy to come by. Perhaps 70 percent of its arms exports, which make up about 30 percent of the world total, go to the region. Syria, Iraq, and Libya, all major clients, were the fourth, fifth, and sixth largest Third World weapons importers between 1977 and 1980. French and British arms sales have also been significant.

A measure of the appalling dimensions of this traffic is that between 1971 and 1980, the Middle East and North Africa, with about 5 percent of the world's population, received over half of the world's foreign military sales. In 1982, it received over one half of all arms imports in the Third World. Since 1973, the number of weapons in the region has more than doubled. Israel, which is considered able to beat any combination of Arab forces, alone has more combat aircraft than West Germany, one third as many tanks as the United States (which has about 60 times more people) and thrice as many as Britain or France. Israel and its most likely Arab adversaries have nearly as many conventional weapons as the Eastern Bloc in all of northern and eastern Europe. If Israel's reserves of 300,000 are included, the Middle East has almost twice the total military manpower of the United States and has close to the 4.7 million for the United States and all the NATO countries excluding Turkey. The region has more combat aircraft than the combined European NATO air forces and considerably more medium-sized tanks than the United States and NATO combined.

According to the Congressional Research Service of the Library of Congress, between 1973 and 1980 the United States, the Soviet Union, and Western Europe provided Middle Eastern and North African states with 14,530 tanks and self-propelled cannons, 21,680 troop carriers, 3370 supersonic combat aircraft, and 26,020 surface-to-air missiles. The highly advanced nature of some of these weapons needs to be emphasized; they include F-15, F-16, F-18, and Mig-25 fighter bombers; M-1, T-72, and Chieftain tanks; "smart" laser guided bombs; extraordinarily sophisticated radar and early warning systems; and modern rocketry. In addition, Israel is believed to have 10 to 27 nuclear bombs stockpiled and to have detonated a test bomb off South Africa in 1979.

Almost continuous conflict has encouraged the growth of a local arms industry. Israel has achieved far more than the Arabs in this respect. In 1980, it was the world's seventh largest arms exporter. Its weapons shipments were worth $1.3 billion, or 40 percent of total exports and the largest single export. Arms manufacture and sales have linked Israel strongly with South Africa and various Central American countries.

The economic and social costs of the Middle Eastern arms race are staggering. In 1981, Saudi Arabia, with a population of only 11 million, spent $27.6 billion on defense, compared to Britain's $28.7 billion, France's $26 billion, and West Germany's $25 billion. On a per capita basis, military expenditures in the Middle East are, on average, five times higher than those in Europe. Of the top 10 countries spending over 10 percent of their GNP on the military, 9 are in the region. Defense expenditures in Israel amounted to 23.2 percent of GNP in 1981, compared to 3 to 5 percent among the leading NATO countries. In Israel, Syria, and Saudi Arabia, almost one third of all government spending is on defense.

To some extent the burden of paying for arms is eased by extensive external assistance, which has increased superpower involvement in the conflict. This is particularly true in the case of Egypt and Israel. Prior to 1973, Egypt was a major recipient of Soviet aid. Between 1973 and 1977 it depended on help from the Arab oil-producing countries, which gave $17.2 billion. This was cut off after Sadat's peace initiative and Egypt turned to the United States, which in fiscal 1984 provided $2.2 billion in (mostly military) aid, or more than to the rest of Africa or to Latin America. On a per capita basis, U.S. aid to Egypt totalled $53, compared to only $0.30 to India. American aid to Israel has been even more lavish, exceeding $28 billion between 1949 and 1984 (with most of this coming since 1973). Israel received $2.3 billion—or about $630 per capita and over $3000 per typical family of five—in 1984. Much of this assistance consists of grants or loans that are forgiven. The importance of this aid cannot be too strongly emphasized. In 1979, it amounted to 20 percent of Israel's total budget and 35 percent of its military budget. In addition, nearly 20 percent of *all* U.S. foreign aid in 1984 went to Israel. Perhaps a more telling statistic is that between 1978 and 1984 the United States granted $30 billion in military, economic, and food aid to Egypt and Israel combined. This amounted to one third of its worldwide total.

Although the stakes are exceptionally high, peace does not seem imminent because of the obduracy and lack of trust on almost every side. Obviously there can be no solution that satisfies everyone. At the very least Israelis and Palestinian Arabs must each recognize the legitimacy of one another's national aspirations and need to live in security. Israel is not going to be wiped off the political map. It is too strong and neither the United States nor the Soviet Union would let this happen. Many Palestinians implicitly accept Israel's existence. If there is to be a solution to the problem they must state this explicitly. The Palestinians are not going to disappear. They are too numerous and their nationalism is too deeply rooted for that to happen. If there is to be a solution to the problem, Israel must concede that Palestinian self-determination cannot be indefinitely postponed. A two-state solution—one in which Israel withdrew to its pre-1967 boundaries and the Palestinians were able to establish a state of their own on the West Bank and Gaza—would by no means be ideal and would require extraordinary patience and trust on the part of both sides. But is there any better long-term solution?

Notes

1. Initially, many Jews opposed the Zionist movement. Some rejected its secular political inspiration and argued that the Return to Zion should await the arrival of the Messiah. Some disliked its nationalist overtones and argued that Judaism was not a nationality but a religion, like Christianity or Islam. Some disagreed with the contention that Jews were unassimilable and feared Zionism would bolster the argument of anti-semites that Jews had split loyalties. Yet others, especially in Russia and Poland, rejected Zionism as reactionary, bourgeois, and defeatist, and they espoused the Marxist view that anti-semitism was a product of capitalism and would vanish with its overthrow.

2. The British government and the Zionist movement exchanged six drafts of the declaration before issuing the final version. Each of its 67 words was carefully discussed. For example, the Zionists had wanted the declaration to say that the British government "accepts the principle that Palestine should be *reconstituted* as *the* national home of the Jewish people" (italics added), which implied historic and exclusive legal rights. The document also used the vague term "a national home" instead of "the national state," even though the Zionists ultimately had the latter in mind. The dismissal of the 700,000 Arabs, who made up 90 percent of the population, as the "existing non-Jewish communities in Palestine" was very much in keeping with attempts to portray the territory as an unpopulated or underpopulated wasteland. It was similarly significant that the letter spoke of safeguarding the Palestinian Arabs' "civil and religious" rights but made no mention of their national, political, or economic ones.

3. Chaim Weizmann, one of Israel's architects, similarly appealed to British colonial

instincts when he wrote: "Should Britain encourage Jewish settlement [in Palestine] . . . we could have in twenty or thirty years a million Jews out there, perhaps more; they would develop the country, bring back civilization . . . and form a very effective guard for the Suez Canal." See Chaim Weizmann, *Trial and Error* (New York: Harper, 1949): 177–178.

4. A British commission investigating Arab grievances noted that land purchased by the JNF was "extraterritorialized" and "ceases to be land from which the Arab can gain any advantage. . . . Not only can he never hope to lease or to cultivate it, but . . . he is deprived for ever from employment on that land. Nor can anyone help him by purchasing the land and restoring it to common use." Quoted in United Nations, *The Origins and Evolution of the Palestine Problem, part 1: 1917–1947* (New York: United Nations, 1978): 43.

5. Quoted in Don Peretz, *The Middle East Today*, 3rd ed. (New York: Holt, Rinehart & Winston, 1978): 279.

6. Following the Peel recommendations, Britain sent out the Woodhead Commission to examine the practicality of partition. The commission concluded that the difficulties involved in partitioning Palestine into Arab and Jewish states were so great that it was not a realistic solution.

7. One of Israel's war heroes, Moshe Dayan, was quite frank about this interrelationship, noting "we came to this country which was already populated by Arabs, and we are establishing a . . . Jewish state here. . . . Jewish villages were built in the place of Arab villages. You do not even know the names of these Arab villages, and I do not blame you, because these geography books no longer exist; not only do the books not exist, the Arab villages are not there either . . . there is not one place built in this country that does not have a former Arab population." Quoted in Edward W. Said, *The Question of Palestine* (New York: Vintage Books, 1980): p. 14. According to one count Israel demolished 432 Arab villages in 1948–49. In the subdistrict of Safad, 77 of the 81 villages were demolished. In Tiberias, it was 23 of 25, in Beisan 32 of 34. See Basheer K. Nijim, "Biblical Zionism and Political Zionism," in Basheer K. Nijim (ed.), *American Church Politics and the Middle East*, pp. 21–40. (Belmont, Mass.: Association of Arab-American University Graduates, Inc., 1982): 31.

8. Yigal Allon, the former Israeli deputy prime minister and foreign minister, described how "we . . . looked for means . . . to cause the tens of thousands of . . . Arabs who remained in Galilee to flee." Jewish mayors were told to "whisper in the ears of some Arabs" that a large Jewish reinforcement was "going to burn all the villages of the Huleh" and that they should escape while they could. Allon continued: "The rumor spread . . . that it is time to flee. The flight numbered myriads. The tactic reached its goal completely." Quoted in David Hirst, *The Gun and the Olive Branch: The Roots of Violence in the Middle East* (London: Faber and Faber Inc., 1977): 141–142.

9. In 1979, an Israeli censorship board prohibited former Prime Minister Yitzhak Rabin from describing in his memoirs the expulsion of 50,000 Palestinian civilians from Ramle and Lydda. Rabin recounted how after discussing what to do about these Arabs with Prime Minister Ben-Gurion, he and Yigal Allon agreed "it was essential to drive the inhabitants out." He admitted "the population . . . did not leave willingly. There was no way of avoiding the use of force." Other Arabs, who "watched and learned the lesson," went voluntarily. See the *New York Times*, 23 October 1979, p. A3.

10. Joseph Weitz, the director of the Jewish National Land Fund, wrote in 1940: "There is no room for both peoples in this country. If the Arabs leave the country, it will be broad and wide open for us. And if the Arabs stay, the country will remain narrow and miserable." Israel could only come about by "transferring the Arabs from here to the neighboring countries, to transfer them all; except maybe for Bethlehem, Nazareth and Old Jerusalem, we must not leave a single village, not a single tribe. . . . And only with such a transfer will the country be able to absorb millions of our brothers." Even Theodor

Herzl anticipated the problem. In his diaries, in 1895, he wrote, "we shall have to spirit the penniless population across the border by procuring employment for it in the transit countries, while denying it any employment in our own country. Both the process of expropriation and the removal of the poor must be carried out discreetly and circumspectly." See Note 7 above: both quoted in Said, op. cit., pp. 99–100, 13.

11. See Note 8 above: quoted in Hirst, op. cit., p. 264.

12. Adam Zagorin, "A House Divided," *Foreign Policy* 48(1982): 115.

13. Within one month of the war Moshe Dayan, the minister of defense, had asserted that "the Gaza Strip is Israel and I think it should become an integral part of the country." Efraim Orni, one of Israel's foremost geographers, wrote that "although occupation of the Golan was dictated by security needs, the region is not alien land." He added, "most [Israeli] geographers regard it as part of Eretz Israel, rather than Syria." Within one month of the war, 150,000 had signed a petition against withdrawal from what were characterized as the "liberated" areas. In October, the council of the right-wing Herut party, which had always opposed Palestine's partition, issued a statement that "the liberated land of Israel is the Jewish state and our right to our ancestral heritage is eternal." A few days later Israel's chief Sephardic Rabbi said, "The land was provided to us by the Almighty, and all our prophets foretold its return to us. Therefore, it is forbidden for any Jew ever to consider returning any part whatsoever of the land of our forefathers." See *Jerusalem Post*, 6 July 1967, p. 1, 25 July 1967, p. 5, 25 October 1967, p. 8, and Don Peretz, "Israel's New Arab Dilemma, *Middle East Journal* 22 (1968): 50.

14. *Jerusalem Post*, 20 January 1970, p. 8.

15. Matityahu Drobles, *Master Plan for the Development of Settlement in Judea and Samaria, 1979–83* (Jerusalem: World Zionist Organization, Department for Rural Settlement, 1978): 2–3. Translated by Americans for Middle East Understanding, Inc.

16. A commentary in a leading Israeli newspaper remarked that "the subsidy is so heavy and massive that it seems that only fools will not build their new homes here." See *Ha'aretz*, 21 December 1982, p. 9. According to a plan implemented by the Housing Ministry in December 1982, settlers are supported on a sliding scale, with the largest subsidies going to those in the most peripheral zones of the West Bank. Just inside the West Bank, a typical apartment might cost $60,000 (one third to one half the cost of a comparable unit in a major Israeli city). But buyers here receive low-interest loans of $20,000. Farther out, where housing is cheaper, assistance might reach $30,000, with part of it a grant and much of it an interest-free loan. The intention, obviously, is to distribute settlers throughout the West Bank. *Christian Science Monitor*, 14 January 1983, p. 3.

17. West Bank Arabs have good ground to be apprehensive, despite their numerical superiority. In October 1982, Mordechai Zipori, the Israeli minister of communications, told a group of Jewish settlers near Nablus on the West Bank: "Don't worry about the demographic density of the Arabs. When I was born in Petah Tikwah [in Israel proper] we were entirely surrounded by Arab villages. They have all since disappeared." Quoted in the *Nation*, 15 January 1983, p. 39.

18. Of 59,793 workers from the West Bank and Gaza in December 1982, 7719 were employed in the Jerusalem area, 3354 in Haifa, 6713 in Sharon, 5994 in the Dan region, 22,439 in Tel Aviv, 4361 in the south, and 5308 in the Negev. See the *Jerusalem Post*, 17 January 1983, p. 3.

19. Quoted in William Claiborne and Edward Cody, *The West Bank: Hostage of History* (Washington, D.C.: Foundation for Middle East Peace, 1980): 25.

20. Begin himself has said that the Green Line only "exists in the imagination of some people. It no longer exists in reality. It disappeared. It is gone." One Israeli official admitted in 1982 that "gradually we have been managing to erase the physical distinction between the coastal area and Judea and Samaria. . . . Give us three or four years and . . . you won't be able to find the West Bank." *Christian Science Monitor*, 4 January 1982, p. 13.

21. Foreign Broadcast Information Service (FBIS), *Daily Report, Middle East and Africa*, 4 May 1982, p. I3.

Selected Bibliography

Abu-Lughod, Janet. "The Demographic Transformation of Palestine," in Ibrahim Abu-Lughod (ed.), *The Transformation of Palestine*, pp. 139–163. Evanston, Ill.: Northwestern University Press, 1971.

———. "Israeli Settlements in Occupied Arab Lands: Conquest to Colony." *Journal of Palestine Studies* 11(1982): 16–54.

American Friends Service Committee. *A Compassionate Peace: A Future for the Middle East*. New York: Hill & Wang, 1982.

Amiran, David H. K. "Jerusalem's Urban Development." *Middle East Review* 13(1981): 53–61.

Amos, John W. *Palestinian Resistance: Organization of a Nationalist Movement*. Elmsford, N.Y.: Pergamon Press Inc., 1980.

Asadi, F. "Some Geographic Elements in the Arab-Israeli Conflict." *Journal of Palestine Studies* 6(1976): 79–91.

Benvenisti, Meron. *The West Bank Data Project: A Survey of Israel's Policies*. Washington, D.C.: American Enterprise Institute for Public Policy Research, 1984.

Brawer, Moshe. "Dissimilarities in the Evolution of Frontier Characteristics along Boundaries of Differing Political and Cultural Regions," in Nurit Kliot and Stanley Waterman (eds.), *Pluralism and Political Geography: People, Territory and State*, pp. 159–172. New York: St. Martin's Press, 1983.

Bull, Vivian A. *The West Bank— Is It Viable?* Lexington, Mass.: D. C. Heath & Co., 1975.

Cobban, Helena. *The Palestine Liberation Organization: People, Power and Politics*. New York: Cambridge University Press, 1984.

Cohen, Saul. *Jerusalem. Bridging the Four Walls: A Geopolitical Perspective*. Boulder, Colo.: Westview Press, 1977.

———. *Israel's Defensible Borders: A Geo-Political Map*. Paper No. 20. Tel Aviv: Jaffee Center for Strategic Studies, 1983.

Cooley, John K. *Green March, Black September: The Story of the Palestinian Arabs*. London: Frank Cass, 1973.

Davis, Uri, Maks, Antonia E. L., and Richardson, John. "Israel's Water Policies." *Journal of Palestine Studies* 9(1980): 3–31.

Efrat, Elisha. "Settlement Pattern and Economic Changes of the Gaza Strip, 1947–1977." *Middle East Journal* 31(1975): 349–356.

Elazar, Daniel J. (ed.). *Judea, Samaria and Gaza: Views on the Present and Future*. Washington, D.C.: American Enterprise Institute for Public Policy Research, 1982.

Elmessiri, Abdelwahab M. *The Land of Promise: A Critique of Political Zionism*. New Brunswick, N.J.: North American Inc., 1977.

Elon, Amos. *The Israelis: Founders and Sons*. New York: Holt, Rinehart & Winston, 1971.

Hale, Gerry A. "Diaspora Versus Ghourba: The Territorial Restructuring of Palestine," in D. Gordon Bennett (ed.), *Tension Areas of the World: A Problem Oriented World Regional Geography*, pp. 129–154. Delray Beach, Fl.: Park Press, 1982.

Harris, William W. *Taking Root: Israeli Settlement in the West Bank, the Golan and Gaza-Sinai, 1967–1980*. New York: John Wiley & Sons, 1980.

Hirst, David. *The Gun and the Olive Branch: The Roots of Violence in the Middle East*. London: Faber and Faber Inc., 1977.

Khalidi, Walid. "Thinking the Unthinkable: A Sovereign Palestinian State." *Foreign Affairs* 56(1978): 695–713.

Khouri, Fred. *The Arab-Israeli Dilemma*, 2nd ed. Syracuse, N.Y.: Syracuse University Press, 1976.

Kliot, Nurit. "Dualism and Landscape Transformation in Northern Sinai—Some Outcomes of the Egypt-Israel Peace Treaty," in Nurit Kliot and Stanley Waterman (eds.), *Pluralism and Political Geography: People, Territory and State*, pp. 173–186. New York: St. Martin's Press, 1983.

Lesch, Ann Mosely. *Arab Politics in Palestine, 1917–1939: The Frustration of a Nationalist Movement*. Ithaca, N.Y.: Cornell University Press, 1979.

Nakhleh, Emile A. *The West Bank and Gaza: Toward the Making of a Palestinian State*. Washington, D.C.: American Enterprise Institute for Public Policy Research, 1979.

———— (ed.). *A Palestinian Agenda for the West Bank and Gaza*. Washington, D.C.: American Enterprise Institute for Public Policy Research, 1980.

Nakhleh, Khalil, and Zureik, Elia (eds.). *The Sociology of the Palestinians*. London: Croom Helm, 1980.

Nijim, Basheer K., and Muammar, Bishara. *Toward the De-Arabization of Palestine/Israel, 1945–1977*. Dubuque, Iowa: Kendall/Hunt Publishing Co. for The Jerusalem Fund for Education and Community Development, 1984.

Quandt, William, Jabbar, Fuad, and Lesch, Ann Mosely. *The Politics of Palestinian Nationalism*. Berkeley: University of California Press, 1973.

Rowley, Gwyn. "The Land in Israel," in Alan D. Burnett and Peter J. Taylor (eds.), *Political Studies from Spatial Perspectives*, pp. 443–465. New York: John Wiley & Sons, 1981.

————. "Space, Territory and Competition—Israel and the West Bank," in Nurit Kliot and Stanley Waterman (eds.), *Pluralism and Political Geography: People, Territory and State*, pp. 187–200. New York: St. Martin's Press, 1983.

Ruedy, John. "Dynamics of Land Acquisition," in Ibrahim Abu-Lughod (ed.), *The Transformation of Palestine*, pp. 119–138. Evanston, Ill.: Northwestern University Press, 1971.

Safran, Nadav. *Israel: The Embattled Ally*. 2nd ed. Cambridge: Harvard University Press, 1981.

Schiff, Ze'ev, and Ya'ari, Ehud. *Israel's Lebanon War*. New York: Simon and Schuster, 1984.

Stork, Joe, and Paul, Jim. "Arms Sales and the Militarization of the Middle East." *MERIP Reports*, No. 112 (February 1983): 5–15. (Special issue on "The Arms Race in the Middle East.")

United Nations. *The Origins and Evolution of the Palestine Problem, Part 1: 1917–1947*. New York: United Nations, 1978.

Van Arkadie, Brian. *Benefits and Burdens: A Report on the West Bank and Gaza Strip Economies Since 1967*. Washington, D.C.: Carnegie Endowment for International Peace, 1977.

10

Petroleum:
The Control of a Natural Resource

Few aspects of the Middle East and North Africa's political geography have not been affected in some way by the region's immense petroleum wealth. Oil is the raison d'être of some Middle Eastern states. It has frequently influenced the delimitation of political boundaries on land and offshore. Because it has accentuated inequalities in the geographic distribution of wealth, it has profoundly altered the balance of power within the region. It has variously provoked disputes between neighbors and encouraged regional cooperation. As the lifeblood of the modern industrial age, oil has also given the region a new and extraordinary global importance. Increasing competition for the region's dwindling oil resources could precipitate a confrontation in the future. Securing the principal production areas and oil transportation routes would be an immediate and obvious goal of both superpowers in any major conflict. The United States has proclaimed its willingness to use force to ensure continued access to the Gulf's oil fields and the nearby Soviet Union is keenly aware of most Western industrialized countries' vulnerability to a curtailment of supplies in any conflagration. Oil, in short, has transformed the political and strategic map as much as the economic one.

To the political geographer, one of the most important questions to be asked about petroleum is: Who controls this natural resource? Questions about control, in turn, lead to ones about power, sovereignty, and exploitation. To the geographer, the most obvious way oil or any other mineral resource is controlled is spatially, through concessions or sovereign territorial rights. At best, such control is only partial however. It may have no relationship to who decides the pace and place of ex-

313

ploration, how much oil is to be produced, for what price it is to be sold, and to whom it is to be sold. Spatial control cannot be divorced from questions about control over production, pricing, and marketing.

The chapter has six main sections. The first places the Middle East and North Africa's petroleum resources in a global context. The next three trace how the control of oil has changed. Initially, a few major multinational companies controlled all of the region's oil resources. After the 1950s, minor independent companies acquired an interest in the area's oil, undermining but by no means ending the majors' domination. Not until the early 1970s did the producing countries themselves really gain meaningful control of their oil. A fifth section assesses the varying dependence of the major consuming regions on Middle Eastern and North African oil. Finally, the control of the vital oil transportation routes that link producing and consuming regions is examined.

The Global Context: A Statistical Profile

Reserves

The Middle East and North Africa are, by every common standard, the single most important oil region in the world. The proven reserves of other parts of the world are small in comparison (Table 10.1).[1] Even large discoveries in Alaska, the Yucatan, and the North Sea have not seriously challenged the Middle East and North Africa's primacy. Moreover, Middle Eastern and North African reserves have increased approximately eightfold since 1950 because, until recently, new discoveries generally exceeded or kept pace with production. Most of the region's oil still remains underground. By contrast, the proven reserves of the United States have been falling both absolutely and proportionately. An American born in the 1930s will likely see some 80 percent of all oil discovered or likely to be discovered in the United States consumed in his or her lifetime (Figure 10.1).

The world's oil deposits are more geographically concentrated even than the preceding figures suggest. Although globally some 30,000 oil fields have been discovered, almost 80 percent of known recoverable oil lies within an estimated 272 giant fields (defined as originally containing at least 500 million barrels) and over half the total lies within only 33 supergiant fields (defined as originally having at least 5 billion barrels.) Significantly, 9 of the world's 10 largest oil fields and 28 of its supergiant fields are located within the Middle East. Most of these lie within the so-called Arabian-Iranian oil province, an area measuring only 800 by 500 miles (1280 by 800 kilometers) (Figure 10.2). Saudi Arabia's Ghawar field (the world's largest) alone has reserves of over 60 billion barrels, at least two times greater than the entire proven reserves of the United States.

Table 10.1
World Oil Reserves, 1985

Region/Country	Estimated Proved Reserves, 1985 (million barrels)	Percentage
Middle East and North Africa	433,739	62.1
Algeria	9,000	
Abu Dhabi[a]	30,500	
Bahrain	170	
Divided (Neutral) Zone	5,420	
Dubai[a]	1,440	
Egypt	3,200	
Iran	48,500	
Iraq	44,500	
Israel	<1	
Jordan	—	
Kuwait	90,000	
Lebanon	—	
Libya	21,100	
Morocco	<.5	
Oman	3,500	
Qatar	3,350	
Ras al-Khaymah[a]	100	
Saudi Arabia	169,000	
Sharjah[a]	450	
Syria	1,450	
Tunisia	1,514	
Turkey	294	
Yemen A.R.	—	
P.D.R Yemen	—	
North America	34,375	4.9
Central and South America	83,315	11.9
Western Europe	24,131	3.4
Sub-Saharan Africa	20,726	2.9
Asia/Pacific	18,530	2.6
Eastern Bloc	84,100	12.0
Total	698,667	100.0[b]

[a]Member of the United Arab Emirates.

[b]Because of rounding, does not add up to 100.0.

Source: Adapted from *Oil and Gas Journal,* 31 December, 1984, pp. 74–75.

Because much of the Middle East's oil lies within a few large fields, most countries in the region have relatively small quantities of oil or none at all. Conversely, only four countries, Saudi Arabia, Kuwait, Iran, and Iraq, together have about 80 percent of the region's reserves, one quarter of the world's reserves, and approximately five times the reserves of the United States.[2]

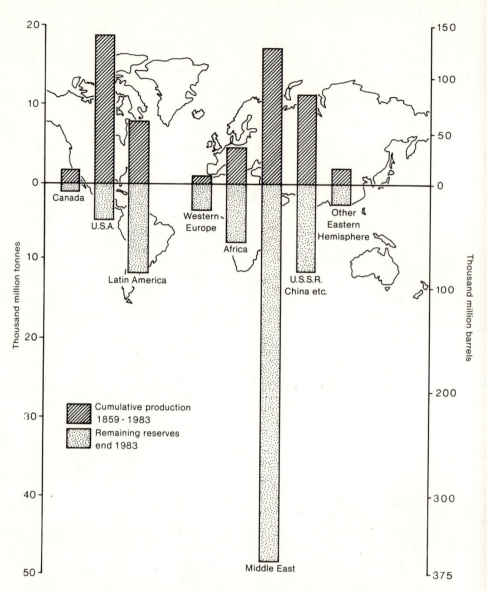

Figure 10.1 World oil reserves versus cumulative production by region. (After *BP Statistical Review of World Energy, 1982*. London: The British Petroleum Company p.l.c., 1982, p. 3.)

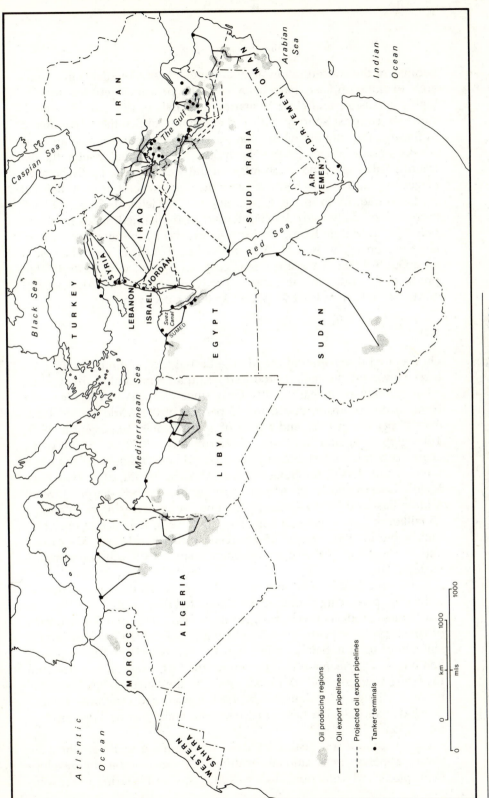

Figure 10.2 Oil fields, facilities, and pipelines in the Middle East and North Africa, 1984.

Competitive Advantages

Because of the concentration of so many giant, shallow fields in a small area, exploration costs have been low. The principal deposits are also highly accessible and close to marine terminals in the Gulf. These advantages contrast sharply with the enormous difficulties encountered in finding and moving oil in such promising but inhospitable areas as Alaska's North Slope and the North Sea. An additional asset is the extraordinarily high production rates for individual wells, partly because of geology and partly because of undivided ownership of individual fields. In Iraq, for example, each well typically yields an average 13,480 barrels of oil daily (b/d). Its counterpart in the United States produces only 17 b/d. Middle East and North African oil is, therefore, exceptionally inexpensive to exploit. A barrel of Saudi Arabian oil, which sold for about $28.00 in early 1985, only costs an estimated $0.10 to $0.20 to produce. By contrast, the costs of producing a barrel of Alaskan and North Sea oil are at least $7.00 and $8.00, respectively.[3]

Production

Oil was first discovered in the Middle East at the beginning of the century. However, the region produced less than 5 percent of the world's oil as recently as the early 1940s. Only since World War II has the area come to the forefront, producing 15 percent of the world's oil in 1950, over 25 percent in 1960, and a peak of approximately 40 percent in 1979. Total global demand has dropped sharply since 1979 as a result of an acute economic recession and price-induced conservation. At the same time, production in the Soviet Union, Mexico, Britain, and other non-Middle Eastern and North African countries has climbed sharply. Overall Middle East and North Africa production, after increasing from almost 15 million b/d in 1968 to 25.1 million b/d in 1979, fell back to only 14.0 million b/d in 1984, or only 25.9 percent of the world total. The causes and implications of this dramatic change since 1979 will be examined in detail later.

Within the Middle East and North Africa, the relative importance of individual producing countries has fluctuated (Figure 10.3). In 1969 the four largest producers were Iran, Saudi Arabia, Libya, and Kuwait, each of which produced between 2.6 million and 3.4 million b/d. The largest shifts have been in Saudi Arabia, which by early 1981 produced 10 million b/d, or approximately 40 percent of the Organization of Petroleum Exporting Countries' (OPEC) total. Recently, the kingdom has borne the brunt of falling global demand. By 1984, it was producing only 4.5 million b/d. Saudi Arabia has, thus, been the main "swing" producer in the region.

Iranian production peaked at about 6 million b/d in 1974, when the Shah's appetite for additional revenues to finance ambitious development plans and arms purchases was at its greatest. During the revolu-

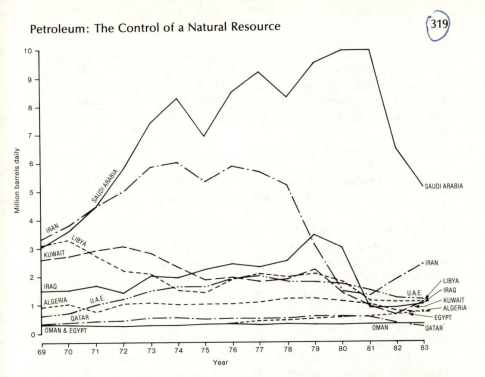

Figure 10.3   Middle East and North African oil production by country, 1969–83. (Based on data in *BP Statistical Review of World Energy, 1982,* London: The British Petroleum Company p.l.c.; and U.S. Department of Energy, Energy Information Administration, *Monthly Energy Review,* Washington, D.C.: U.S. Government Printing Office, various issues.)

tion production plummeted, reaching only 600,000 b/d by late 1980. Since Iraq's invasion, Iran has tried to boost output to pay for its war effort. By 1984, it was producing 2.2 million b/d, making it the region's second largest producer again. Its bid for a larger share of a shrinking market forced Saudi Arabia to cut production to keep the market in balance.

Iraqi production climbed from about 1.5 million b/d in 1969 to 3.4 million b/d a decade later, when an attempt was made to exploit Iran's troubles. The Gulf war has had a devastating impact. Many facilities have been damaged or destroyed and export routes blocked. In October 1980, production fell to only 150,000 b/d. Although Iraqi production recovered somewhat, it was still well below capacity in 1984 (about 1.2 million b/d).

Kuwait's production peaked in the early 1970s at about 3 million b/d, after which the shaykhdom cut back output to conserve reserves. Its large financial reserves made such reductions easy to bear. Nevertheless, by 1984, market conditions compelled Kuwait to produce only 925,000 b/d, far less than even it wanted and only a quarter of what it produced a few years previously.

Libya, too, produces considerably less than it once did. However, like

Iran, it broke OPEC's ranks in 1982 and sought to maintain revenues by boosting output (1.1 million b/d in 1984) and by offering deep price discounts. Generally, production levels in other Middle Eastern and North African countries (United Arab Emirates [U.A.E.], Algeria, Egypt, Syria, Oman, Qatar, and Bahrain) have been both lower and more stable.

The Evolution of the Pre–World War II Concession Map: The Entry of the Majors

Effective ownership of Middle Eastern and North African oil has changed radically in recent years. Until the early 1970s, seven giant, vertically integrated companies—five American, one British, and one Anglo-Dutch—produced over 80 percent of the region's oil. Their paramountcy rested on the concession system whereby, in return for a royalty payment or a share of profits with a host government, they were given the right to produce oil within a specific geographic area for a fixed period. Most of these concessions were obtained before the region's oil wealth was fully apparent. Furthermore, they were typically negotiated with, or imposed on, fledgling, impecunious, and often weak or colonially controlled governments, which virtually surrendered sovereignty to the companies by granting them exclusive oil rights over most or all of their territories for several decades. The companies were able to decide the pace and place of exploration, how much oil to produce, how to dispose of it, and more or less what to charge for it. Because they usually had concessions in several countries and produced oil jointly, they were able to transcend, subvert, or evade the authority of individual governments and to ignore political boundaries almost completely. The early concessions were, thus, a dominant element of each country's political geographic substructure.

The Great Carve-up

The first concession of any lasting significance in the region was granted in 1901 by the government of Iran to William Knox D'Arcy.[4] It covered almost the entire country and was to last for 60 years. When initial explorations proved unsuccessful, D'Arcy formed a syndicate with the Burmah Oil Company to keep operating. After oil was struck at Masjid-i-Sulaiman in 1908, it was renamed the Anglo-Persian Oil Company (and eventually British Petroleum [BP]).[5] Despite modifications of the original concession in 1933, with a reduction of the concession area to 100,000 square miles (259,000 square kilometers), Iranian oil production remained firmly and exclusively in the hands of this one British company until 1951.

Ultimately, the concession in neighboring Iraq was more significant.

It was here that the pattern of creating joint production companies to save costs, reduce mutually destructive competition, and orchestrate supplies was first established. In 1914 BP, Royal Dutch-Shell, and the Deutsche Bank formed the Turkish Petroleum Company (TPC) to obtain oil rights in Mesopotamia. Because of World War I, final negotiations over this concession were never completed. After hostilities ended, the British government expropriated the German share of TPC and, in a classic horsetrade, awarded it to the French in return for the transfer of the oil-rich Mosul area—which fell within the French zone in the Sykes-Picot agreement—to British-controlled Iraq. TPC's concession was ratified in 1925 before an autonomous Iraqi government had been constituted.

This exclusionary Anglo-French arrangement angered the major U.S. oil companies, who believed serious global oil shortages were imminent and sought access to new nondomestic sources. With the support of the U.S. State Department, which advocated an "Open Door" policy among the Allies, they persuaded the British to expand TPC's membership. In 1928, several U.S. companies, including Exxon, Mobil, and Gulf, were admitted to TPC, which was renamed the Iraqi Petroleum Company (IPC). The concessions of IPC and its wholly owned subsidiaries covered virtually the entire country until 1961.

IPC's parent companies tried to perpetuate and extend their collusive control over the region's oil resources through the Red Line Agreement. Within an area delimited on a map by a red line (practically all of the Middle East to the east of Egypt, with the exception of Iran and Kuwait), the IPC companies agreed they would only obtain concessions jointly.[6] The IPC group could not prevent other companies from obtaining oil rights in the region however. Accordingly, the Red Line Agreement directly and indirectly influenced the evolution of concession patterns in what proved to be the richest oil-bearing region of all, the Arabian peninsula.

The earliest concessions in the peninsula were purchased by Frank Holmes, who then tried to sell them to larger companies. In 1925, he acquired oil exploration rights on Bahrain. Unable to interest BP or Exxon in the concession, he sold it to Gulf Oil Co. However, Gulf was bound by the Red Line Agreement. After failing to bring in the other IPC members, it sold the concession to Standard of California (Socal), which was not a party to the Red Line Agreement.

After Socal struck oil in Bahrain in 1932, it naturally turned its attention to oil prospects in Saudi Arabia only 20 miles (32 kilometers) away. At this juncture, an anxious IPC made a bid for the Saudi concession to prevent a glut, forestall competitors, and avoid making the same mistake of passing up an opportunity. However, Socal offered far better terms to King Ibn Saud and in 1933 won rights over 320,000 square miles (829,000 square kilometers) of Saudi Arabia for 60 years. It subsequently sold a one-half interest in its Saudi Arabian and Bahrain concessions to Texaco, which had the foreign market outlets it needed. When the magnitude of Saudi Arabia's deposits became apparent, Exxon and Mobil grew apprehensive that Aramco—Socal and Texaco's joint production company in Saudi Arabia—would undercut them on the market with cheap, abundant oil. In addition, they were keen to gain access to Saudi Arabia's huge oil fields themselves. For their part, Socal and Texaco wanted access to Exxon and Mobil's better distribution network and needed capital to build a pipeline to the Mediterranean coast. But before Exxon and Mobil could enter Aramco, they had to cancel the Red Line Agreement. The remaining IPC members only consented to this in 1948 after Exxon and Mobil agreed to long-term contracts to buy some of their Iranian, Iraqi, and Kuwaiti oil.

When Gulf purchased Holmes's concession rights in Bahrain, it also took over his option in Kuwait, which fell outside the Red Line Agreement and, therefore, did not have to be sold off when other IPC participants showed no interest. However, BP felt it had the first right of refusal on any concession in Kuwait because of a prior commitment from the ruler of this British protectorate. Although the company was not keen to produce great quantities of Kuwaiti oil itself, in view of its ample sources in Iran and Iraq, it was anxious to prevent Gulf from doing so. Gulf and BP, therefore, briefly vied for the concession, bidding its price upwards in the process. They soon realized that cooperation would better serve their interests. When the concession was finally awarded in 1934, it went to both companies, which formed the Kuwait Oil Company (KOC) to produce the oil.[7]

The Oil Company Cartel

Before World War II, control of the region's oil by a cartel of foreign companies was complete and encompassed every phase of operations. The major companies alone had the technology, organization, expertise, and capital to find, exploit, transport, refine, and market the oil. Consequently, they were able to create an economic world almost divorced from geographic reality. Working together, they orchestrated production *regionally*, adjusting output in the individual countries in accordance with their global needs.[8] The only map that really mattered to them was the concession map because they could so easily ignore boundary lines on the political map. Because of joint concession ownership patterns and secret cartel arrangements dating from the 1928 Achnacarry Agreement, the companies eventually became so interdependent that serious competition among them was inevitably curtailed, if not eliminated (Figure 10.4).[9]

Oligopolistic control placed the oil companies in a strong position vis-à-vis individual Middle Eastern governments, as was graphically illustrated whenever there were disagreements over royalty payments or concession terms. The companies typically responded to any serious attempt by a host government to challenge their power by holding back

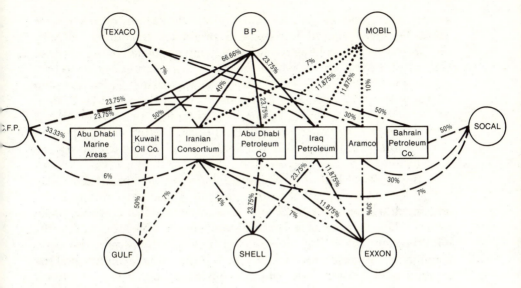

Figure 10.4   Oil company links, late 1970s.

F.P. = Compagnie française des Pétroles

production or exploration. Because they had concession interests in several countries they could easily obtain crude elsewhere without disrupting supplies. The producing countries, conversely, were vulnerable in any dispute because they depended on one company or consortium of companies for a high proportion of their revenues.

The Iranian crisis of 1951–54 illustrates the weakness of individual governments in the face of a united front of companies. Because BP was the sole concessionaire in Iran, it was a frequent target of nationalist criticism. In 1951, the Iranian parliament passed an oil nationalization bill. BP reacted by leading a boycott of all Iranian oil by the major companies. Deprived of buyers and without the ability to transport, refine, and distribute its own crude, Iran produced only 8 to 9 million barrels in 1952, compared to 243 million barrels in 1950. BP easily made up for this loss by increasing production in Iraq and in Kuwait. The governments of these countries obviously benefited from the additional revenues. The crisis was resolved after a Central Intelligence Agency (CIA)-supported coup d'état brought a more compliant Iranian government to power. Although Iran retained ownership of all oil fields and refineries, after 1954 the oil was produced by a new joint production company called the Consortium. Significantly, the Consortium included all the seven majors for the first time.

Pricing and Royalties

For many years, the oil company cartel arbitrarily set the price of Middle Eastern oil to equal that of U.S. oil, which was considerably more expensive to produce. Besides making Middle Eastern oil even more profitable, this protected domestic U.S. producers. In addition, all Middle Eastern oil was sold as though it actually originated along the U.S. Gulf of Mexico coastline, which inflated transportation costs. According to this "Gulf-plus" system, the buyer was charged for "phantom freight." This could produce ludicrous results. Cheap Middle Eastern oil was sold to nearby India, for instance, as though it had been shipped from Texas or Louisiana. Not until the British government complained during World War II was a second Middle Eastern pricing reference point introduced.

During the first half of this century, the companies paid fixed royalties to the producing countries for their oil. These payments typically amounted to a miniscule $0.22 to $0.25 a barrel. In 1950, however, Saudi Arabia followed Venezuela's example and sought a 50-50 split of profits with the companies. This arrangement subsequently became the norm throughout the region for two decades. "Profit" was taken to equal the arbitrarily set "posted price" of oil, minus production costs. As a result of the new arrangement, Aramco's payments to the Saudi government rose from $0.22 to $0.80 per barrel and Saudi revenues increased from $39.2 million in 1949 to $111.7 million in 1950. However, Aramco succeeded in obtaining a ruling from the U.S. Internal Revenue Service that these additional payments were taxes, not royalties, and could, therefore, be fully subtracted from corporate taxes owed to the United States. In other words, Aramco's U.S. tax bill decreased in equal measure that its payments to Saudi Arabia increased. The American taxpayer footed its higher bill for Saudi oil. Because this practice was adopted elsewhere in the Middle East and North Africa, U.S. oil companies operating overseas were spared an estimated $14 billion in U.S. taxes between 1950 and 1978.

The Evolution of the Post–World War II Concession Map: The Entry of the Independents

Although the major companies continued to dominate Middle Eastern and North African oil production until the early 1970s, their absolute control over the region's resources was increasingly challenged by the host governments and by smaller competitors in the post–World War II period.

New Concession Arrangements

Because Middle Eastern oil was enormously profitable, so-called independent companies—those without global production, transportation, refining, and marketing systems—soon sought their own concessions. Few areas had not already been claimed by the majors, however, so independents had to content themselves mainly with the Neutral Zone between Saudi Arabia and Kuwait, offshore areas of the Gulf, tracts relinquished by the majors, and countries just beginning to open up their territories for exploration.

Independents made their entrance in 1948–49 in the Neutral Zone, where the Kuwaiti concession was awarded to Aminoil, a syndicate of U.S. independents, and the Saudi concession to J. P. Getty, the multimillionaire. To the majors' embarassment, these smaller operators offered far better terms to the producing governments. The influx of American independents accelerated in 1955 when nine were given a risk-free, lucrative 5 percent share of the Consortium in Iran, where the oil had already been discovered and they could piggyback the majors.

The greatest opportunity for the independents came in Libya, which was a tabula rasa. Libya was determined that the seven majors not monopolize its concessions, as elsewhere, and initially awarded 51 tracts to 17 companies, many of them minor independents. Because concession areas were often small and fragmented, the Libyan concession map was extremely complex and quite different from any other in the Middle East, where vast undivided tracts were the general rule. In addition, concessions were granted for shorter terms and if left undeveloped had eventually to be relinquished to the Libyan government, which could auction them off again. When oil began to flow, more than half of it was produced by independents. This had a profoundly destabilizing effect on the global oil market.

Most of the independents entering the region were American. However, rising consumption in Europe and Japan led small, often state-owned companies from these areas to seek concessions too. The agreements they reached with the host governments or their newly formed national oil companies were increasingly favorable to the producing countries. In 1957, ENI, the Italian state-owned company, established a precedent by forming a joint venture with the National Iranian Oil Company (NIOC). ENI would pay all exploration costs. Half of any oil discovered would be owned by NIOC but sold for it by ENI; the remaining half would be owned by ENI but taxed at the prevailing 50 percent rate. The effective profit split, therefore, was 75–25, instead of the usual 50-50. Similar partnerships followed throughout the region.

After 1966, an even more radical arrangement was introduced, first in Iran and then elsewhere, whereby the company merely operated as a contractor providing a service and not as a concessionaire. In these partnerships, the producing country owned all oil, but the company could purchase some of the output it produced at a discount.

The Birth of OPEC

Throughout the 1950s and 1960s, oil consumption grew dramatically in the United States, Western Europe, and Japan. Nonetheless, this was a time of oil glut. As long as the seven majors tightly controlled production, they could maintain a stable, orderly market and balance supply and demand relatively easily. But when independents gained access to Middle Eastern and especially Libyan oil, the majors were powerless to prevent a surplus. Because independents were not vertically integrated and had poor outlets for their new-found oil, the quickest way they could gain a place in a market dominated by the giant companies was by cutting prices. To make matters worse, in 1959 the United States imposed quotas limiting oil imports to approximately 15 percent of total consumption to protect politically powerful domestic producers. Middle Eastern and North African oil flooded into Europe instead, aggravating the glut. At a time when Middle Eastern and North African oil was inexpensive, plentiful, and largely controlled by U.S. companies, America was rapidly depleting its own reserves and effectively subsidizing Europe and Japan's economic boom.

Because oil company payments to Middle Eastern and North African countries were based on an artificial *posted* price, government revenues were not initially affected by glut-related decreases in the *market* price of oil. When the actual price exceeded the posted price, as it did in the early 1950s, the companies benefited because they calculated their 50-50 profit split from the latter. But when the actual price fell below the posted price, which it did during the glut, the companies suffered a serious drop in revenues and found themselves getting much less than 50 percent of profits.[10] The only way they could restore their profit margins was by unilaterally cutting the posted price. Obviously this would also slash payments to the producing countries. The first cut of $0.18 a barrel in 1959 chopped the four main producing countries' annual revenues by 10 percent. Immediately following a second cut of $0.10 a barrel in 1960, five countries—Saudi Arabia, Iraq, Kuwait, Iran, and Venezuela—met in Baghdad and established OPEC. They had begun to learn a lesson from the companies: singly they were weak, together they might be strong.

The Price and Ownership Revolution:
The Entry of the Producing Governments

During its first decade, OPEC succeeded only in gaining more members and in preventing further unilateral cuts in the posted price. It did not pose a serious threat to the companies, and its members showed few tangible signs of being able to cooperate in matters of importance. OPEC's disunity and disorganization were sharply exposed during the 1967 Arab-Israeli War, when non-Arab members capitalized on an Arab embargo of major Western-consuming countries by increasing their own production. Only in the 1970s did OPEC emerge as a quasi-cartel with control over pricing and output. How did this revolution occur and what role did geographic factors play in it? For that matter, why was OPEC's heyday so brief?

The Pivotal Role of Libya

The 1967 Arab-Israeli War had a profound and lasting effect on the world's oil industry. The Suez Canal's closure lengthened the tanker trip from the Gulf to Western Europe from approximately 6500 miles (10,400 kilometers) to 11,300 miles (18,100 kilometers) because vessels now had to go around the Cape of Good Hope in South Africa. This disruption encouraged new exploration in the North Sea, Mexico, and Alaska, and it accentuated the locational advantages of African producing countries west of the canal.

The main beneficiary of the canal's closure was unquestionably Libya, especially once a civil war reduced Nigeria's oil production. Whereas a tanker took 62 days to make the round trip between the Gulf and Rotterdam, it could make a round trip between Libya and Rotterdam in only 16 days. Moreover, Libya was close to refineries in Italy and France. At a time of increasing awareness about pollution, Libyan oil had the added advantage of a low sulfur content. For all these reasons, Libyan oil production climbed dramatically. In 1968 alone, output increased by 50 percent. Europe especially grew highly dependent on Libyan oil.

The risks inherent in this situation were underlined when young, radical nationalist officers overthrew Libya's conservative, pro-Western monarch in September 1969. The new regime immediately began negotiations to raise the posted price. The companies refused Libya's initial request for an additional $0.40 per barrel, a laughably small amount by today's standards. However, independents with few alternate sources of oil were vulnerable to pressure. Realizing this, Libya ordered several of them, notably Occidental, to cut back production or face nationalization.

By September 1970, Libyan production had fallen by over 1 million b/d. This cutback coincided with, and exacerbated, a tightening market. Demand in Europe was higher than expected. The longer haul around the Cape of Good Hope had aggravated a tanker shortage. The trans-Arabian oil pipeline (Tapline) was out of operation. Finally, U.S. production had peaked and could no longer close the gap between supply and demand. All spare production capacity lay within the OPEC countries. In these circumstances, the companies, one by one, acceded to Libya's demands.

Libya's modest victory served primarily to inspire other OPEC countries to push for higher prices too. As a result of the Tehran and Tripoli agreements of 1971 between OPEC and the companies, posted prices were raised between $0.33 and $0.90 and the tax rate on profits was increased from 50 percent to 55 percent. Significantly, the companies now negotiated price changes with the producing countries as a bloc rather than individually, which limited the ability of these companies to play producers off against one another as in the past.

The Price Shocks of 1973 and 1979

In retrospect, the 1970–71 increases were minor and caused little economic dislocation. The real turning point occurred during the 1973 Arab-Israeli War, when OPEC took advantage of a tight market and raised prices by 70 percent from $3.01 to $5.12 per barrel. In addition, the Organization of Arab Petroleum Exporting Countries (OAPEC), which had been formed in 1968, cut production and imposed an embargo on the United States and the Netherlands because of their support for Israel. During the resulting shortage, bids for oil on the open market reached unprecedented levels. In December 1973, the OPEC countries increased the posted price again by 128 percent to $11.65 per barrel (Figure 10.5). Significantly, they did not consult the companies. In only three months, the price of oil had quadrupled.

For the next five years, prices remained relatively stable as a result of higher OPEC production and decreased demand in most major consuming countries. As recently as 1978, the price of a barrel of oil was only $12.70. In fact, when adjusted for inflation and the dollar's decreasing value, the real price of oil fell substantially during this period. However, in 1978–79, a second major price explosion accompanied the Iranian revolution. Although Saudi Arabia and Iraq increased production to make up for some of the 5 million b/d drop in Iranian output, this was not enough to eliminate the shortfall. Once again, prices on the open market soared. OPEC responded by raising prices in stages, so that by July 1980, oil from certain countries fetched $37.00 per barrel.

The fifteenfold price increase since 1972 has had far-reaching consequences for both producing and consuming countries, bringing about one of the greatest geographic transfers of wealth in history. Countries that were among the world's least developed and poorest a few years ago now count among the world's most influential and richest, even if their sudden fabulous prosperity has accentuated social and geographic inequalities and often has been bewildering and disruptive.

Saudi Arabia graphically illustrates what has happened. In 1972, Saudi oil exports were valued at $4.2 billion. By 1974, they were worth $31.2 billion. In 1981, they totalled almost $113 billion, a twenty-seven-fold increase in a decade and well over $10,000 per capita. Despite massive arms purchases, ambitious development plans, conspicuous consumption of imported consumer goods, and lavish expenditures on social services, Saudi Arabia still has financial reserves of $150 billion and a huge and, until recently, a mounting balance of payments surplus. In 1984, however, oil revenues declined to only $43 billion.

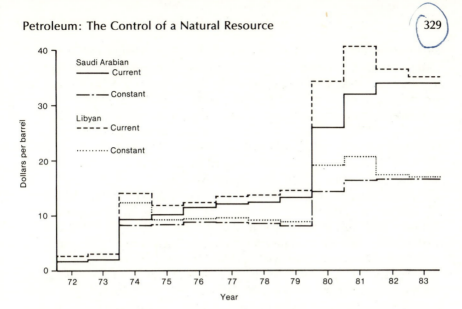

Figure 10.5   World oil prices, 1972–83. (Based on data in U.S. Department of Energy, Energy Information Administration, *Monthly Energy Review;* and *Weekly Petroleum Status Report,* Washington, D.C.: U.S. Government Printing Office, various issues.)

Participation and Nationalization

The producing countries' ability to set prices unilaterally and collectively was only one manifestation of their more active involvement in all phases of the oil industry after the early 1970s. The most significant change, perhaps, was in the concession system, which the producing countries viewed as an unacceptable vestige of colonialism. Even the most conservative regimes vowed eventually to end what they saw as oil company exploitation. However, until circumstances changed radically in the early 1970s, most producing countries acted cautiously, mindful of the lessons of the Iranian nationalization crisis in the early 1950s and of the difficulties of producing oil without the companies.

In 1968, the OPEC countries formally announced their intention to seek participation in the companies that produced their oil. When a seller's market developed a few years later, this goal became realizable and Saudi Arabia, Iraq, Kuwait, Abu Dhabi, and Qatar opened negotiations with the companies. The resulting 1972 General Agreement on Participation granted the signatory countries an immediate 25 percent stake in the concession companies and provided for their majority ownership by 1982. In return, the companies would be able to buy back a proportion of the producing country's share of crude output at a discount. Thus, their continued access to oil, a vital concern, was assured.

However, events overtook the agreement. Kuwait failed to ratify it

and demanded new negotiations with KOC on greater initial participation. In 1974, it obtained a 60 percent stake in the company. The following year, it took it over completely, compensating BP and Gulf and
permitting them to buy oil at a discount in return for their continued
technical assistance. Although Saudi Arabia, Qatar, and Abu Dhabi did
ratify the 1972 agreement, Kuwait's success, among other things, also
led them to seek accelerated majority ownership. By the end of 1974,
all these countries controlled 60 percent of their respective concessionaire companies. Qatar and Saudi Arabia subsequently negotiated
100 percent ownership. Abu Dhabi, conversely, contented itself with
60 percent participation only. Elsewhere in the Arabian peninsula,
Bahrain took full control of the Bahrain Petroleum Co. (BAPCO) in
1978; Oman favored a limited 60 percent participation.

Neither Libya nor Iran were parties to the General Agreement on
Participation. However, in both countries the status of the companies
has been fundamentally altered. Between 1973 and 1974, Libya either
seized 51 percent of the companies operating in the country or nationalized them outright. In Iran, as a result of a complex 1972 agreement,
NIOC assumed management control over all production, whereas operations were handled by the Consortium's new service company, Iranian Oil Service Co. (IOSCO). The Consortium companies purchased
any oil that NIOC did not itself keep to trade. After the revolution, the
role of foreign oil companies was still further reduced and links with
the former Consortium companies are now limited to a few sales contracts.

Although most producing countries still rely on the major companies
for their technical expertise and for marketing much of their oil, they
have increasingly been bypassing them altogether. National oil companies like NIOC, the Kuwait National Oil Company, the Libyan National Oil Company, and Saudi Arabia's Petromin have been gaining
experience and trying to move downstream into refining, transportation, and distribution. The producing countries have also been selling
more of their oil directly to other governments or bartering it for technology, capital goods, technical assistance, weapons, and even food. In
addition, determined efforts are being made to replace foreign experts,
especially in such countries as Iraq and Algeria.[11]

The Demise of OPEC?

Some 70 years after oil was first discovered in the region, Middle Eastern and North African producing countries, for a brief few years, appeared to have acquired the wherewithal to do what they wanted with
it. However, a series of developments greatly undermined their power
in the early 1980s and even led to speculation that OPEC might collapse.

The price increases of the 1970s had several major consequences. First, they accelerated the trend among the major industrial countries to use energy more efficiently. Second, they aborted these same countries' fragile economic recovery and contributed to the worst recession the world has seen since the 1930s depression. This slowdown further reduced oil consumption. Third, they gave added impetus to the major consuming countries' efforts to diversify their energy sources and encouraged greater use of coal and, in some cases, nuclear power. Finally, they caused non-OPEC oil production to soar.[12] Consequently, although total world oil production fell slightly from 55.6 million b/d in 1973 to 54.0 million b/d in 1984, OPEC production fell precipitously from 30.9 million b/d (about 56 percent of the world total) to only 17.4 million b/d (about 32 percent of the total). OPEC's drop in production was especially dramatic after 1980, when its output was still 26.9 million b/d. This seriously affected revenues; whereas OPEC sales totaled $278.6 billion in 1980, they fell about 30 percent to under $200 billion by 1982.

As long as the world's demand for oil was growing or stable and the OPEC countries' revenues were generally adequate for their needs, OPEC functioned reasonably well, despite major differences and tensions among its members. It was never a cartel in the strict sense of the word because it never assigned strict production quotas to its members. However, when demand began to fall, the divergent interests of its members threatened to destroy it. The OPEC countries' needs differ radically. Some, like Saudi Arabia and Kuwait, have vast financial reserves and can withstand production cutbacks without too much difficulty. These two countries are believed to earn $20 billion and $10 billion, respectively, each year just on interest from their overseas investments. Others, like the United Arab Emirates (U.A.E.), have extremely high production in relation to their small populations. Iran and Algeria (and outside the region Nigeria and Indonesia) have large populations in relation to their production levels and revenues (Table 10.2). The inherent contradictions within OPEC have been seriously aggravated by political tensions, most notably between Iran and Iraq, Iran and Saudi Arabia, and Saudi Arabia and Libya. Indeed, given these differences, the organization's longevity is in itself a major achievement.

Disagreements about how OPEC's falling production should be divided up were inevitable. In March 1982, the organization agreed for the first time ever to limit production to 17.5 million b/d to keep prices firm. Equally important, it established production quotas. However, within four months, certain countries were flagrantly exceeding their quotas and offering deep discounts of $3 to $4 per barrel in order to increase their market share and maintain revenues. Ironically, the principal offenders were the two so-called "radical" countries that did most to unleash the price explosion: Iran and Libya.

In December 1982, the OPEC countries agreed to keep production at 18.5 million b/d through 1983. However, this agreement was meaning-

Table 10.2
Value of Oil Exports, 1983

Country	Oil Exports ($ millions)	Oil Exports per Capita ($)
Algeria[a]	11,104	519
Bahrain[a]	444	1,110
Egypt[a]	1,720	37
Iran	19,770	451
Iraq	9,599	640
Kuwait	8,713	5,446
Libya	11,054	2,987
Oman	4,096	4,096
Qatar	3,031	10,103
Saudi Arabia	47,362	4,385
Syria[a]	1,041	103
Tunisia	790	113
United Arab Emirates	12,580	8,387

[a] 1982 data.

Source: Based on data in *International Financial Statistics*. Washington, D.C.:
International Monetary Fund, December 1984; and *1984 World Population Data
Sheet*. Washington, D.C.: Population Reference Bureau, 1984.

less because they could not apportion national production ceilings. Another OPEC meeting, in January 1983, broke up in disarray, without production quotas or an agreement to stop deep discounting. By early 1983 the future of OPEC was uncertain and the possibility of a downward price spiral seemed imminent after Nigeria broke OPEC ranks and reduced what it charged by several dollars. This obliged Gulf producers to follow suit. Eventually, in March 1983, OPEC, to regain control over the world market and prevent the situation getting out of hand, for the first time in its history cut prices by 15 percent to $29 for a barrel of benchmark Saudi light crude. Production quotas were also set, although these could not be enforced. A $6 drop in the price of a barrel of oil could cost OPEC $35 billion in lost revenues in one year. For each $1.00 drop in price, Mexico's annual revenues fall by $600 million, Nigeria's by $450 million. At the same time, the United States import bill is shaved by $2 billion for each $1.00 drop in price. In January 1985, nine OPEC countries approved an additional modest price cut averaging 43 cents a barrel, but control of the market continued to slip from their hands.

The Consumers

While the production of oil is highly concentrated among a handful of countries, so also is its consumption. In 1984, only seven countries—

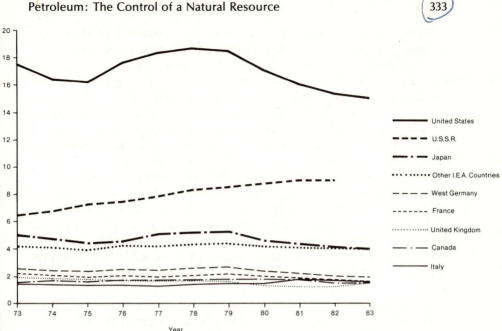

Figure 10.6   Oil consumption in major industrial countries, 1973–83. (Based on data in *BP Statistical Review of World Energy*, London: The British Petroleum Company, various years; and U.S. Department of Energy, Energy Information Administration, *Monthly Energy Review*, Washington, D.C.: U.S. Government Printing Office, various issues.)

the United States, Canada, Japan, West Germany, France, Italy, and Britain—consumed roughly 50 percent of total world production. The U.S.S.R., Eastern Europe, and the 20 members of the International Energy Agency—formed by the Organization of Economic Cooperation and Development (OECD) after the 1973 crisis to coordinate energy policies among the industrialized Western nations—together consumed over 80 percent of the world's oil. Nevertheless, the major consuming countries differ markedly in their degree of dependence on Middle Eastern and North African oil.

The United States

The United States is by far and away the world's largest consumer of energy (Figure 10.6). With 5 percent of the world's population, it devours about 30 percent of its oil. Its per capita consumption is two times greater than that of West Germany. The United States has 40 percent of the world's cars. Because of their average size and weight, these consume one half of all gasoline used in automobiles.

U.S. oil consumption increased from 5.4 million b/d in 1947, when it accounted for one third of all energy, to a peak of 18.8 million b/d in

1979, by which time it was the source of almost one half of all energy. However, domestic production has fallen since 1970, even with Alaska coming onstream. By 1984, U.S. wells pumped only 8.7 million b/d— less than in 1967 and far short of total demand. The gap between production and consumption has been closed through imports, which more than doubled from 3.4 million b/d and 24 percent of all oil consumed in 1970 to a peak of 8.4 million b/d and 46 percent of all oil consumed in 1979. The bill for these rising imports, which coincided with the two price explosions, was enormous. In 1972, petroleum imports totaled $4.3 billion, or $19 for each American. By 1979 the cost had lept thirteenfold to $56.5 billion, or $254 per capita. Moreover, during the 1970s, the United States became steadily more dependent on Middle Eastern and North African oil, despite the 1973 Arab embargo. In 1972, before the crisis, Iran and the Arab members of OPEC provided 672,000 b/d, or 14 percent of all U.S. imports and a meager 4 percent of total consumption. By 1979, they supplied 3.3 million b/d and 40 percent of all imports.

The pattern has changed drastically since 1979. Deep recession has, as noted, cut consumption. At the same time, conservation and greater energy efficiency have made their mark. By 1984, the United States was consuming about 15 to 20 percent less oil than in 1979, when the level of economic activity was about the same. When the 1973 oil crisis began, some experts estimated that U.S. oil consumption in 1990 would approach 40 million b/d. In 1984, however, it was using approximately 15.5 million b/d, or about what it used in 1970.

An equally significant change has been in the level and source of imports. In 1979, imports totaled 8.4 million b/d. By 1984 they had fallen 40 percent to 5.4 million b/d. Whereas the United States was importing almost one half of the oil it consumed in 1979, by 1983 imports accounted for less than one third. In addition, Middle Eastern and North African OPEC members supplied approximately 900,000 b/d only, or less than 20 percent of imports and less than 6 percent of total consumption (Figure 10.7). Since 1979, the United States has sought out non-OPEC sources for its oil. Surprisingly, by late 1982 Britain was (briefly) the second largest supplier after Mexico, providing substantially more than even Saudi Arabia. Clearly U.S. dependence on Middle Eastern and North African oil has lessened dramatically. The discovery of a huge field off the California coast and the storage of 350 million barrels in the Strategic Petroleum Reserve—salt domes in Texas and Louisiana— may further this trend. Nevertheless, unanticipated events could change the situation quickly and the United States cannot ignore what happens to Middle Eastern and North African oil.

Japan

Japan's predicament is, in many ways, far more serious than that of the United States because it obtains 72 percent of its energy from oil and

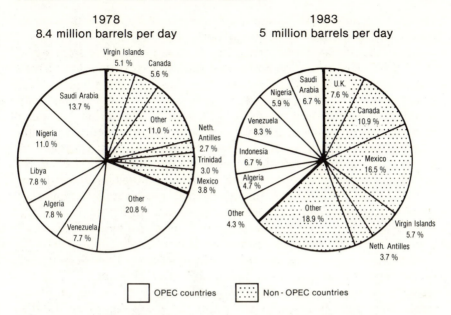

Figure 10.7   U.S. oil imports by source, 1978 versus 1983. (Based on data in U.S. Department of Energy, Energy Information Administration, *Monthly Energy Review*, Washington, D.C.: U.S. Government Printing Office, various issues; and *Christian Science Monitor*, 28 January 1983.)

virtually all of this is imported. Its excessive dependence on foreign oil is quite recent and dates from a massive shift from coal after World War II.[13] Almost 70 percent of Japan's oil comes from the Middle East and North Africa, making it perhaps the most vulnerable of all the industrialized countries to political pressures and to price rises.

There seem to be few obvious alternatives to this situation. Japan has virtually no known oil of its own and lacks large coal reserves. It has responded to the energy crisis by adopting strict conservation measures, cultivating friendly ties with Middle Eastern and North African producers, and attempting to diversify its sources of oil. In the future, it will likely increase imports from the U.S.S.R., China, and Southeast Asia.

Western Europe

Western Europe, like Japan, switched from indigenous coal to cheaper imported oil after World War II. As a result, oil consumption lept from only 4.2 million b/d in 1960 to a peak of 15.1 million b/d in 1973. Today, Western Europe is more oil dependent than the United States but less so than Japan. However, there are great differences within the region. In 1983, oil was the source of 37 percent of British energy, but it provided 44 percent of West German, 49 percent of French, 64 percent of Italian, and 66 percent of Greek energy.

The risks associated with converting Europe's economies from a coal to oil base were amply demonstrated during each of the Arab-Israeli wars in 1956, 1967, and 1973, when supplies were disrupted or curtailed. At the time of the most recent embargo, which was directed only at the Netherlands and the United States but affected all European countries, Britain obtained over 75 percent of its oil imports from the Middle East and North Africa, France 80 percent, West Germany 85 percent, and Italy 90 percent. After prices quadrupled, the need to reduce this dependence became acute. Consumption fell by almost 1 percent annually, both because of price-related conservation—a gallon of gasoline costs between two and three times more in Europe than in the United States—and because of the substitution of alternate sources of energy, particularly natural gas and nuclear power.[14]

Although most European countries have lessened their dependence on oil imports from the Middle East and North Africa since 1973, in the near future only Britain and Norway will not rely on the region for an appreciable portion of their energy. For these two countries, the discovery of oil in the North Sea could not have been more opportune. Until 1975, Britain produced negligible amounts of oil. By 1984, it produced 2.4 million b/d, or more than any Middle Eastern and North African country except Saudi Arabia. Production exceeded local requirements in 1980. Nevertheless, the combined proven reserves of Britain and Norway are only 21 billion barrels, compared to the Middle East and North Africa's 434 billion barrels.

The Soviet Union

The Soviet Union has been the world's largest oil producer since 1974 and oil is its principal export. Therefore, it has had little direct interest in Middle East oil. But how long Soviet energy autarky will last is a matter of considerable debate.

The CIA predicts a serious shortfall by 1990, when the Soviet Union will become a net importer of 3.5 million b/d. In such a case, the Middle East will be an obvious source. However, the U.S. Defense Intelligence Agency claims the Soviet Union's energy prospects are highly favorable and that it will be able to increase production and exports for the foreseeable future. Whereas the CIA says the U.S.S.R. has proven reserves of 35 billion barrels, the Defense Intelligence Agency puts the figure at 80 to 85 billion barrels. Which analysis is correct has of course profound implications for the Middle East.[15]

The Geography and Politics of Oil Transportation

A vast oil transportation network is necessary to link the world's main producing regions in the Middle East and North Africa with the main

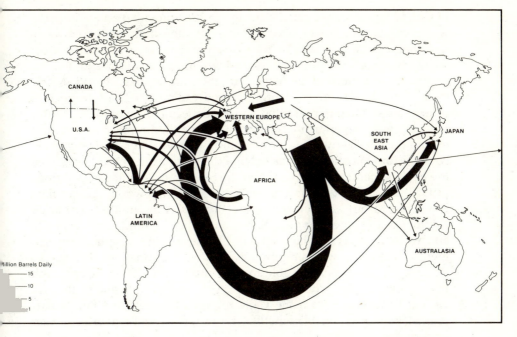

Figure 10.8   The movement of oil, 1981. (After *BP Statistical Review of World Energy, 1982*. London: The British Petroleum Company p.l.c., 1982, pp. 14–15.)

consuming regions in the industrialized West. These oil shipment routes are long, vulnerable lifelines to both producers and consumers. The importance of this flow is such that it bulks large in the superpowers' global mental maps.

Tankers

Most crude oil is transported by tankers along a few well-defined ocean routes (Figure 10.8). Almost 80 percent of all tanker voyages begin in the Middle East, mainly in the Gulf. As one would expect, almost all tanker trips end in Europe (49 percent), the United States (23 percent), or Japan (14 percent). So massive is this movement of oil that it makes up over one half of all seaborne trade measured by ton-mile. The strategic consequences of shipping so much of the industrialized world's oil through what are sometimes nervously portrayed as chokepoints at the Straits of Hormuz and Bab al-Mandab have been discussed in an earlier chapter.

Oil transportation routes and technology have changed substantially since the mid-1960s. Prior to the 1967 Arab-Israeli War, tankers sailing between the Gulf and Europe transited the Suez Canal. By 1966, crude oil and petroleum products comprised 86 percent of all tonnage going north through that waterway. The realignment of routes around the Cape of Good Hope after the canal's closure in 1967 provided added impetus to a revolution in tanker size. Before 1960, almost all oil tankers were less than 65,000 deadweight tons (dwt) and most were smaller than 45,000 dwt. Such vessels were increasingly incapable of transporting the enormous quantities of oil needed by the industrialized world. Moreover, they were relatively inefficient and expensive. The introduction of ever-larger tankers permitted substantial economies of scale.[16] After the 1967 war, supertanker construction expanded rapidly and vessels exceeding 200,000 dwt became the norm. Tankers over 200,000 dwt accounted for almost three quarters of all new tonnage in the 1970s, raising environmental concerns. When the Suez Canal resumed operations in 1975, it could not accommodate 75 percent of the world's tanker fleet compared to only 25 percent before the 1967 war. In 1981, crude oil shipments accounted for only 27 percent of northbound goods tonnage and were considerably below their 1966 level. The Egyptian government is presently widening and deepening the canal, so that supertankers will eventually be able to pass through it. Nevertheless, high transit fees, a new pipeline across Egypt, and the possibility that diverting traffic away from the Cape route will aggravate a tanker surplus make it questionable whether the waterway will regain its former importance.

Pipelines

Pipelines play an important role in oil transportion because they can greatly shorten tanker voyages and, in certain instances, bypass strategic bottlenecks (see Figure 10.2). However, they are expensive to construct, inflexible, and singularly vulnerable to disruption. Frequent closures have underscored their unreliability and reduced their usefulness.

Until recently, one of the major lines in the Middle East was the 1068-mile (1709-kilometer) Tapline, which transported up to 500,000 b/d from eastern Saudi Arabia to Sidon in Lebanon. Completed in 1950, it cut about 2000 miles (3200 kilometers) from the tanker trip to Europe. The saving was even greater after 1967, when tankers from the Gulf had to circumnavigate Africa. However, Tapline has been plagued by stoppages, especially since 1969. The line traverses Jordan, Syria, the occupied Golan Heights, and Lebanon. As a result, it has been hostage to numerous disputes over transit fees and has had the misfortune to pass through a major war zone. In 1969, Palestinian guerillas sabotaged the line in the Golan Heights. The Syrian government refused to allow repairs and used the closure to press for higher transit fees. Pumping resumed only after the Tapline Company agreed to increase its annual payments to Syria. Soon after operations resumed, however, the flow of oil through the line plummeted, falling from 422,000 b/d in 1973 to 233,000 b/d in 1974 and to between only 26,000 b/d and 55,000 b/d in the three following years. This precipitous drop reflected a virtual suspension of pumping during the Lebanese civil war and the increasing cost advantages of exporting oil directly from Gulf terminals. In 1973, less than 6 percent of Aramco's oil was exported through Tapline, far less proportionately than in the 1950s and 1960s. Indeed, after 1975, the line was used only to deliver small amounts of oil to the local Jordanian and Lebanese markets. Tapline's future is uncertain.

The closure of the Suez Canal in 1967 and the supertanker revolution gave birth to two new pipelines. The first was a 162-mile (260-kilometer) Israeli line between Eilat on the Gulf of Aqaba and Ashkelon on the Mediterranean. In 1970, the first year of operation, approximately 220,000 b/d went through the line. By 1972, its capacity was almost 600,000 b/d, or more than that of Tapline. However, the line has obvious political disadvantages and the Arab League has threatened to boycott any oil company using it. Iran was the main user until the revolution. Now Israel has been deprived of even this source of oil so that the line's useful life may be over.

The second pipeline designed to offer an alternative to the Cape route is Egypt's 208-mile (333-kilometer) Sumed line, which runs between the Gulf of Suez and the Mediterranean and was completed in 1977. Throughput in the early 1980s was considerably below 1.6 million b/d capacity and less than transited the canal before its closure. Sumed's flow represents only a fraction of all crude currently leaving the Middle East via the Cape route. Until 1981, all Gulf oil using Sumed had first to pass through the narrow Bab al-Mandab.

A key addition to the Middle East's pipeline network opened in 1981. This is Saudi Arabia's 754-mile (1206-kilometer) Petroline, which links the oil-producing Eastern Province with the port of Yanbu on the Red Sea and has a capacity of 1.85 million b/d. When used in conjunction with Sumed, it will enable approximately one third of all Saudi oil produced each year to be shipped out of the region without having to go through the Hormuz or Bab al-Mandab straits, around the Cape, or via Lebanon and Syria. Barring a major dispute between Egypt and Saudi Arabia, this simple link, which cuts 3000 miles (4800 kilometers) off the Cape route, seems destined to become one of the most important oil transportation routes in coming decades because of its immense geopolitical advantages.[17] Capacity may eventually be doubled. Saudi Arabia has also looked into the possibility with Iraq, the U.A.E., and Oman of building a line from Ras Tanura to the Gulf of Oman, thus bypassing the Strait of Hormuz.

Iraq's Special Problems

Of all Middle Eastern producing states, Iraq is perhaps the most dependent on international pipelines for exporting its oil because it has almost no coastline and its large Kirkuk oil fields are as close to the Mediterranean as the Gulf.

Iraq's first small pipeline, completed in 1934, went from Kirkuk to Haditha and then branched to Haifa in Palestine and Tripoli in Lebanon. Immediately after World War II, work started on second parallel lines. The one to Haifa was never completed because of the 1948–49 Arab-Israeli War. Furthermore, all Arab oil exports through Haifa were terminated after Israel's creation, so that Iraq had to await the upgrading of the existing route to Tripoli and the completion of an additional alternate one to Baniyas in Syria.

Until recently, Iraq exported almost all its oil through these lines to Tripoli and Baniyas. Syria, without much oil of its own, has made the most of this. The Kirkuk-Mediterranean lines have been interrupted more frequently than any others in the region. They were first closed for several months during the 1956 Suez crisis after Syria sabotaged them in retaliation for the invasion of Egypt by Britain, France, and Israel. The Syrian government closed them again in 1966 after failing to obtain higher transit fees. Pumping resumed only after IPC, the owner of the line, agreed to increase its payments to Syria by 50 percent. Syria secured yet another increase in transit dues in 1971 after threatening to close the lines again. The following year, after Iraq nationalized IPC, Syria took complete ownership of all IPC lines and installations within its territory.

An even more serious stoppage of the Kirkuk-Mediterranean lines lasted from 1976 to 1979 as a result of a complex payments dispute and political disagreements. This time, Syria had little leverage over Iraq. By the early 1970s pipeline transit fees made up about 25 percent of all domestic revenues in Syria. The closure cost Syria $136 million in 1977 alone, so that it was anxious to resolve the dispute. Although Iraq suffered, too, past experience had led it to diversify its export routes and expand its own Gulf ports. Four months before the lines through Syria were closed, Iraq opened a new strategic pipeline between Haditha and Al-Faw on the Gulf, thus bypassing the Mediterranean route completely.

Seeking to reduce its dependence on Syria still further, Iraq also signed an agreement with Turkey in 1975 to construct a 613-mile (980-kilometer) pipeline to Dortyol on the Mediterranean. Oil started flowing in 1977. The line's present capacity of 700,000 b/d may eventually be increased. However, this pipeline has had its problems too. Nothing was pumped for much of 1978 because of Turkey's inability to pay Iraq a $225 million oil bill. Later in the year, the line was closed once more by two explosions and a fire, which some Iraqis intimated might have been started by Syria. In September 1980, Kurdish rebels took advantage of the Iraqi-Iranian war to sabotage the line yet again. This was the *sixth* time it had been blown up since its opening.

Iraq signed an agreement with Syria to reopen the Kirkuk-Baniyas line in February 1979. Significantly, although the capacity of this line is over 1.1 million b/d, Iraq pumped only 200,000 to 300,000 b/d in 1979 and 1980, underlining its determination never again to become so dependent on trans-Syrian routes. Iraq's fortunes took another turn for the worse, however, as a result of its war with Iran. Before the war, roughly one third of Iraq's daily oil exports of 3.7 million b/d flowed through the Syrian and Turkish pipelines, with the remainder leaving through its Gulf terminals. After the shipment of oil through Iraq's Gulf terminals became impossible, it was forced to depend entirely on its Mediterranean outlets. The branch line to Tripoli, via Homs in Syria, had been closed since 1976 as a result of the Lebanese civil war. In December 1981, after a six-year stoppage, it was reopened. Within a week, the line was blown up near the Syrian border and the Tripoli refinery was set ablaze. Shi'i supporters of the Khumayni regime in Iran were the most likely attackers because anything that interfered with the flow of Iraqi oil would help Tehran's war effort. In March 1982, the Iraqi line to Lebanon was blown up a second time.

Iraq's most serious problem has been the bitter enmity with Syria, which openly backs Iran in the Gulf war. Because Syria needed about 175,000 b/d from Iraq for its own refineries and benefited from transit payments, initially it did not interfere with the flow of oil from its neighbor. However, in March 1982, Iran agreed to supply Syria with 175,000 b/d, making dependence on Iraq unnecessary. In return, Syria provided Iran with weapons and, most important, closed the Kirkuk-Baniyas line, which had been carrying almost 700,000 b/d. This left only the Turkish line, which was already almost at capacity, as a major export route. Iraq was left with no choice but to slash production. Deprived of much of its oil revenues, it has depended heavily on aid from other Arab countries for its war effort. They, in turn, have repeatedly tried to persuade Syria to reopen the line.

Even before Syria's closure of the Kirkuk-Baniyas line, Iraq had been searching for new alternate routes. In 1984, it signed an agreement with Jordan to construct a 1 million b/d pipeline to Aqaba. Aqaba, incidently, is vulnerable to blockage at the Strait of Tiran and is virtually on the Israeli border. Iraq sought U.S. assurances that Israel would not attack the new line. Iraq has also investigated the possibility of constructing a large line with a 1 million b/d capacity through Kuwait; this could continue down the eastern littoral of the Arabian peninsula. Kuwait has agreed in principle to such a project. The line through Turkey has also been expanded. The most interesting proposal, though, is to lay a new line from southern Iraq to Yanbu, on Saudi Arabia's Red Sea coastline. Plans for this line, which may have a capacity of 1.6 million b/d, are well advanced. Iraq's threats to abandon its Kirkuk-Baniyas line no longer seem unrealistic.

Conclusion

The age of oil will be a relatively short one. Much of the Middle East and North Africa's petroleum will probably have been depleted within a century. Large discoveries outside the Middle East and North Africa will most likely reduce its relative global importance and undermine OPEC's power. Nevertheless, for several decades, the region will continue to be the world's chief producing area.

Since oil's discovery, the balance between demand and supply has usually been precarious. Gluts have alternated with shortages. As a result, the balance of power between buyers and sellers has also changed. There is no reason to believe that it will not change again. No one in 1970 could possibly have guessed what cataclysmic developments would befall the world's oil industry in the next decade. By the same token, it is easy to be lulled by the adequate supply and stable prices of the early 1980s. Time and again, unforeseen political events have suddenly disrupted the market and altered the balance of power. Why not again? Although it is unlikely, what would be the consequences of the closure of the Strait of Hormuz? What if Iran severed Iraq's remaining pipeline to Turkey or Iraq destroyed Iran's Gulf terminals? What would be the result of a revolution in Saudi Arabia?

When a cartel of major multinational companies controlled every facet of production and marketing, they could orchestrate supply to their maximum advantage. Now the producing countries nominally control their oil, while still depending symbiotically on the companies to handle it for them. Notwithstanding OPEC, their cooperation has been limited, with the result that their efforts to calibrate production to changing market conditions have not been completely successful. Consequently, they still run the risk of losing control over the pricing of oil, without which ownership remains partial at best. They are clearly aware of this danger and may yet devise a more permanent and fair way of assigning production quotas. At the same time, OPEC's future demise cannot be ruled out. Although its members have an obvious and admitted self-interest in perpetuating and strengthening the organization, formidable political and other tensions divide them. The issue of control is by no means finally settled.

Notes

1. Geologists distinguish between *proven, probable, possible,* and *speculative* reserves. Obviously, proven reserves offer the most conservative measure, but significantly understate the world's oil supply. The Middle East and North Africa's share of the world's proven oil reserves are not at all the same thing as its share of the world's actual total oil.

2. One should treat reserve statistics cautiously because they are generated by the oil companies or the producing governments, not by independent agencies. The statistics can be inflated or deflated to serve a particular economic or political purpose. There is a widespread belief that Saudi Arabia and Iraq have consistently underplayed the extent of their deposits.

3. Major U.S. oil companies spent $175 billion exploring for oil between 1973 and 1983, and most of their efforts were outside the Middle East and North Africa. In 1982, Exxon's

exploration costs per barrel of oil found were over $5.00, Texaco's $9.50, and Standard Oil of California's (Socal's) more than $12.00.

4. In return for D'Arcy's right to "search for, obtain, exploit, develop, render suitable for trade, carry away and sell" petroleum and natural gas, the Persian government got £20,000 in cash, £20,000 in shares, 16 percent of net profits, and a small annual payment.

5. Throughout this chapter the current names of the oil companies are used for clarity. For example, Mobil was originally called Standard of New York and Exxon called Standard of New Jersey.

6. The origin of the agreement's name is interesting. The participants agreed not to exploit oil in the old Ottoman Empire. But at first no one seemed sure what that empire's limits were. Reputedly, Nubar Gulbenkian, the Armenian oil magnate, "sent out for a large map of the Middle East, laid it on the table in front of the delegates, and then drew a line around the area with a red pencil. 'That was the Ottoman Empire which I knew in 1914,' he said. 'And I ought to know. I was born in it, lived in it, served it. If anyone knows better, carry on.' " So is history made. See Leonard Mosley, *Power Play: Oil in the Middle East* (Baltimore: Penguin Books, 1974): 50.

7. One of the most readable and colorful accounts of how the major oil companies came to dominate Middle Eastern oil concessions is in Anthony Sampson's *The Seven Sisters: The Great Oil Companies and The World They Shaped* (New York: Bantam Books Inc., 1976): 52–134 especially.

8. The best analysis of this collusion is still by John M. Blair, *The Control of Oil* (New York: Pantheon Books Inc., 1976). See pp. 101–113 in particular for a fascinating account of the complex and sophisticated mechanisms used by the companies to control production.

9. This agreement, sometimes called the "As-Is" Agreement, was hammered out among the oil companies to prevent a world oil glut and mutually destructive competition. Essentially, they agreed to accept their present market shares and to limit production increases.

10. To take a simple, much exaggerated example: if the posted price of a barrel of oil was $1.00 and the actual market price $2.00, the host government got 50 percent of the posted price of $1.00, or $0.50. The company obviously got $2.00, the actual selling price, minus the $0.50 it paid the host government, or $1.50. However, if the market price fell to only $0.75, the host government still got 50 percent of the unchanged posted price, or $0.50, whereas the company got only $0.25.

11. The 10 member states of OAPEC plan nearly to double their refining capacity. Kuwait recently purchased Gulf Oil's Rotterdam refinery and 750 service stations in Belgium, Luxembourg, and the Netherlands.

12. Between 1973 and 1984, production in Mexico climbed from 465,000 b/d to 2.7 million b/d, in Britain from 2000 b/d to 2.4 million b/d, in China from 1 million b/d to 2.2 million b/d, and in the Soviet Union from 8.5 million b/d to 12.2 million b/d.

13. In 1950, oil contributed only 7 percent of all energy requirements and coal 60 percent. Even by 1957, Japan consumed only 300,000 b/d of oil. Consumption then increased spectacularly, reaching 5.2 million b/d by 1979. As in other industrialized countries, it dropped to 4.3 million b/d by 1983.

14. Gas was in the process of becoming a major energy source in Europe well before the 1973 oil price explosion as a result of the development of fields in the Netherlands, rising imports from the Soviet Union, and, most important, large discoveries in the North Sea. Between 1968 and 1978, the amount of gas used in Western Europe increased over four times. The growth was even more dramatic in certain countries. For example, in Britain, where gas now provides almost 20 percent of all energy compared to only 1.5 percent in 1970, consumption rose almost thirteenfold.

Several countries, particularly France, Belgium, Sweden, and West Germany, have increased their reliance on nuclear power since 1973. This has been controversial, however, and popular opposition is likely to retard or even halt further expansion, except perhaps in France. By the early 1980s, Western Europe obtained well under 5 percent of its energy from nuclear power plants.

15. In December 1981, a Swedish organization reported that a major discovery had been made at Bezhenov in Western Siberia. It placed the field's size at 4200 billion barrels, or *six* times total proved worldwide reserves. Although the report was ridiculed by Western experts, the U.S. intelligence estimate, which is classified, has been characterized nonetheless as "colossal."

16. In 1954, it cost approximately $2.25 to ship a barrel of oil 11,000 miles (17,600 kilometers). Two decades later it cost only $1.00. Transporting a barrel of oil from the Gulf to Europe in a 250,000 dwt tanker costs less than half as much as in a 50,000 dwt one.

17. Petroline is, however, expensive to use. Its tariff of $0.60 per barrel is double what its customers had expected but necessary to pay for the line's high construction costs ($1.6 billion).

Selected Bibliography

American Petroleum Institute. *Basic Petroleum Data Book*. Washington, D.C.: American Petroleum Institute, 1979.

Anthony, John Duke (ed.). *The Middle East: Oil, Politics, and Development*. Washington, D.C.: American Enterprise Institute for Public Policy Research, 1975.

Bill, James A., and Stookey, Robert W. *Politics and Petroleum: The Middle East and the United States*. Brunswick, Ohio: King's Court Communications, Inc., 1975.

Blair, John M. *The Control of Oil*. New York: Pantheon Books Inc., 1976.

British Petroleum. Public Affairs and Information Department. *BP Statistical Review of the World Oil Industry*. London: British Petroleum, 1978–1980.

————. *BP Statistical Review of World Energy*. London: British Petroleum, 1981–1984.

Conant, Melvin A., and Gold, Fern R. *The Geopolitics of Energy*. Boulder, Colo.: Westview Press, 1978.

Engler, Robert. *The Brotherhood of Oil: Energy Policy and the Public Interest*. Chicago: University of Chicago Press, 1977.

Flower, Andrew R. "World Oil Production." *Scientific American* 238(March 1978): 42–49.

International Petroleum Encyclopedia, 1979. Tulsa, Okla.: Petroleum Publishing Co., 1979.

Longrigg, Stephen H. *Oil in the Middle East: Its Discovery and Development*, 3rd ed. London: Oxford University Press, 1968.

Mikdashi, Zuhayr. *A Financial Analysis of the Middle East Oil Concessions, 1901–1965*. New York: Praeger Publishers, 1966.

Miller, E. Willard. "Oil and Money: How OPEC Changes the Wealth of Nations." *Focus* 30(November–December 1979): 1–17.

Mosley, Leonard. *Power Play: Oil in the Middle East*. Baltimore: Penguin Books, 1974.

Nehring, Richard. *Giant Oil Fields and World Oil Resources*. Santa Monica, Calif.: Rand Corporation, 1978.

Odell, Peter R. *Oil and World Power*, 7th ed. London: Penguin Books, 1983.

Organization of Arab Petroleum Exporting Countries. *Annual Statistical Report*. Kuwait: OAPEC, 1972–1982.

Rustow, Dankwart, and Mugno, John F. *OPEC: Success and Prospects*. New York: New York University Press, 1976.

Sampson, Anthony. *The Seven Sisters: The Great Oil Companies and the World They Shaped*. New York: Bantam Books Inc., 1976.

Sherbiny, N.A., and Tessler, M.A. (eds.). *Arab Oil: Impact on the Arab Countries and Global Implications*. New York: Praeger Publishers, 1976.

Shwadran, Benjamin. *The Middle East, Oil and the Great Powers*. New York: John Wiley & Sons, 1973.

Stobaugh, Robert, and Yergin, Daniel (eds.). *Energy Future: Report of the Energy Project of the Harvard Business School*. New York: Random House, 1979.

Stocking, George W. *Middle East Oil*. Nashville, Tenn.: Vanderbilt University Press, 1970.

Stork, Joe. *Middle East Oil and the Energy Crisis*. New York: Monthly Review Press, 1975.

U.S. Department of Energy. Energy Information Administration. *Monthly Energy Review*. Washington, D.C.: U.S. Government Printing Office, 1977–1984.

———. *Quarterly Report*. Washington, D.C.: U.S. Government Printing Office, 1978–1982.

———. *Annual Report to Congress, 1979*. Vol. 2: Data. Washington, D.C.: U.S. Government Printing Office, 1979.

———. *International Petroleum Annual, 1978*. Washington, D.C.: U.S. Government Printing Office, 1980.

———. *The Petroleum Resources of the Middle East*. Washington, D.C.: U.S. Government Printing Office, 1983.

Vicker, Ray. *The Kingdom of Oil*. New York: Charles Scribner's Sons, 1974.

Workshop on Alternative Energy Strategies. *Energy: Global Prospects, 1985–2000*. New York: McGraw-Hill, 1977.

11

Conclusion

We feel that a look forward is more appropriate than a look back at this point. How might the region's political map change in the coming decades? Will some of the conflicts we have discussed be resolved? What new problems may emerge?

The Future Political Map

The Middle East and North Africa is a region of constant, rapid change. Today's political map is extraordinarily young when considered in the context of the region's recorded history. Who, 100 years ago, could possibly have predicted how the contemporary political landscape would look? It is sobering to recollect how much has happened even in the last 20 years: Arab-Israeli wars in 1967 and 1973 (with their associated territorial changes); Israel's 1982 invasion and occupation of southern Lebanon; the Egyptian-Israeli peace treaty; the Iran-Iraq War; civil wars in the Yemen Arab Republic, Sudan, Cyprus, Iraq, Jordan, and Lebanon; Turkey's invasion of Cyprus; a fifteenfold explosion in the price of oil; a revolution in Iran; the toppling of the Libyan monarchy; the assassination of President Sadat of Egypt; the Soviet invasion of nearby Afghanistan; and the resurgence of Islamic fundamentalism. Will the next 20 years be as momentous? Does the past suggest only the futility of attempting to look into the future?

Obviously, one cannot predict the kind of sudden jolts the Middle East and North Africa or any other region periodically experiences. The only certain thing is that such political earthquakes will continue to occur. Change must be anticipated if one is to view the world realistically. With these caveats in mind, looking forward need not be an exercise in folly.

The partitioning of the Middle East and North Africa's land area is virtually complete. The state system, which revolutionized the political organization of space, is here to stay. Despite serious national integration problems in Lebanon, Sudan, Cyprus, Iraq, and elsewhere, new sovereign states seem unlikely to emerge as a result of further territorial division. Lebanon is a candidate for de facto partition by occupying powers more than for de jure division into Muslim and Christian states. Kurdish demands for statehood will most likely remain unfulfilled. Similarly, Polisario's chances of creating a western Sahara state in areas currently claimed by Morocco seem increasingly remote. The only exception might be the birth of an independent Palestinian state on the West Bank, but for this to happen opinion within Israel must change radically. Even the establishment or survival of new states as a result of the fusion of two or more existing ones does not appear probable in the near future.

This is not to say that the political map will not change. Although new states may not be created, the lines that define them might be adjusted slightly here and there, either through force or by mutual agreement. The most significant changes would probably be associated with another Arab-Israeli war or, conversely, a peace agreement between Israel, Jordan, and Syria. In time, land boundaries in the Middle East and North Africa will, with certain notable exceptions, be agreed on and properly surveyed using modern techniques. Boundary lines will be more deeply etched in the landscape. The vagueness or ambiguity that still exists in a few parts of the Arabian peninsula where boundaries remain undefined will be eliminated. In the future, most disputes will be diseases of the body, not the skin. Most current boundary disputes can, and probably will, be solved. The Iran-Iraq disagreement may be an exception because it is enmeshed in a much broader, bitter quarrel. Functional disputes seem destined to recur between antagonistic neighbors, like Syria and Iraq, impeding spatial interaction regionally. Possibly, there will be a growing discrepancy between permeable boundaries (in the Arabian peninsula) and impermeable ones (between Egypt and Libya, Iran and Iraq, and Israel and Syria for instance).

Transboundary resource disputes may become more common. The Middle East and North Africa's population will double within 40 years or so. Competition for the region's limited water resources can, therefore, be expected to intensify. Lebanon fears Israel will divert the Litani, whereas Syria fears its enemy to the southwest has its eyes on the Orontes. West Bank Arabs complain that Jewish settlers are mining their groundwater. The Nile, Euphrates, and Jordan rivers might similarly figure increasingly in political disputes. Conversely, the question of how to allocate water fairly and rationally could stimulate regional cooperation. The pumping of water from Iraq's rivers to arid Jordan would strengthen the bond between the two countries for instance. The need to use the Euphrates's waters more efficiently could spur Iraq and Syria to set aside their political differences. Joint Arab-Israeli development of the Jordan River basin could be one obvious benefit of peace.

The partitioning of the oceans is at a fairly early stage. The possibilities for future conflict and cooperation are, therefore, infinite. As states bring offshore areas and their resources under their direct control, maritime boundary disagreements may multiply. Uninhabited islands, particularly in the Red Sea and Gulf, will acquire a new significance and become a focus of disputes as states strive to project their power seaward. Coastal states may also try to restrict external activity (of superpower navies or oil supertanker traffic for instance) as their maritime interests grow. The significance of the various strategic straits will likely change. The construction of new oil pipelines across the Arabian peninsula will lessen the relative importance of the Straits of Hormuz and Bab al-Mandab. Simultaneously, the Suez Canal might regain some of its former importance as an oil shipment route. The Turkish and Gibraltar straits are quiet today but have a high potential to become geostrategic flashpoints. The oceans also offer unprecedented opportunities for regional cooperation. All coastal states clearly have a responsibility to protect their maritime environments as well as a self-interest in doing so. The Gulf states paid a high cost for not being able to cooperate over the cleanup of a huge oil spill in 1983. Pacts among the Mediterranean, Gulf, and Red Sea states might encourage them to view the seas they rim as a shared resource and perhaps serve as vehicles for more ambitious economic cooperation. As coastal states become increasingly aware of the strategic importance of offshore areas, they may also create regional security pacts, no doubt with self-interested assistance from superpowers.

Although the process of partitioning the Middle East and North Africa's land areas may be virtually complete, the process of integrating the spaces defined by partition lines is far from over. At the national level, the territorial integration problems of many countries in the region are a function of their youthfulness and will lessen as communication networks expand, national space economies develop, and central governments accumulate more power. However, change does not occur in only one direction. Integration is not an inevitable consequence of modernization. Indeed, modernization can sometimes aggravate tensions within culturally diverse societies by intensifying competition. Lebanon, after all, is among the most modern of all Middle Eastern states by many criteria.

Not all heterogeneous countries can expect serious integration problems in the future. Many can however: Lebanon, Sudan, and Cyprus come immediately to mind. Sunni-Shi'i and native-nonnative differences may also present intractable unity problems in certain Arabian peninsula states. Countries with large Kurdish populations can expect problems too. One country where sectarian tensions could explode is Syria; resentment over the perceived Alawi monopolization of power runs deep. Could Syria be the next Lebanon? Israel's integration problems similarly deserve close attention. The rift between Ashkenazi and Sephardic Jews could widen. The more serious cleavage between Jews and Arabs also seems destined to grow. Increased civil strife seems assured if Israel pursues its current policies in the occupied territories.

Prospects for future regional integration are mixed. On the one hand, no substantial reorganization of the political map is foreseen. Occasionally, two or more countries may try to unite politically. If the past is any guide, these efforts will not be successful for long unless they are based on loose federation. The pan-Arabist dream of creating a single Arab nation-state will not be fulfilled, certainly in our lifetimes, and most probably never. On the other hand, functional links within the Arab world will continue to multiply. Increased spatial interaction in the form of trade, migration, capital flows, cultural exchanges, and political consultation will bind the region's constituent parts more closely together. The growing network of regional institutions will solidify these bonds. Increased subregional cooperation also seems likely, particularly in the Arabian peninsula. Although political differences seem to preclude closer cooperation within the Maghreb and Fertile Crescent at present, political change could revitalize prospects.

It sometimes seems as though the Arab-Israeli dispute is insoluble. The proverbial man in the street often throws up his hands in despair, asserting that the conflict has gone on for thousands of years, thereby implying that it will continue for many more (in reality it is quite recent in origin). Or he might suggest (again mistakenly) that conflict and hatred are endemic to the Middle East. If he is from outside the region, particularly Europe, he might do well to examine his own history first, especially over the last century. The world has seen many far longer, bloodier, and more tangled conflicts than the one between the Arabs and Israelis. Things can change. Only 40 years ago the United States and Britain were allies of the Soviet Union, fighting Germany and Japan. No one needs to be reminded of how many millions of Europeans have died and been uprooted in this century's wars or how many times the European political map has been redrawn.

This is not to suggest that solving the Arab-Israeli dispute will be easy. In certain respects the passage of time makes a settlement more difficult. Approximately half of all Arabs in the West Bank and Gaza have been born since the Israeli occupation began. A growing percentage of Israelis also cannot remember a time when they did not control these areas. With each year, it becomes more difficult for Israel to hand land back. Passions will continue to run deep. Outstanding issues, such as Israel's desire to live within secure borders and the Palestinians' need for their own state, must be settled before peace has any chance of succeeding. We believe that any settlement, if it is to offer hope of lasting peaceful coexistence, must be based on territorial compromise. We favor a two-state solution: one state for Israeli Jews; another in the West Bank and Gaza Strip for Palestinian Arabs. We favor also an internationalized Jerusalem. Many—perhaps most—Middle Easterners as well as many scholars would not agree with this formula. Formidable obstacles stand in the way of such a solution. Consequently, although we believe the conflict is solvable, we also feel that it will not actually soon be settled. The direction of events depends on many things. Will Egypt ultimately reject peace with Israel and rejoin Arab ranks, which could decisively alter the military balance? Or will it persuade other Arab states that its approach is the most realistic and rewarding? How would major political change in Jordan or Israel alter the equation? Will the United States or the Palestinians change their position? Will the 1990s bring yet another war, as did the 1940s, 1950s, 1960s, 1970s, and 1980s? Will the region's ominous and accelerating militarization continue?

It seems unlikely that the Middle East and North Africa will ever again be as important as they were in the 1970s in shaping the world's energy situation. They will continue to supply a significant percentage of the world's oil, but exploration in other regions, conservation in the consuming countries, and growing dependence on other forms of energy will diminish their relative global importance. A few years ago, all the talk was of oil shortages. Now it all seems to be about surpluses. It would be foolhardy, however, to assume the energy crisis is behind us. Previous projections of energy supply and demand have often been spectacularly wrong because unforeseen political events can change market conditions abruptly. Surprises cannot, indeed should not, be ruled out.

Middle Eastern and North African countries will increasingly extract, refine, transport, and market their oil themselves. Nevertheless, foreign oil companies will continue to play an important role in the region as contractors and middlemen. The transportation of oil will change significantly because of the construction of several new pipelines across the Arabian peninsula. As previously noted, less oil will transit the Straits of Hormuz and Bab al-Mandab, lessening their locational importance. Little Iraqi oil will probably pass through Syria to the Mediterranean. The widening and deepening of the Suez Canal will reduce the significance of the Cape route for tankers.

A Research Agenda

In preparing this book, we have been struck by how few studies political geographers have conducted on the Middle East and North Africa, even on traditional subjects such as boundaries. Many of the works we consulted were written by political scientists, historians, and economists, and they did not have an explicitly geographic focus. There is an urgent need for more political geographic research in the region. Numerous topics quickly come to mind.

Our knowledge about the origins and even placement of past political boundaries remains remarkably incomplete. Research on the antecedents of modern boundaries from maps, archival records, and treaties would be of considerable interest to area specialists. Similarly, much research remains to be done on the evolution and status of existing boundaries, particularly disputed ones. Although these topics fall within the old formal-structural tradition, they are nonetheless important.

Empirical studies on boundary functions are practically nonexistent and much needed. How is a particular boundary perceived by those living on either side of it? How does it affect spatial interaction patterns and hinterland delimitation? How permeable is it? To what extent do functional disputes and laborious border-crossing formalities disrupt trade and other transactions? What is the effect of television and radio broadcasts beamed across the boundary? If the boundary is disputed, can geography suggest a better, or less stress-inducing, location?

Political geographers have much to contribute technically to the solution of offshore boundary problems. For example, they can help to define historic bays, opposite coasts, and the location of median lines where these may be required. Many potential offshore disputes over islands, resources, and boundaries need to be investigated more thoroughly. The whole question of marine pollution and the collective response of coastal states to this threat demands greater attention. How have the Gulf countries dealt with oil spills? How could their efforts be improved? Changes in traffic through the strategic straits could be monitored to detect trends and provide indications of any shift in their locational significance. Where are the vessels going to and coming from, and what are their cargoes? To what extent are perceived risks of passage through the straits reflected in higher insurance rates? The way in which Jordan and Iraq have coped with their limited ocean access also requires further study.

Research on national integration involves sensitive and controversial issues, and it is restricted as a result. Most countries in the region do not like to draw attention to their internal divisions, fearing publicity serves to legitimize and promote cleavages. Statistical data on the geographic distribution of ethnic groups or ethnic inequalities are, by and large, not gathered for this very reason. The motives of outsiders seeking to conduct research on interethnic relations will be questioned. In most cases, field research simply will not be possible. For instance, Syria would never permit anyone to study Alawi-Sunni relations. Saudi Arabia (or any other country in the Arabian peninsula) would not allow research on the status of the Shi'is. Iraq would disallow any investigation of Sunni-Shi'i-Kurdish relations. However, there is much that can be done if the researcher treads carefully and avoids obviously sensitive subjects. An examination of spatial interaction patterns within a country—measured by the movement of people or goods, for example—could offer useful clues about the level of territorial integration and might even help to identify regional cleavages. Spatial inequities might also be measured. Many countries publish geographic data in their annual statistical abstracts or decennial censuses on the distribution of physicians, infant mortality, life expectancy, teachers, schools, literacy, electric consumption, automobile ownership, and many other variables that could be used in factor analysis. The problem of inequality within Middle Eastern and North African countries is acute and politically explosive. Political geographers can make a significant contribution to understanding and measuring it.

Regional integration is a fertile area for research. In particular, political geographers could profitably study spatial interaction patterns within the region: trade, labor migration, tourism, capital flows, aid patterns, transportation links, political visits, and the like. They could also investigate the actual performance of regional institutions. What is the impact of joint ventures on regional integration? Prospects for subregional integration could be assessed and methods for achieving this could be suggested. Actual integration experiments, such as the failed United Arab Republic and the so-far successful United Arab Emirates, could be compared and evaluated.

Political geographers have done a fair amount of research on the Arab-Israeli conflict and related matters. Nevertheless, research opportunities abound. The process and extent of Israeli land expropriation on the West Bank needs to be thoroughly studied and documented. Other possible topics include: the geographic viability of an independent Palestinian state on the West Bank; the extent of emigration from the occupied territories; the implications of Israel's heavy reliance on Arab workers from the West Bank and Gaza; the effect of Jewish colonization of the occupied territories on Arab agriculture; competition for and use of water from the West Bank's aquifers; the changing geographic distribution and legal position of Palestinians within the Arab world; the evolution of the Palestinian state-idea; and differences between Jewish and Arab mental maps. A multitude of additional subjects come to mind. Political geographers have a vital role to play in describing, analyzing, and helping to solve the Arab-Israeli conflict.

In the matter of petroleum, topics for further political geographic research are perhaps not so obvious. Nevertheless, they exist. The evolution of concession maps within individual countries could be profitably traced. Much also remains to be known about the role of the oil companies in determining the location of international boundaries on land and offshore. How did the concession map shape the political map? The question of how transboundary oil fields are exploited needs systematic study. To what extent have political and strategic considerations entered into locational decisions about which oil fields to exploit or where export terminals and refineries should be built and oil pipelines laid? In particular, how has the Iran-Iraq War affected petroleum development in the region? The transportation of oil, especially the changing importance of different pipelines, could be examined in more detail.

This list is intended to be illustrative rather than comprehensive. We have not even mentioned the possibilities for research in subject areas we were unable to include in this book (for example, local administration, locational conflict, electoral geography, and decision-making). Our point is simply that much still remains to be explored. If we have stimulated interest in the subject and illustrated the importance of a geographic perspective in understanding political phenomena in the region, we will have met our principal goals.

Index

Boldface page numbers indicate figures.